Night Shift

Other Baby Blues® Books from Andrews McMeel Publishing

Guess Who Didn't Take a Nap?
I Thought Labor Ended When the Baby Was Born
We Are Experiencing Parental Difficulties . . . Please Stand By
Night of the Living Dad
I Saw Elvis in My Ultrasound
One More and We're Outnumbered!
Check, Please . . .
threats, bribes & videotape
If I'm a Stay-at-Home Mom, Why Am I Always in the Car?
Lift and Separate
I Shouldn't Have to Scream More Than Once!
Motherhood Is Not for Wimps
Baby Blues®: Unplugged
Dad to the Bone
Never a Dry Moment
Two Plus One Is Enough
Playdate: Category 5
Our Server Is Down
Something Chocolate This Way Comes
Briefcase Full of Baby Blues

Treasuries

The Super-Absorbent Biodegradable Family-Size Baby Blues®
Baby Blues®: Ten Years and Still in Diapers
Butt-Naked Baby Blues®
Wall-to-Wall Baby Blues®
Driving Under the Influence of Children
Framed!

Night Shift

Baby Blues® 23 Scrapbook

By
Rick Kirkman
& Jerry Scott

Andrews McMeel
Publishing, LLC

Kansas City

Baby Blues® is syndicated internationally by King Features Syndicate, Inc. For information, write King Features Syndicate, Inc., 300 West Fifty-Seventh Street, New York, NY 10019.

Night Shift copyright © 2007 by Baby Blues Partnership. All rights reserved. Printed in the United States of America. No part of this book may be used or reproduced in any manner whatsoever without written permission except in the case of reprints in the context of reviews. For information, write Andrews McMeel Publishing, LLC, an Andrews McMeel Universal company, 4520 Main Street, Kansas City, Missouri 64111.

07 08 09 10 11 BBG 10 9 8 7 6 5 4 3 2 1

ISBN: 978-0-7407-6842-2
ISBN: 0-7407-6842-5

Library of Congress Catalog Card Number: 2007925330

www.andrewsmcmeel.com

Find *Baby Blues*® on the Web at
www.babyblues.com.

——— **ATTENTION: SCHOOLS AND BUSINESSES** ———

Andrews McMeel books are available at quantity discounts with bulk purchase for educational, business, or sales promotional use. For information, please write to: Special Sales Department, Andrews McMeel Publishing, LLC, 4520 Main Street, Kansas City, Missouri 64111.

To Dr. Barbara Silton, for making a difference.
—J.S.

To my bandmates, who've grown from teenage rock & rollers to family men, always remaining staunch supporters of my work.
This one's for you: Bob, Gary and John.
—R.K

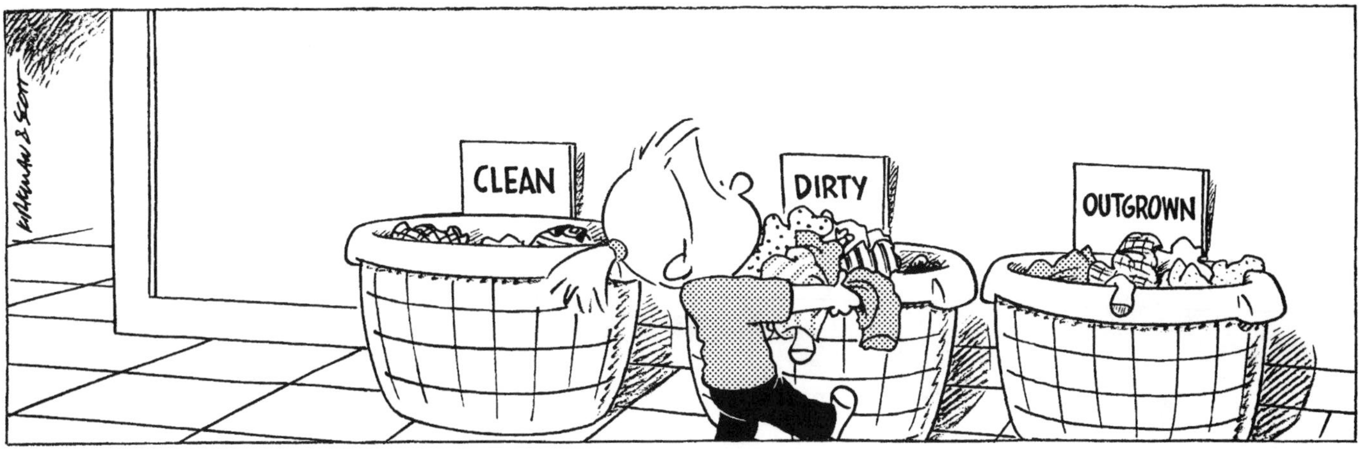
CLEAN
DIRTY
OUTGROWN

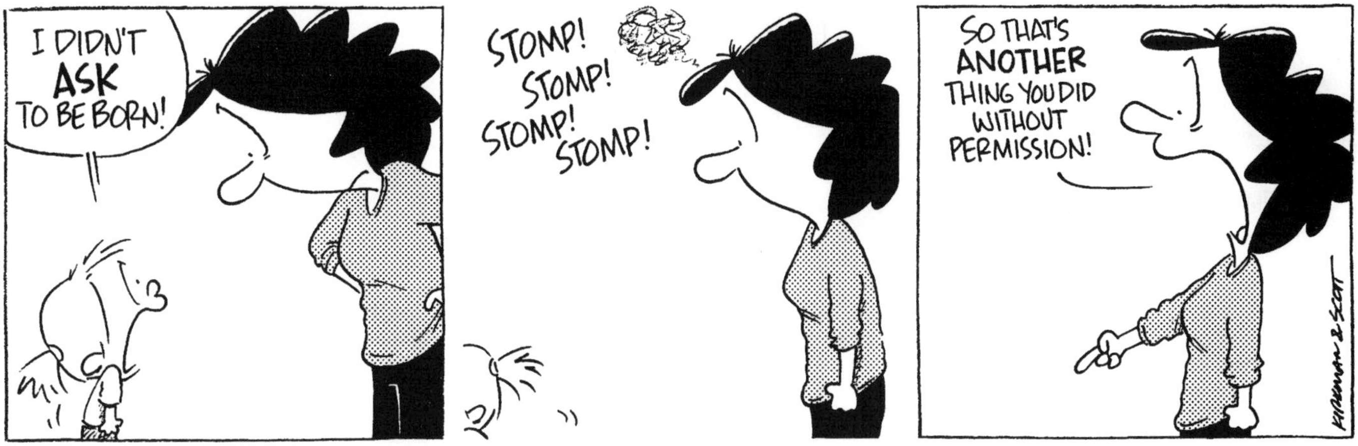
I DIDN'T **ASK** TO BE BORN!
STOMP! STOMP! STOMP! STOMP!
SO THAT'S **ANOTHER** THING YOU DID WITHOUT PERMISSION!

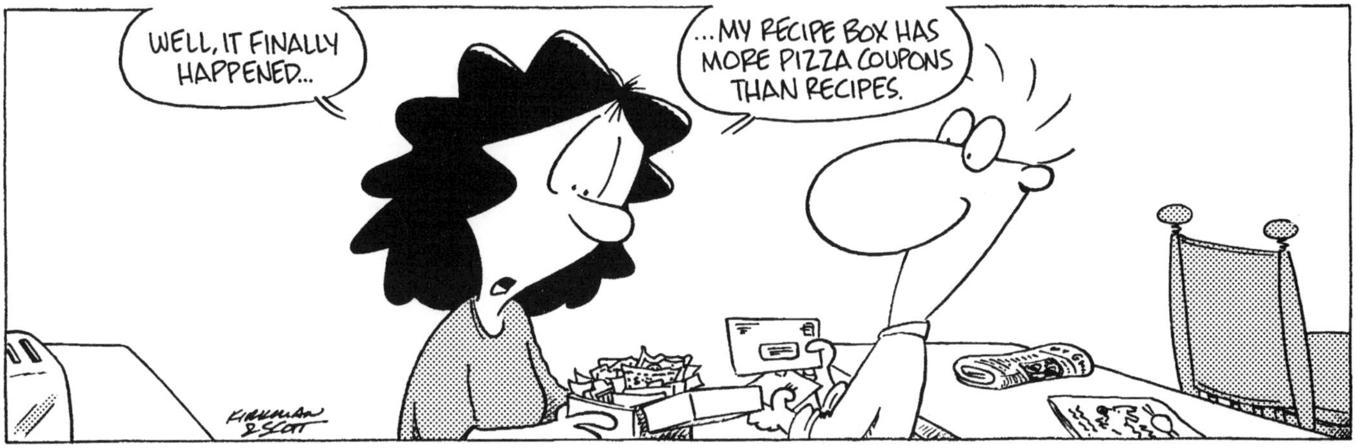
WELL, IT FINALLY HAPPENED...
...MY RECIPE BOX HAS MORE PIZZA COUPONS THAN RECIPES.

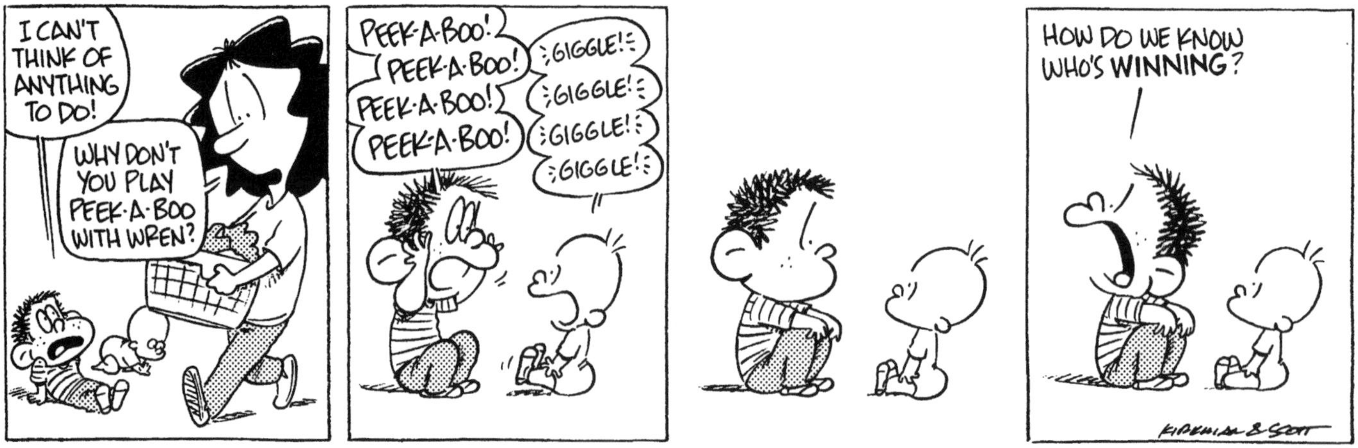
I CAN'T THINK OF ANYTHING TO DO!
WHY DON'T YOU PLAY PEEK-A-BOO WITH WREN?
PEEK-A-BOO! PEEK-A-BOO! PEEK-A-BOO! PEEK-A-BOO!
GIGGLE! GIGGLE! GIGGLE! GIGGLE!
HOW DO WE KNOW WHO'S **WINNING**?

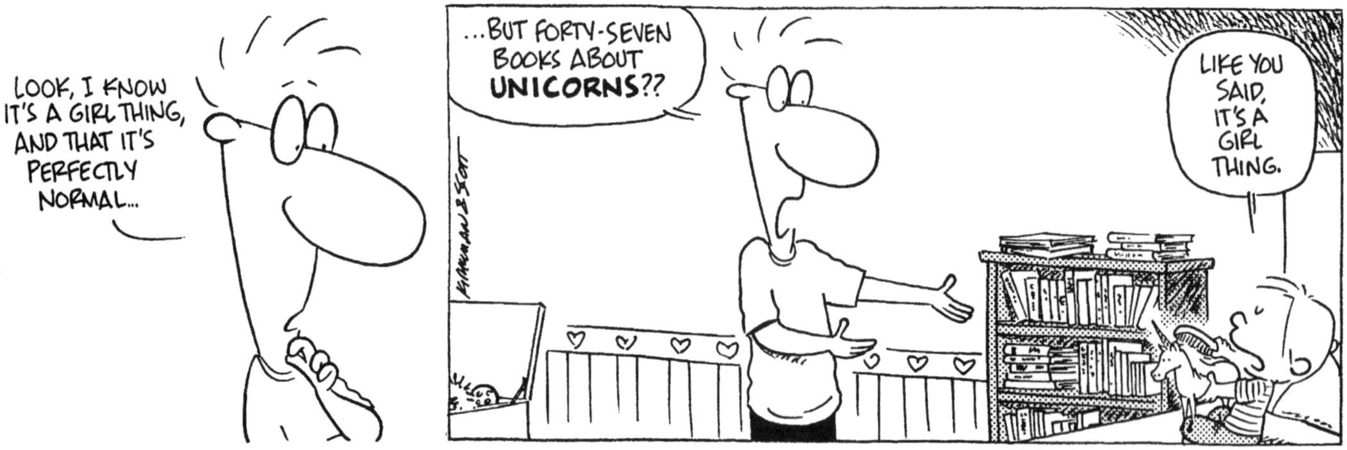
LOOK, I KNOW IT'S A GIRL THING, AND THAT IT'S PERFECTLY NORMAL...
...BUT FORTY-SEVEN BOOKS ABOUT **UNICORNS**??
LIKE YOU SAID, IT'S A GIRL THING.

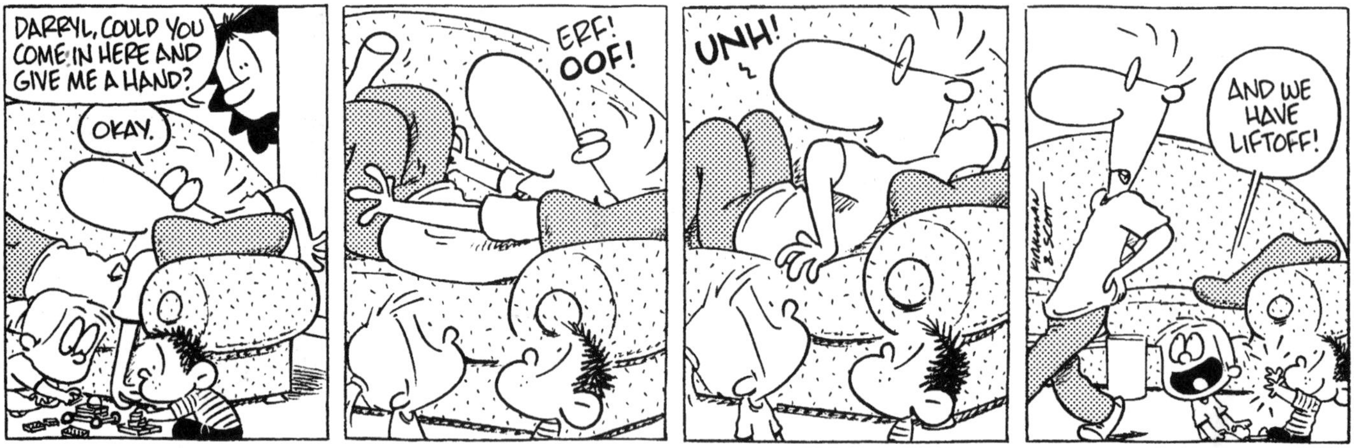
DARRYL, COULD YOU COME IN HERE AND GIVE ME A HAND?
OKAY.
ERF! **OOF!**
UNH!
AND WE HAVE LIFTOFF!

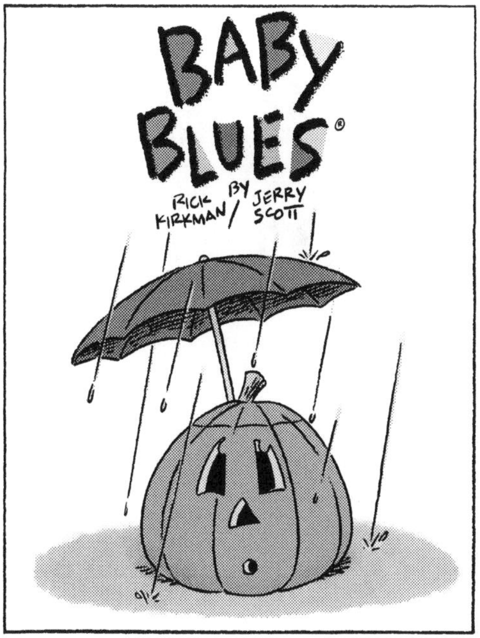
BABY BLUES®
BY RICK KIRKMAN / JERRY SCOTT

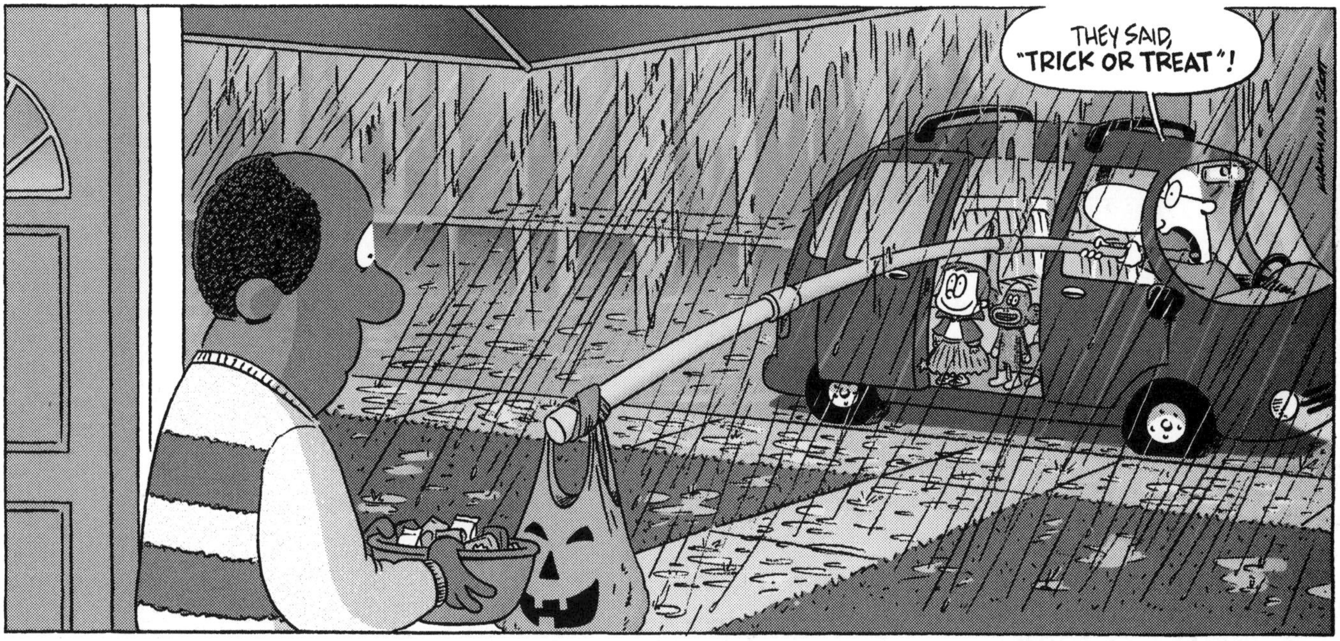
THEY SAID, "TRICK OR TREAT"!

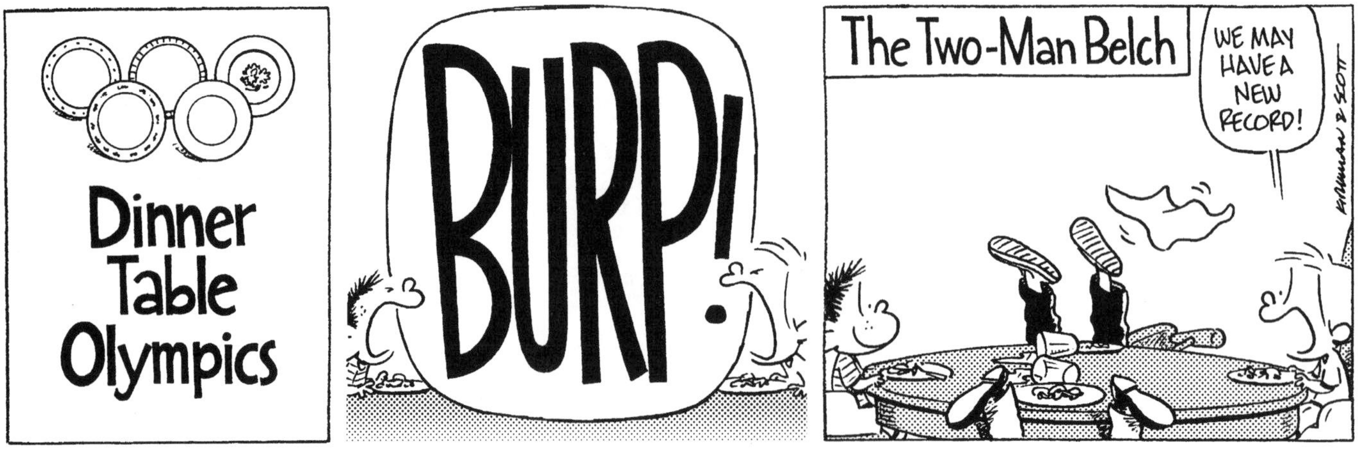
Dinner Table Olympics
BURP!
The Two-Man Belch
WE MAY HAVE A NEW RECORD!
KIRKMAN & SCOTT

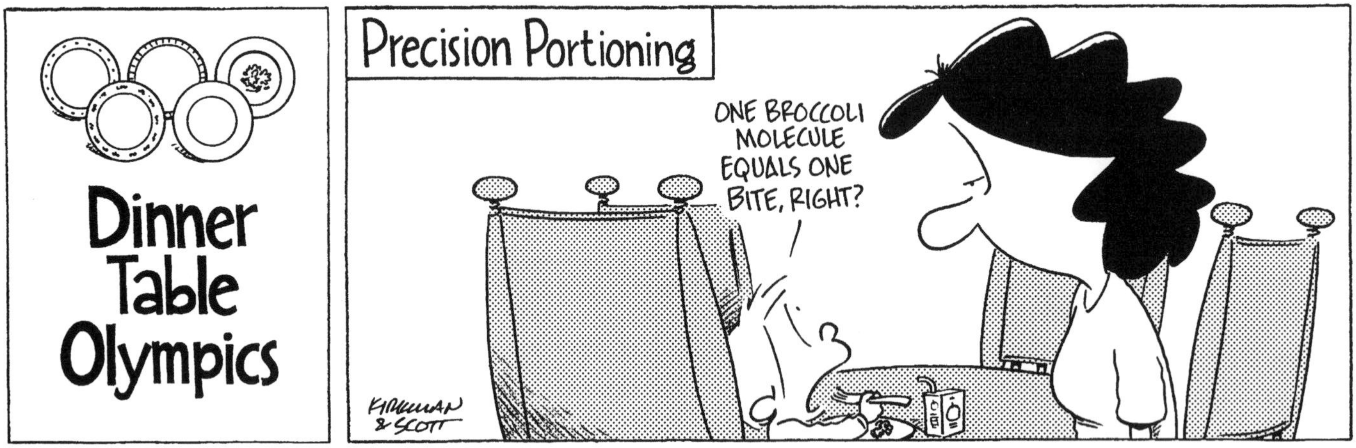
Dinner Table Olympics
Precision Portioning
ONE BROCCOLI MOLECULE EQUALS ONE BITE, RIGHT?
KIRKMAN & SCOTT

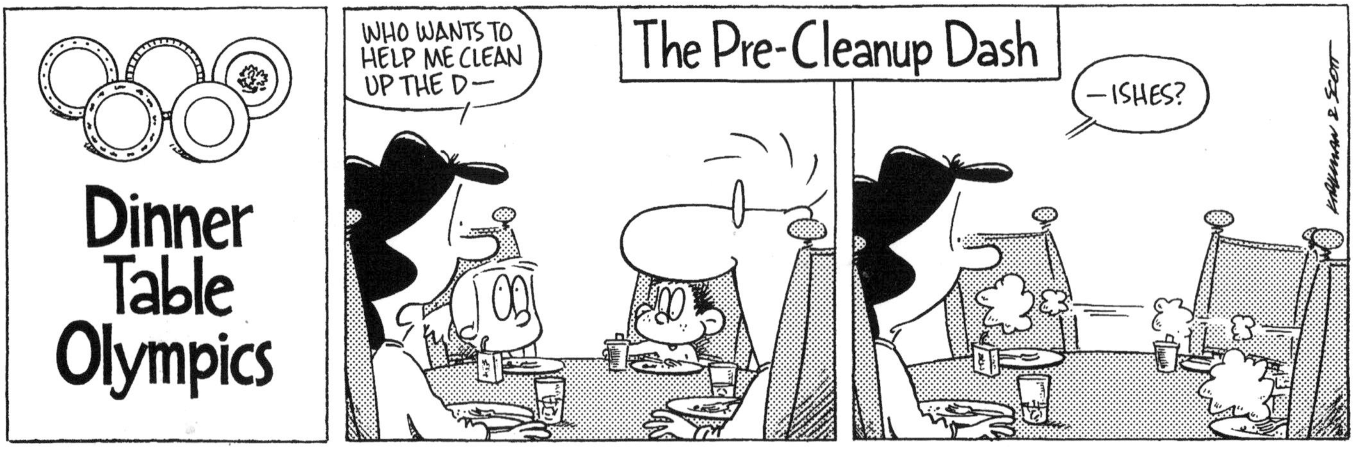
Dinner Table Olympics
WHO WANTS TO HELP ME CLEAN UP THE D—
The Pre-Cleanup Dash
—ISHES?
KIRKMAN & SCOTT

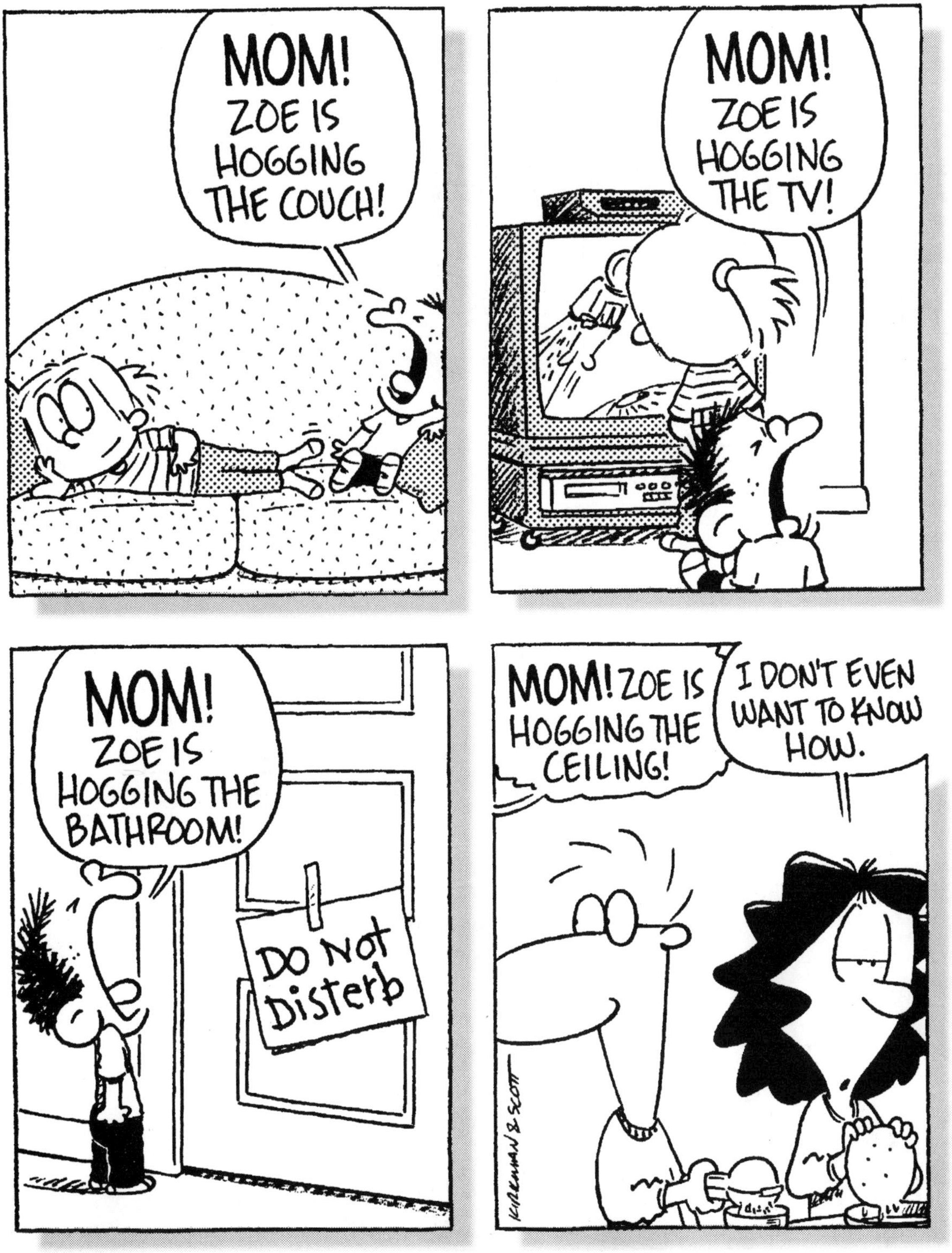
MOM! ZOE IS HOGGING THE COUCH!
MOM! ZOE IS HOGGING THE TV!
MOM! ZOE IS HOGGING THE BATHROOM!
Do Not Disterb
MOM! ZOE IS HOGGING THE CEILING!
I DON'T EVEN WANT TO KNOW HOW.
KIRKMAN & SCOTT

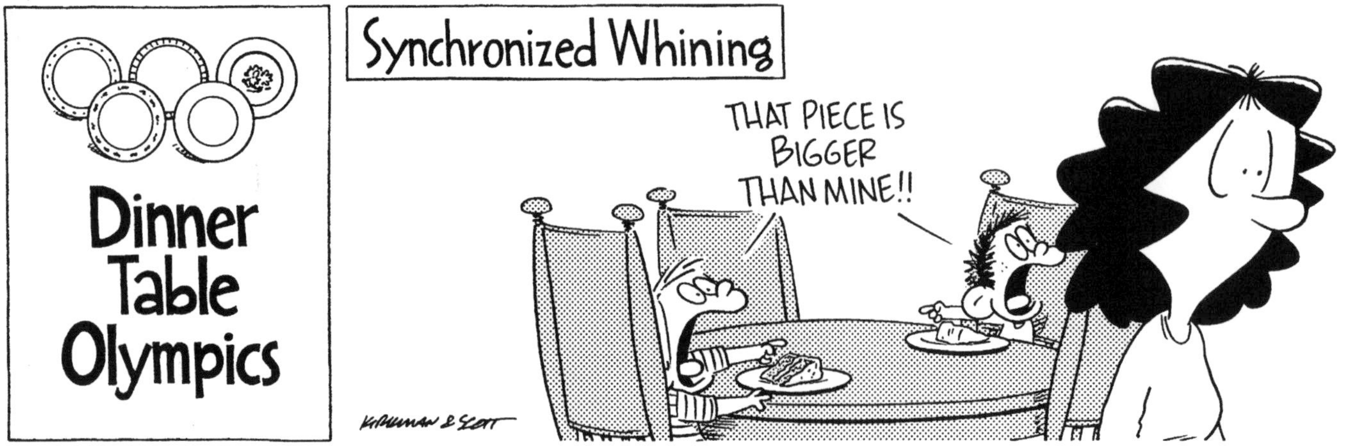
Dinner Table Olympics
Synchronized Whining
THAT PIECE IS BIGGER THAN MINE!!
KIRKMAN & SCOTT

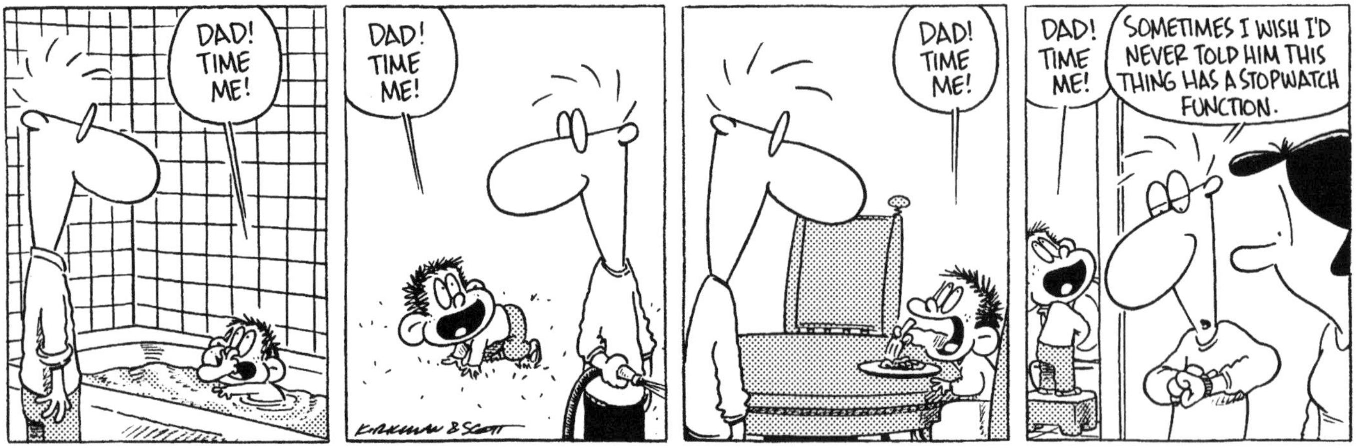
DAD! TIME ME!
DAD! TIME ME!
KIRKMAN & SCOTT
DAD! TIME ME!
DAD! TIME ME!
SOMETIMES I WISH I'D NEVER TOLD HIM THIS THING HAS A STOPWATCH FUNCTION.

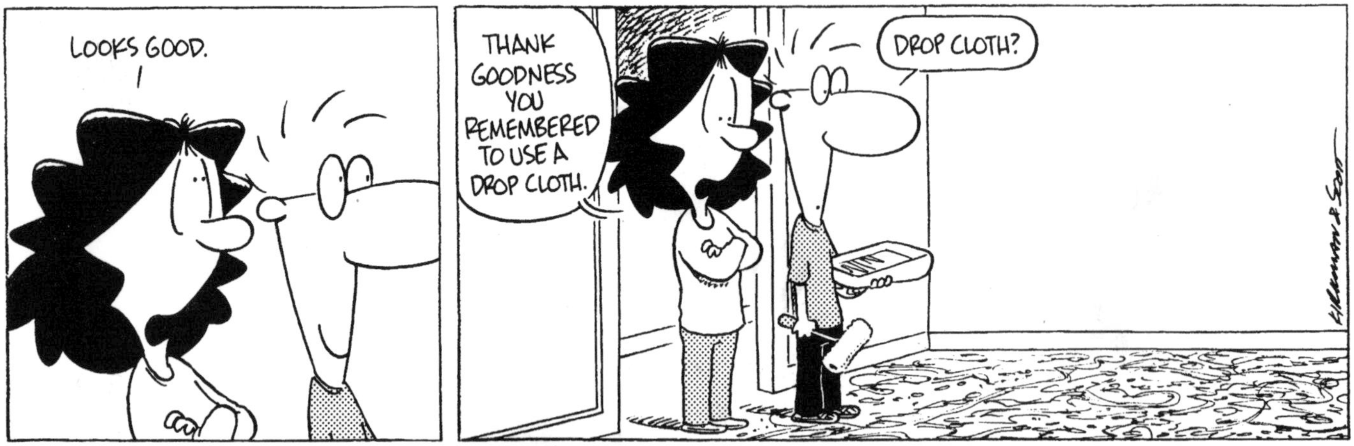
LOOKS GOOD.
THANK GOODNESS YOU REMEMBERED TO USE A DROP CLOTH.
DROP CLOTH?
KIRKMAN & SCOTT

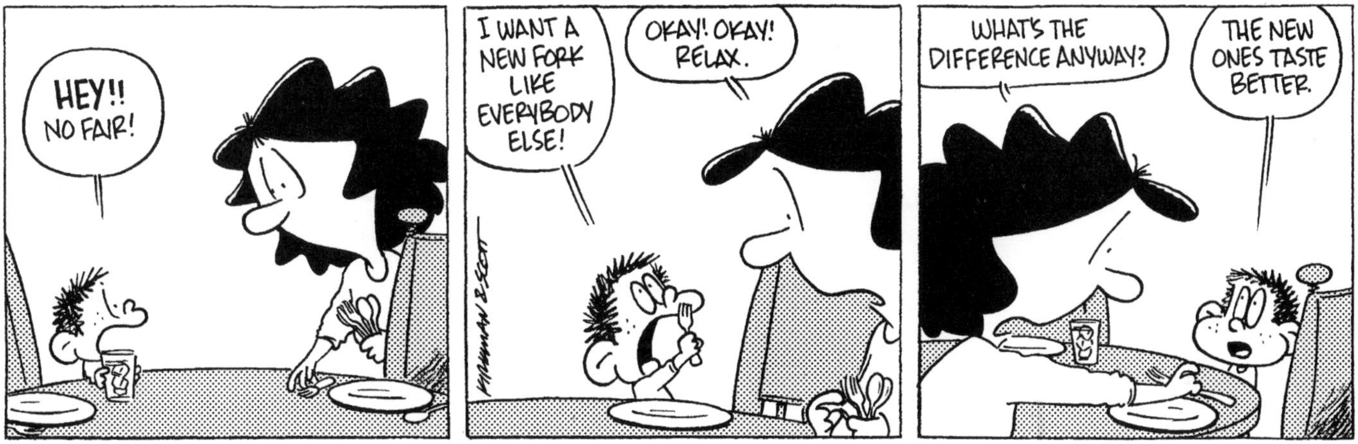
HEY!! NO FAIR!
I WANT A NEW FORK LIKE EVERYBODY ELSE!
OKAY! OKAY! RELAX.
WHAT'S THE DIFFERENCE ANYWAY?
THE NEW ONES TASTE BETTER.

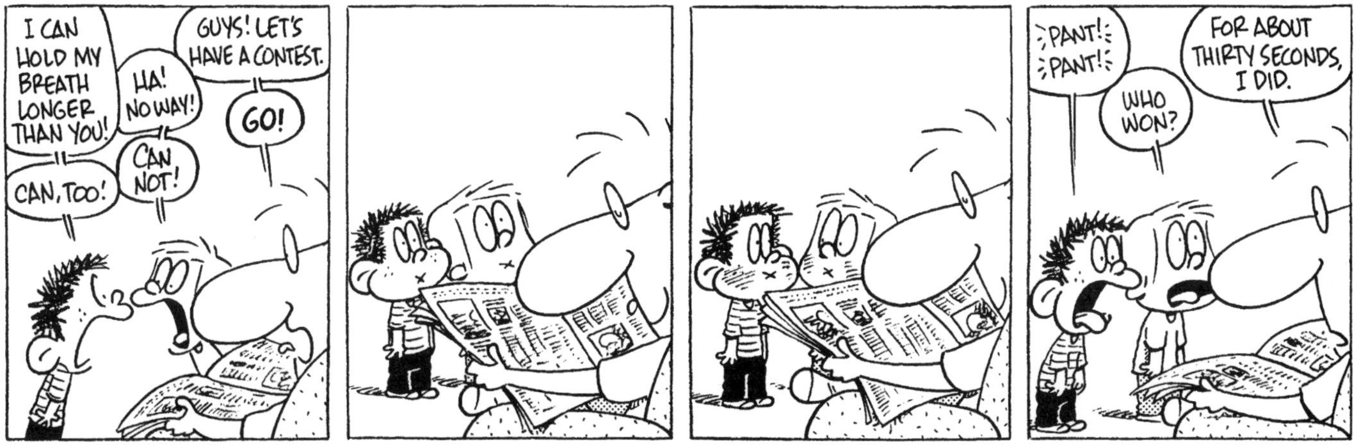
I CAN HOLD MY BREATH LONGER THAN YOU!
HA! NO WAY!
CAN, TOO!
CAN NOT!
GUYS! LET'S HAVE A CONTEST.
GO!
PANT! PANT!
WHO WON?
FOR ABOUT THIRTY SECONDS, I DID.

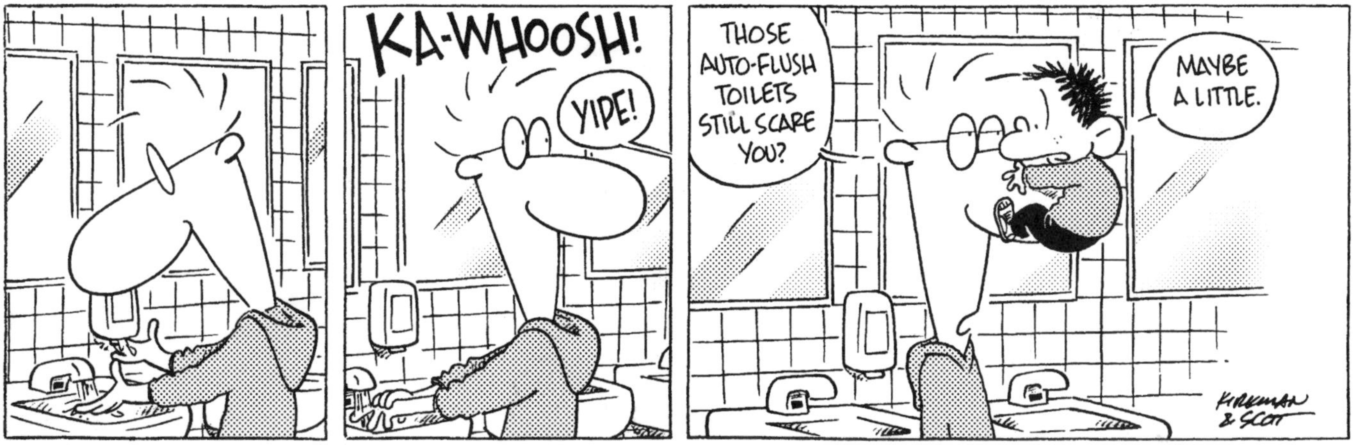
KA-WHOOSH!
YIPE!
THOSE AUTO-FLUSH TOILETS STILL SCARE YOU?
MAYBE A LITTLE.
KIRKMAN & SCOTT

Baby Blues
Rick Kirkman by Jerry Scott

Cheese Logs 'n Nose Studs!
RINGTONES UP THE YIN YANG
Tattoos for Tots
IS IT JUST ME, OR DO YOU FEEL LIKE WE'RE STARTING TO DRIFT A LITTLE OUT OF THE MAINSTREAM?
KIRKMAN & SCOTT

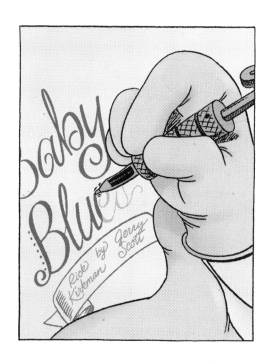

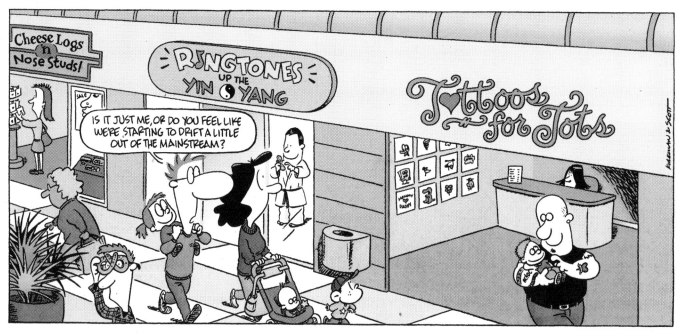

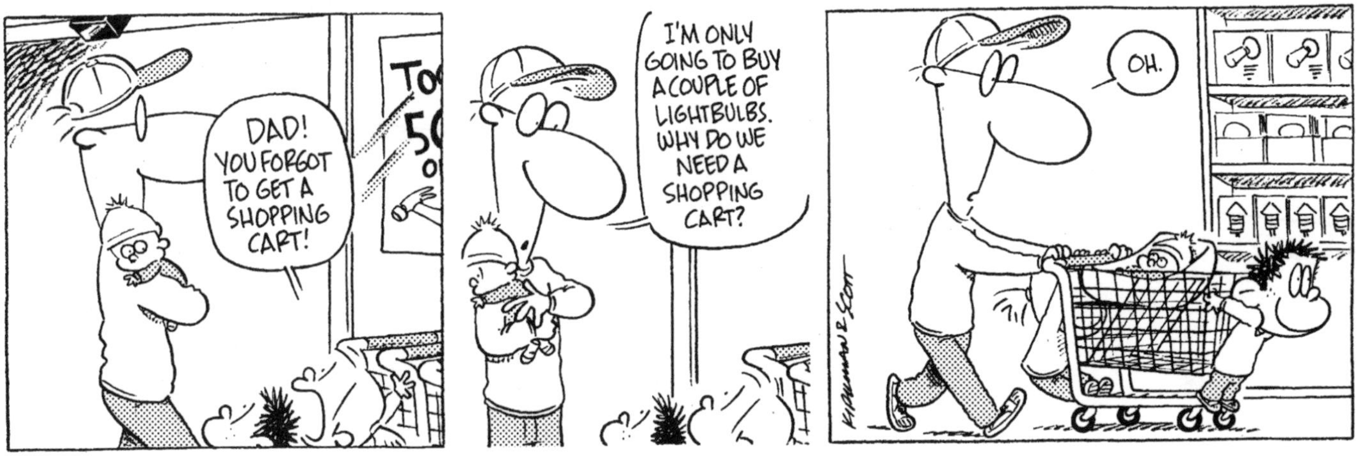
DAD! YOU FORGOT TO GET A SHOPPING CART!
I'M ONLY GOING TO BUY A COUPLE OF LIGHTBULBS. WHY DO WE NEED A SHOPPING CART?
OH.
KIRKMAN & SCOTT

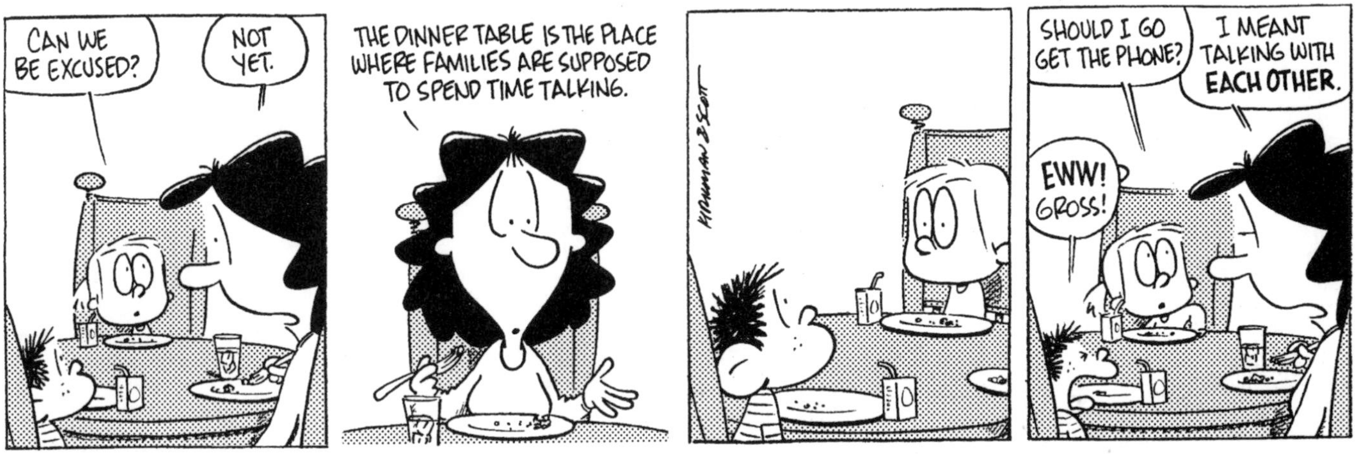
CAN WE BE EXCUSED?
NOT YET.
THE DINNER TABLE IS THE PLACE WHERE FAMILIES ARE SUPPOSED TO SPEND TIME TALKING.
KIRKMAN & SCOTT
SHOULD I GO GET THE PHONE?
I MEANT TALKING WITH **EACH OTHER**.
EWW! GROSS!

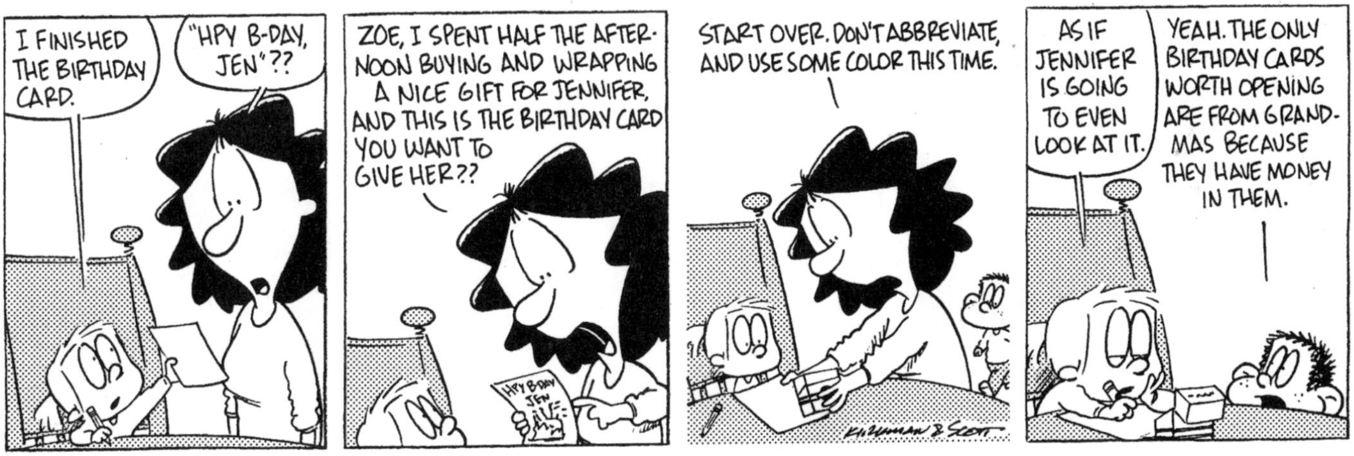
I FINISHED THE BIRTHDAY CARD.
"HPY B-DAY, JEN"??
ZOE, I SPENT HALF THE AFTERNOON BUYING AND WRAPPING A NICE GIFT FOR JENNIFER, AND THIS IS THE BIRTHDAY CARD YOU WANT TO GIVE HER??
HPY B-DAY JEN
START OVER. DON'T ABBREVIATE, AND USE SOME COLOR THIS TIME.
KIRKMAN & SCOTT
AS IF JENNIFER IS GOING TO EVEN LOOK AT IT.
YEAH. THE ONLY BIRTHDAY CARDS WORTH OPENING ARE FROM GRANDMAS BECAUSE THEY HAVE MONEY IN THEM.

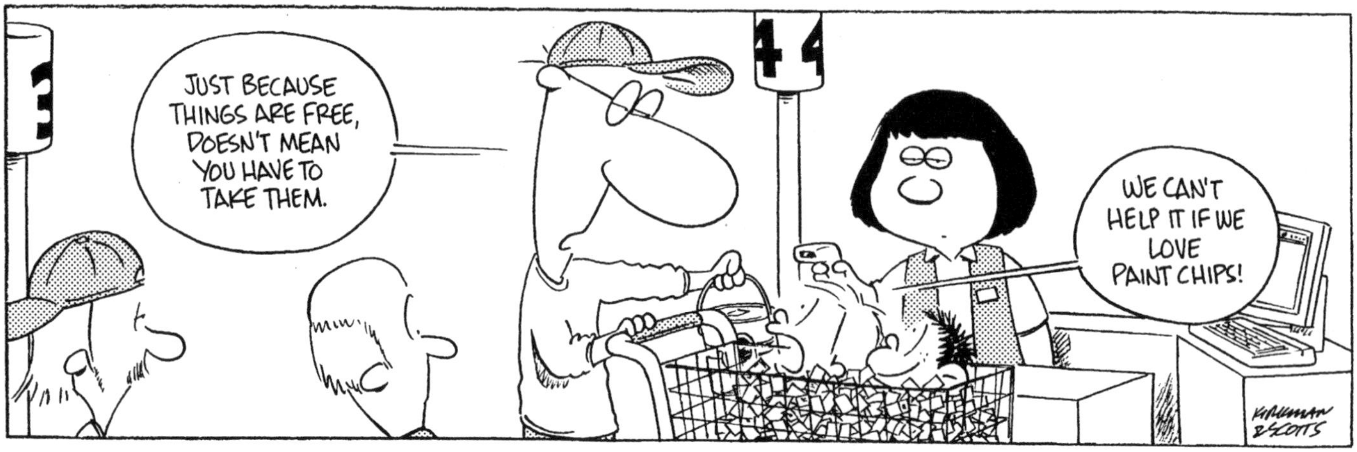
JUST BECAUSE THINGS ARE FREE, DOESN'T MEAN YOU HAVE TO TAKE THEM.
WE CAN'T HELP IT IF WE LOVE PAINT CHIPS!

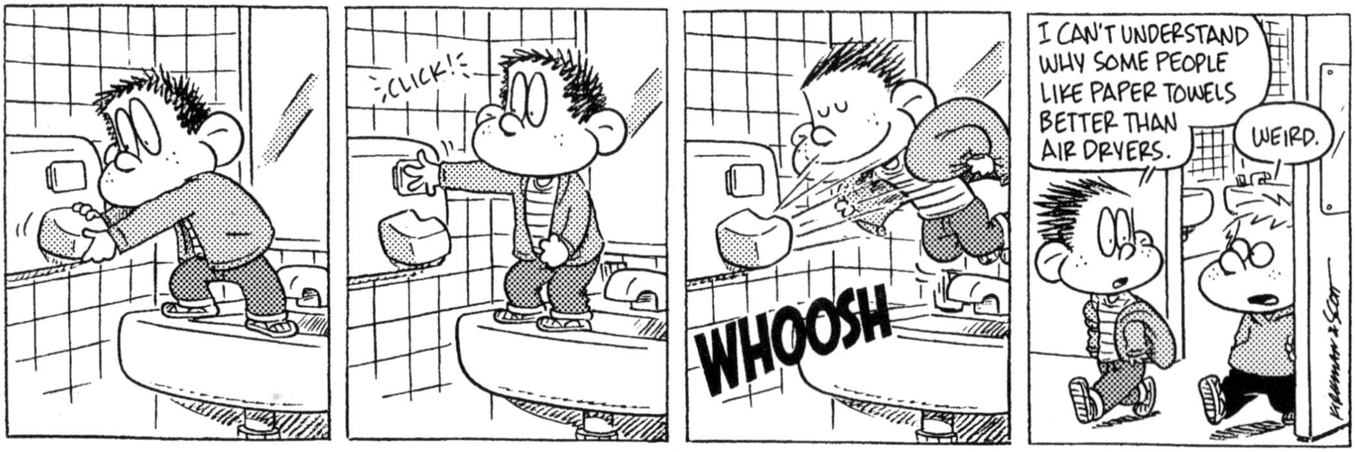
CLICK!
WHOOSH
I CAN'T UNDERSTAND WHY SOME PEOPLE LIKE PAPER TOWELS BETTER THAN AIR DRYERS.
WEIRD.

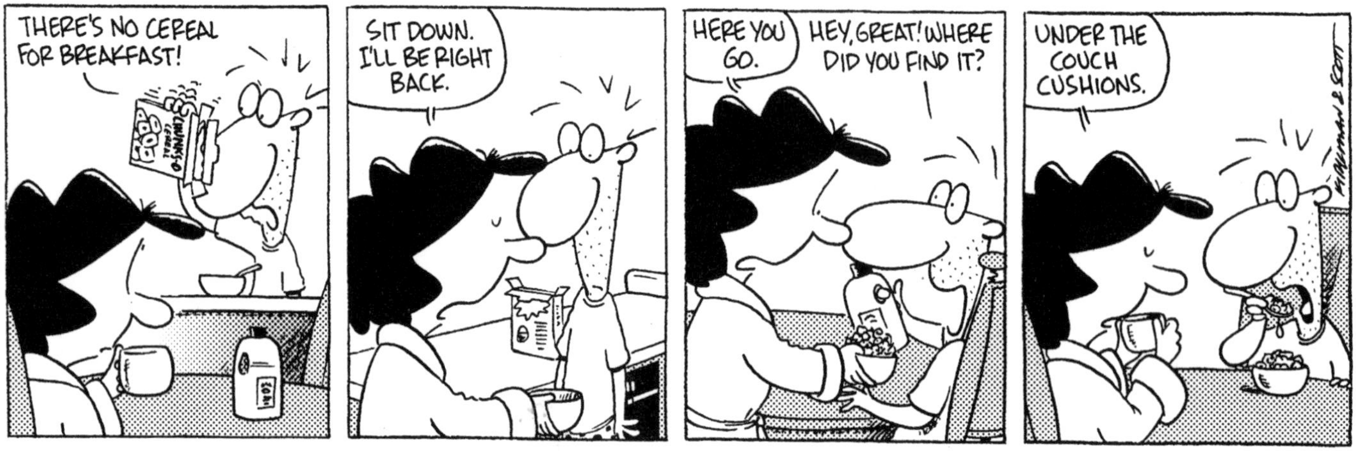
THERE'S NO CEREAL FOR BREAKFAST!
SIT DOWN. I'LL BE RIGHT BACK.
HERE YOU GO.
HEY, GREAT! WHERE DID YOU FIND IT?
UNDER THE COUCH CUSHIONS.

BABY BLUES®
RICK KIRKMAN / BY / JERRY SCOTT

WHOA!
IS IT POSSIBLE?
ZOE AND HAMMIE ARE AT PLAYDATES, AND WREN IS TAKING A NAP.
WE ACTUALLY HAVE SOME DOWNTIME!
KIRKMAN & SCOTT
HOW COME **YOUR** DOWNTIME IS ALWAYS **DOWN**, AND **MY** DOWNTIME IS ALWAYS **UP**?

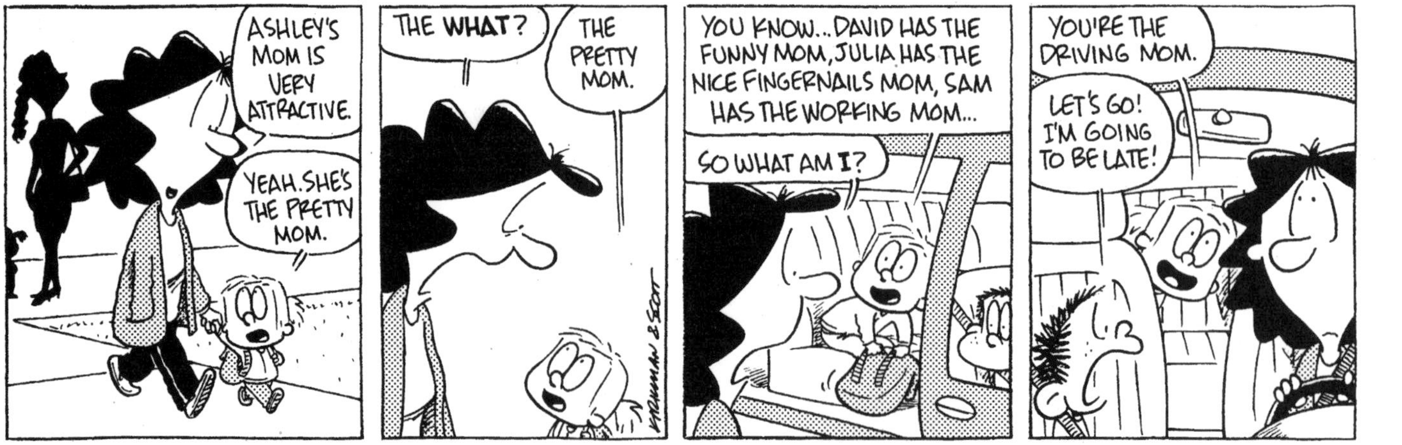
ASHLEY'S MOM IS VERY ATTRACTIVE.
YEAH. SHE'S THE PRETTY MOM.
THE **WHAT**?
THE PRETTY MOM.
YOU KNOW... DAVID HAS THE FUNNY MOM, JULIA HAS THE NICE FINGERNAILS MOM, SAM HAS THE WORKING MOM...
SO WHAT AM **I**?
YOU'RE THE DRIVING MOM.
LET'S GO! I'M GOING TO BE LATE!

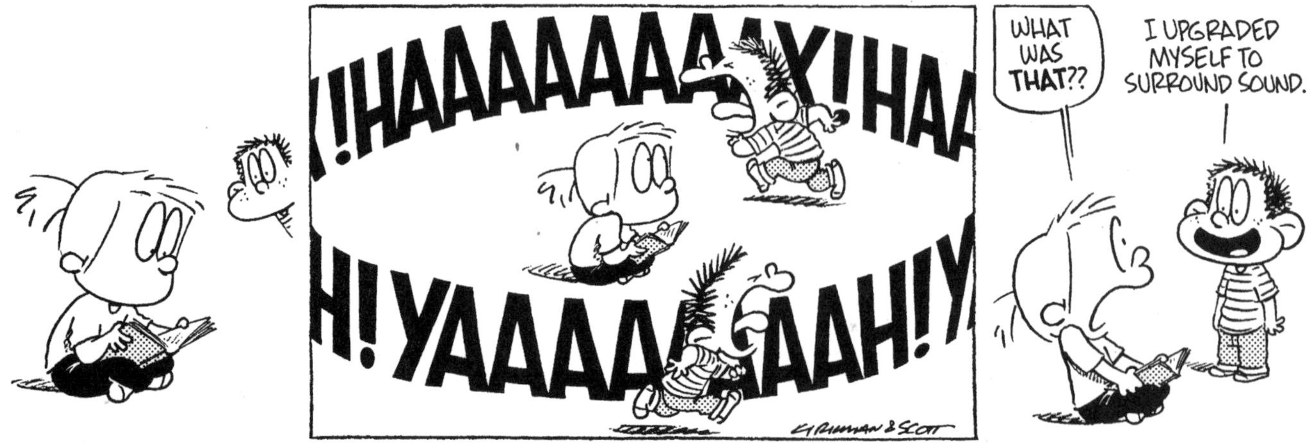
Y!HAAAAAAAA
Y!HAA
H! YAAAA
AAH!
WHAT WAS **THAT**??
I UPGRADED MYSELF TO SURROUND SOUND.

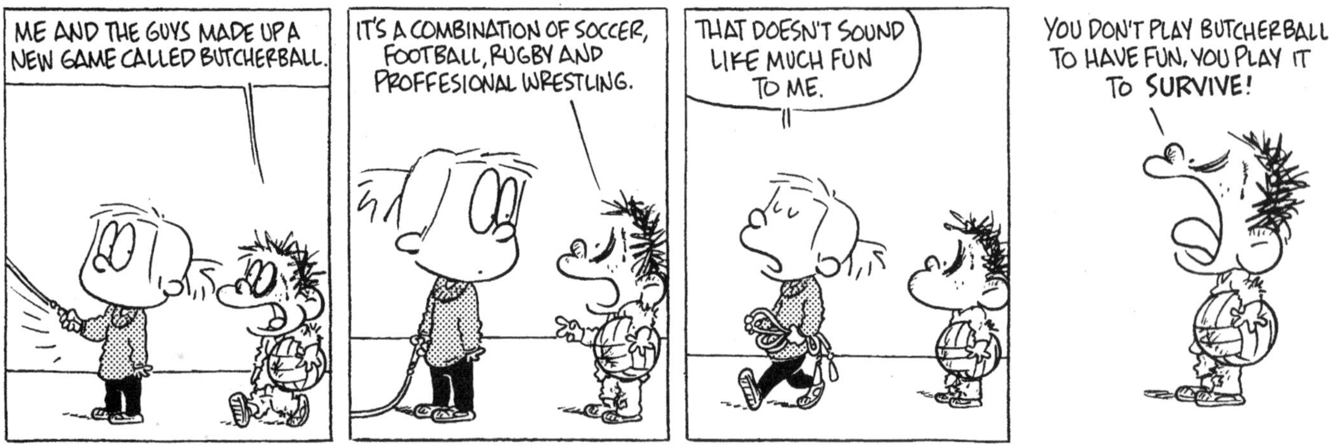
ME AND THE GUYS MADE UP A NEW GAME CALLED BUTCHERBALL.
IT'S A COMBINATION OF SOCCER, FOOTBALL, RUGBY AND PROFFESIONAL WRESTLING.
THAT DOESN'T SOUND LIKE MUCH FUN TO ME.
YOU DON'T PLAY BUTCHERBALL TO HAVE FUN, YOU PLAY IT TO **SURVIVE**!

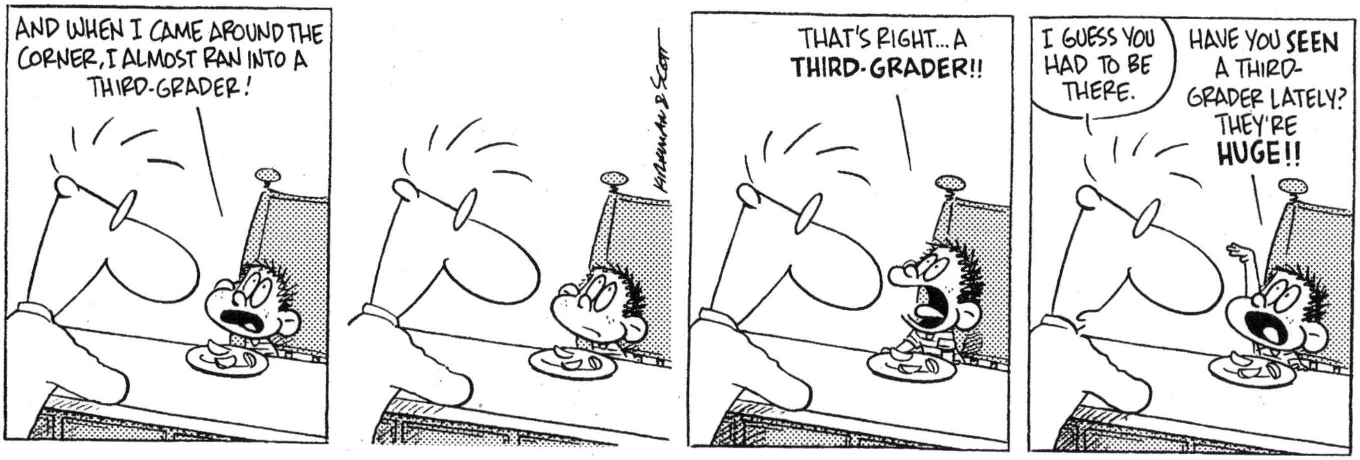
AND WHEN I CAME AROUND THE CORNER, I ALMOST RAN INTO A THIRD-GRADER!
KIRKMAN & SCOTT
THAT'S RIGHT... A **THIRD-GRADER!!**
I GUESS YOU HAD TO BE THERE.
HAVE YOU **SEEN** A THIRD-GRADER LATELY? THEY'RE **HUGE!!**

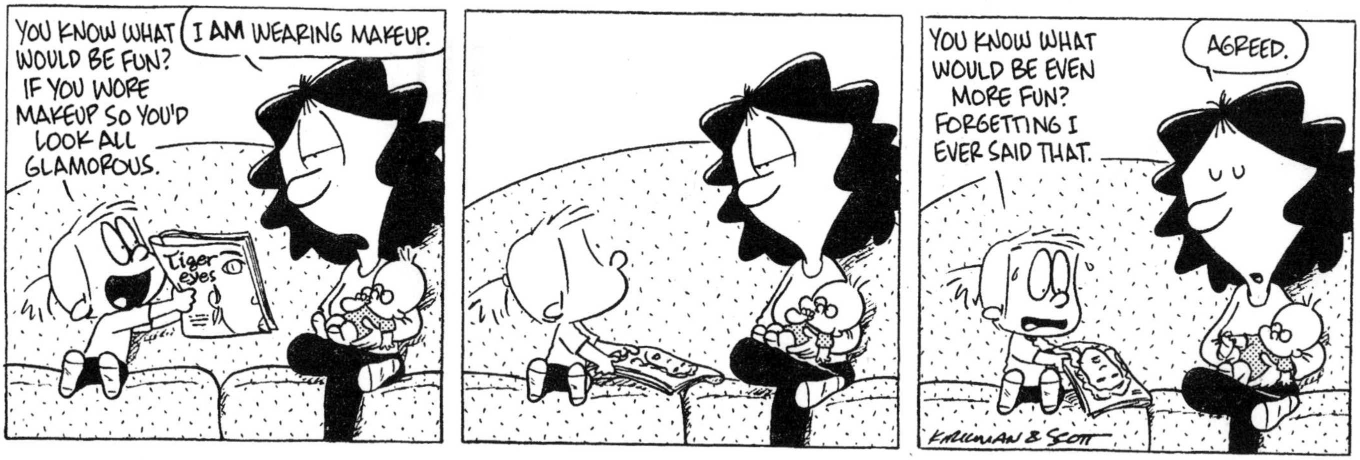
YOU KNOW WHAT WOULD BE FUN? IF YOU WORE MAKEUP SO YOU'D LOOK **ALL** GLAMOROUS.
I **AM** WEARING MAKEUP.
Tiger eyes
YOU KNOW WHAT WOULD BE EVEN MORE FUN? FORGETTING I EVER SAID THAT.
AGREED.
KIRKMAN & SCOTT

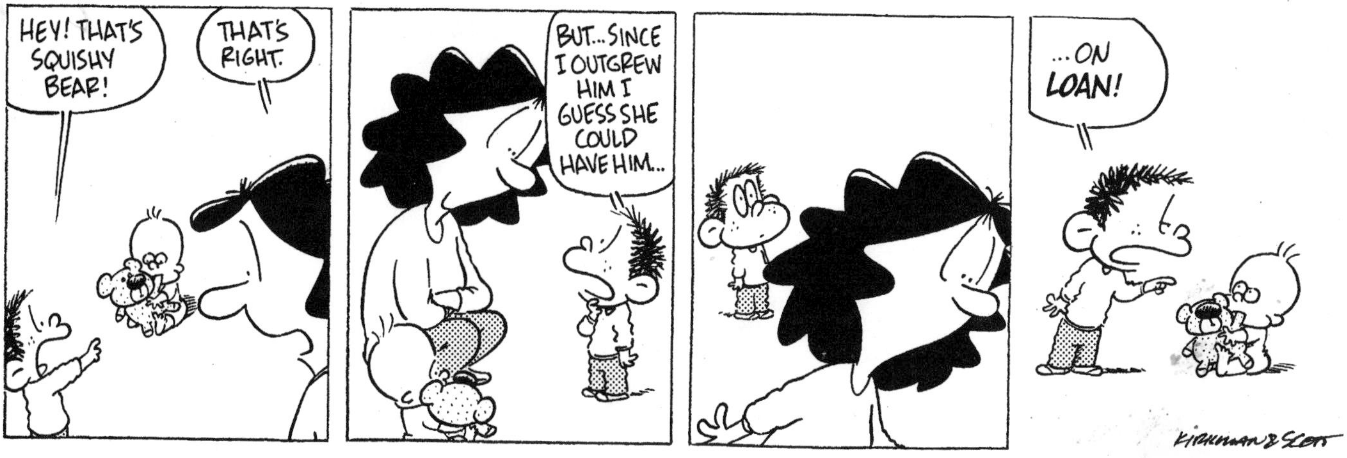
HEY! THAT'S SQUISHY BEAR!
THAT'S RIGHT.
BUT... SINCE I OUTGREW HIM I GUESS SHE COULD HAVE HIM...
...ON **LOAN!**
KIRKMAN & SCOTT

What were they thinking?
CASE NO. 1006
BERRY MEDLEY
OH. HERE'S THE LID.
KIRKMAN & SCOTT

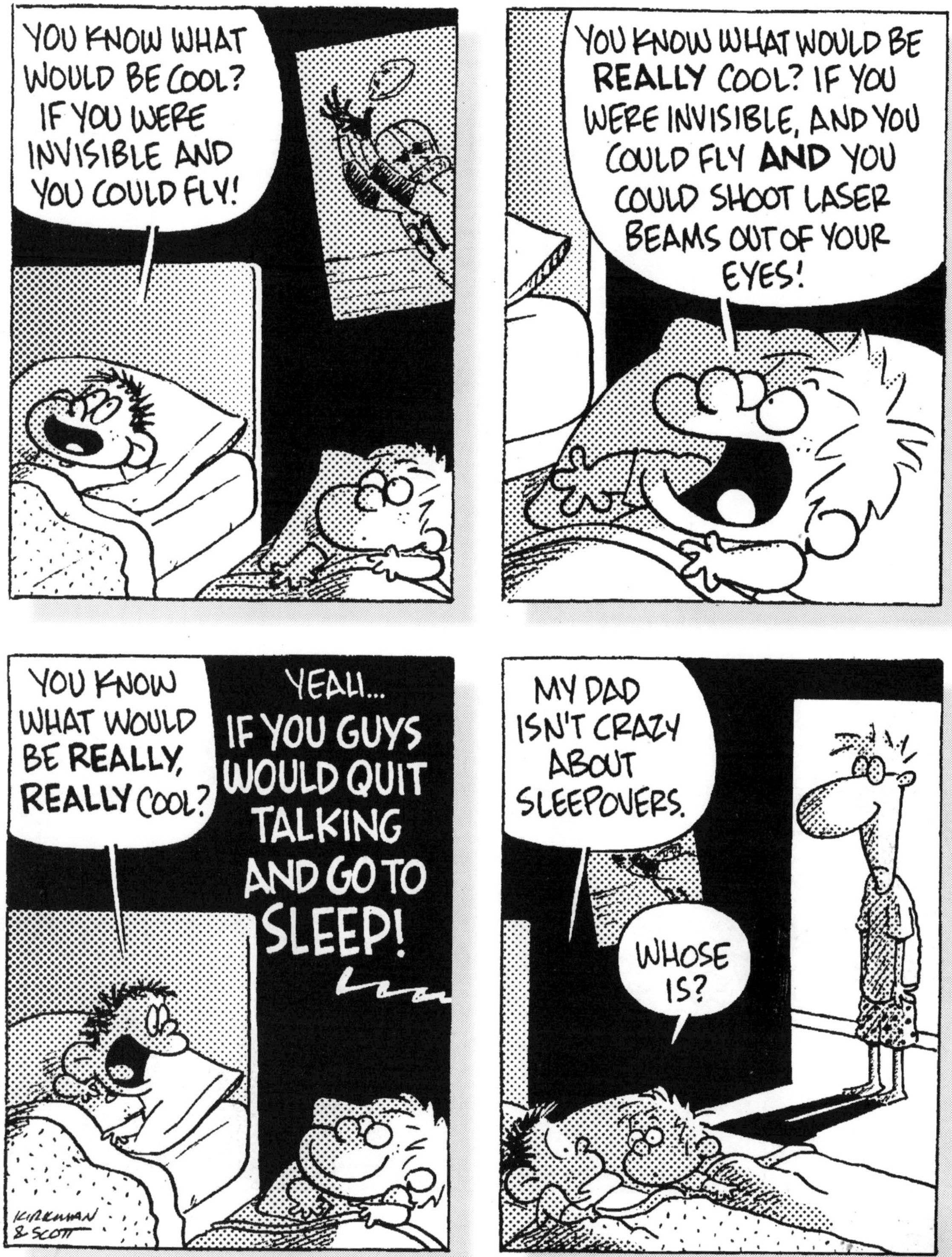
YOU KNOW WHAT WOULD BE COOL? IF YOU WERE INVISIBLE AND YOU COULD FLY!
YOU KNOW WHAT WOULD BE REALLY COOL? IF YOU WERE INVISIBLE, AND YOU COULD FLY AND YOU COULD SHOOT LASER BEAMS OUT OF YOUR EYES!
YOU KNOW WHAT WOULD BE REALLY, REALLY COOL?
YEAH... IF YOU GUYS WOULD QUIT TALKING AND GO TO SLEEP!
KIRKMAN & SCOTT
MY DAD ISN'T CRAZY ABOUT SLEEPOVERS.
WHOSE IS?

BABY BLUES®
BY
RICK KIRKMAN / JERRY SCOTT

SHUF SHUFFLE SH HUFFLE SHUF UFFLE SHUF FFLE SHUFF FFLE SHUFFLE SH SHUFFLE SH SHUFFLE S LE SHUF
BA-ZAP!
KIRKMAN & SCOTT
IT WAS AN ACCIDENT.

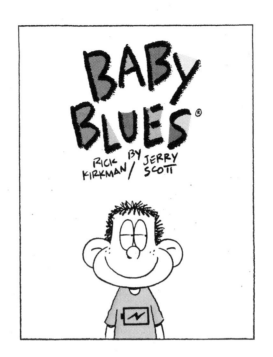

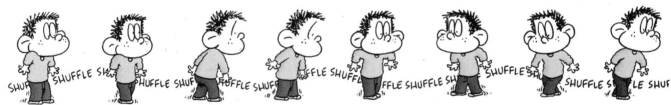

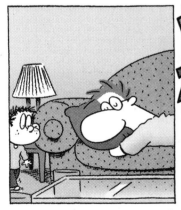

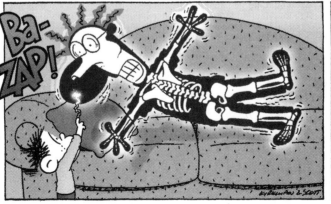

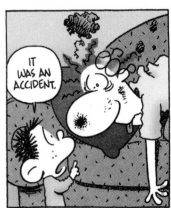

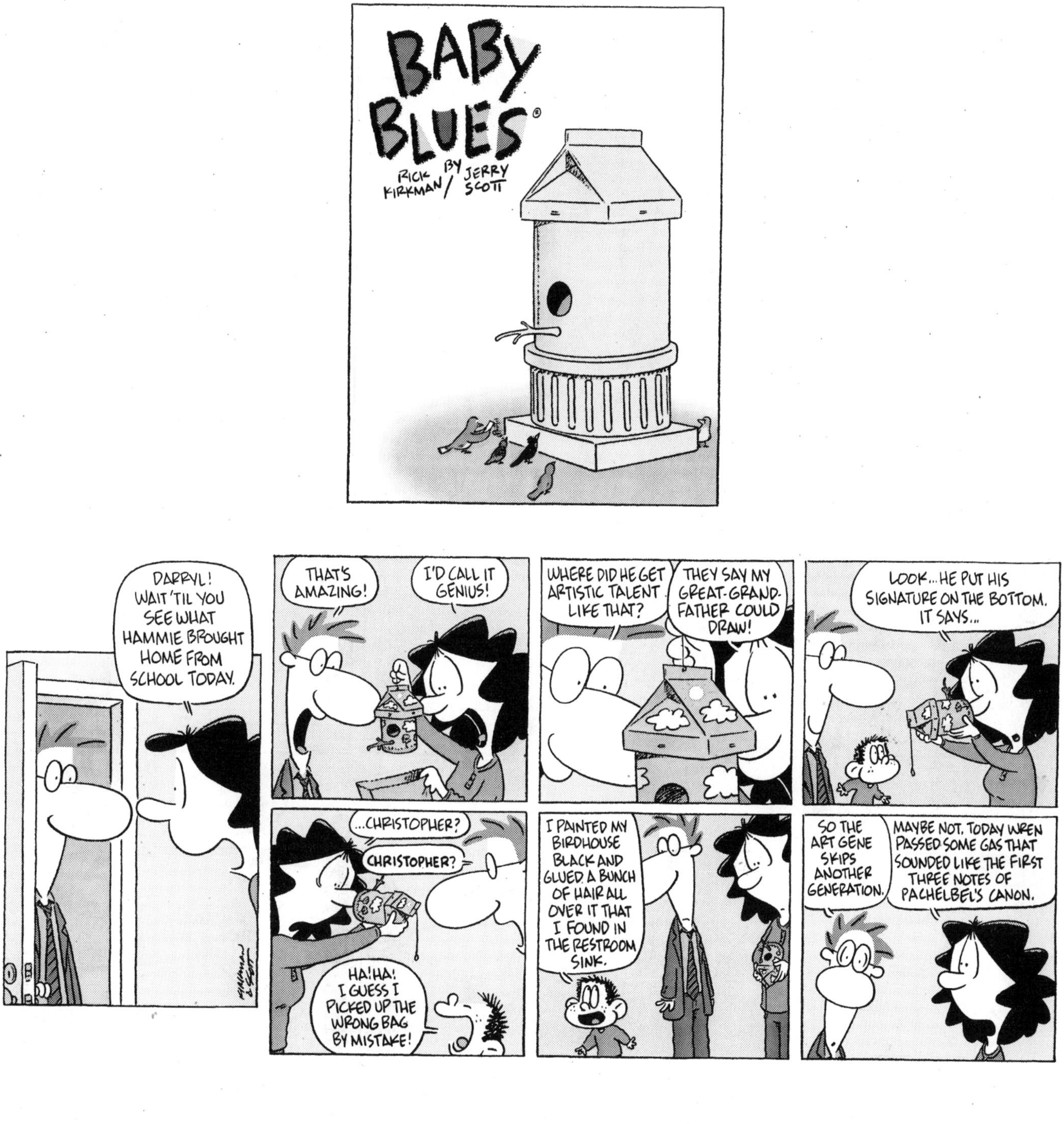
BABY BLUES®
BY RICK KIRKMAN / JERRY SCOTT
DARRYL! WAIT 'TIL YOU SEE WHAT HAMMIE BROUGHT HOME FROM SCHOOL TODAY.
THAT'S AMAZING!
I'D CALL IT GENIUS!
WHERE DID HE GET ARTISTIC TALENT LIKE THAT?
THEY SAY MY GREAT-GRAND-FATHER COULD DRAW!
LOOK... HE PUT HIS SIGNATURE ON THE BOTTOM. IT SAYS...
...CHRISTOPHER?
CHRISTOPHER?
HA! HA! I GUESS I PICKED UP THE WRONG BAG BY MISTAKE!
I PAINTED MY BIRDHOUSE BLACK AND GLUED A BUNCH OF HAIR ALL OVER IT THAT I FOUND IN THE RESTROOM SINK.
SO THE ART GENE SKIPS ANOTHER GENERATION.
MAYBE NOT. TODAY WREN PASSED SOME GAS THAT SOUNDED LIKE THE FIRST THREE NOTES OF PACHELBEL'S CANON.

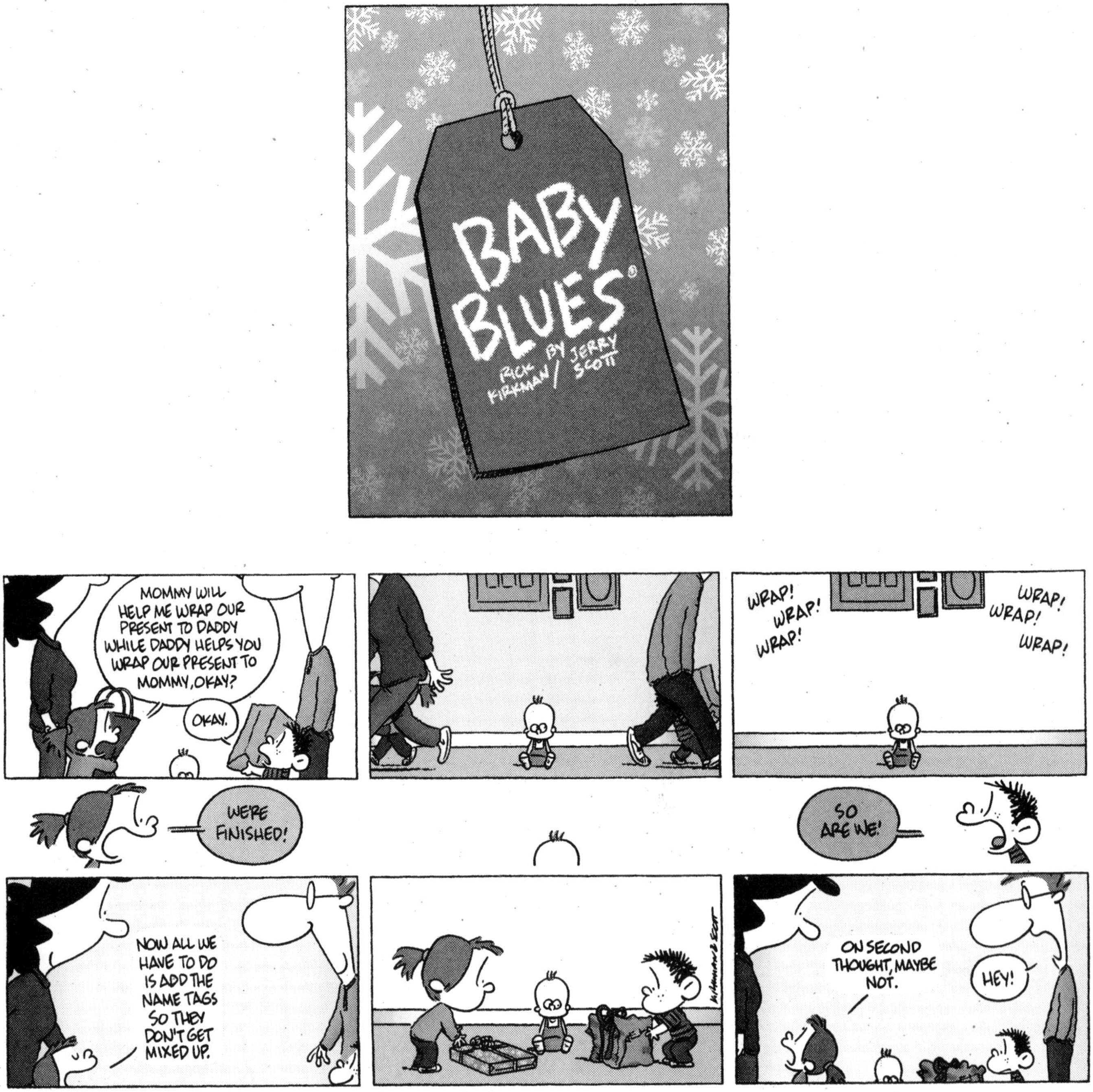
BABY BLUES®
RICK KIRKMAN / BY JERRY SCOTT
MOMMY WILL HELP ME WRAP OUR PRESENT TO DADDY WHILE DADDY HELPS YOU WRAP OUR PRESENT TO MOMMY, OKAY?
OKAY.
WRAP! WRAP! WRAP!
WRAP! WRAP! WRAP!
WE'RE FINISHED!
SO ARE WE!
NOW ALL WE HAVE TO DO IS ADD THE NAME TAGS SO THEY DON'T GET MIXED UP.
ON SECOND THOUGHT, MAYBE NOT.
HEY!

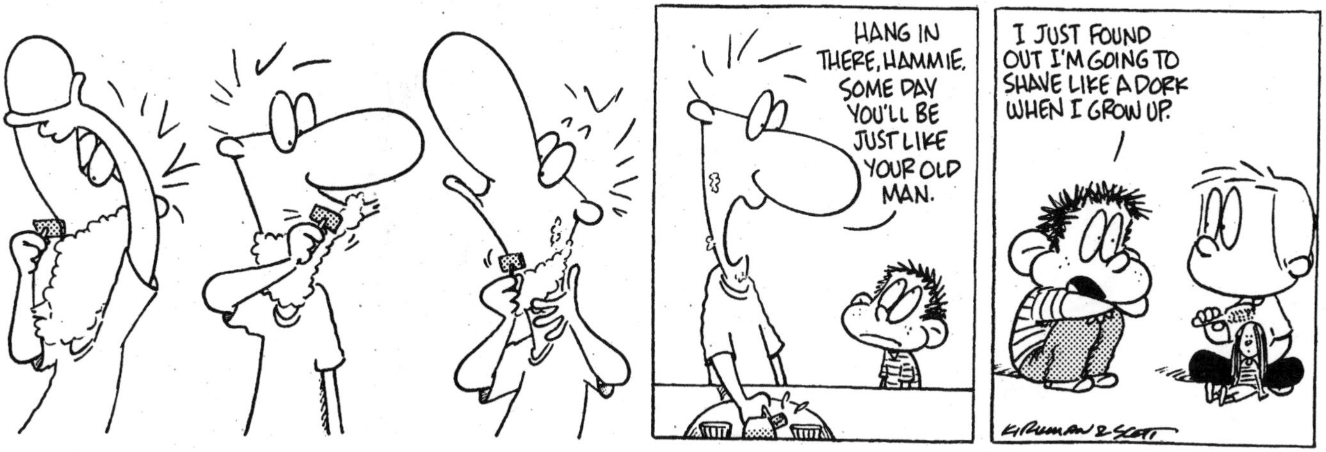
HANG IN THERE, HAMMIE. SOME DAY YOU'LL BE JUST LIKE YOUR OLD MAN.
I JUST FOUND OUT I'M GOING TO SHAVE LIKE A DORK WHEN I GROW UP.
KIRKMAN & SCOTT

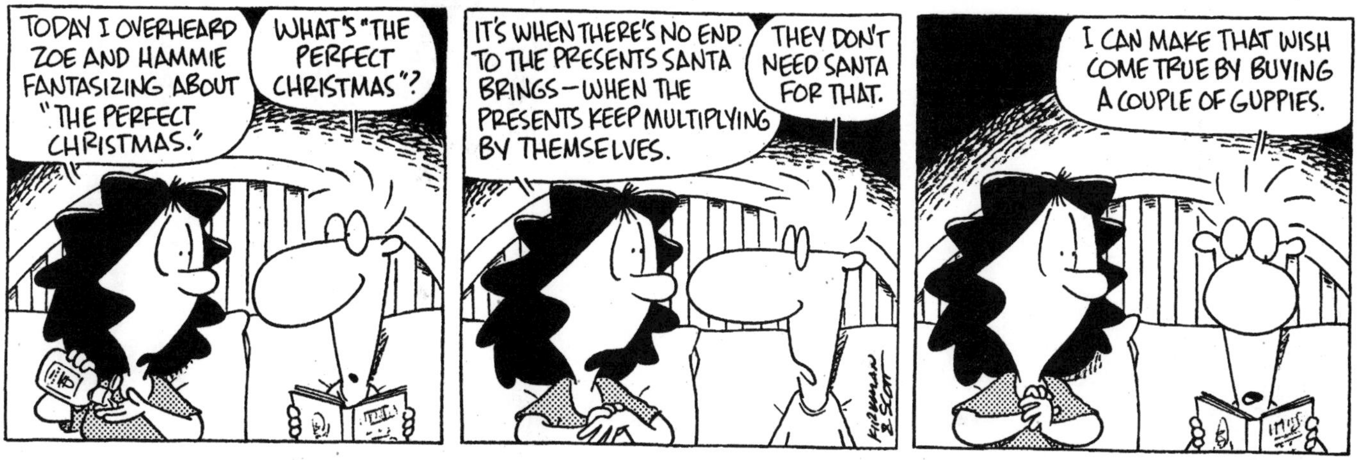
TODAY I OVERHEARD ZOE AND HAMMIE FANTASIZING ABOUT "THE PERFECT CHRISTMAS."
WHAT'S "THE PERFECT CHRISTMAS"?
IT'S WHEN THERE'S NO END TO THE PRESENTS SANTA BRINGS—WHEN THE PRESENTS KEEP MULTIPLYING BY THEMSELVES.
THEY DON'T NEED SANTA FOR THAT.
KIRKMAN & SCOTT
I CAN MAKE THAT WISH COME TRUE BY BUYING A COUPLE OF GUPPIES.

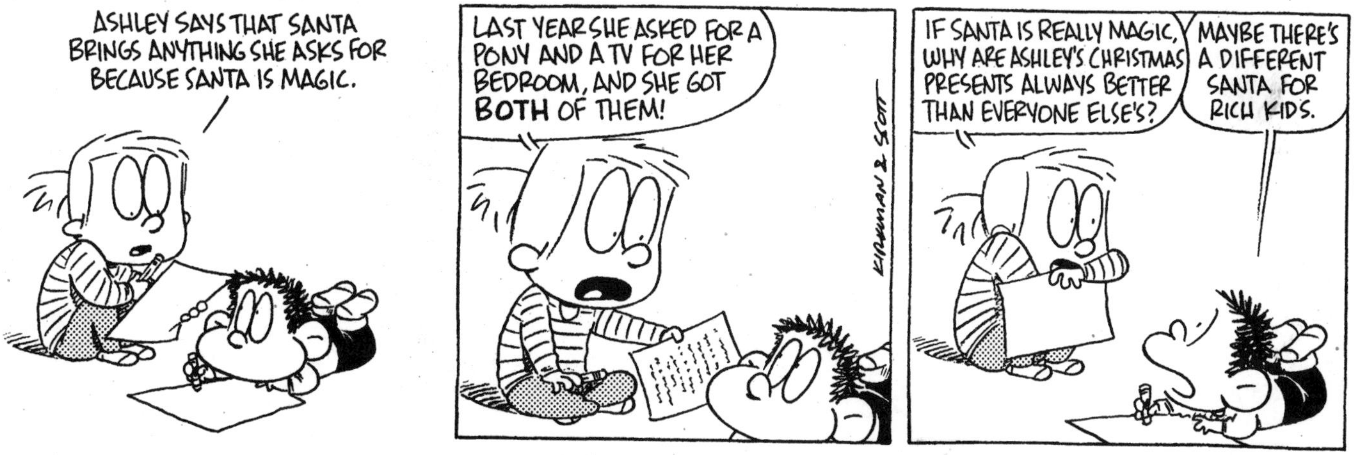
ASHLEY SAYS THAT SANTA BRINGS ANYTHING SHE ASKS FOR BECAUSE SANTA IS MAGIC.
LAST YEAR SHE ASKED FOR A PONY AND A TV FOR HER BEDROOM, AND SHE GOT **BOTH** OF THEM!
KIRKMAN & SCOTT
IF SANTA IS REALLY MAGIC, WHY ARE ASHLEY'S CHRISTMAS PRESENTS ALWAYS BETTER THAN EVERYONE ELSE'S?
MAYBE THERE'S A DIFFERENT SANTA FOR RICH KIDS.

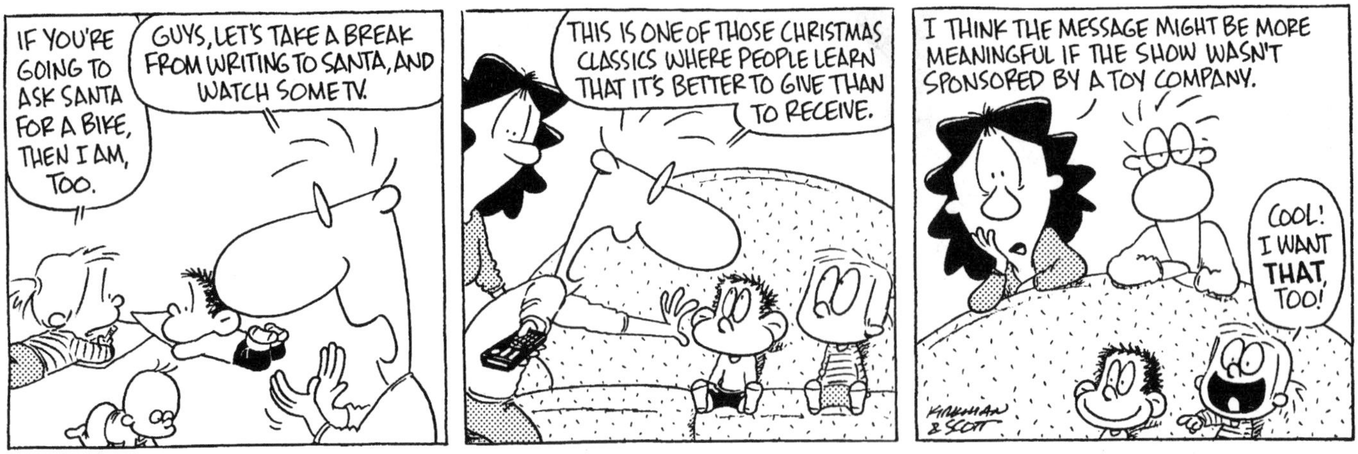

IF YOU'RE GOING TO ASK SANTA FOR A BIKE, THEN I AM, TOO.
GUYS, LET'S TAKE A BREAK FROM WRITING TO SANTA, AND WATCH SOME TV.
THIS IS ONE OF THOSE CHRISTMAS CLASSICS WHERE PEOPLE LEARN THAT IT'S BETTER TO GIVE THAN TO RECEIVE.
I THINK THE MESSAGE MIGHT BE MORE MEANINGFUL IF THE SHOW WASN'T SPONSORED BY A TOY COMPANY.
COOL! I WANT **THAT**, TOO!

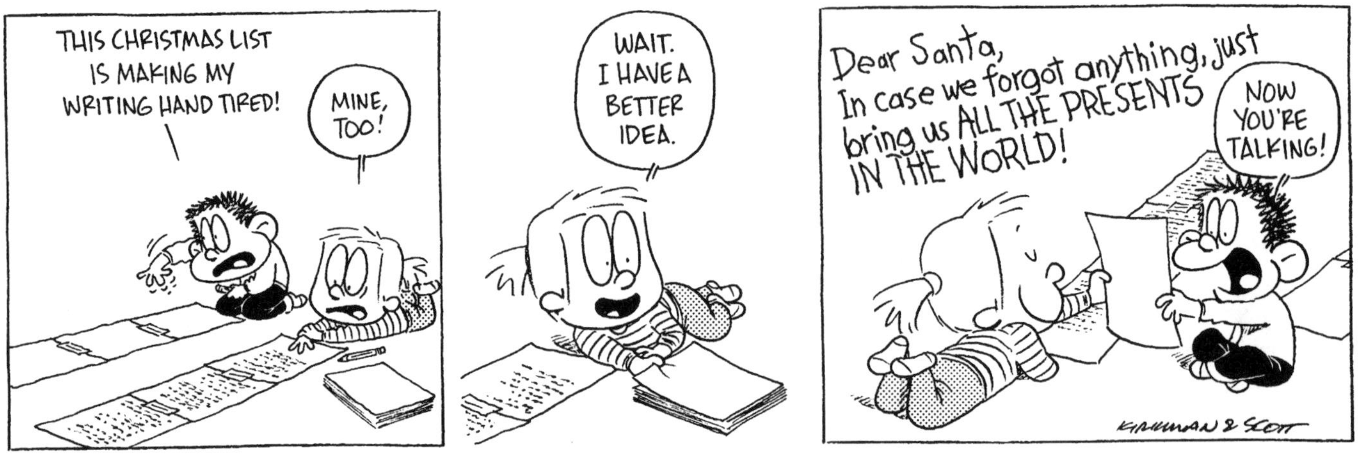

THIS CHRISTMAS LIST IS MAKING MY WRITING HAND TIRED!
MINE, TOO!
WAIT. I HAVE A BETTER IDEA.
Dear Santa,
In case we forgot anything, just bring us ALL THE PRESENTS IN THE WORLD!
NOW YOU'RE TALKING!

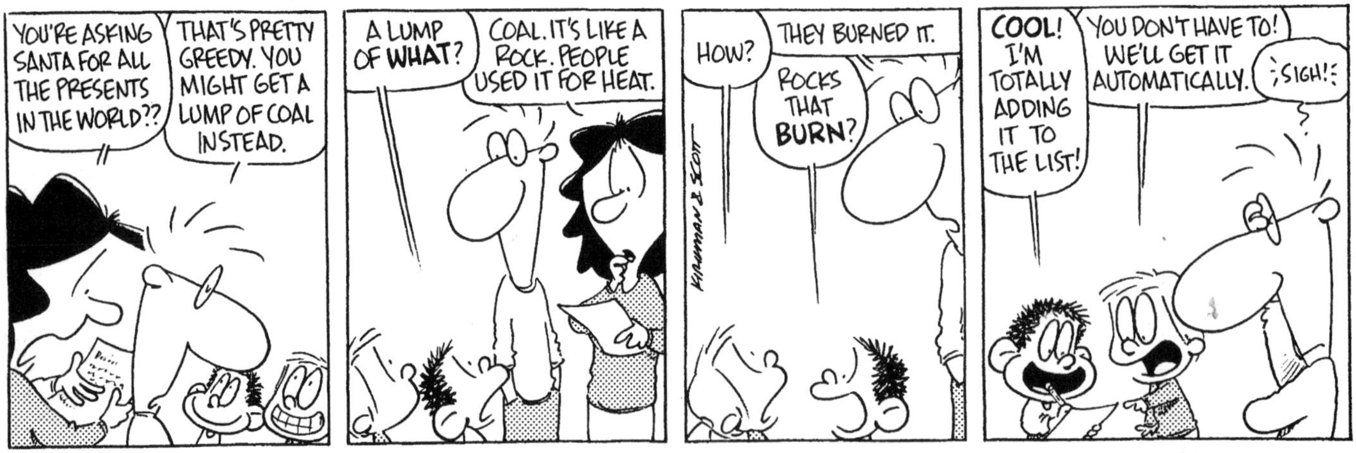

YOU'RE ASKING SANTA FOR ALL THE PRESENTS IN THE WORLD??
THAT'S PRETTY GREEDY. YOU MIGHT GET A LUMP OF COAL INSTEAD.
A LUMP OF **WHAT**?
COAL. IT'S LIKE A ROCK. PEOPLE USED IT FOR HEAT.
HOW?
THEY BURNED IT.
ROCKS THAT **BURN**?
COOL! I'M TOTALLY ADDING IT TO THE LIST!
YOU DON'T HAVE TO! WE'LL GET IT AUTOMATICALLY.
SIGH!

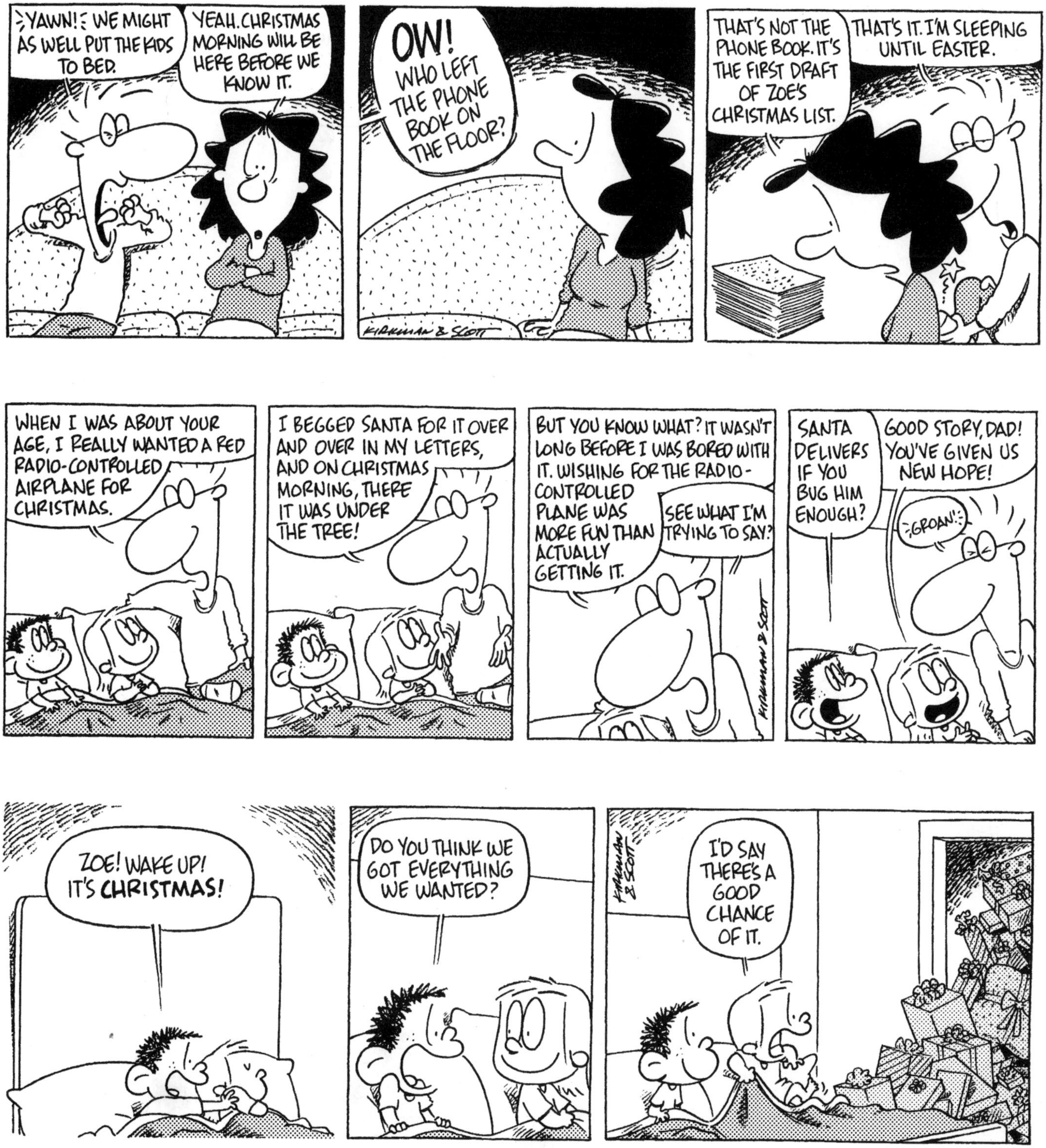
YAWN! WE MIGHT AS WELL PUT THE KIDS TO BED.
YEAH. CHRISTMAS MORNING WILL BE HERE BEFORE WE KNOW IT.
OW! WHO LEFT THE PHONE BOOK ON THE FLOOR?
KIRKMAN & SCOTT
THAT'S NOT THE PHONE BOOK. IT'S THE FIRST DRAFT OF ZOE'S CHRISTMAS LIST.
THAT'S IT. I'M SLEEPING UNTIL EASTER.
WHEN I WAS ABOUT YOUR AGE, I REALLY WANTED A RED RADIO-CONTROLLED AIRPLANE FOR CHRISTMAS.
I BEGGED SANTA FOR IT OVER AND OVER IN MY LETTERS, AND ON CHRISTMAS MORNING, THERE IT WAS UNDER THE TREE!
BUT YOU KNOW WHAT? IT WASN'T LONG BEFORE I WAS BORED WITH IT. WISHING FOR THE RADIO-CONTROLLED PLANE WAS MORE FUN THAN ACTUALLY GETTING IT.
SEE WHAT I'M TRYING TO SAY?
KIRKMAN & SCOTT
SANTA DELIVERS IF YOU BUG HIM ENOUGH?
GOOD STORY, DAD! YOU'VE GIVEN US NEW HOPE!
GROAN!
ZOE! WAKE UP! IT'S CHRISTMAS!
DO YOU THINK WE GOT EVERYTHING WE WANTED?
KIRKMAN & SCOTT
I'D SAY THERE'S A GOOD CHANCE OF IT.

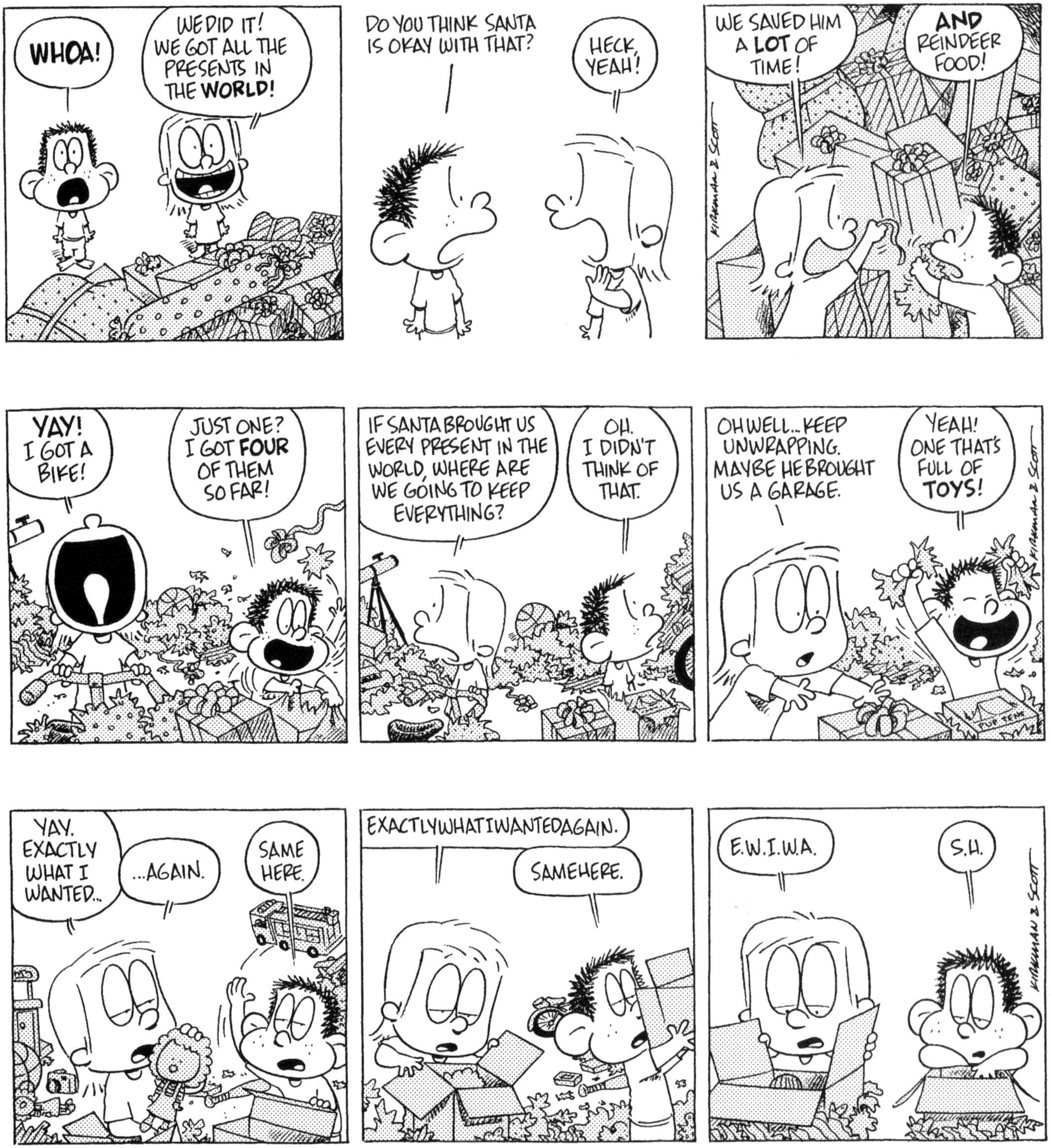
WHOA!
WE DID IT! WE GOT ALL THE PRESENTS IN THE **WORLD**!
DO YOU THINK SANTA IS OKAY WITH THAT?
HECK, YEAH!
WE SAVED HIM A **LOT** OF TIME!
AND REINDEER FOOD!
KIRKMAN & SCOTT
YAY! I GOT A BIKE!
JUST ONE? I GOT **FOUR** OF THEM SO FAR!
IF SANTA BROUGHT US EVERY PRESENT IN THE WORLD, WHERE ARE WE GOING TO KEEP EVERYTHING?
OH. I DIDN'T THINK OF THAT.
OH WELL... KEEP UNWRAPPING. MAYBE HE BROUGHT US A GARAGE.
YEAH! ONE THAT'S FULL OF **TOYS**!
KIRKMAN & SCOTT
YAY. EXACTLY WHAT I WANTED...
...AGAIN.
SAME HERE.
EXACTLYWHATIWANTEDAGAIN.
SAMEHERE.
E.W.I.W.A.
S.H.
KIRKMAN & SCOTT

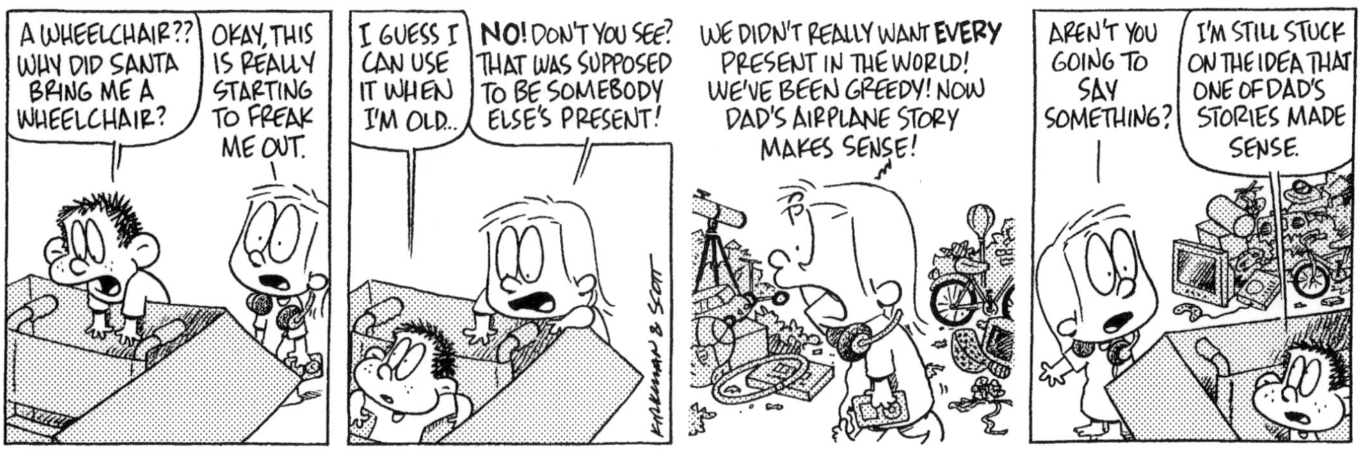
A WHEELCHAIR?? WHY DID SANTA BRING ME A WHEELCHAIR?
OKAY, THIS IS REALLY STARTING TO FREAK ME OUT.
I GUESS I CAN USE IT WHEN I'M OLD...
NO! DON'T YOU SEE? THAT WAS SUPPOSED TO BE SOMEBODY ELSE'S PRESENT!
WE DIDN'T REALLY WANT EVERY PRESENT IN THE WORLD! WE'VE BEEN GREEDY! NOW DAD'S AIRPLANE STORY MAKES SENSE!
AREN'T YOU GOING TO SAY SOMETHING?
I'M STILL STUCK ON THE IDEA THAT ONE OF DAD'S STORIES MADE SENSE.

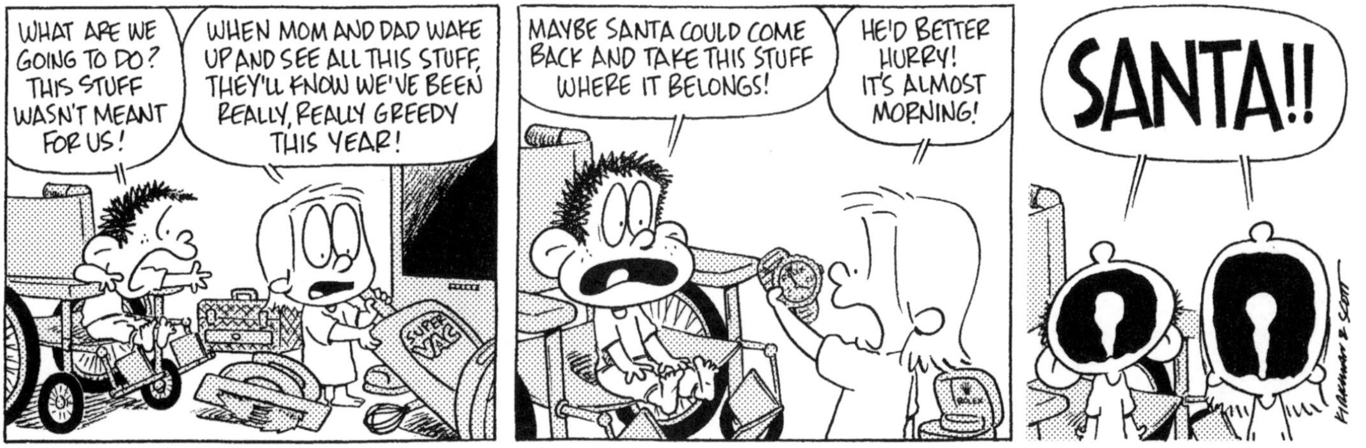
WHAT ARE WE GOING TO DO? THIS STUFF WASN'T MEANT FOR US!
WHEN MOM AND DAD WAKE UP AND SEE ALL THIS STUFF, THEY'LL KNOW WE'VE BEEN REALLY, REALLY GREEDY THIS YEAR!
SUPER VAC
MAYBE SANTA COULD COME BACK AND TAKE THIS STUFF WHERE IT BELONGS!
HE'D BETTER HURRY! IT'S ALMOST MORNING!
SANTA!!

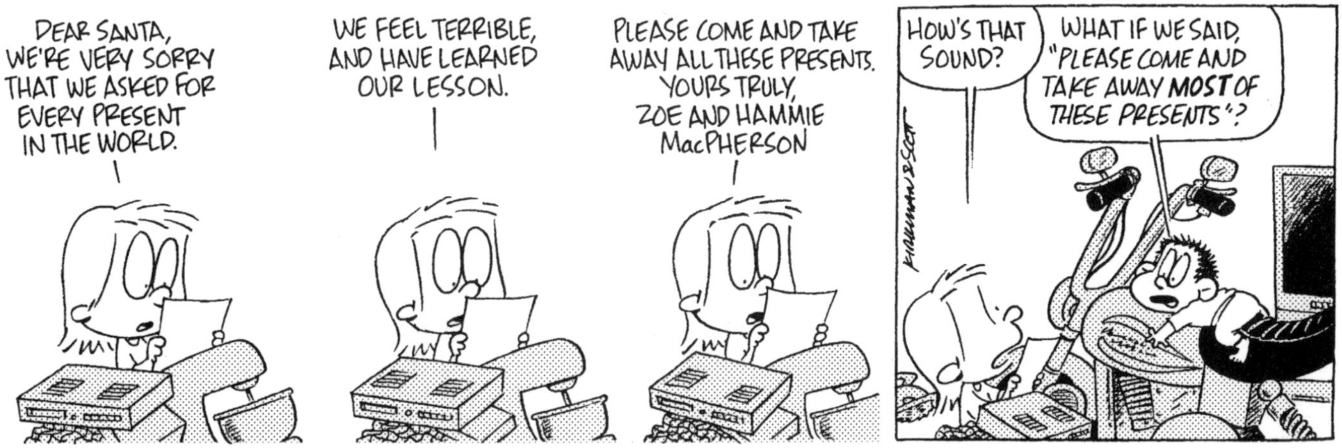
DEAR SANTA, WE'RE VERY SORRY THAT WE ASKED FOR EVERY PRESENT IN THE WORLD.
WE FEEL TERRIBLE, AND HAVE LEARNED OUR LESSON.
PLEASE COME AND TAKE AWAY ALL THESE PRESENTS. YOURS TRULY, ZOE AND HAMMIE MacPHERSON
HOW'S THAT SOUND?
WHAT IF WE SAID, "PLEASE COME AND TAKE AWAY MOST OF THESE PRESENTS"?

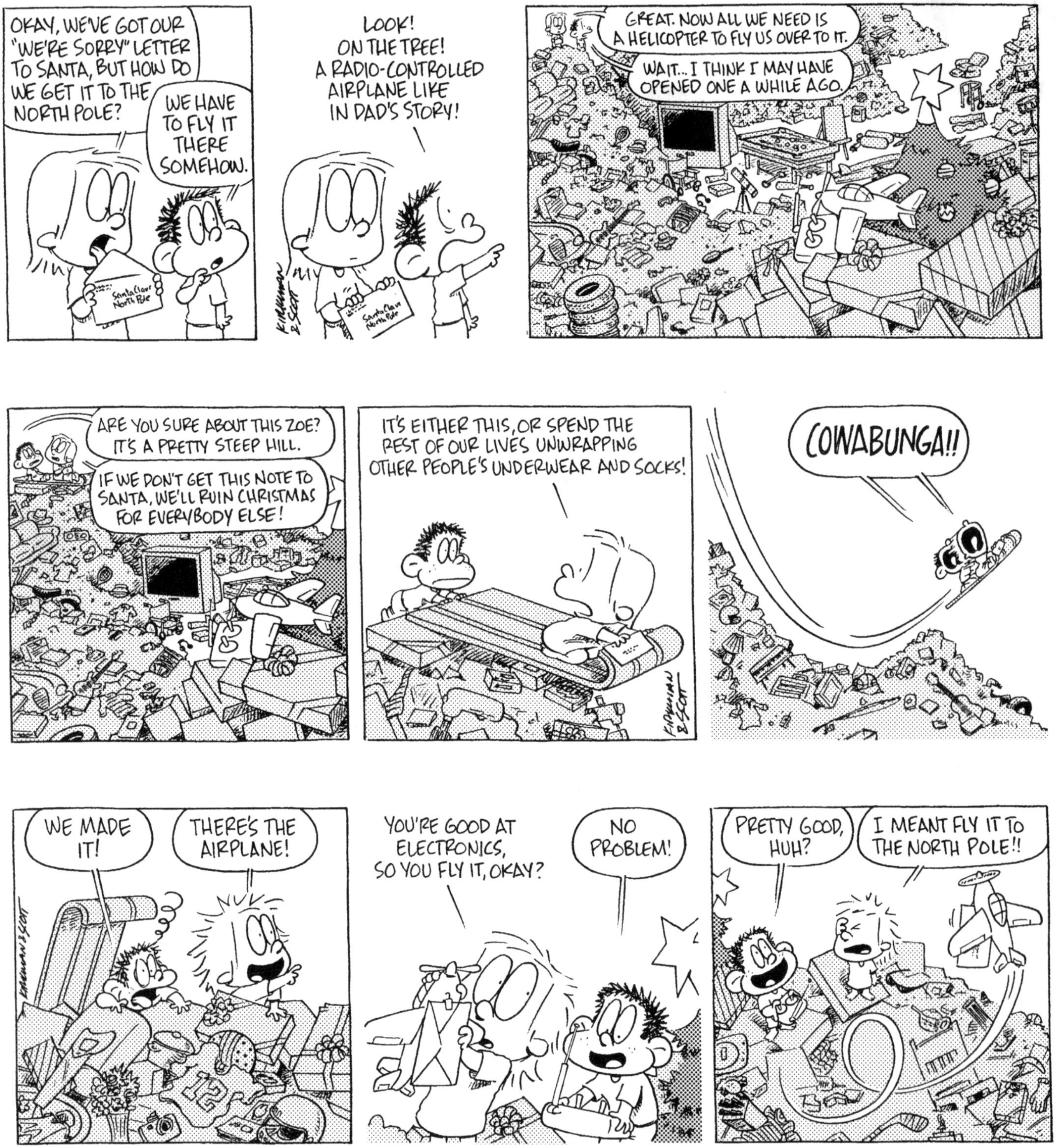

OKAY, WE'VE GOT OUR "WE'RE SORRY" LETTER TO SANTA, BUT HOW DO WE GET IT TO THE NORTH POLE?
WE HAVE TO FLY IT THERE SOMEHOW.
Santa Claus North Pole
LOOK! ON THE TREE! A RADIO-CONTROLLED AIRPLANE LIKE IN DAD'S STORY!
GREAT. NOW ALL WE NEED IS A HELICOPTER TO FLY US OVER TO IT.
WAIT... I THINK I MAY HAVE OPENED ONE A WHILE AGO.
ARE YOU SURE ABOUT THIS ZOE? IT'S A PRETTY STEEP HILL.
IF WE DON'T GET THIS NOTE TO SANTA, WE'LL RUIN CHRISTMAS FOR EVERYBODY ELSE!
IT'S EITHER THIS, OR SPEND THE REST OF OUR LIVES UNWRAPPING OTHER PEOPLE'S UNDERWEAR AND SOCKS!
COWABUNGA!!
WE MADE IT!
THERE'S THE AIRPLANE!
YOU'RE GOOD AT ELECTRONICS, SO YOU FLY IT, OKAY?
NO PROBLEM!
PRETTY GOOD, HUH?
I MEANT FLY IT TO THE NORTH POLE!!

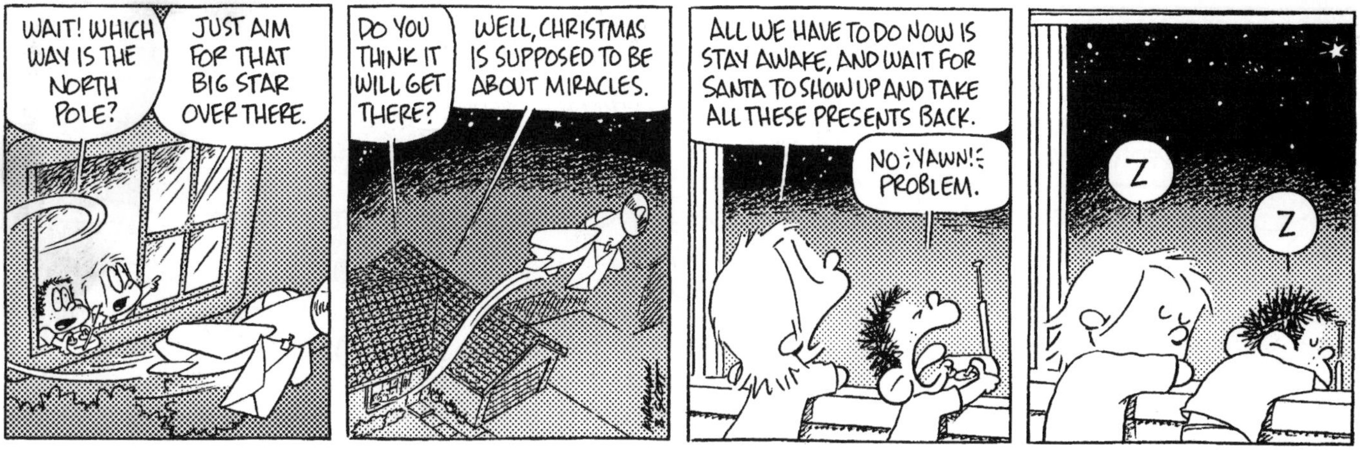
WAIT! WHICH WAY IS THE NORTH POLE?
JUST AIM FOR THAT BIG STAR OVER THERE.
DO YOU THINK IT WILL GET THERE?
WELL, CHRISTMAS IS SUPPOSED TO BE ABOUT MIRACLES.
ALL WE HAVE TO DO NOW IS STAY AWAKE, AND WAIT FOR SANTA TO SHOW UP AND TAKE ALL THESE PRESENTS BACK.
NO *YAWN!* PROBLEM.
Z
Z

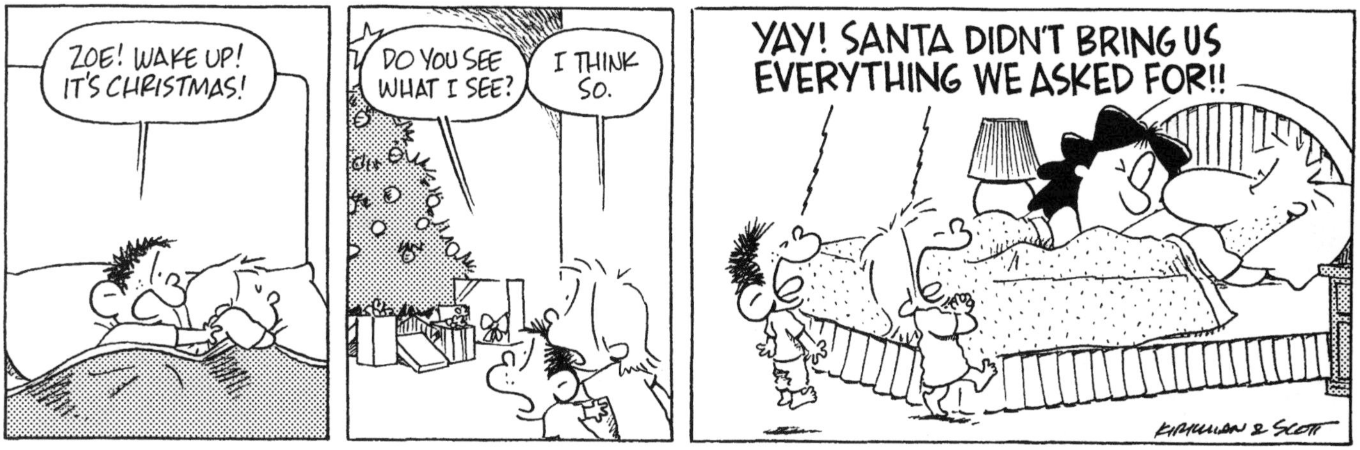
ZOE! WAKE UP! IT'S CHRISTMAS!
DO YOU SEE WHAT I SEE?
I THINK SO.
YAY! SANTA DIDN'T BRING US EVERYTHING WE ASKED FOR!!
KIRKMAN & SCOTT

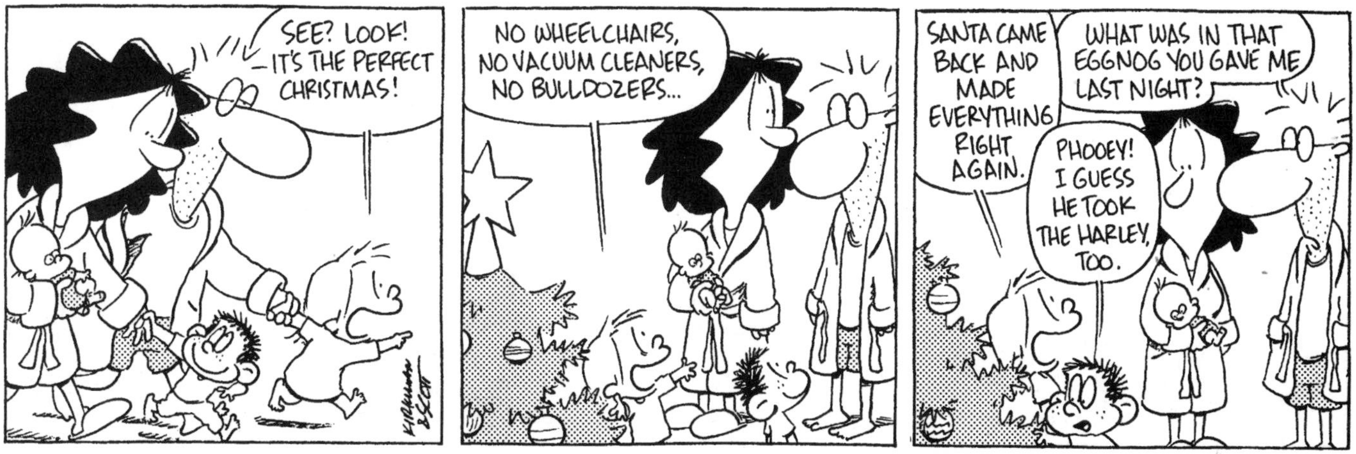
SEE? LOOK! IT'S THE PERFECT CHRISTMAS!
NO WHEELCHAIRS, NO VACUUM CLEANERS, NO BULLDOZERS...
SANTA CAME BACK AND MADE EVERYTHING RIGHT AGAIN.
WHAT WAS IN THAT EGGNOG YOU GAVE ME LAST NIGHT?
PHOOEY! I GUESS HE TOOK THE HARLEY, TOO.

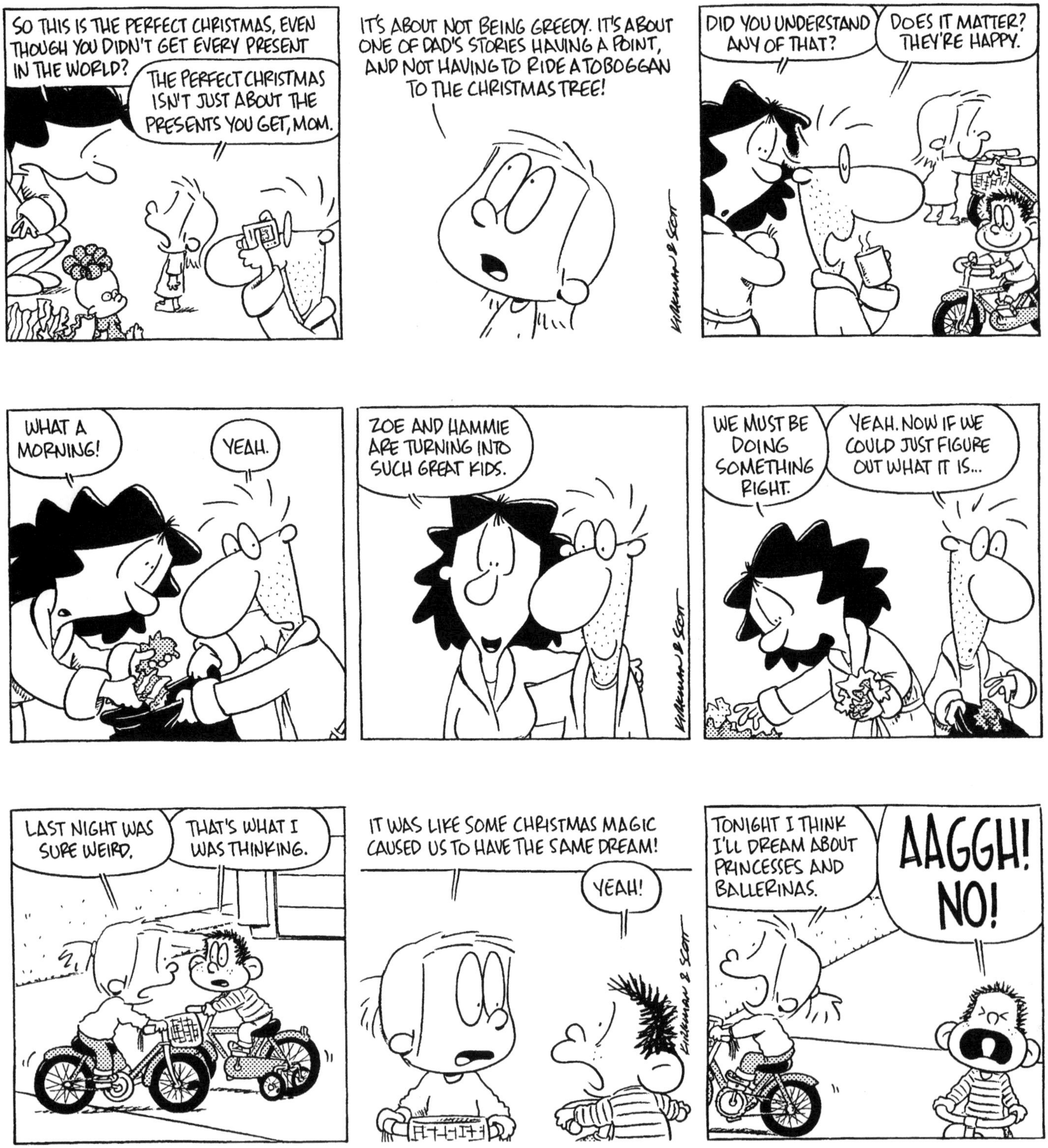
SO THIS IS THE PERFECT CHRISTMAS, EVEN THOUGH YOU DIDN'T GET EVERY PRESENT IN THE WORLD?
THE PERFECT CHRISTMAS ISN'T JUST ABOUT THE PRESENTS YOU GET, MOM.
IT'S ABOUT NOT BEING GREEDY. IT'S ABOUT ONE OF DAD'S STORIES HAVING A POINT, AND NOT HAVING TO RIDE A TOBOGGAN TO THE CHRISTMAS TREE!
DID YOU UNDERSTAND ANY OF THAT?
DOES IT MATTER? THEY'RE HAPPY.
WHAT A MORNING!
YEAH.
ZOE AND HAMMIE ARE TURNING INTO SUCH GREAT KIDS.
WE MUST BE DOING SOMETHING RIGHT.
YEAH. NOW IF WE COULD JUST FIGURE OUT WHAT IT IS...
LAST NIGHT WAS SURE WEIRD.
THAT'S WHAT I WAS THINKING.
IT WAS LIKE SOME CHRISTMAS MAGIC CAUSED US TO HAVE THE SAME DREAM!
YEAH!
TONIGHT I THINK I'LL DREAM ABOUT PRINCESSES AND BALLERINAS.
AAGGH! NO!

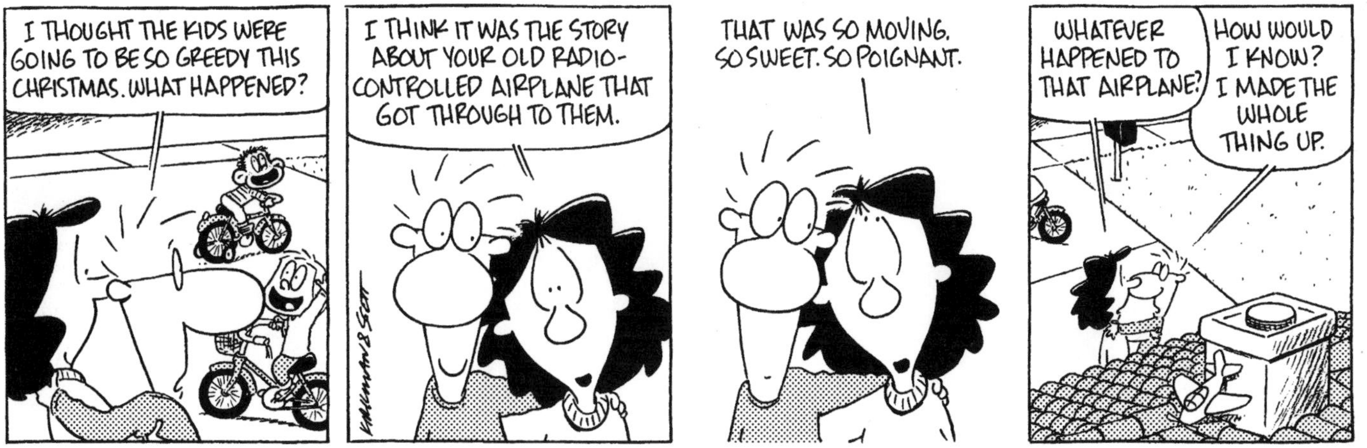
I THOUGHT THE KIDS WERE GOING TO BE SO GREEDY THIS CHRISTMAS. WHAT HAPPENED?
I THINK IT WAS THE STORY ABOUT YOUR OLD RADIO-CONTROLLED AIRPLANE THAT GOT THROUGH TO THEM.
THAT WAS SO MOVING. SO SWEET. SO POIGNANT.
WHATEVER HAPPENED TO THAT AIRPLANE?
HOW WOULD I KNOW? I MADE THE WHOLE THING UP.

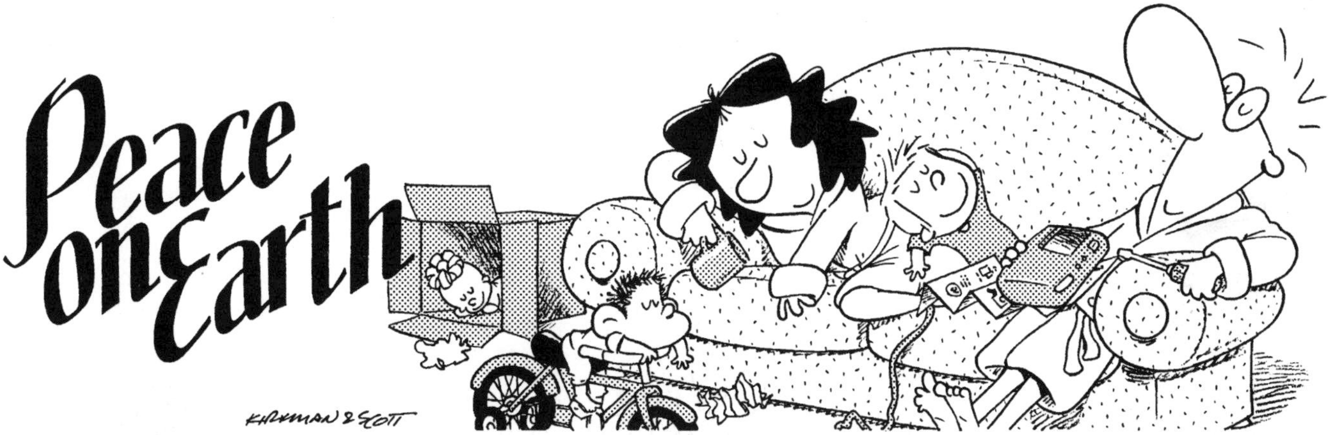
Peace on Earth
KIRKMAN & SCOTT

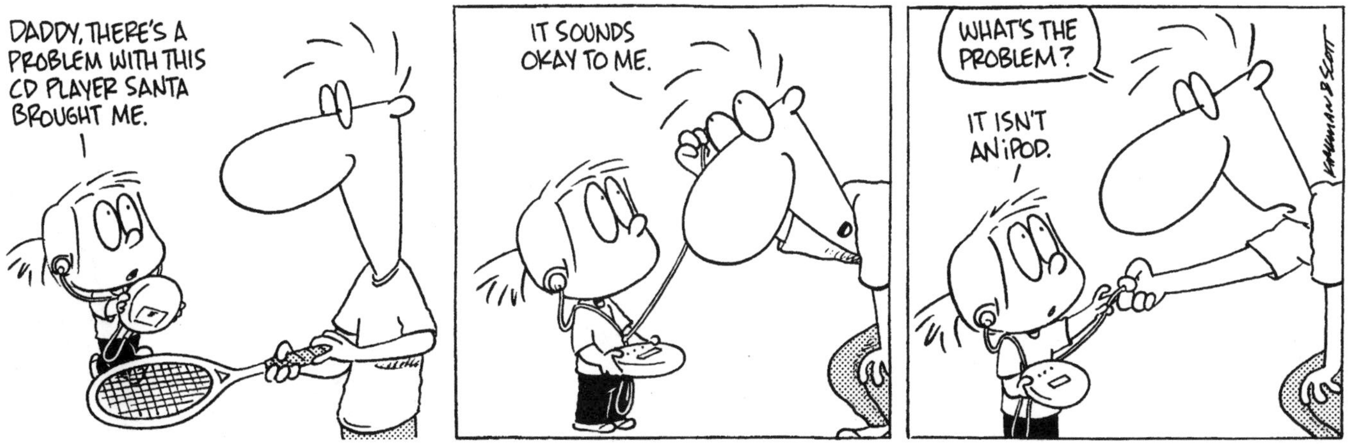
DADDY, THERE'S A PROBLEM WITH THIS CD PLAYER SANTA BROUGHT ME.
IT SOUNDS OKAY TO ME.
WHAT'S THE PROBLEM?
IT ISN'T AN iPOD.

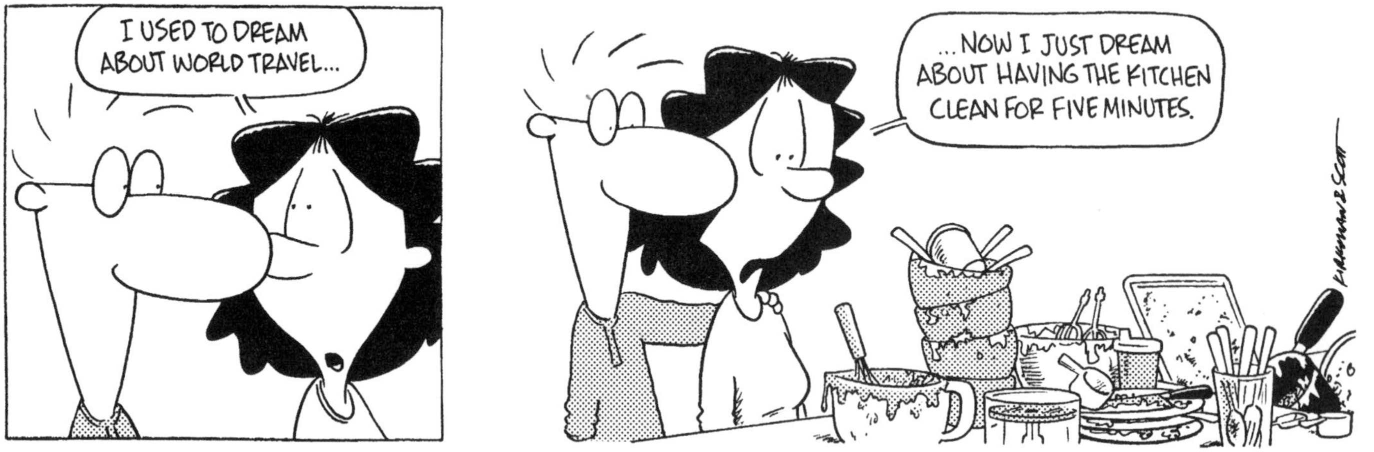
I USED TO DREAM ABOUT WORLD TRAVEL...
...NOW I JUST DREAM ABOUT HAVING THE KITCHEN CLEAN FOR FIVE MINUTES.

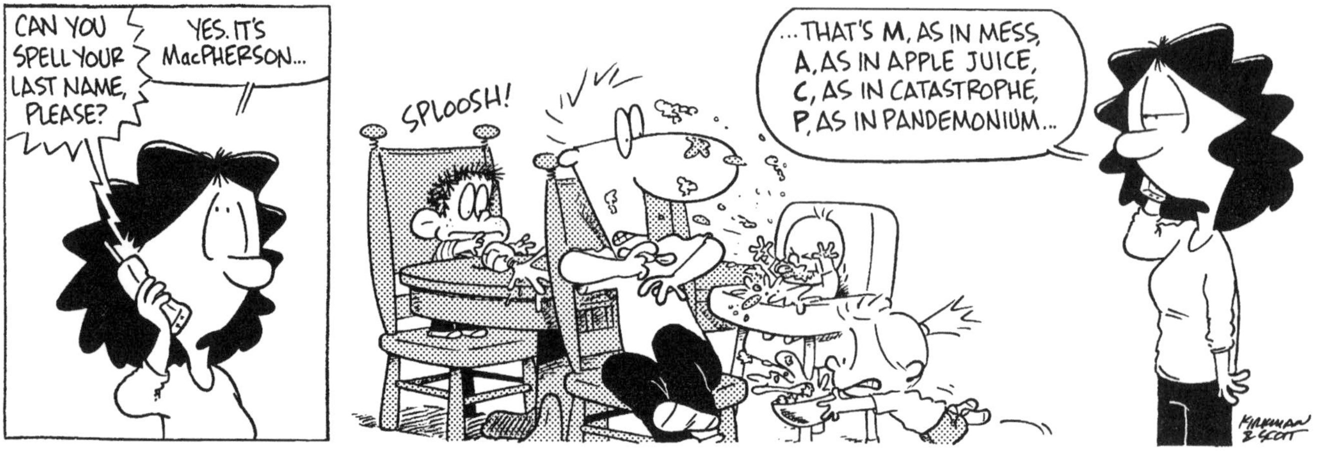
CAN YOU SPELL YOUR LAST NAME, PLEASE?
YES. IT'S MacPHERSON...
SPLOOSH!
...THAT'S M, AS IN MESS, A, AS IN APPLE JUICE, C, AS IN CATASTROPHE, P, AS IN PANDEMONIUM...

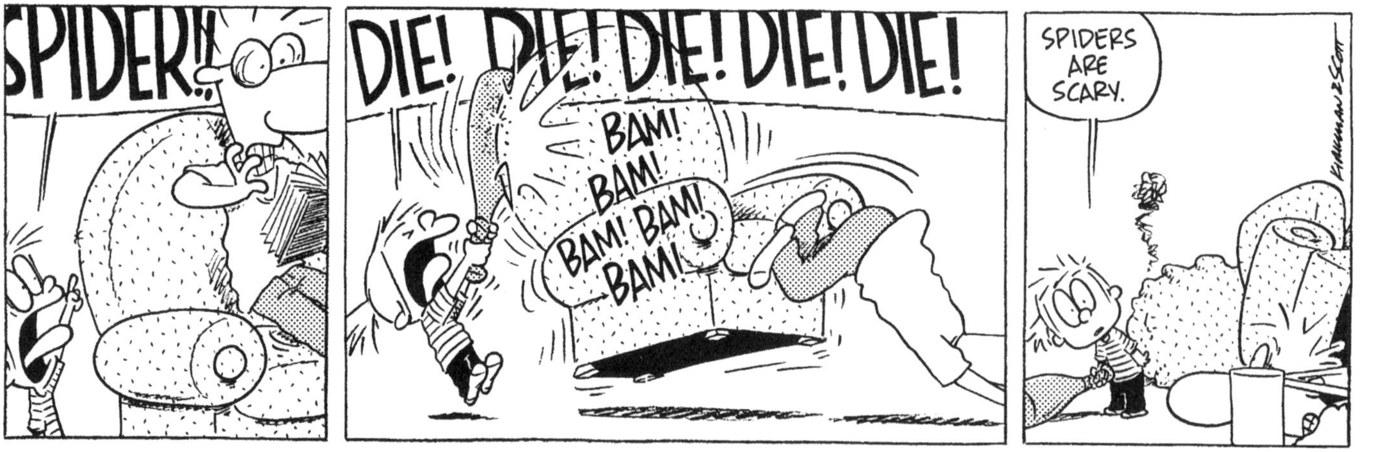
SPIDER!!
DIE! DIE! DIE! DIE! DIE!
BAM! BAM! BAM! BAM! BAM!
SPIDERS ARE SCARY.

NOW PLAYING
BABY BLUES®
IN COLOR
NOW PLAYING
BABY BLUES®
IN COLOR

IT'S TRUE... WE DO SAVE A FORTUNE ON BABYSITTERS.
AND IT DOESN'T TAKE ANY GAS.
AND WE DON'T HAVE TO BUY TICKETS.
OR PAY FOR PARKING.
HI.
HI.
KIRKMAN & SCOTT
BUT TRADING HOUSES WITH THE NEIGHBORS TO WATCH A DVD ISN'T THE SAME THING AS A DATE.
HEY, GOING OUT IS GOING OUT.

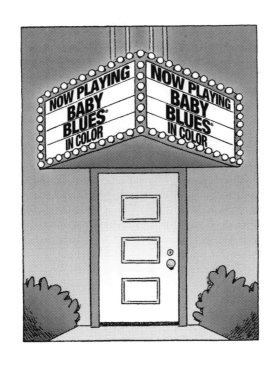

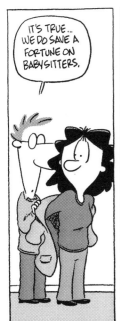

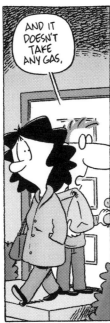

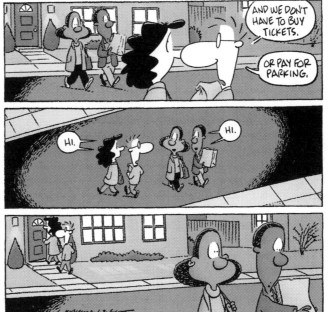

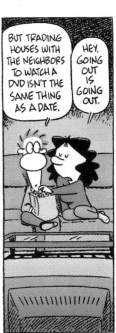

BABY BLUES®
BY
RICK KIRKMAN / JERRY SCOTT

AWWW! WREN IS BLOWING SPIT BUBBLES!
BURBLE BURBLE
HAMMIE! THAT'S GROSS!
HEE! HEE! SHE SURE LIKES THE WARM SUN.
DON'T YOU HAVE SOMETHING TO DO, HAMMIE?
HA! HA! LOOK AT THAT MUG!
IF YOU KEEP IT UP, YOUR FACE IS GOING TO FREEZE LIKE THAT.
YOU HAD YOUR TURN BEING THE CUTE ONE. IT'S TIME TO MOVE ON.
IT STINKS BEING THE MIDDLE CHILD.
KIRKMAN & SCOTT

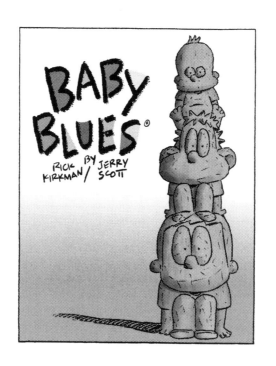

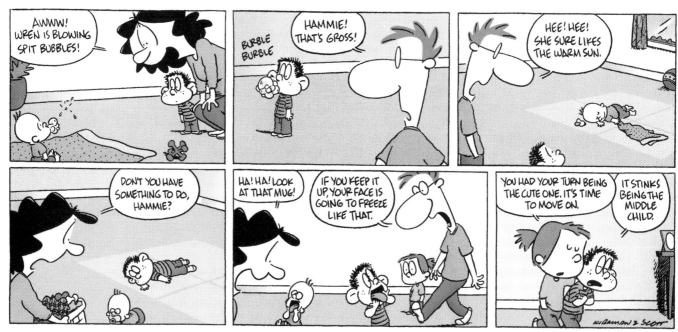

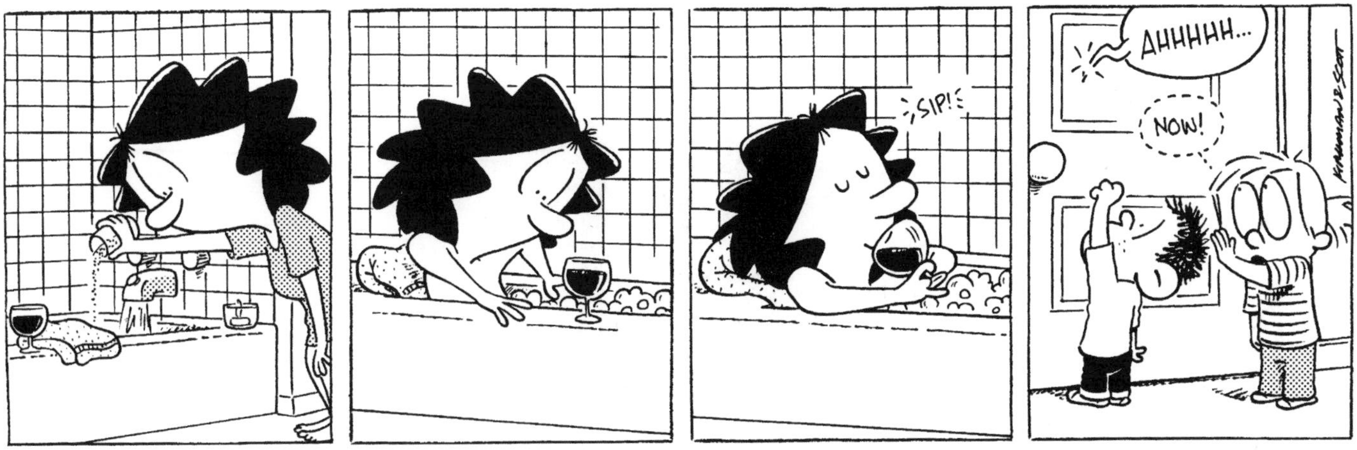
SIP!
AHHHHH...
NOW!

THE WINDOW OF CONVERSATIONAL OPPORTUNITY CONTINUES TO SHRINK...

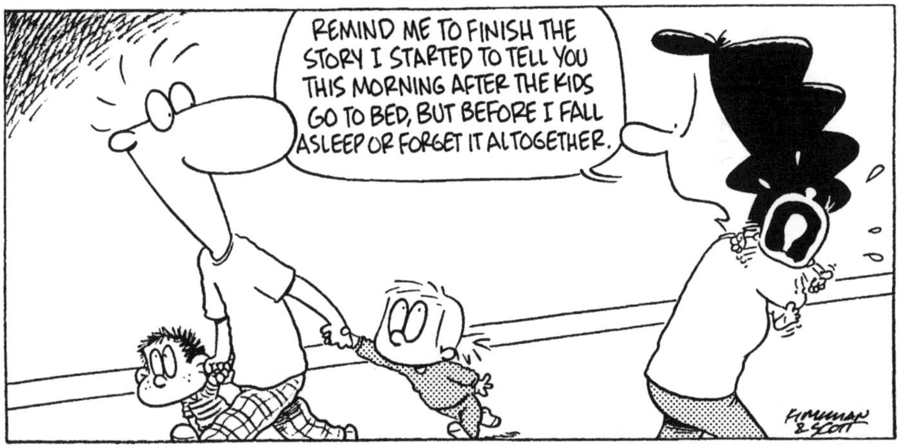
REMIND ME TO FINISH THE STORY I STARTED TO TELL YOU THIS MORNING AFTER THE KIDS GO TO BED, BUT BEFORE I FALL ASLEEP OR FORGET IT ALTOGETHER.

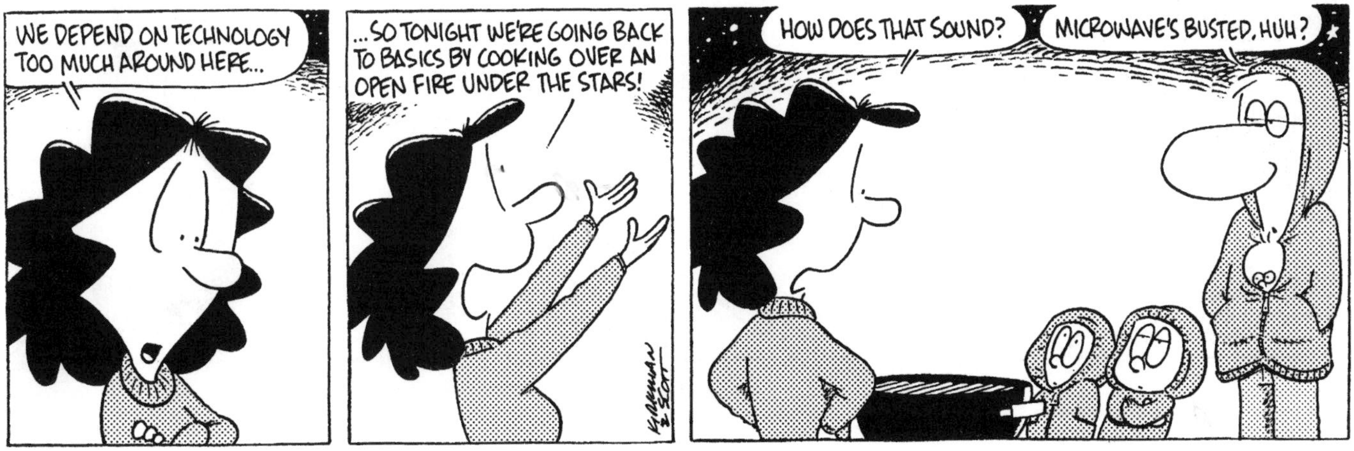
WE DEPEND ON TECHNOLOGY TOO MUCH AROUND HERE...
...SO TONIGHT WE'RE GOING BACK TO BASICS BY COOKING OVER AN OPEN FIRE UNDER THE STARS!
HOW DOES THAT SOUND?
MICROWAVE'S BUSTED, HUH?

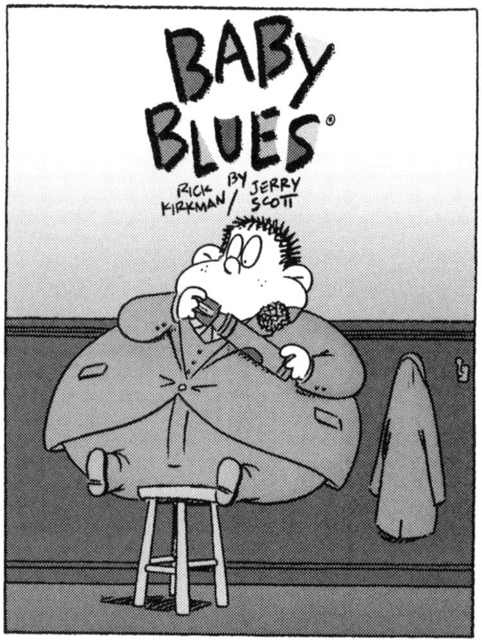
BABY BLUES®
BY RICK KIRKMAN / JERRY SCOTT

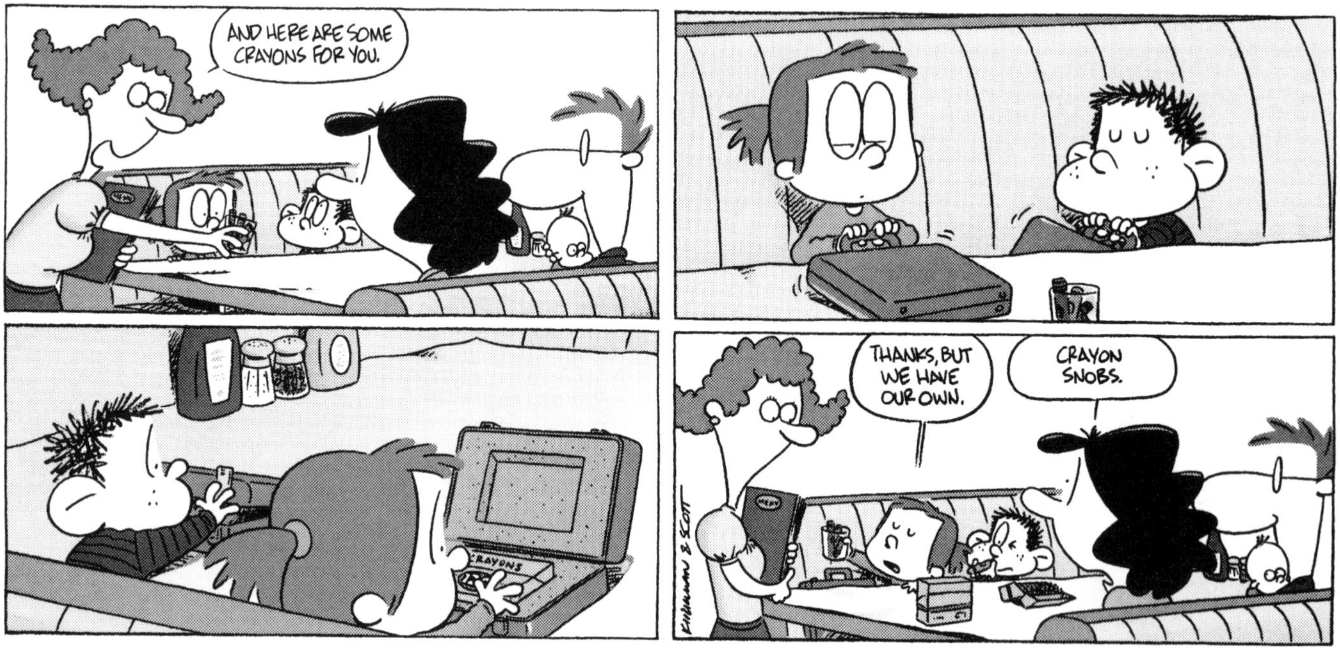
AND HERE ARE SOME CRAYONS FOR YOU.
CRAYONS
THANKS, BUT WE HAVE OUR OWN.
CRAYON SNOBS.
KIRKMAN & SCOTT

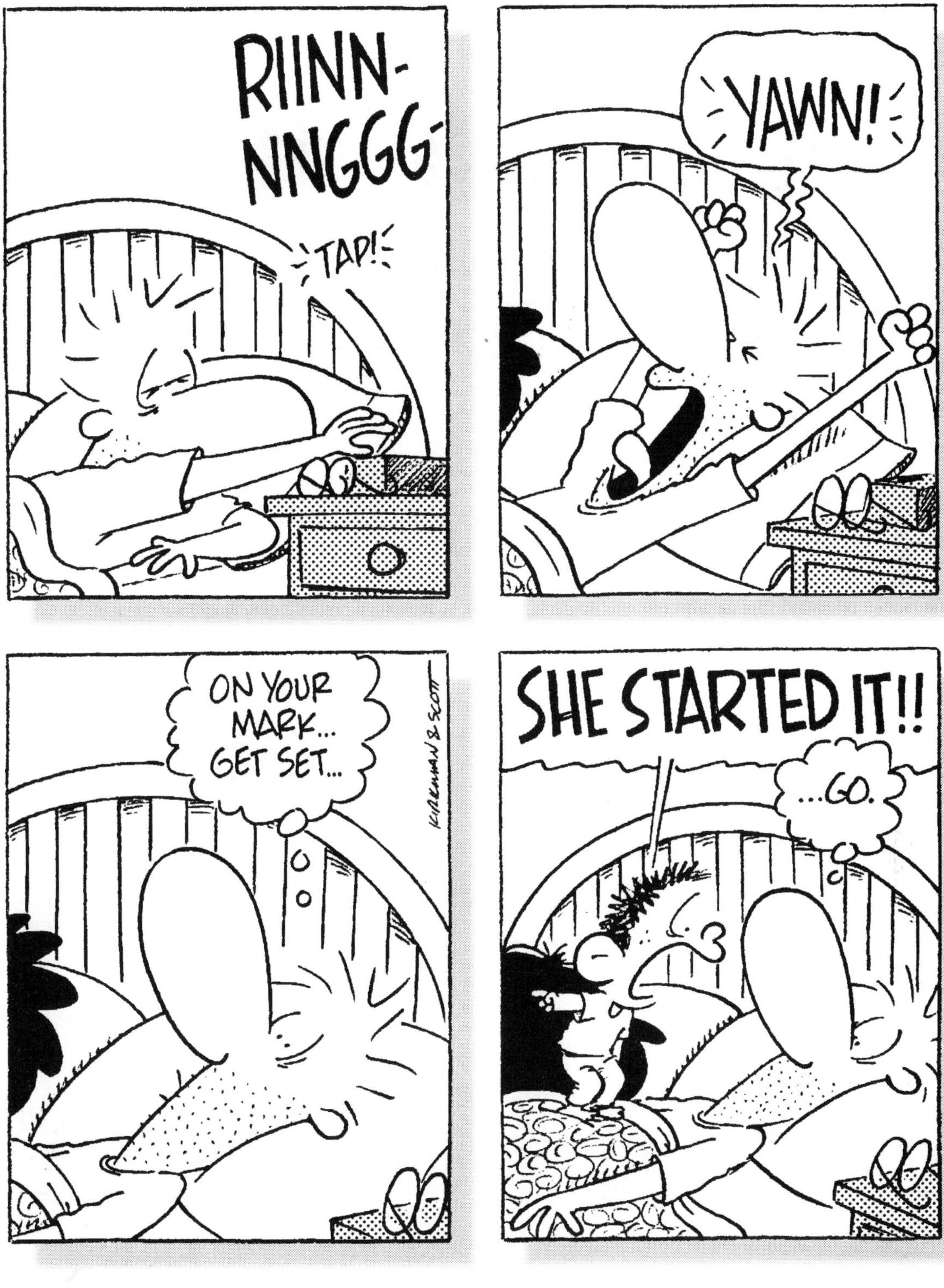
RIINN-
NNGGG-
TAP!
YAWN!
ON YOUR MARK... GET SET...
KIRKMAN & SCOTT
SHE STARTED IT!!
...GO.

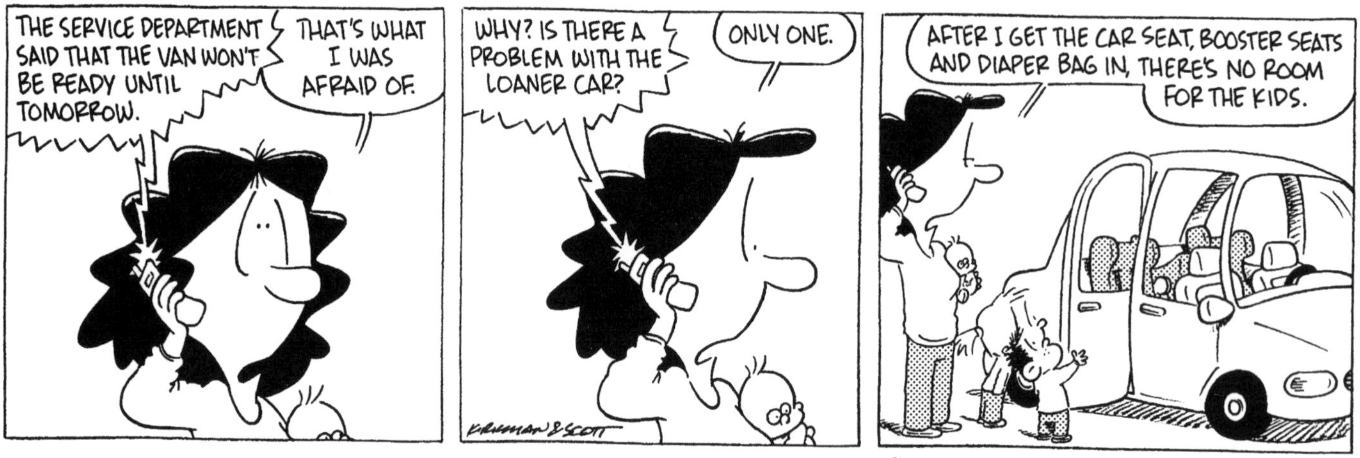
THE SERVICE DEPARTMENT SAID THAT THE VAN WON'T BE READY UNTIL TOMORROW.
THAT'S WHAT I WAS AFRAID OF.
WHY? IS THERE A PROBLEM WITH THE LOANER CAR?
ONLY ONE.
KIRKMAN & SCOTT
AFTER I GET THE CAR SEAT, BOOSTER SEATS AND DIAPER BAG IN, THERE'S NO ROOM FOR THE KIDS.

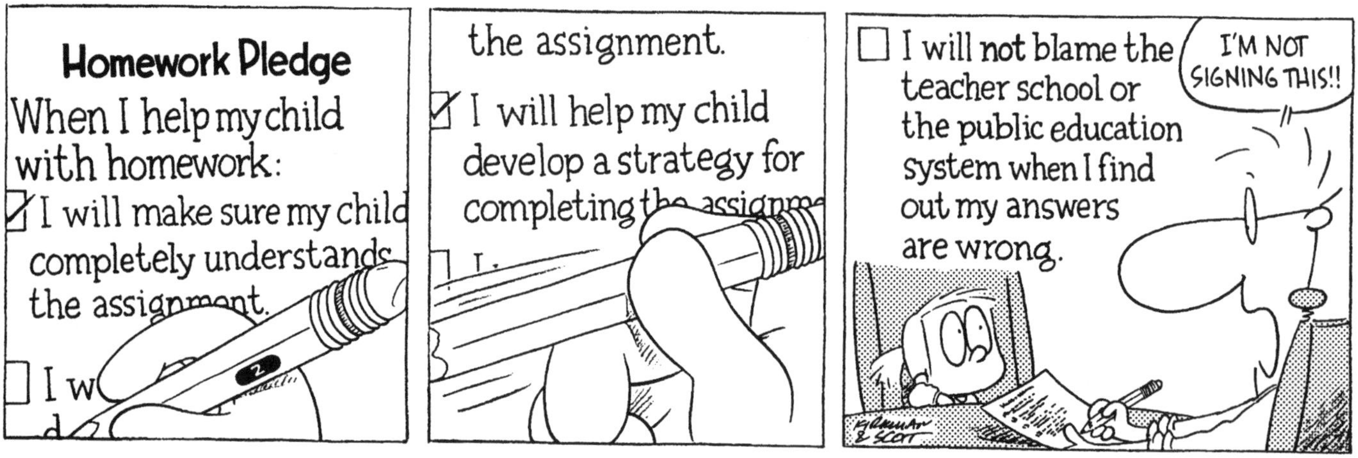
Homework Pledge
When I help my child with homework:
I will make sure my child completely understands the assignment.
the assignment.
I will help my child develop a strategy for
I will not blame the teacher school or the public education system when I find out my answers are wrong.
I'M NOT SIGNING THIS!!
KIRKMAN & SCOTT

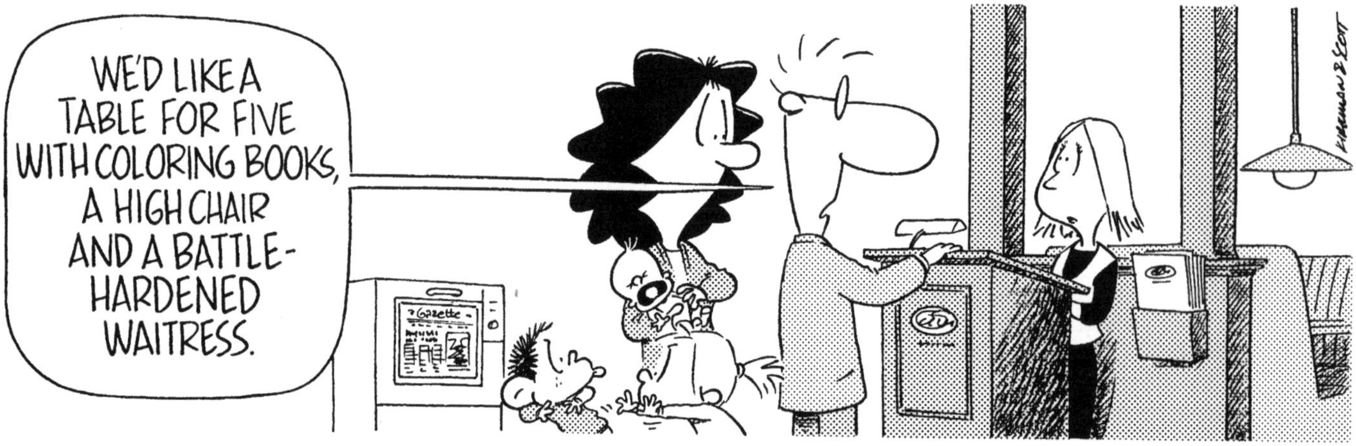
WE'D LIKE A TABLE FOR FIVE WITH COLORING BOOKS, A HIGH CHAIR AND A BATTLE-HARDENED WAITRESS.
Gazette
KIRKMAN & SCOTT

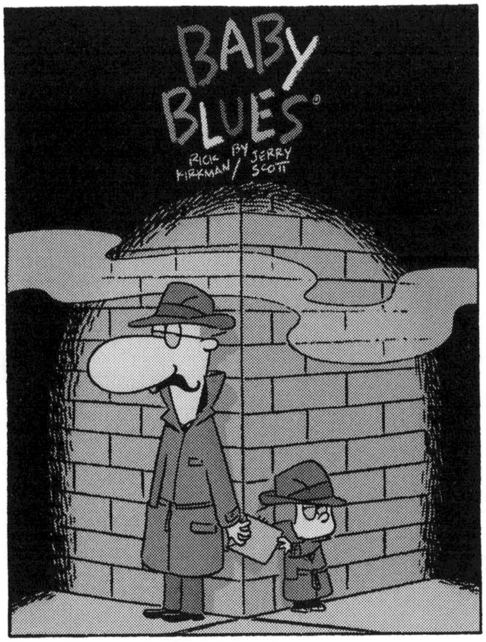
BABY BLUES®
BY RICK KIRKMAN / JERRY SCOTT

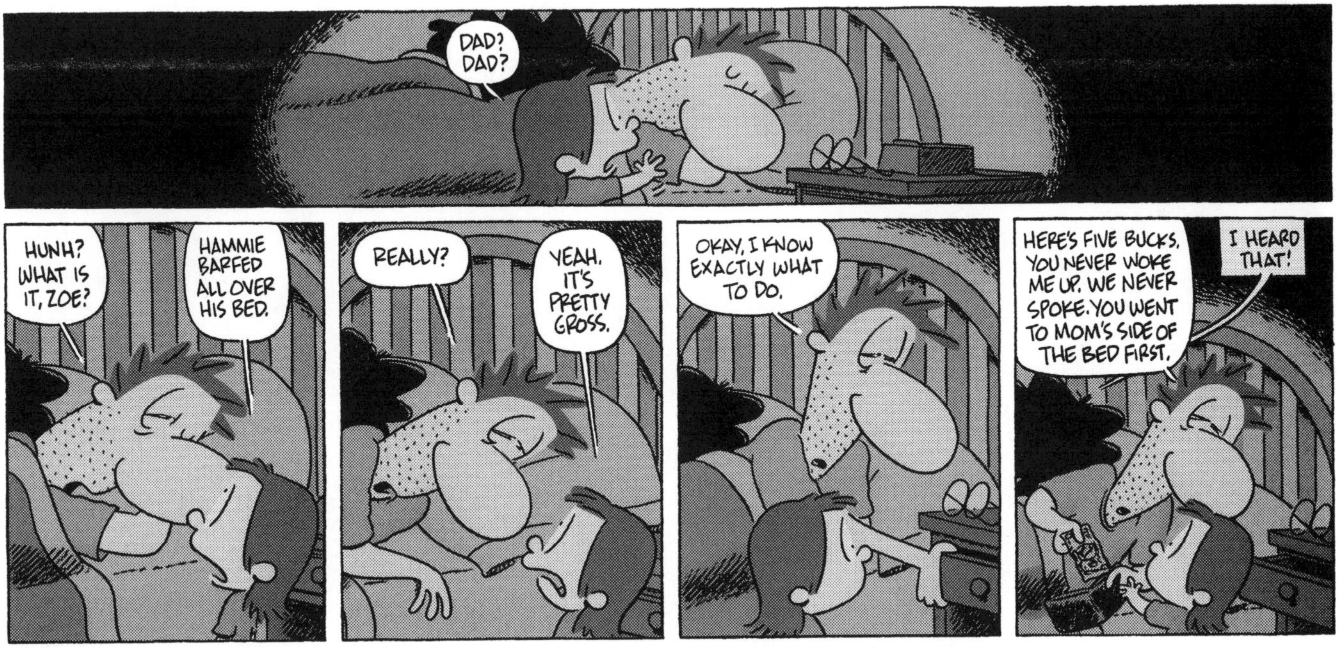
DAD? DAD?
HUNH? WHAT IS IT, ZOE?
HAMMIE BARFED ALL OVER HIS BED.
REALLY?
YEAH. IT'S PRETTY GROSS.
OKAY, I KNOW EXACTLY WHAT TO DO.
HERE'S FIVE BUCKS. YOU NEVER WOKE ME UP. WE NEVER SPOKE. YOU WENT TO MOM'S SIDE OF THE BED FIRST.
I HEARD THAT!

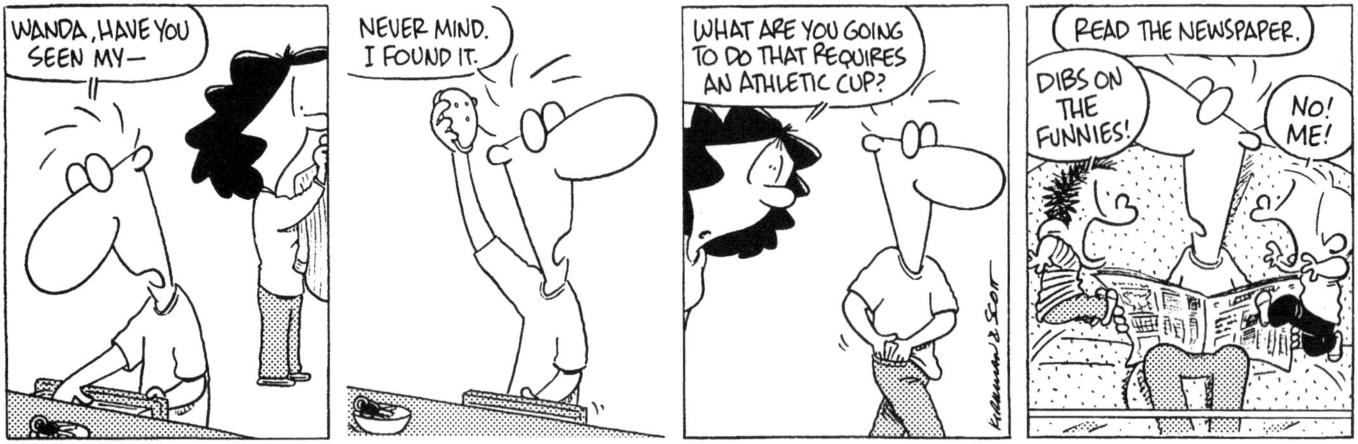
WANDA, HAVE YOU SEEN MY—
NEVER MIND. I FOUND IT.
WHAT ARE YOU GOING TO DO THAT REQUIRES AN ATHLETIC CUP?
READ THE NEWSPAPER.
DIBS ON THE FUNNIES!
NO! ME!

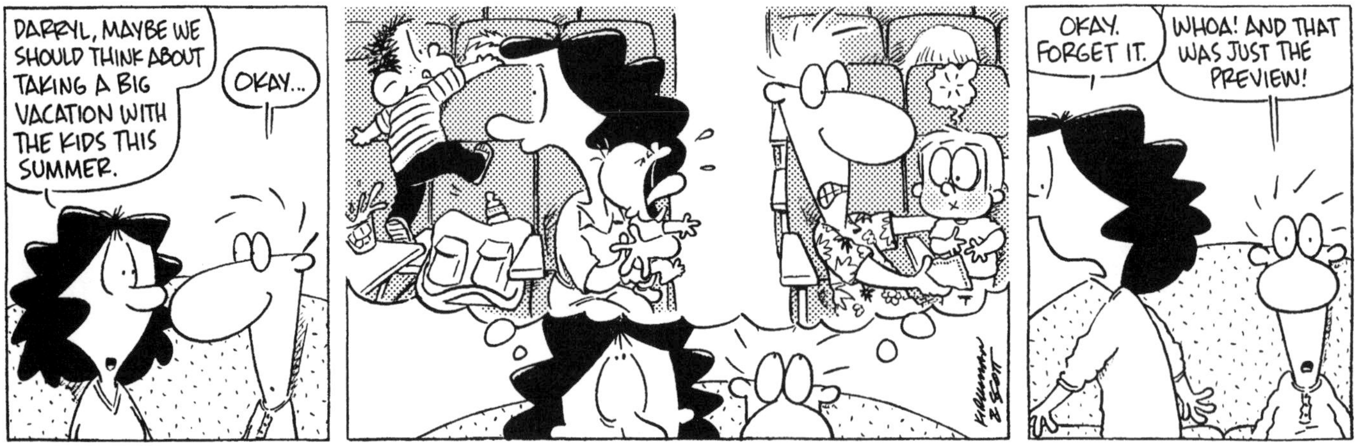
DARRYL, MAYBE WE SHOULD THINK ABOUT TAKING A BIG VACATION WITH THE KIDS THIS SUMMER.
OKAY...
OKAY. FORGET IT.
WHOA! AND THAT WAS JUST THE PREVIEW!

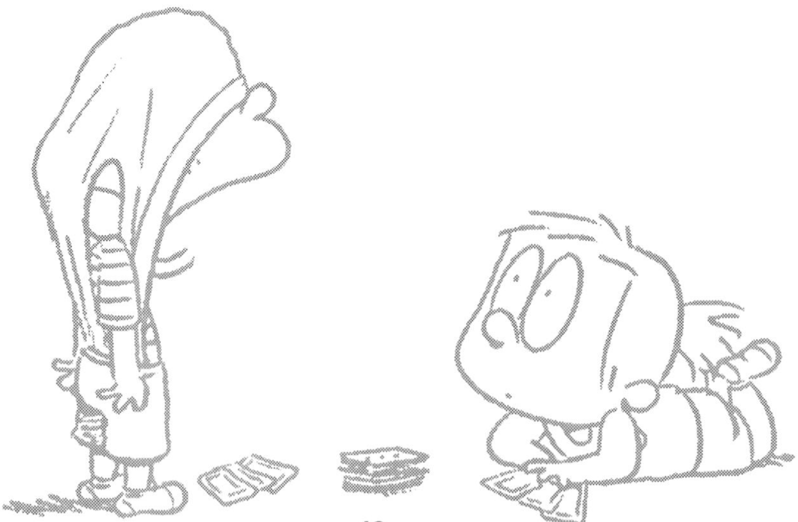

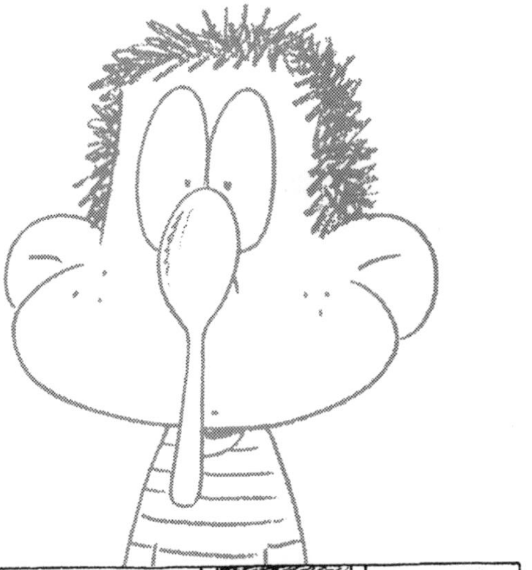

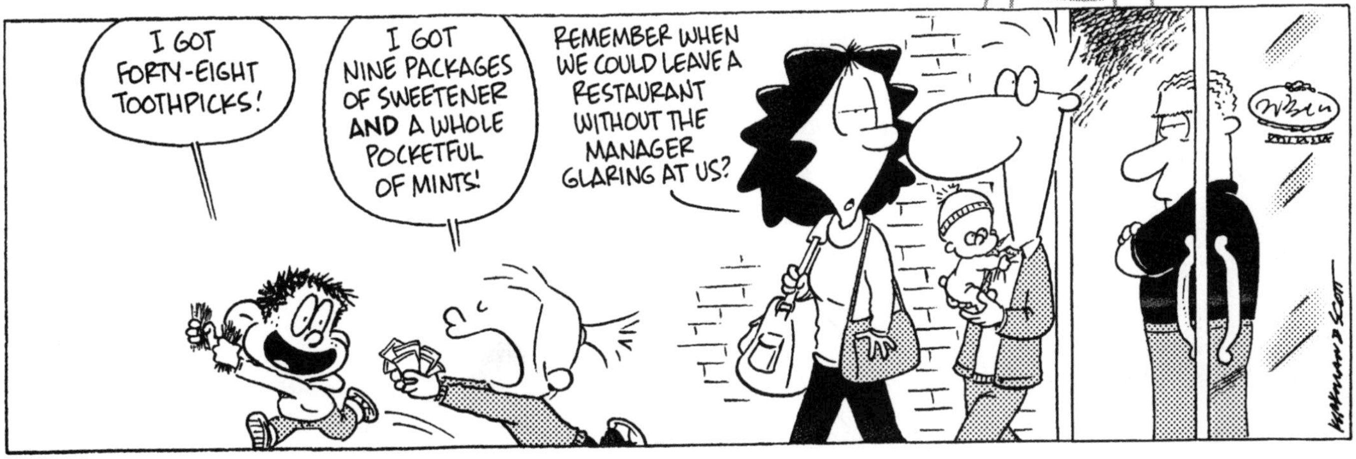

I GOT FORTY-EIGHT TOOTHPICKS!
I GOT NINE PACKAGES OF SWEETENER **AND** A WHOLE POCKETFUL OF MINTS!
REMEMBER WHEN WE COULD LEAVE A RESTAURANT WITHOUT THE MANAGER GLARING AT US?

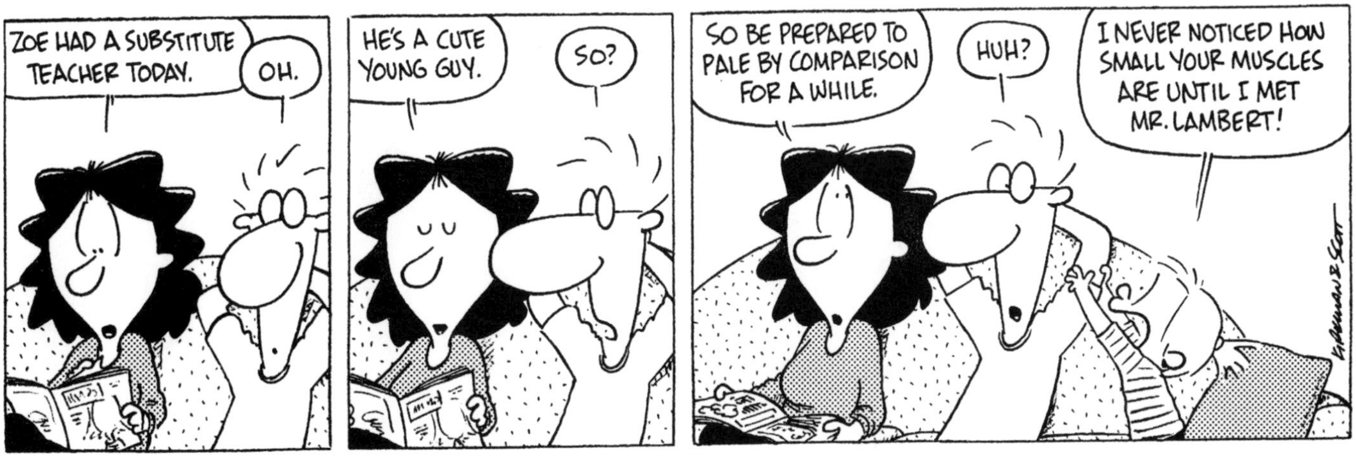

ZOE HAD A SUBSTITUTE TEACHER TODAY.
OH.
HE'S A CUTE YOUNG GUY.
SO?
SO BE PREPARED TO PALE BY COMPARISON FOR A WHILE.
HUH?
I NEVER NOTICED HOW SMALL YOUR MUSCLES ARE UNTIL I MET MR. LAMBERT!

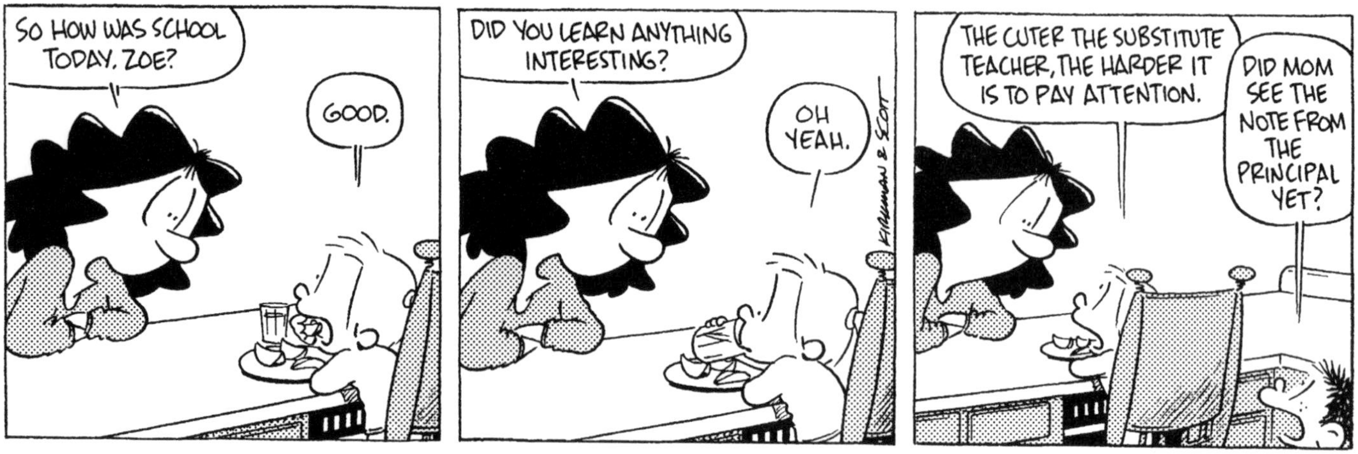
SO HOW WAS SCHOOL TODAY, ZOE?
GOOD.
DID YOU LEARN ANYTHING INTERESTING?
OH YEAH.
KIRKMAN & SCOTT
THE CUTER THE SUBSTITUTE TEACHER, THE HARDER IT IS TO PAY ATTENTION.
DID MOM SEE THE NOTE FROM THE PRINCIPAL YET?

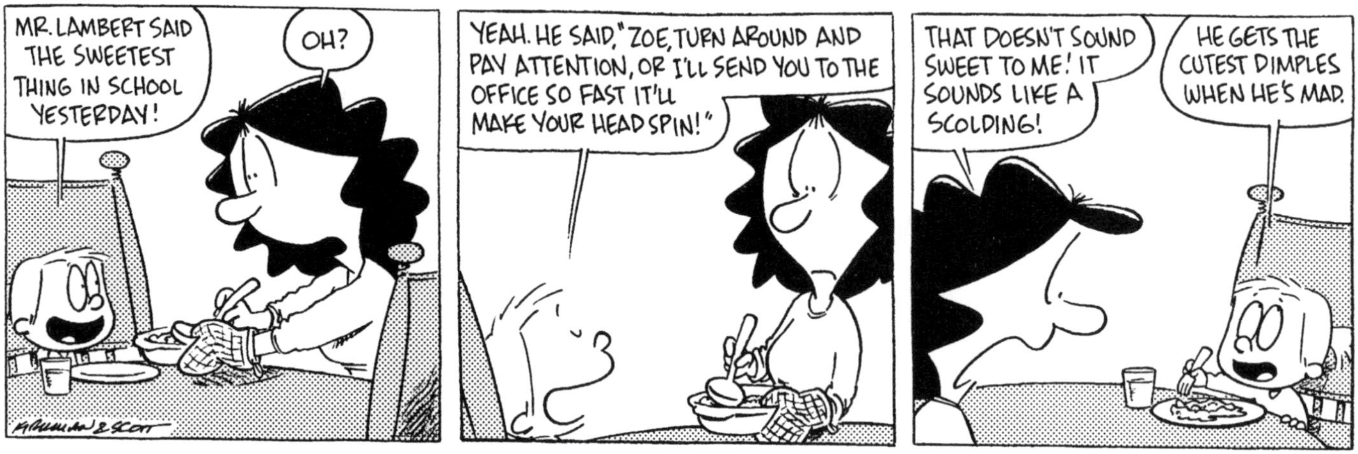
MR. LAMBERT SAID THE SWEETEST THING IN SCHOOL YESTERDAY!
OH?
YEAH. HE SAID, "ZOE, TURN AROUND AND PAY ATTENTION, OR I'LL SEND YOU TO THE OFFICE SO FAST IT'LL MAKE YOUR HEAD SPIN!"
THAT DOESN'T SOUND SWEET TO ME! IT SOUNDS LIKE A SCOLDING!
HE GETS THE CUTEST DIMPLES WHEN HE'S MAD.
KIRKMAN & SCOTT

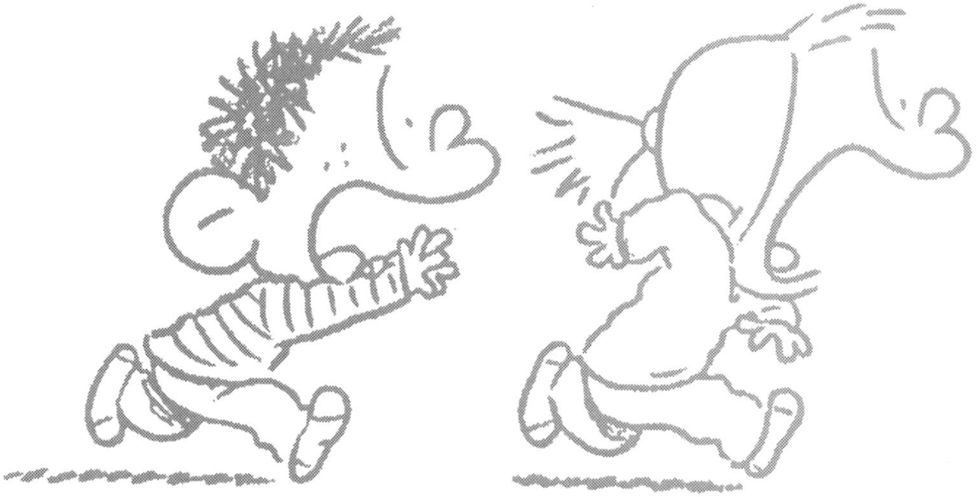

BABY BLUES®
RICK KIRKMAN / BY / JERRY SCOTT

DING-DONG
YO!
COME ON IN, MIKE.
YOU'RE RIGHT ON TIME. THEY JUST KICKED OFF.
BEER?
SURE.
GRAB THE DIP, WILL YA?
OH, AND IF I WERE YOU, I'D LEAVE MY HAT ON.
RIGHT.

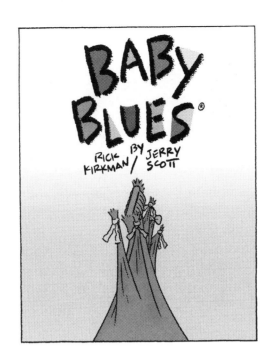

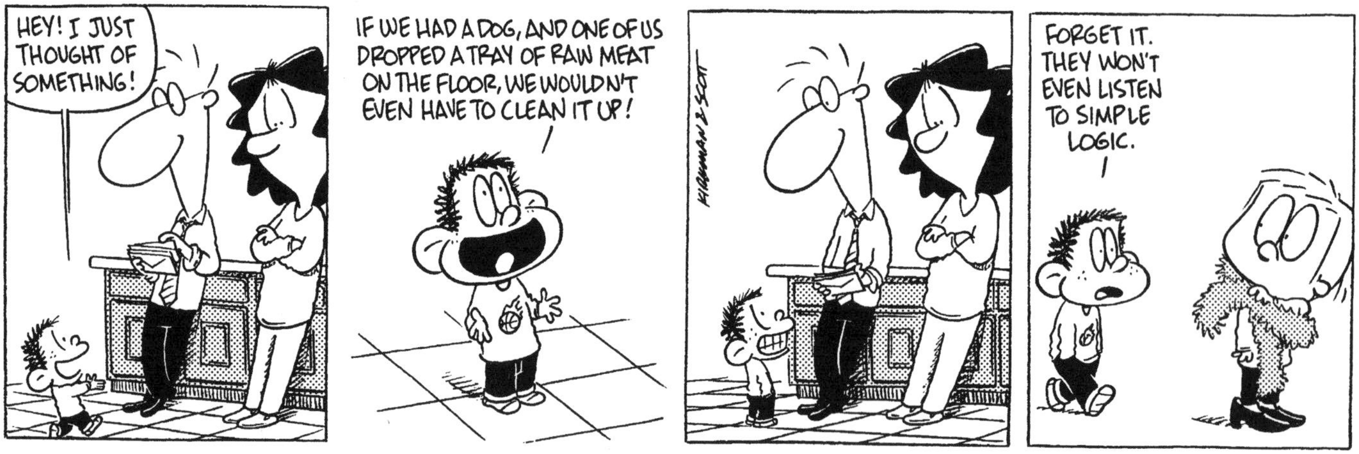
HEY! I JUST THOUGHT OF SOMETHING!
IF WE HAD A DOG, AND ONE OF US DROPPED A TRAY OF RAW MEAT ON THE FLOOR, WE WOULDN'T EVEN HAVE TO CLEAN IT UP!
FORGET IT. THEY WON'T EVEN LISTEN TO SIMPLE LOGIC.

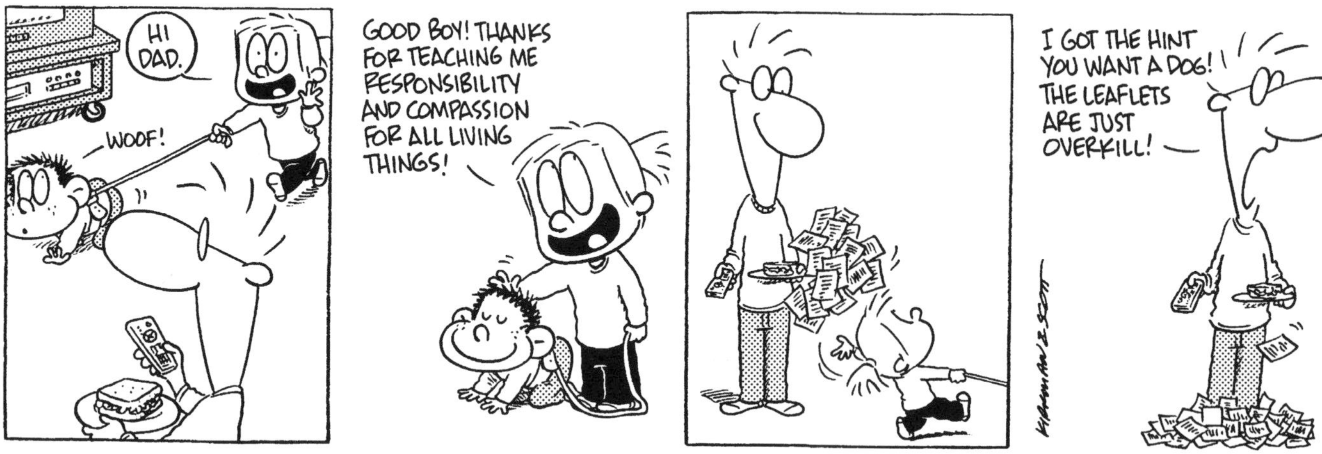
HI DAD.
WOOF!
GOOD BOY! THANKS FOR TEACHING ME RESPONSIBILITY AND COMPASSION FOR ALL LIVING THINGS!
I GOT THE HINT YOU WANT A DOG! THE LEAFLETS ARE JUST OVERKILL!

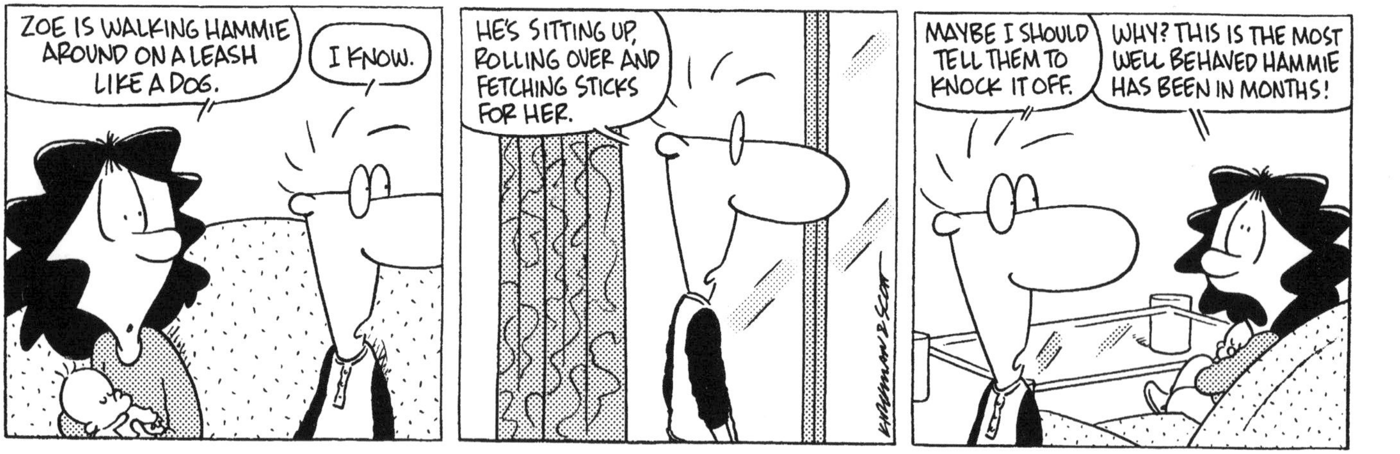
ZOE IS WALKING HAMMIE AROUND ON A LEASH LIKE A DOG.
I KNOW.
HE'S SITTING UP, ROLLING OVER AND FETCHING STICKS FOR HER.
MAYBE I SHOULD TELL THEM TO KNOCK IT OFF.
WHY? THIS IS THE MOST WELL BEHAVED HAMMIE HAS BEEN IN MONTHS!

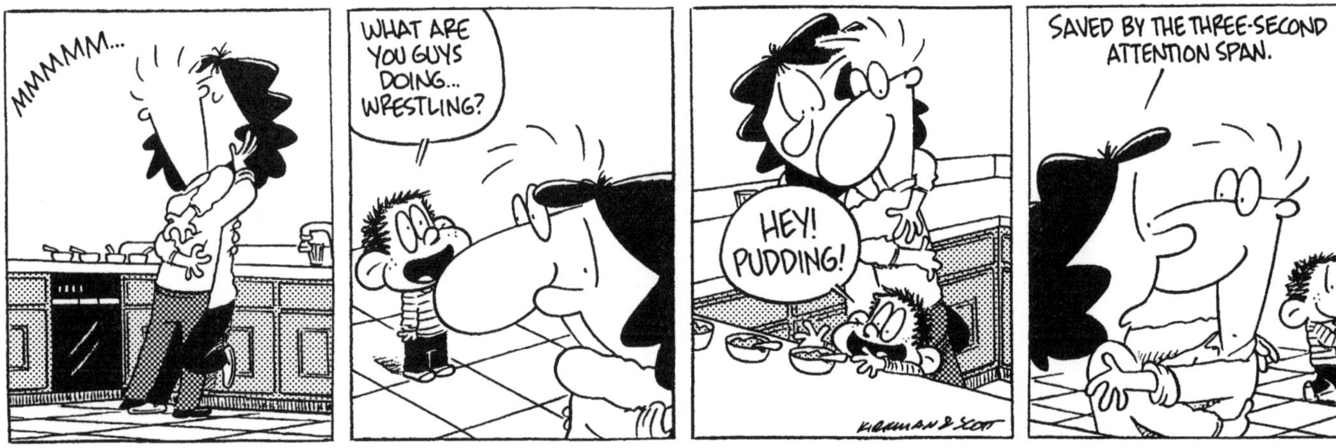
MMMMM...
WHAT ARE YOU GUYS DOING... WRESTLING?
HEY! PUDDING!
SAVED BY THE THREE-SECOND ATTENTION SPAN.

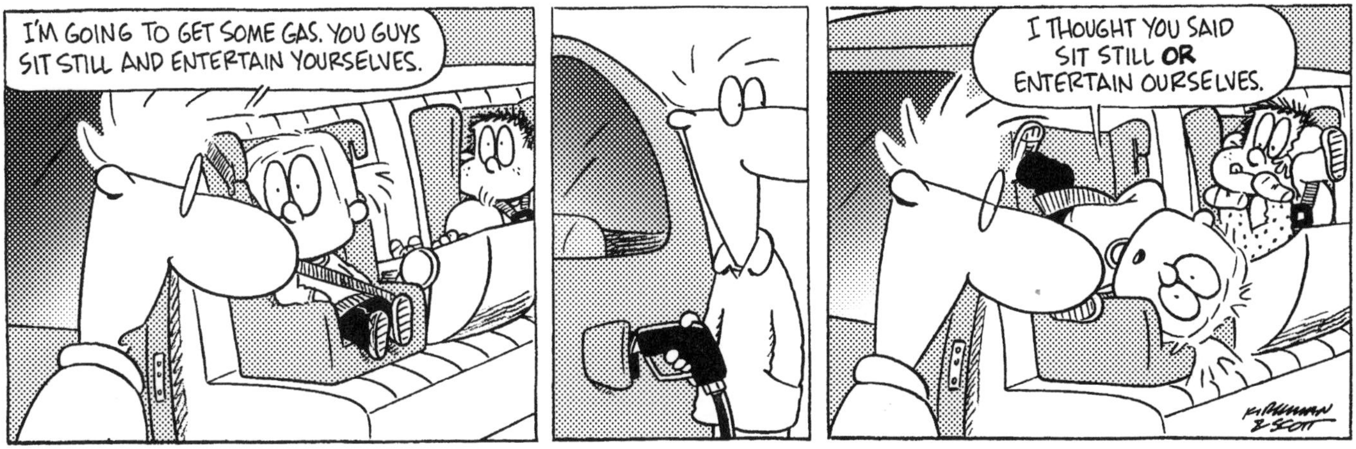
I'M GOING TO GET SOME GAS. YOU GUYS SIT STILL AND ENTERTAIN YOURSELVES.
I THOUGHT YOU SAID SIT STILL **OR** ENTERTAIN OURSELVES.

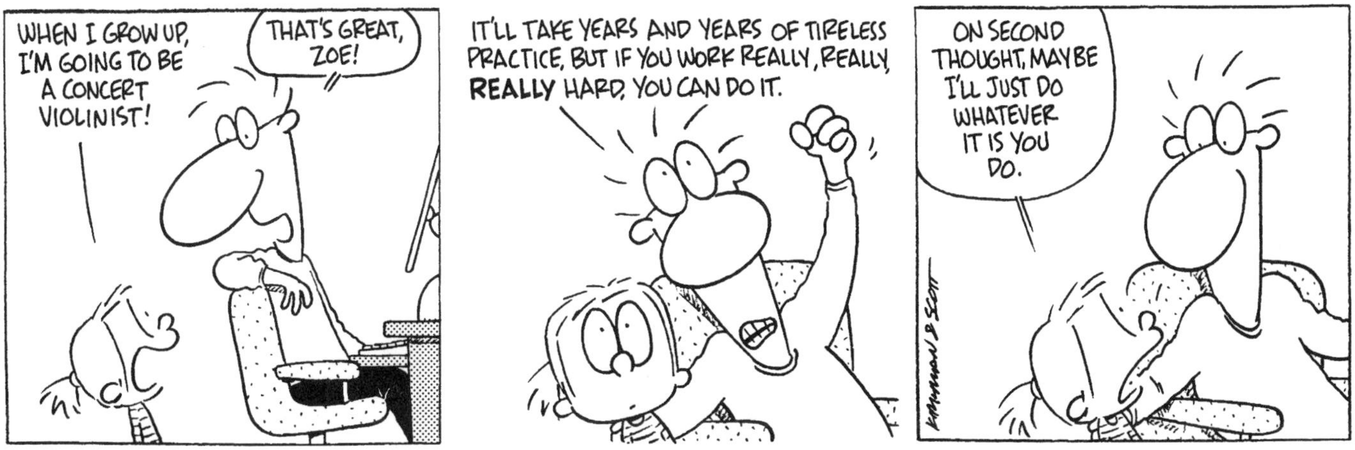
WHEN I GROW UP, I'M GOING TO BE A CONCERT VIOLINIST!
THAT'S GREAT, ZOE!
IT'LL TAKE YEARS AND YEARS OF TIRELESS PRACTICE, BUT IF YOU WORK REALLY, REALLY, **REALLY** HARD, YOU CAN DO IT.
ON SECOND THOUGHT, MAYBE I'LL JUST DO WHATEVER IT IS YOU DO.

BABY BLUES®

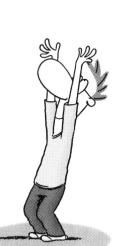

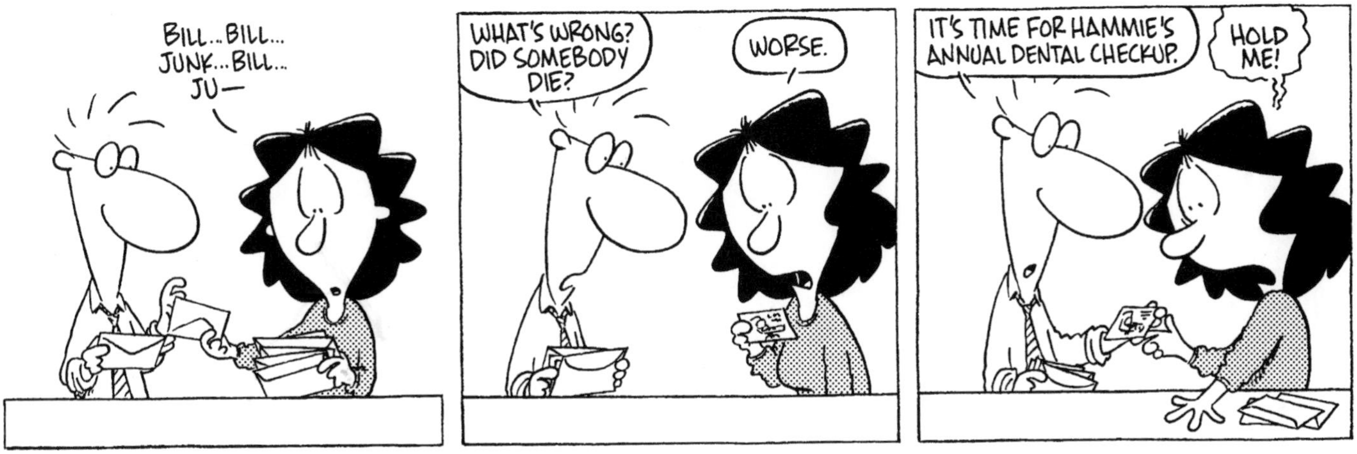
BILL...BILL...
JUNK...BILL...
JU—
WHAT'S WRONG? DID SOMEBODY DIE?
WORSE.
IT'S TIME FOR HAMMIE'S ANNUAL DENTAL CHECKUP.
HOLD ME!

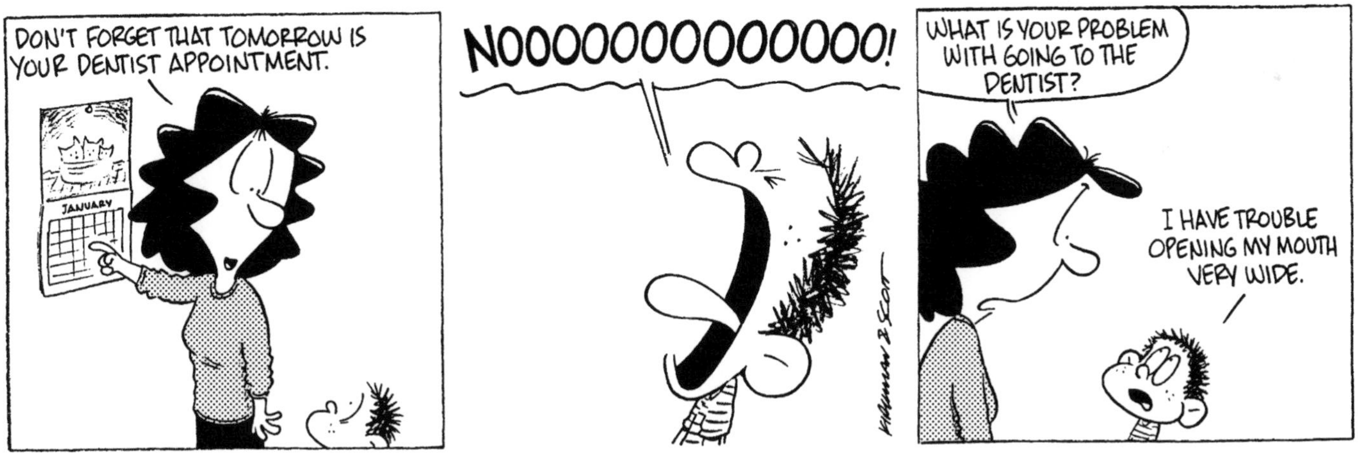
DON'T FORGET THAT TOMORROW IS YOUR DENTIST APPOINTMENT.
JANUARY
NOOOOOOOOOOOOO!
WHAT IS YOUR PROBLEM WITH GOING TO THE DENTIST?
I HAVE TROUBLE OPENING MY MOUTH VERY WIDE.

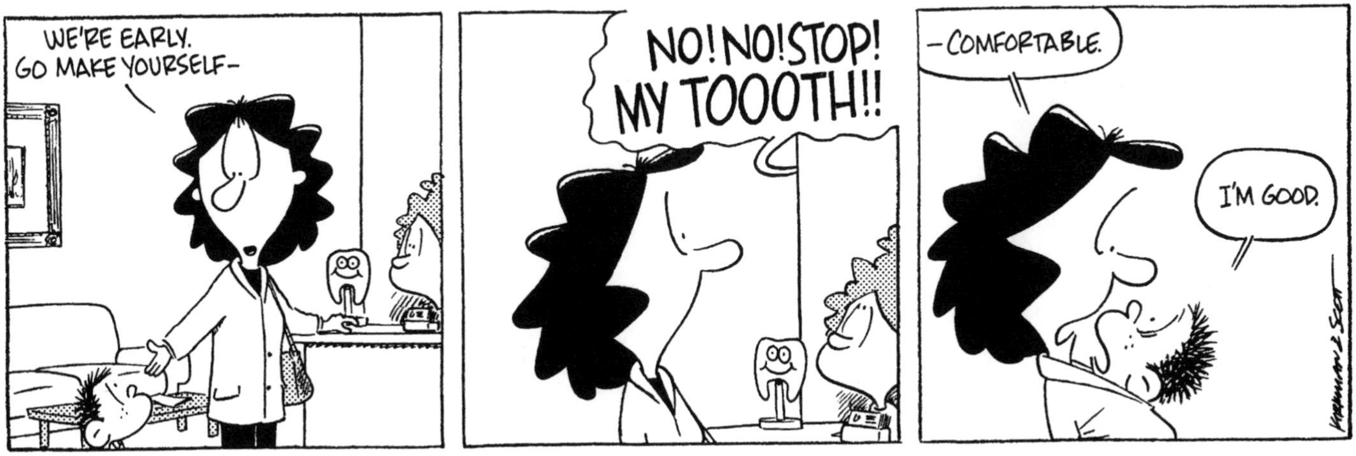
WE'RE EARLY. GO MAKE YOURSELF—
NO! NO! STOP! MY TOOOTH!!
—COMFORTABLE.
I'M GOOD.

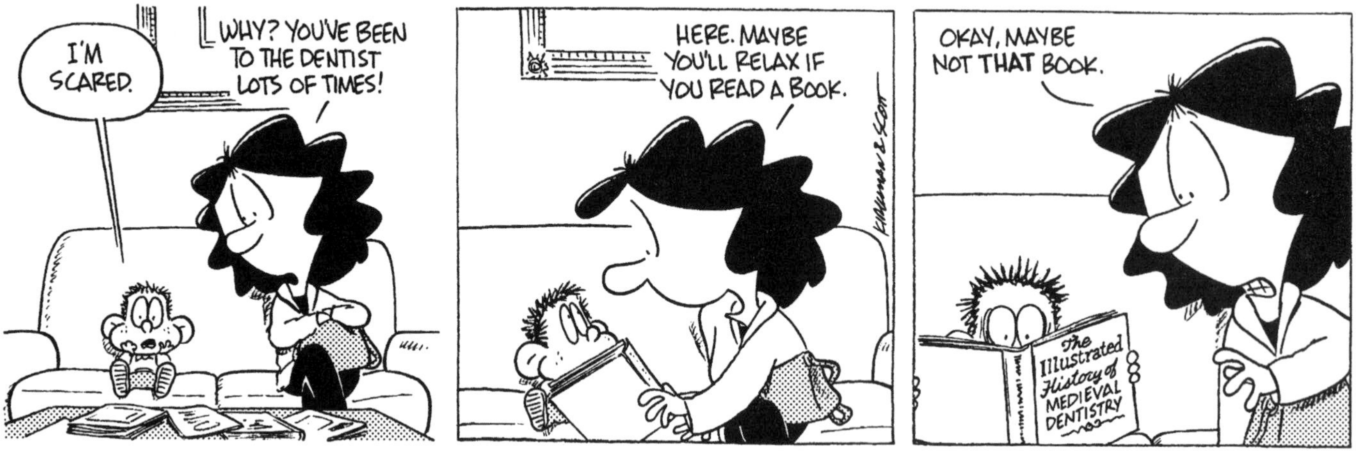
I'M SCARED.
WHY? YOU'VE BEEN TO THE DENTIST LOTS OF TIMES!
HERE. MAYBE YOU'LL RELAX IF YOU READ A BOOK.
OKAY, MAYBE NOT **THAT** BOOK.
The Illustrated History of MEDIEVAL DENTISTRY

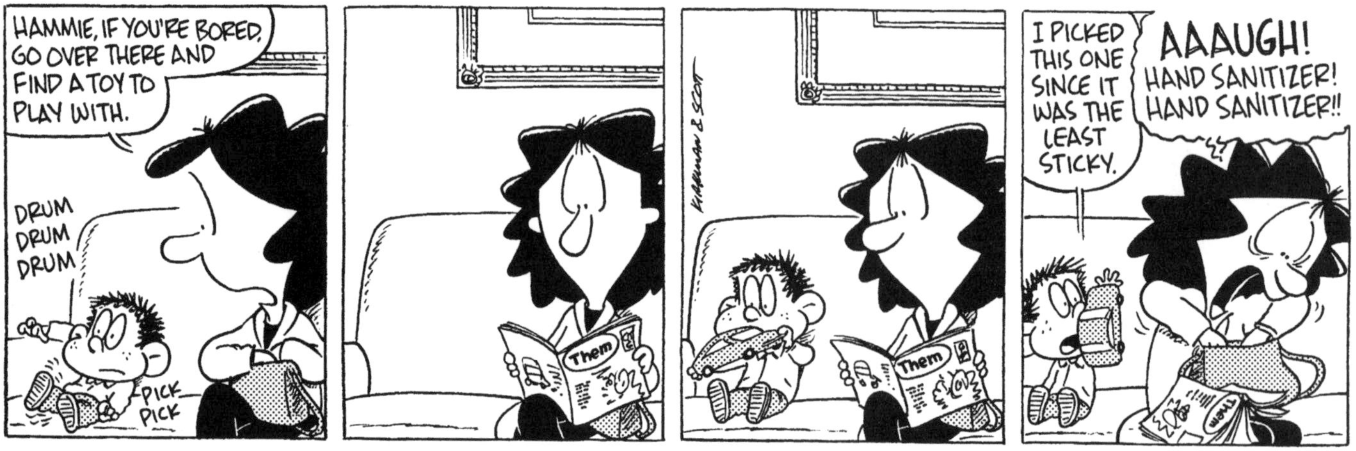
HAMMIE, IF YOU'RE BORED, GO OVER THERE AND FIND A TOY TO PLAY WITH.
DRUM DRUM DRUM
PICK PICK
Them
I PICKED THIS ONE SINCE IT WAS THE LEAST STICKY.
AAAUGH! HAND SANITIZER! HAND SANITIZER!!

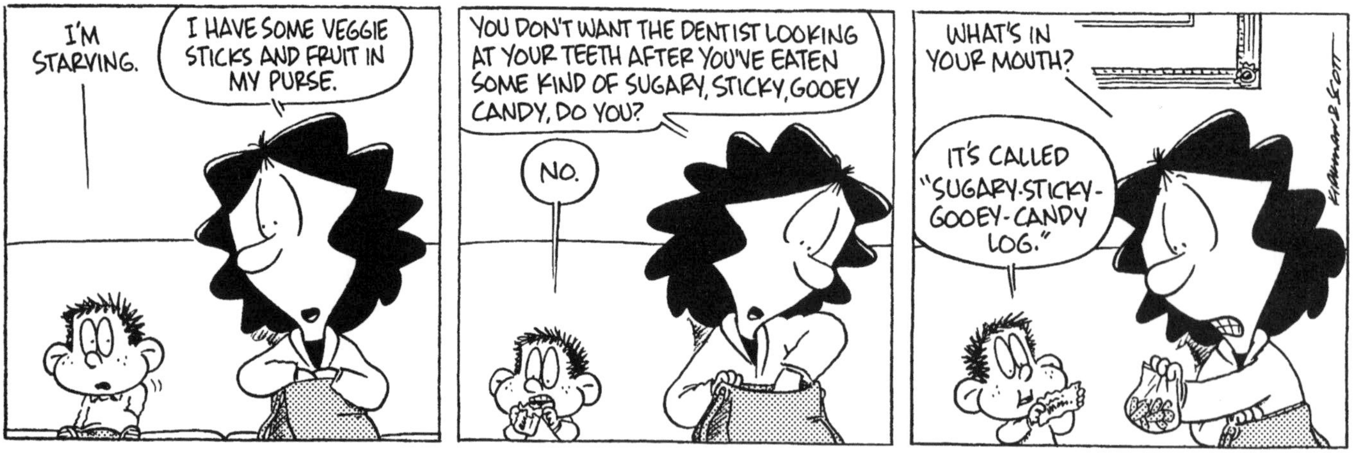
I'M STARVING.
I HAVE SOME VEGGIE STICKS AND FRUIT IN MY PURSE.
YOU DON'T WANT THE DENTIST LOOKING AT YOUR TEETH AFTER YOU'VE EATEN SOME KIND OF SUGARY, STICKY, GOOEY CANDY, DO YOU?
NO.
WHAT'S IN YOUR MOUTH?
IT'S CALLED "SUGARY-STICKY-GOOEY-CANDY LOG."

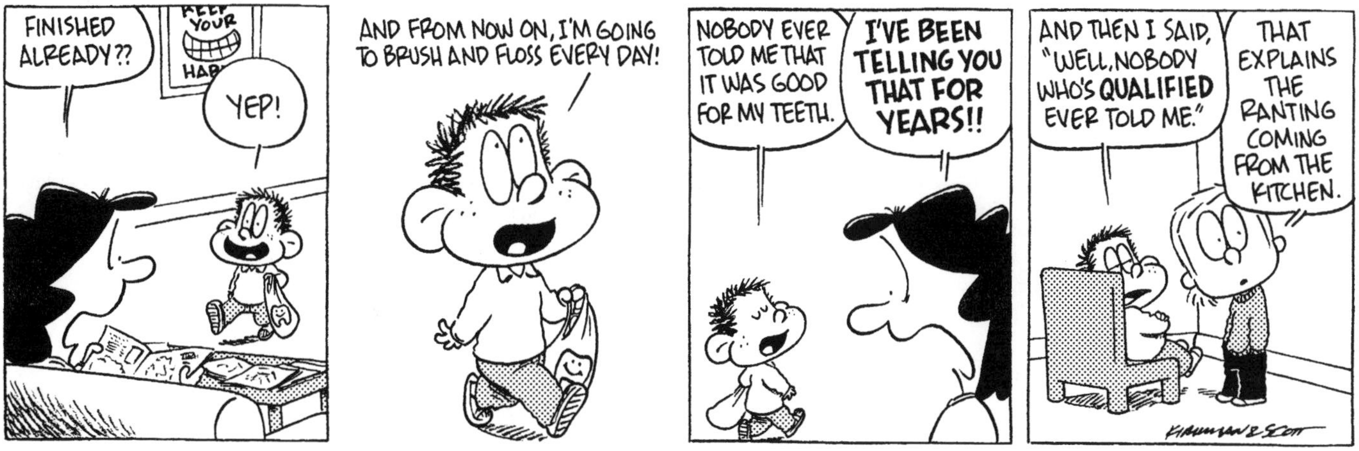
FINISHED ALREADY??
YEP!
AND FROM NOW ON, I'M GOING TO BRUSH AND FLOSS EVERY DAY!
NOBODY EVER TOLD ME THAT IT WAS GOOD FOR MY TEETH.
I'VE BEEN TELLING YOU THAT FOR YEARS!!
AND THEN I SAID, "WELL, NOBODY WHO'S QUALIFIED EVER TOLD ME."
THAT EXPLAINS THE RANTING COMING FROM THE KITCHEN.
KIRKMAN & SCOTT

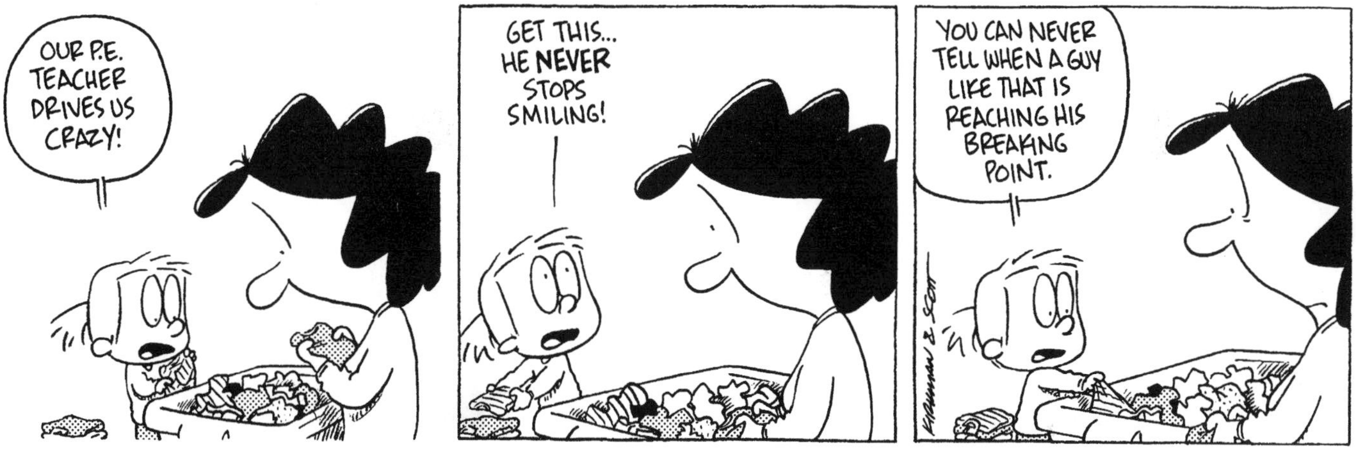
OUR P.E. TEACHER DRIVES US CRAZY!
GET THIS... HE NEVER STOPS SMILING!
YOU CAN NEVER TELL WHEN A GUY LIKE THAT IS REACHING HIS BREAKING POINT.
KIRKMAN & SCOTT

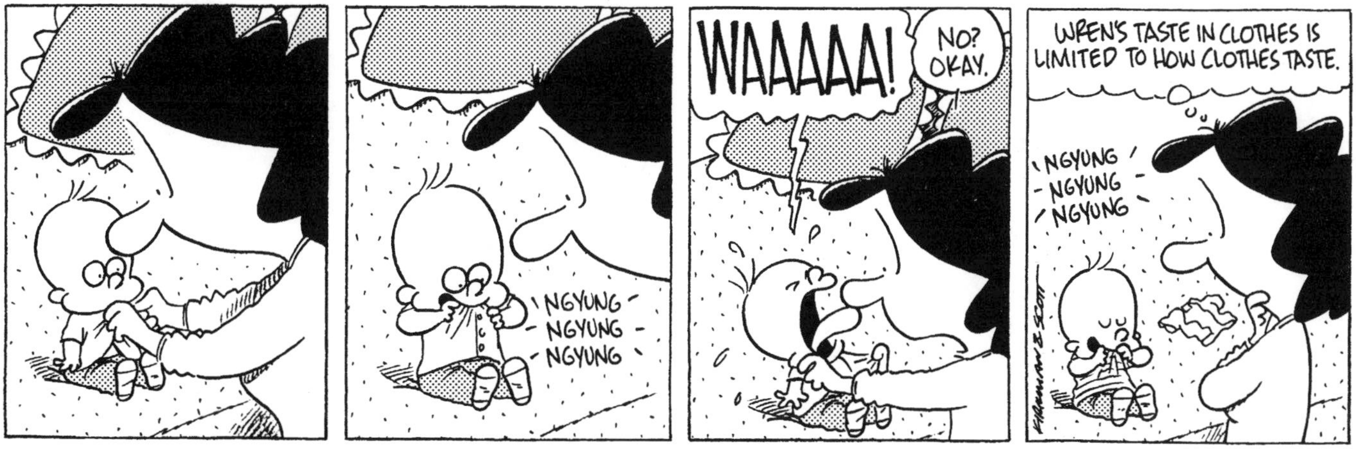
NGYUNG NGYUNG NGYUNG
WAAAAA!
NO? OKAY.
WREN'S TASTE IN CLOTHES IS LIMITED TO HOW CLOTHES TASTE.
NGYUNG NGYUNG NGYUNG
KIRKMAN & SCOTT

BABY BLUES®
BY RICK KIRKMAN / JERRY SCOTT

YOU MUST BE THE SMARTEST DAD IN THE WORLD!
WELL, I DO MY BEST.
SERIOUSLY... HOW DID YOU KNOW 36 MINUS 9 EQUALS 27?
IT JUST CAME TO ME.
AMAZING!
HOW DOES IT FEEL TO BE THE SMARTEST DAD IN THE WORLD?
TEMPORARY.
HA! HA! LOOK AT THE WAY MY TEACHER SPELLED "POLY-NUCLEOTIDE"!
KIRKMAN & SCOTT

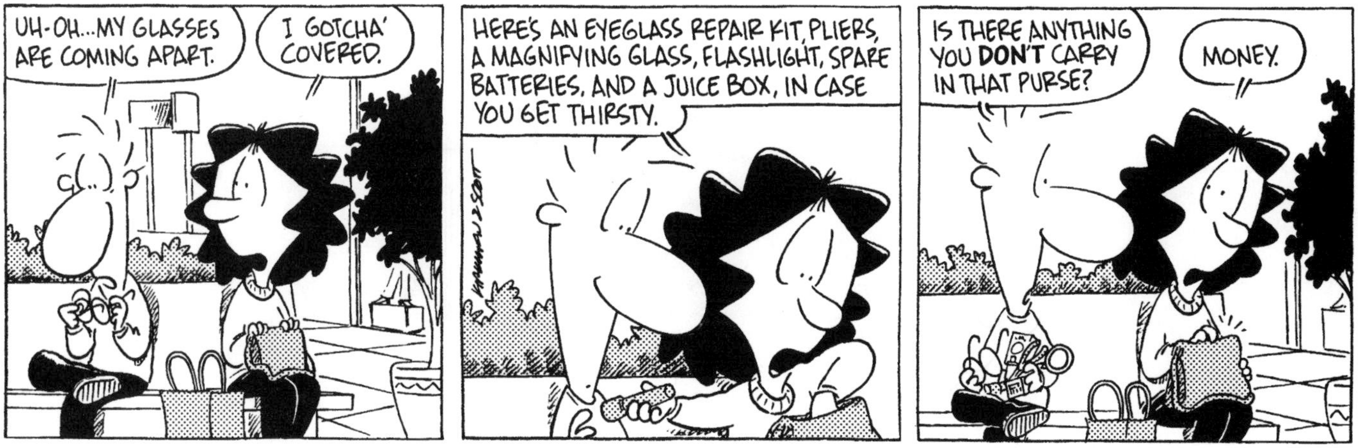
UH-OH...MY GLASSES ARE COMING APART.
I GOTCHA' COVERED.
HERE'S AN EYEGLASS REPAIR KIT, PLIERS, A MAGNIFYING GLASS, FLASHLIGHT, SPARE BATTERIES, AND A JUICE BOX, IN CASE YOU GET THIRSTY.
IS THERE ANYTHING YOU **DON'T** CARRY IN THAT PURSE?
MONEY.

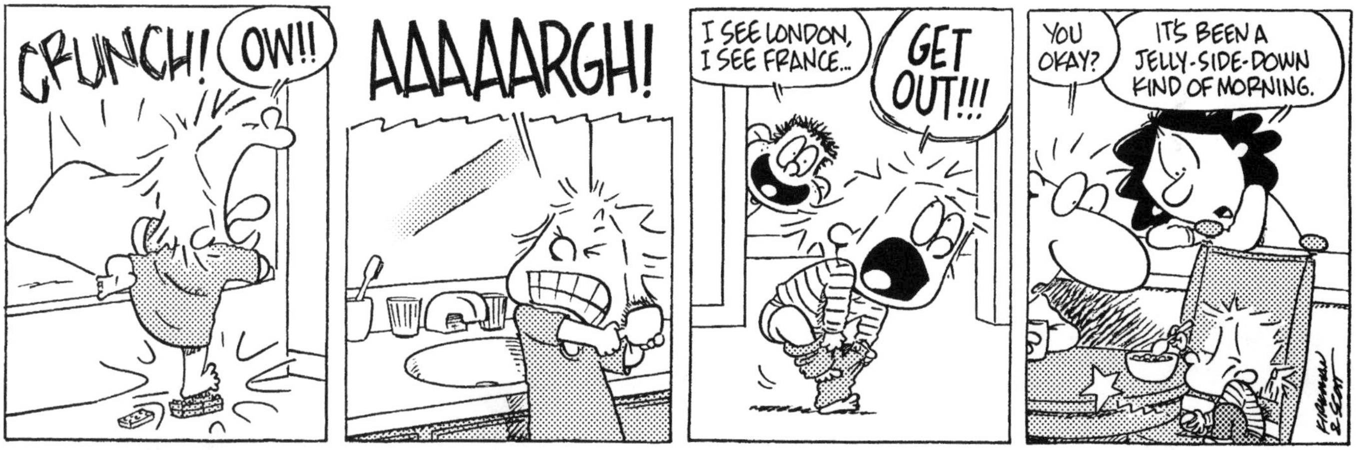
CRUNCH!
OW!!
AAAAARGH!
I SEE LONDON, I SEE FRANCE...
GET OUT!!!
YOU OKAY?
IT'S BEEN A JELLY-SIDE-DOWN KIND OF MORNING.

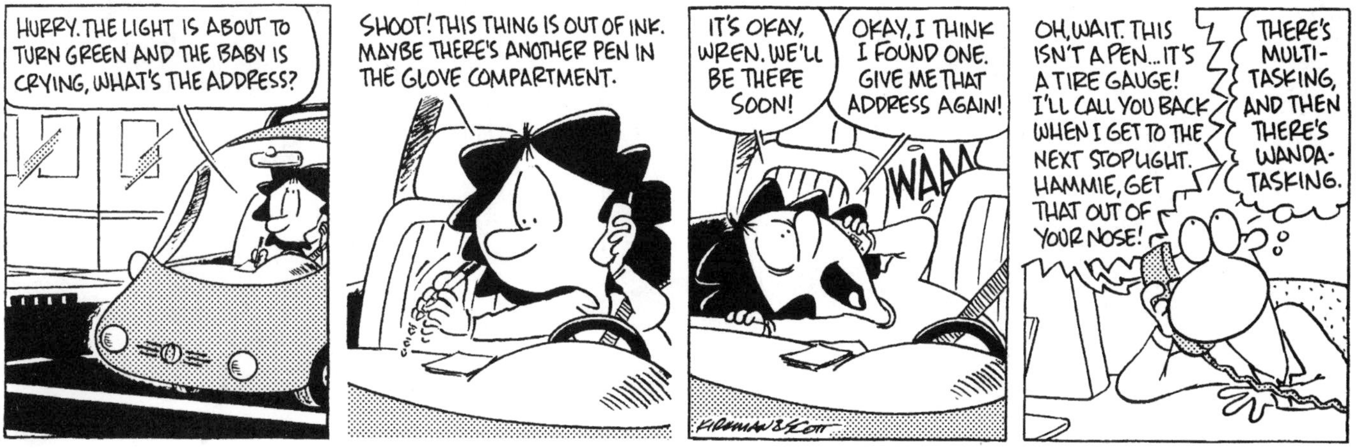
HURRY. THE LIGHT IS ABOUT TO TURN GREEN AND THE BABY IS CRYING, WHAT'S THE ADDRESS?
SHOOT! THIS THING IS OUT OF INK. MAYBE THERE'S ANOTHER PEN IN THE GLOVE COMPARTMENT.
IT'S OKAY, WREN. WE'LL BE THERE SOON!
OKAY, I THINK I FOUND ONE. GIVE ME THAT ADDRESS AGAIN!
WAA
OH, WAIT. THIS ISN'T A PEN...IT'S A TIRE GAUGE! I'LL CALL YOU BACK WHEN I GET TO THE NEXT STOPLIGHT. HAMMIE, GET THAT OUT OF YOUR NOSE!
THERE'S MULTI-TASKING, AND THEN THERE'S WANDA-TASKING.

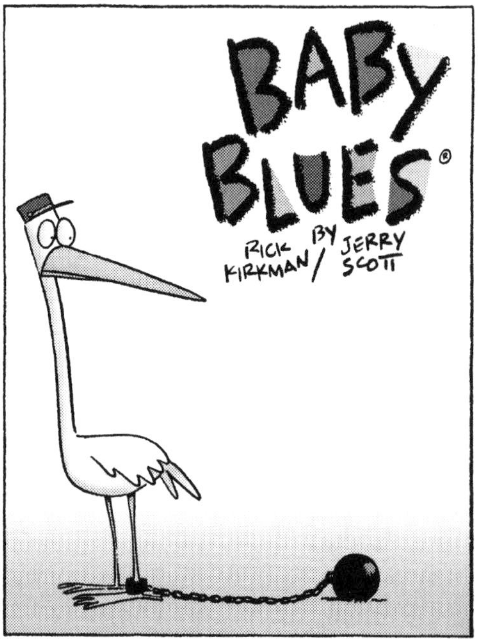
BABY BLUES®
BY RICK KIRKMAN / JERRY SCOTT

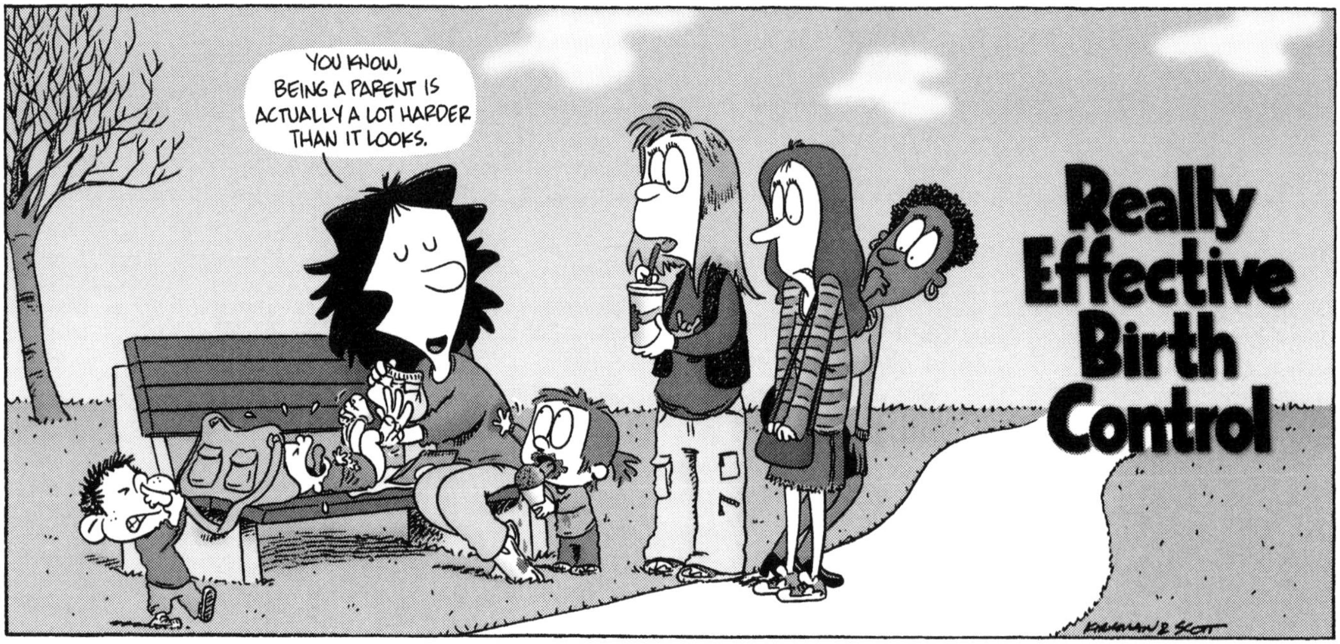
YOU KNOW, BEING A PARENT IS ACTUALLY A LOT HARDER THAN IT LOOKS.
Really Effective Birth Control
KIRKMAN & SCOTT

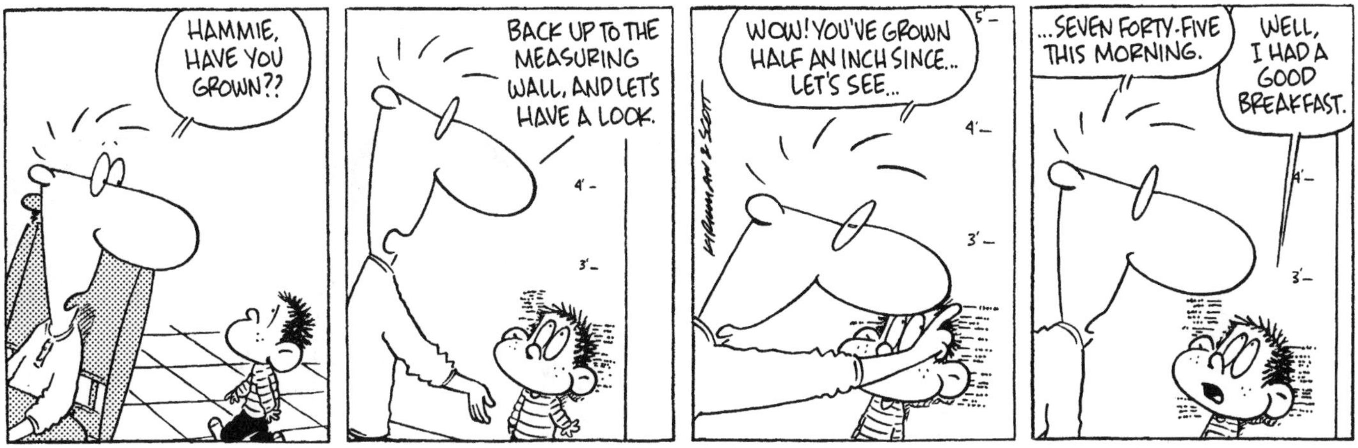
HAMMIE, HAVE YOU GROWN??
BACK UP TO THE MEASURING WALL, AND LET'S HAVE A LOOK.
WOW! YOU'VE GROWN HALF AN INCH SINCE... LET'S SEE...
...SEVEN FORTY-FIVE THIS MORNING.
WELL, I HAD A GOOD BREAKFAST.

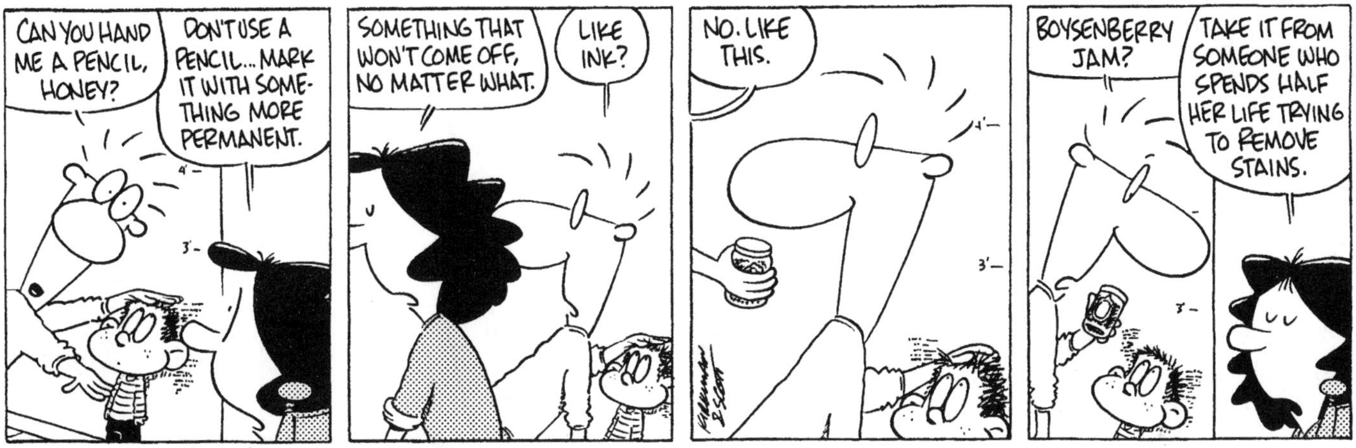
CAN YOU HAND ME A PENCIL, HONEY?
DON'T USE A PENCIL... MARK IT WITH SOMETHING MORE PERMANENT.
SOMETHING THAT WON'T COME OFF, NO MATTER WHAT.
LIKE INK?
NO. LIKE THIS.
BOYSENBERRY JAM?
TAKE IT FROM SOMEONE WHO SPENDS HALF HER LIFE TRYING TO REMOVE STAINS.

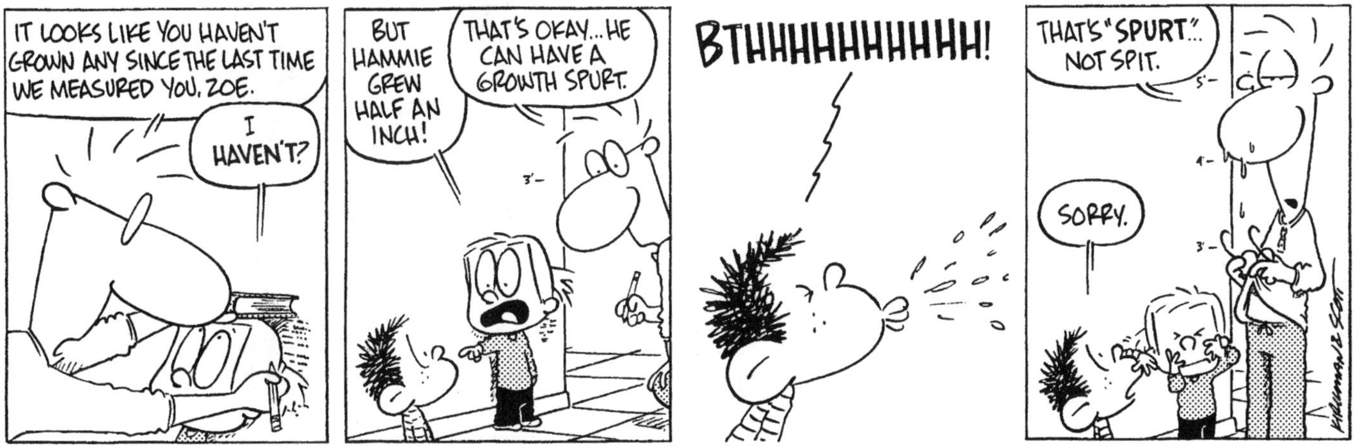
IT LOOKS LIKE YOU HAVEN'T GROWN ANY SINCE THE LAST TIME WE MEASURED YOU, ZOE.
I HAVEN'T?
BUT HAMMIE GREW HALF AN INCH!
THAT'S OKAY... HE CAN HAVE A GROWTH SPURT.
BTHHHHHHHHHH!
THAT'S "SPURT." NOT SPIT.
SORRY.

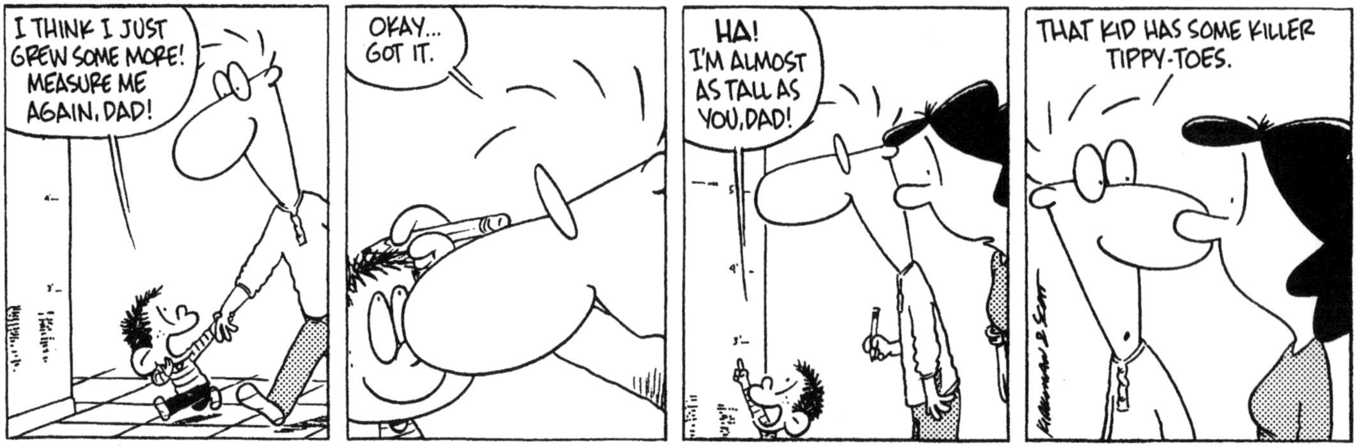
I THINK I JUST GREW SOME MORE! MEASURE ME AGAIN, DAD!
OKAY... GOT IT.
HA! I'M ALMOST AS TALL AS YOU, DAD!
THAT KID HAS SOME KILLER TIPPY-TOES.
KIRKMAN & SCOTT

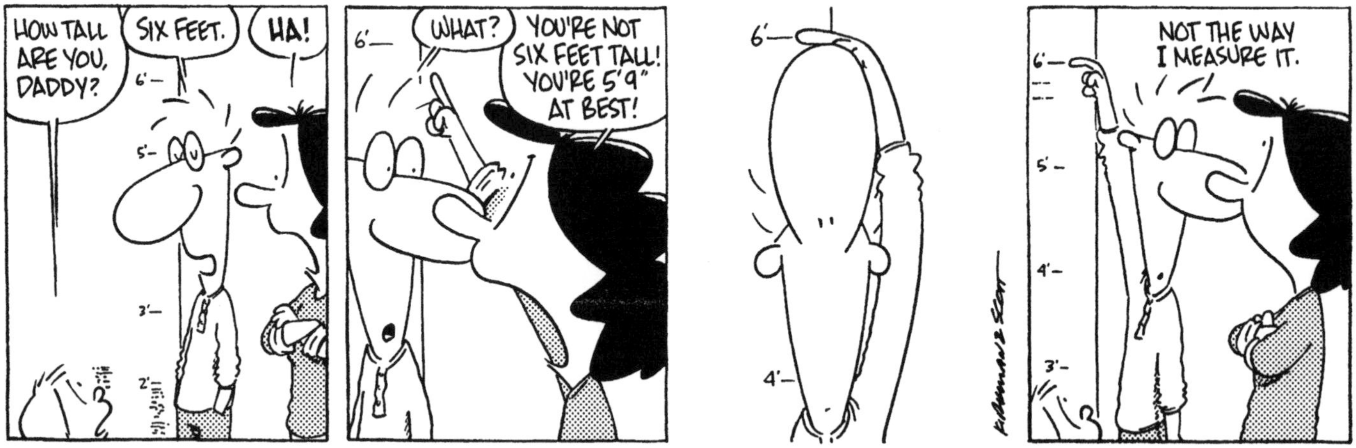
HOW TALL ARE YOU, DADDY?
SIX FEET.
HA!
WHAT?
YOU'RE NOT SIX FEET TALL! YOU'RE 5'9" AT BEST!
NOT THE WAY I MEASURE IT.
KIRKMAN & SCOTT

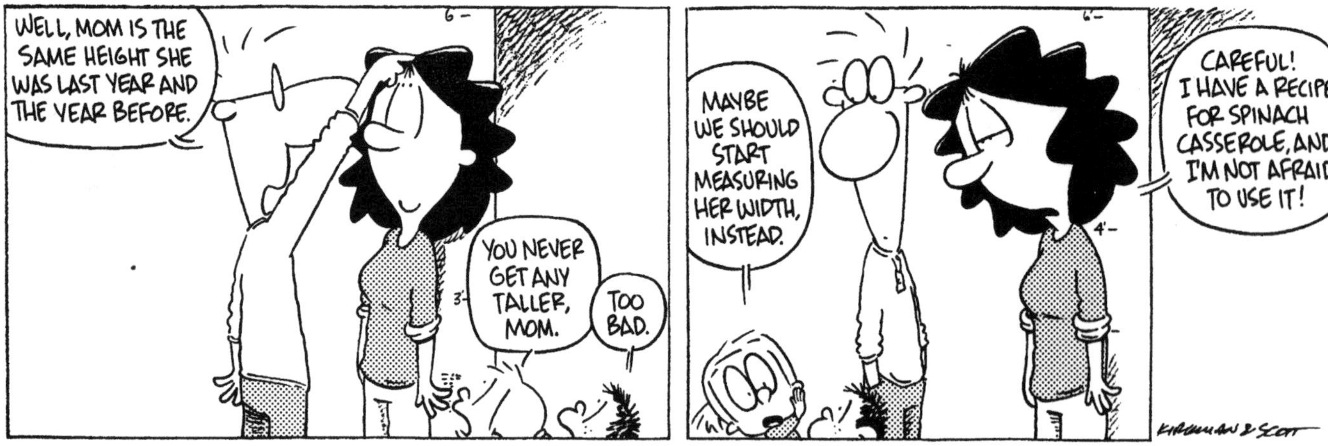
WELL, MOM IS THE SAME HEIGHT SHE WAS LAST YEAR AND THE YEAR BEFORE.
YOU NEVER GET ANY TALLER, MOM.
TOO BAD.
MAYBE WE SHOULD START MEASURING HER WIDTH, INSTEAD.
CAREFUL! I HAVE A RECIPE FOR SPINACH CASSEROLE, AND I'M NOT AFRAID TO USE IT!
KIRKMAN & SCOTT

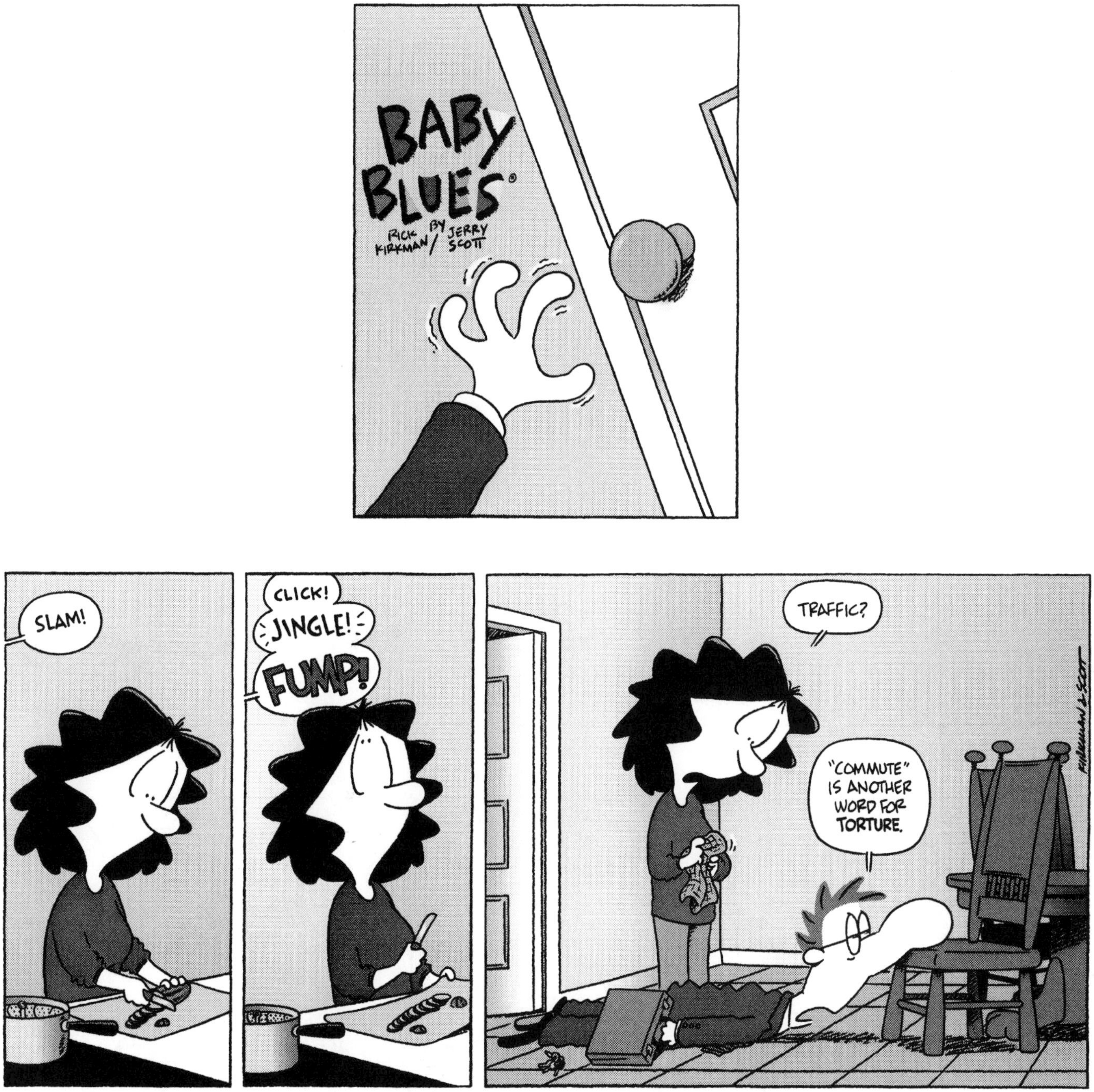
BABY BLUES®
RICK KIRKMAN / BY JERRY SCOTT
SLAM!
CLICK!
JINGLE!
FUMP!
TRAFFIC?
"COMMUTE" IS ANOTHER WORD FOR TORTURE.
KIRKMAN & SCOTT

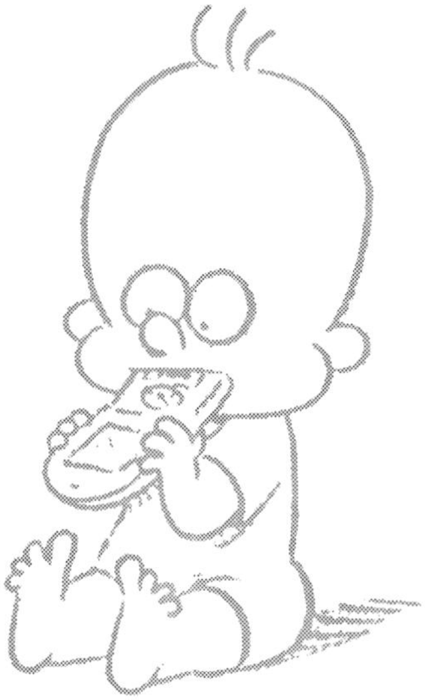

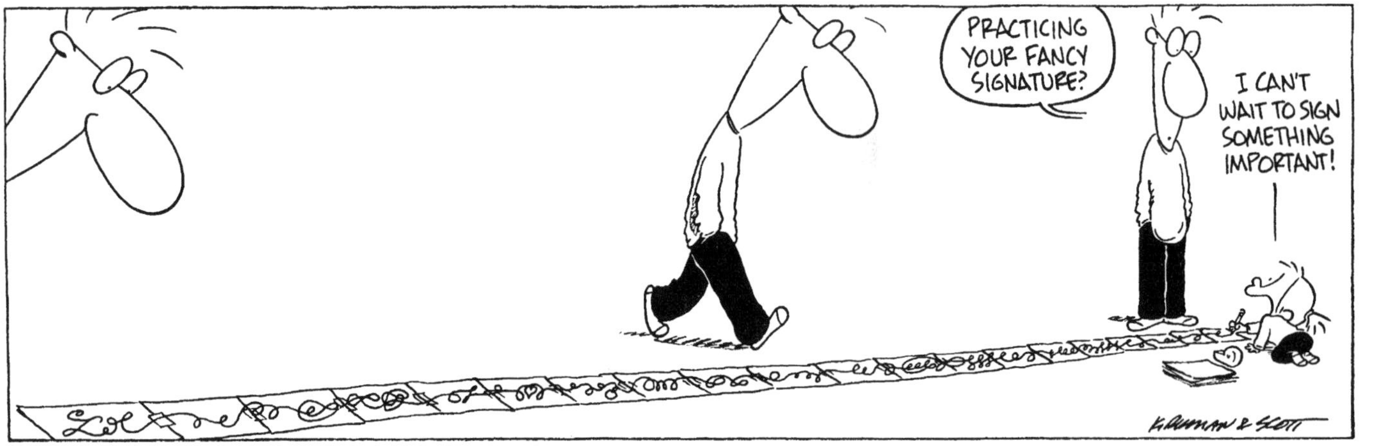
PRACTICING YOUR FANCY SIGNATURE?
I CAN'T WAIT TO SIGN SOMETHING IMPORTANT!
KIRKMAN & SCOTT

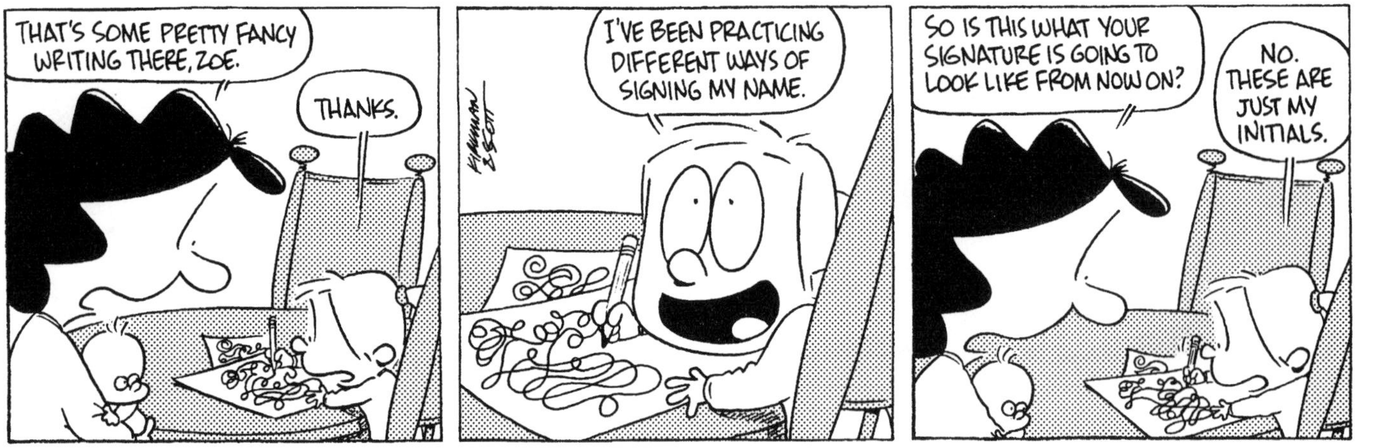
THAT'S SOME PRETTY FANCY WRITING THERE, ZOE.
THANKS.
I'VE BEEN PRACTICING DIFFERENT WAYS OF SIGNING MY NAME.
SO IS THIS WHAT YOUR SIGNATURE IS GOING TO LOOK LIKE FROM NOW ON?
NO. THESE ARE JUST MY INITIALS.

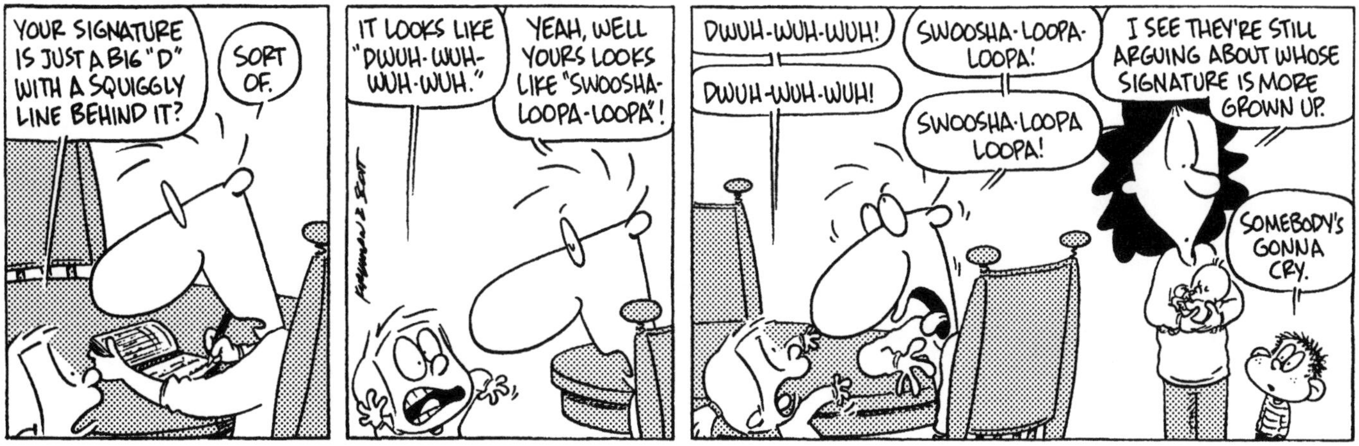

YOUR SIGNATURE IS JUST A BIG "D" WITH A SQUIGGLY LINE BEHIND IT?
SORT OF.
IT LOOKS LIKE "DWUH-WUH-WUH-WUH."
YEAH, WELL YOURS LOOKS LIKE "SWOOSHA-LOOPA-LOOPA"!
DWUH-WUH-WUH!
DWUH-WUH-WUH!
SWOOSHA-LOOPA-LOOPA!
SWOOSHA-LOOPA LOOPA!
I SEE THEY'RE STILL ARGUING ABOUT WHOSE SIGNATURE IS MORE GROWN UP.
SOMEBODY'S GONNA CRY.

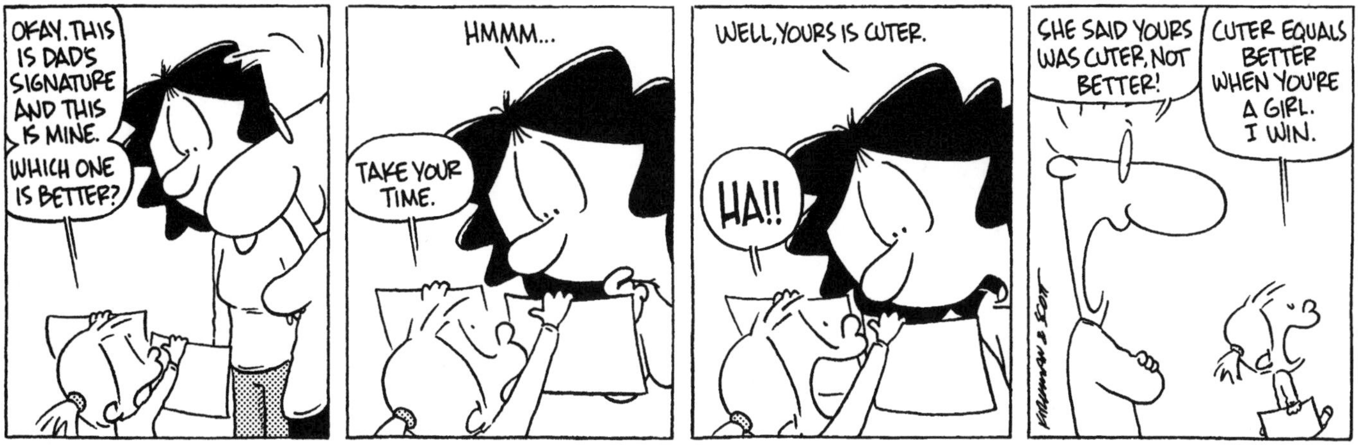

OKAY. THIS IS DAD'S SIGNATURE AND THIS IS MINE.
WHICH ONE IS BETTER?
HMMM...
TAKE YOUR TIME.
WELL, YOURS IS CUTER.
HA!!
SHE SAID YOURS WAS CUTER, NOT BETTER!
CUTER EQUALS BETTER WHEN YOU'RE A GIRL. I WIN.

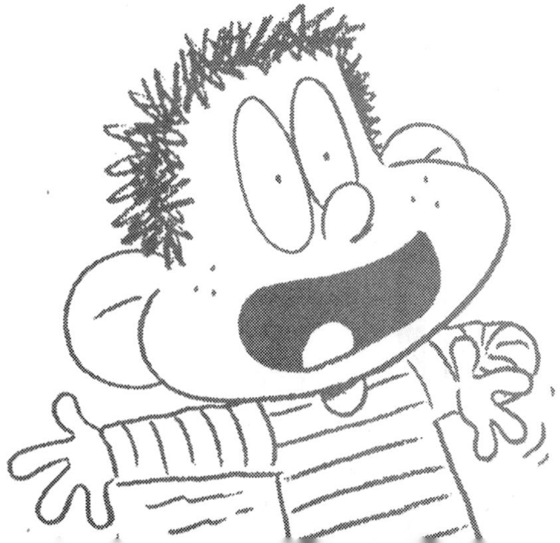

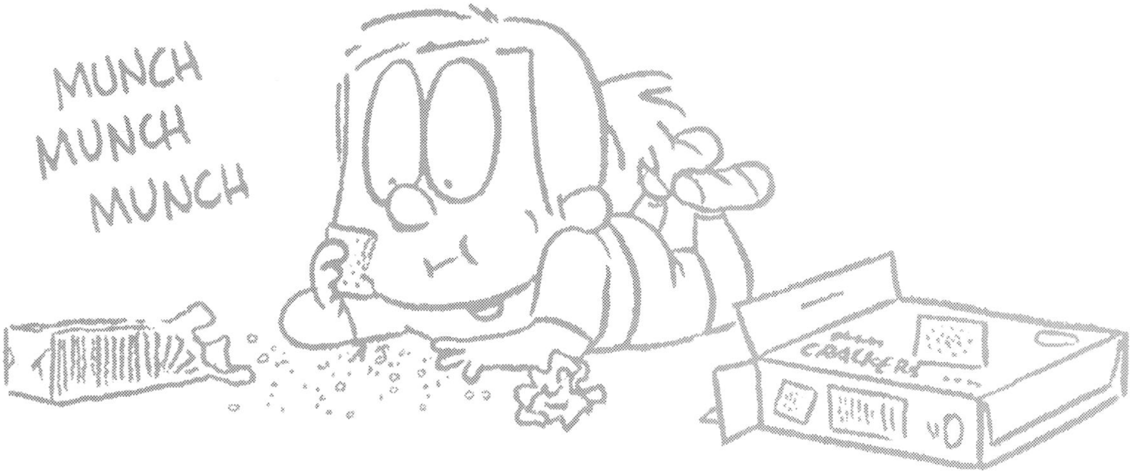
MUNCH
MUNCH
MUNCH

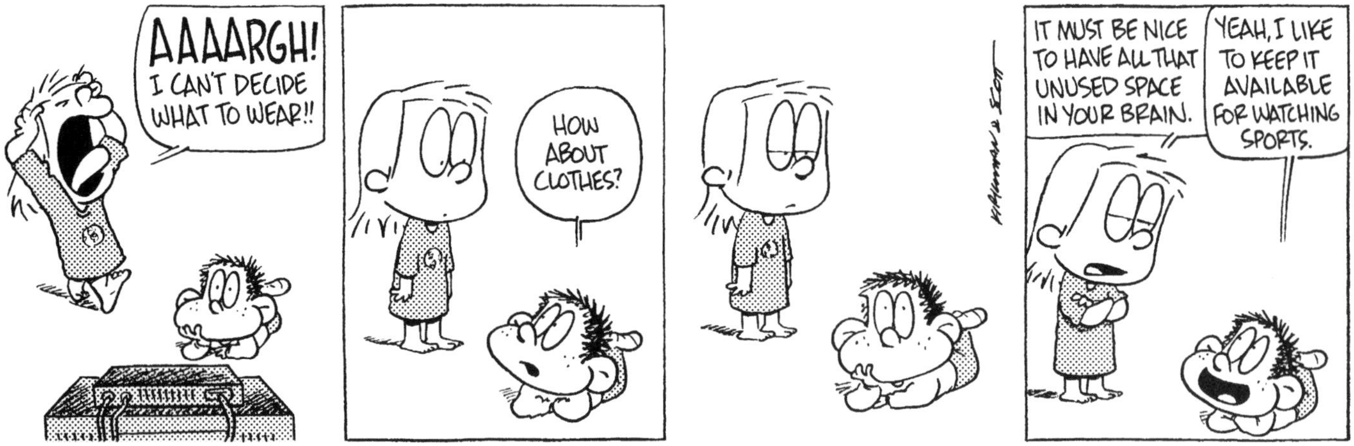
AAAARGH! I CAN'T DECIDE WHAT TO WEAR!!
HOW ABOUT CLOTHES?
IT MUST BE NICE TO HAVE ALL THAT UNUSED SPACE IN YOUR BRAIN.
YEAH, I LIKE TO KEEP IT AVAILABLE FOR WATCHING SPORTS.

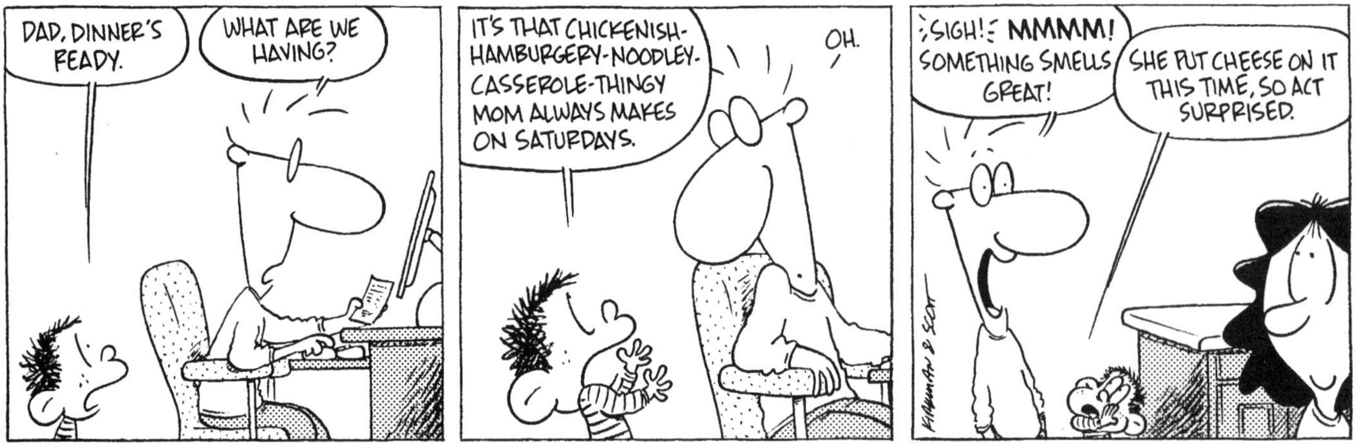
DAD, DINNER'S READY.
WHAT ARE WE HAVING?
IT'S THAT CHICKENISH-HAMBURGERY-NOODLEY-CASSEROLE-THINGY MOM ALWAYS MAKES ON SATURDAYS.
OH.
SIGH! MMMM! SOMETHING SMELLS GREAT!
SHE PUT CHEESE ON IT THIS TIME, SO ACT SURPRISED.

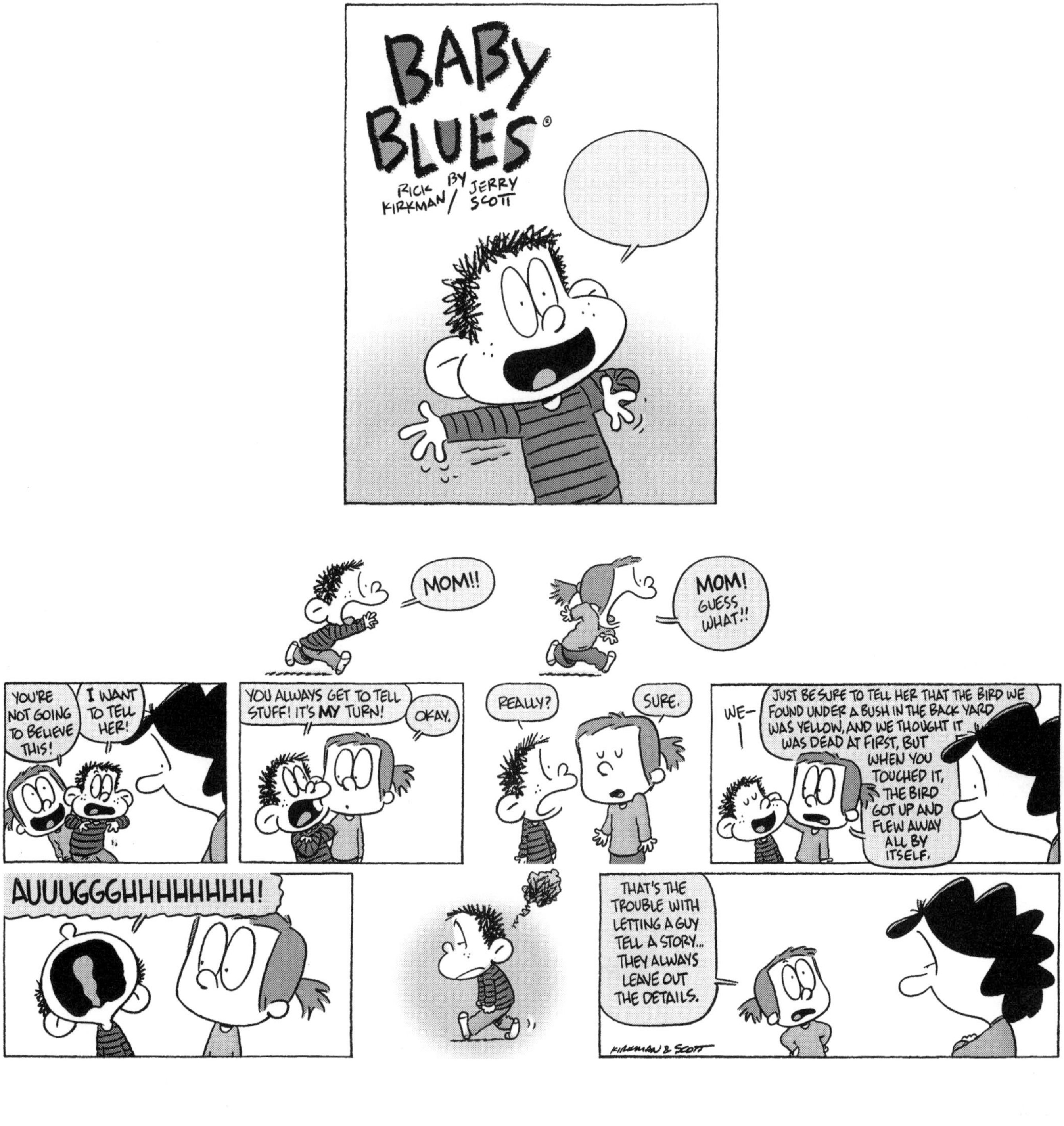
BABY BLUES®
BY RICK KIRKMAN / JERRY SCOTT
MOM!!
MOM! GUESS WHAT!!
YOU'RE NOT GOING TO BELIEVE THIS!
I WANT TO TELL HER!
YOU ALWAYS GET TO TELL STUFF! IT'S MY TURN!
OKAY.
REALLY?
SURE.
WE—
JUST BE SURE TO TELL HER THAT THE BIRD WE FOUND UNDER A BUSH IN THE BACK YARD WAS YELLOW, AND WE THOUGHT IT WAS DEAD AT FIRST, BUT WHEN YOU TOUCHED IT, THE BIRD GOT UP AND FLEW AWAY ALL BY ITSELF.
AUUUGGGHHHHHHHH!
THAT'S THE TROUBLE WITH LETTING A GUY TELL A STORY... THEY ALWAYS LEAVE OUT THE DETAILS.
KIRKMAN & SCOTT

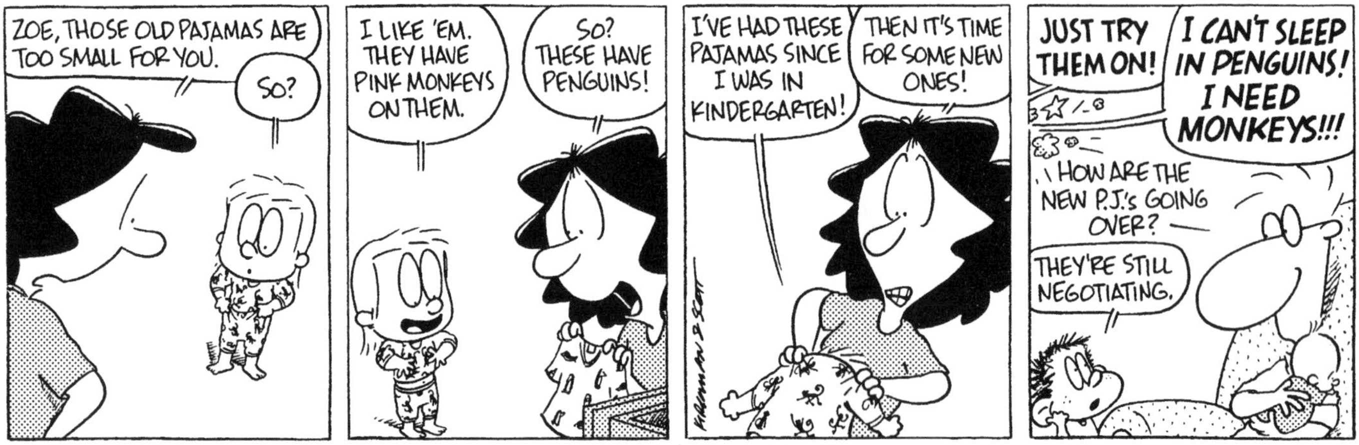
ZOE, THOSE OLD PAJAMAS ARE TOO SMALL FOR YOU.
SO?
I LIKE 'EM. THEY HAVE PINK MONKEYS ON THEM.
SO? THESE HAVE PENGUINS!
I'VE HAD THESE PAJAMAS SINCE I WAS IN KINDERGARTEN!
THEN IT'S TIME FOR SOME NEW ONES!
JUST TRY THEM ON!
I CAN'T SLEEP IN PENGUINS! I NEED MONKEYS!!!
HOW ARE THE NEW P.J.'s GOING OVER?
THEY'RE STILL NEGOTIATING.

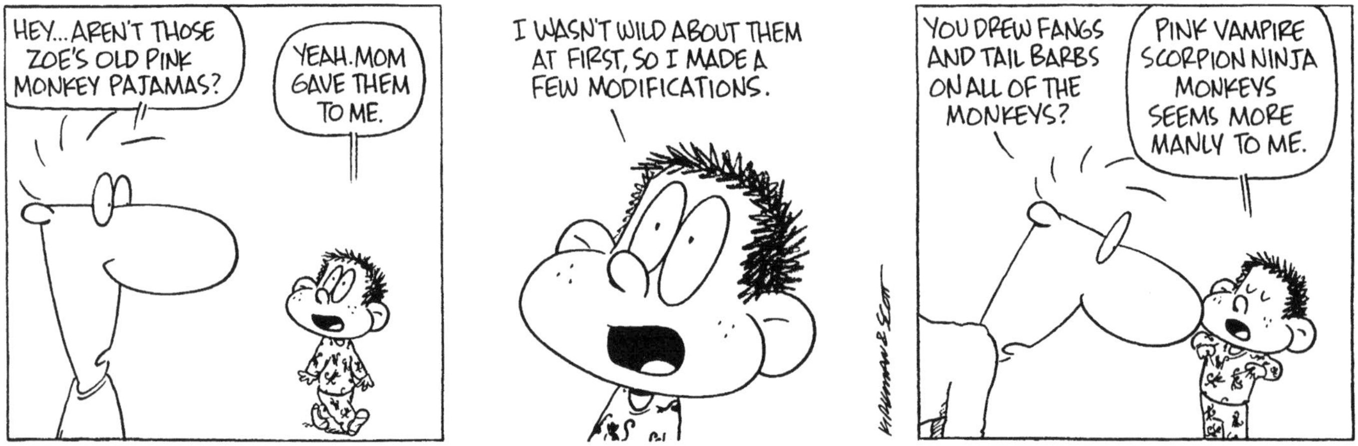
HEY... AREN'T THOSE ZOE'S OLD PINK MONKEY PAJAMAS?
YEAH. MOM GAVE THEM TO ME.
I WASN'T WILD ABOUT THEM AT FIRST, SO I MADE A FEW MODIFICATIONS.
YOU DREW FANGS AND TAIL BARBS ON ALL OF THE MONKEYS?
PINK VAMPIRE SCORPION NINJA MONKEYS SEEMS MORE MANLY TO ME.

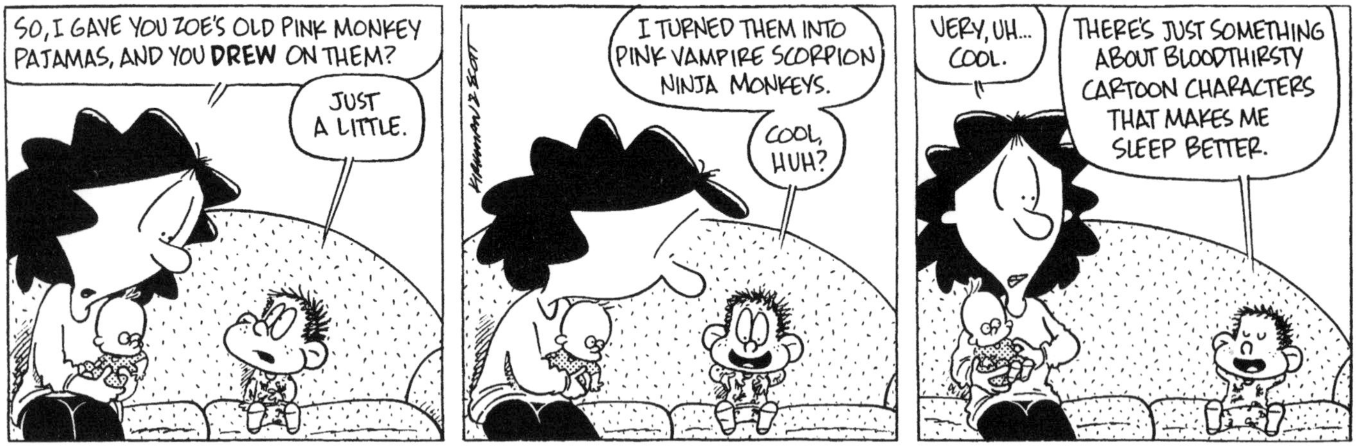
SO, I GAVE YOU ZOE'S OLD PINK MONKEY PAJAMAS, AND YOU **DREW** ON THEM?
JUST A LITTLE.
I TURNED THEM INTO PINK VAMPIRE SCORPION NINJA MONKEYS.
COOL, HUH?
VERY, UH... COOL.
THERE'S JUST SOMETHING ABOUT BLOODTHIRSTY CARTOON CHARACTERS THAT MAKES ME SLEEP BETTER.

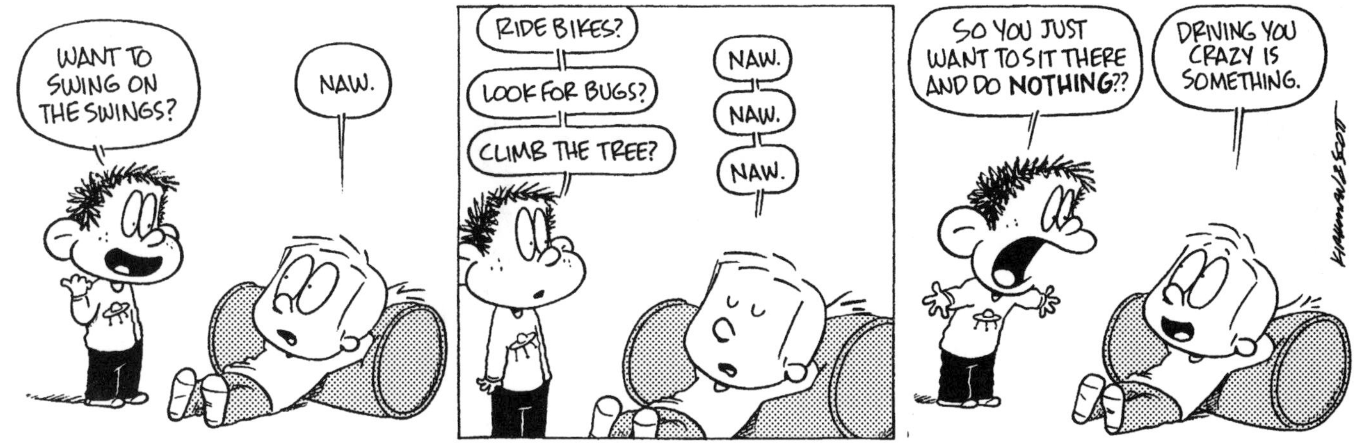
WANT TO SWING ON THE SWINGS?
NAW.
RIDE BIKES?
LOOK FOR BUGS?
CLIMB THE TREE?
NAW.
NAW.
NAW.
SO YOU JUST WANT TO SIT THERE AND DO **NOTHING**??
DRIVING YOU CRAZY IS SOMETHING.

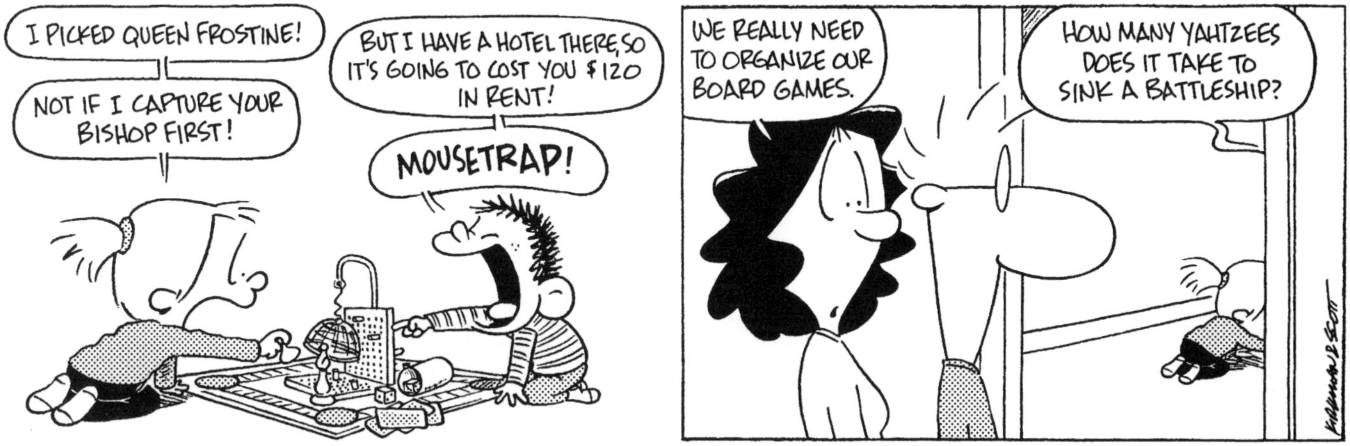
I PICKED QUEEN FROSTINE!
NOT IF I CAPTURE YOUR BISHOP FIRST!
BUT I HAVE A HOTEL THERE, SO IT'S GOING TO COST YOU $120 IN RENT!
MOUSETRAP!
WE REALLY NEED TO ORGANIZE OUR BOARD GAMES.
HOW MANY YAHTZEES DOES IT TAKE TO SINK A BATTLESHIP?

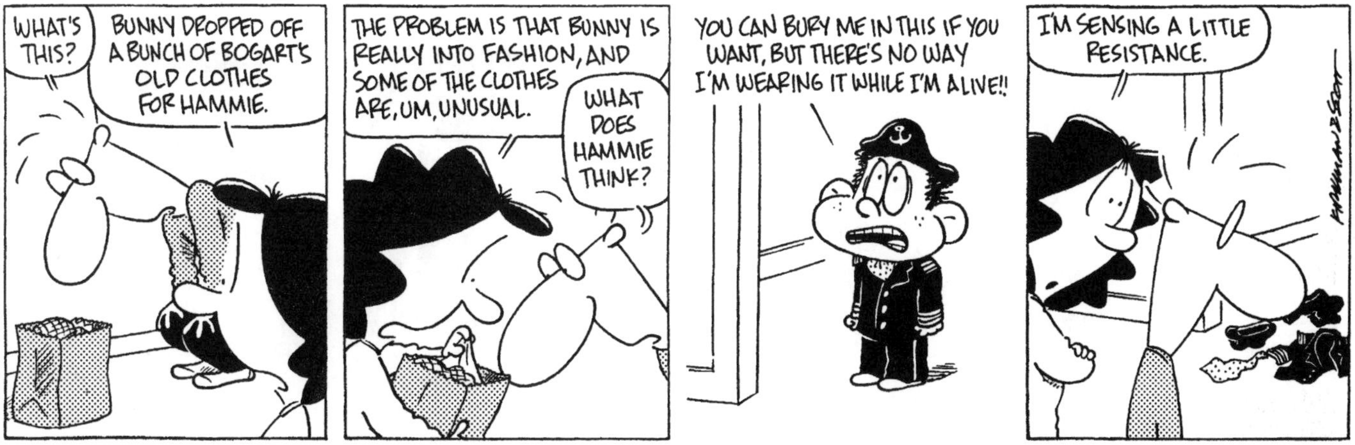
WHAT'S THIS?
BUNNY DROPPED OFF A BUNCH OF BOGART'S OLD CLOTHES FOR HAMMIE.
THE PROBLEM IS THAT BUNNY IS REALLY INTO FASHION, AND SOME OF THE CLOTHES ARE, UM, UNUSUAL.
WHAT DOES HAMMIE THINK?
YOU CAN BURY ME IN THIS IF YOU WANT, BUT THERE'S NO WAY I'M WEARING IT WHILE I'M ALIVE!!
I'M SENSING A LITTLE RESISTANCE.

BABY BLUES®
BY RICK KIRKMAN / JERRY SCOTT

SNIFF!
WAA-CHOOO!
KIRKMAN & SCOTT
SIGH!

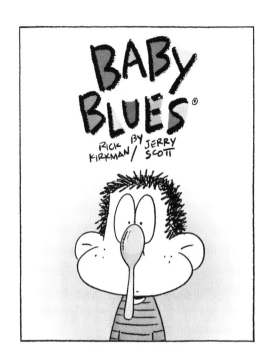

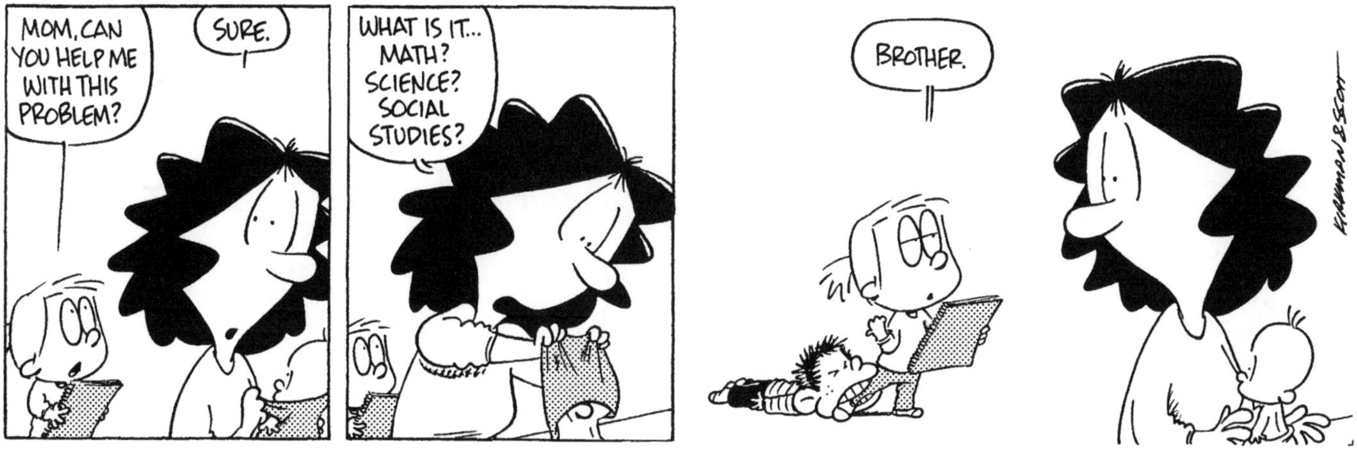
MOM, CAN YOU HELP ME WITH THIS PROBLEM?
SURE.
WHAT IS IT... MATH? SCIENCE? SOCIAL STUDIES?
BROTHER.
KIRKMAN & SCOTT

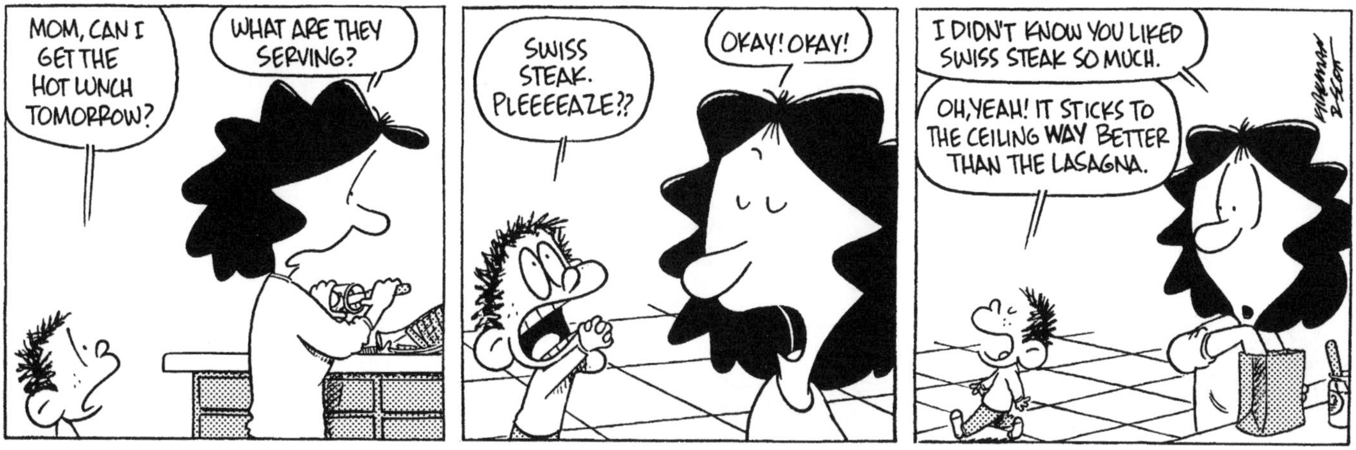
MOM, CAN I GET THE HOT LUNCH TOMORROW?
WHAT ARE THEY SERVING?
SWISS STEAK. PLEEEEAZE??
OKAY! OKAY!
I DIDN'T KNOW YOU LIKED SWISS STEAK SO MUCH.
OH, YEAH! IT STICKS TO THE CEILING WAY BETTER THAN THE LASAGNA.

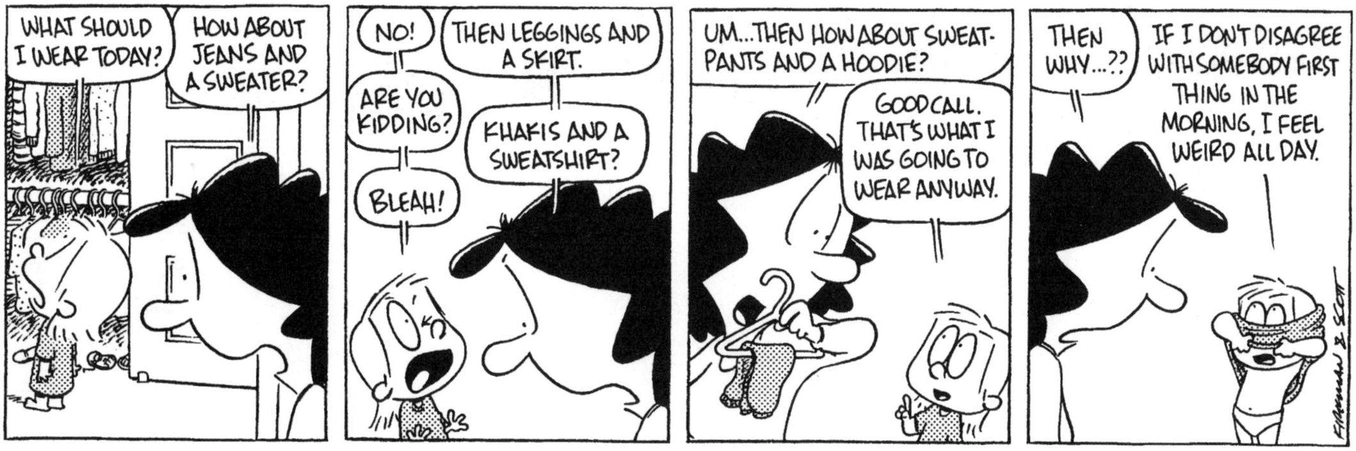
WHAT SHOULD I WEAR TODAY?
HOW ABOUT JEANS AND A SWEATER?
NO!
ARE YOU KIDDING?
BLEAH!
THEN LEGGINGS AND A SKIRT.
KHAKIS AND A SWEATSHIRT?
UM...THEN HOW ABOUT SWEAT-PANTS AND A HOODIE?
GOOD CALL. THAT'S WHAT I WAS GOING TO WEAR ANYWAY.
THEN WHY...??
IF I DON'T DISAGREE WITH SOMEBODY FIRST THING IN THE MORNING, I FEEL WEIRD ALL DAY.

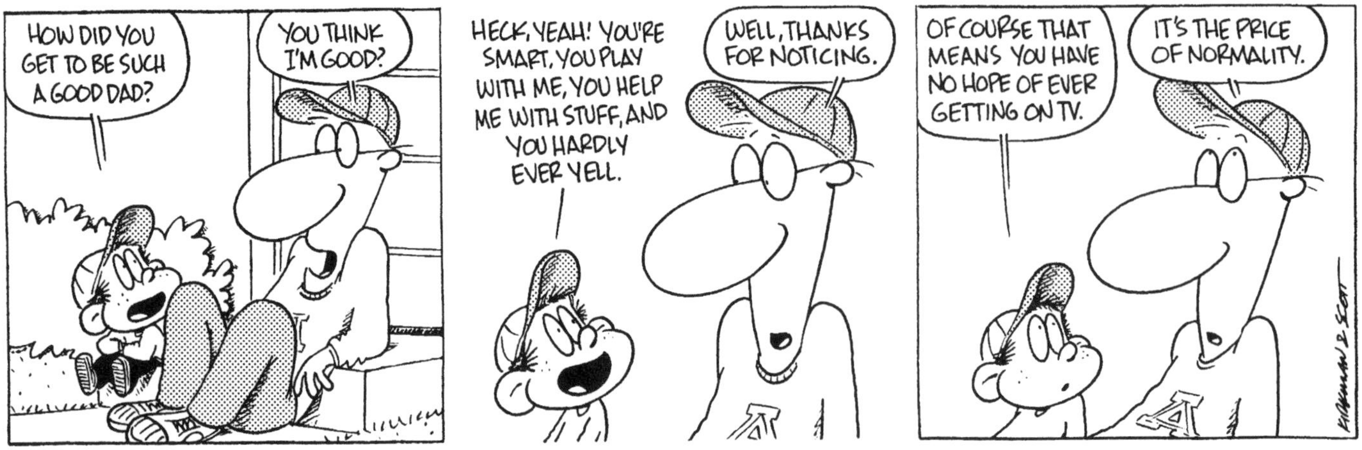
HOW DID YOU GET TO BE SUCH A GOOD DAD?
YOU THINK I'M GOOD?
HECK, YEAH! YOU'RE SMART, YOU PLAY WITH ME, YOU HELP ME WITH STUFF, AND YOU HARDLY EVER YELL.
WELL, THANKS FOR NOTICING.
OF COURSE THAT MEANS YOU HAVE NO HOPE OF EVER GETTING ON TV.
IT'S THE PRICE OF NORMALITY.
KIRKMAN & SCOTT

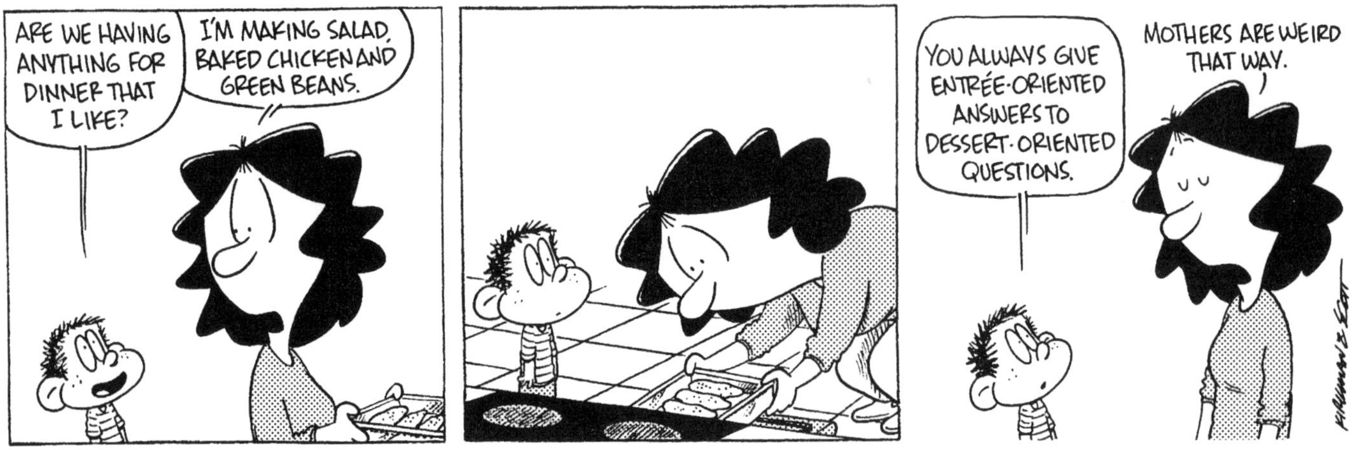
ARE WE HAVING ANYTHING FOR DINNER THAT I LIKE?
I'M MAKING SALAD, BAKED CHICKEN AND GREEN BEANS.
YOU ALWAYS GIVE ENTRÉE-ORIENTED ANSWERS TO DESSERT-ORIENTED QUESTIONS.
MOTHERS ARE WEIRD THAT WAY.
KIRKMAN & SCOTT

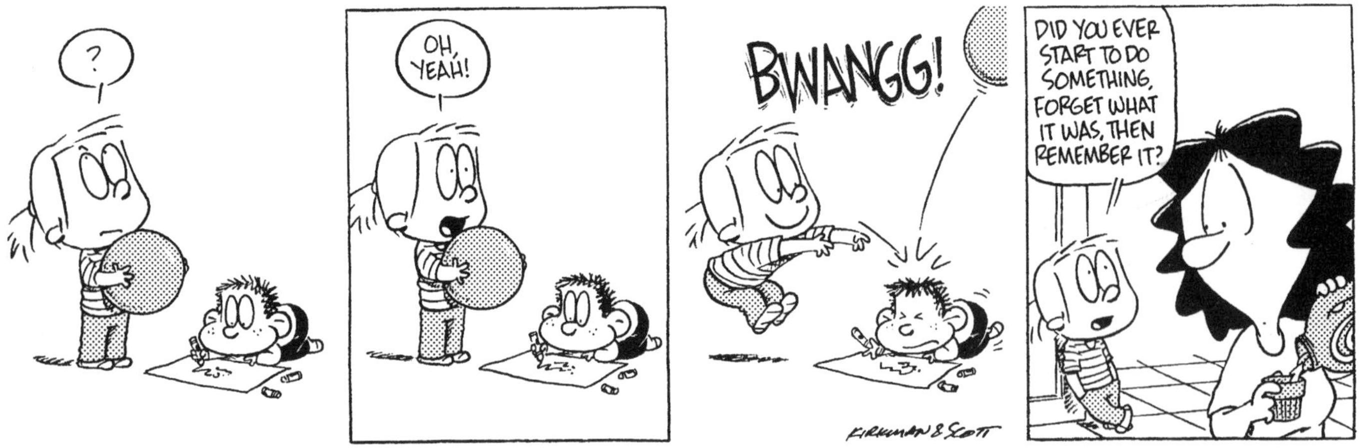
?
OH, YEAH!
BWANGG!
DID YOU EVER START TO DO SOMETHING, FORGET WHAT IT WAS, THEN REMEMBER IT?
KIRKMAN & SCOTT

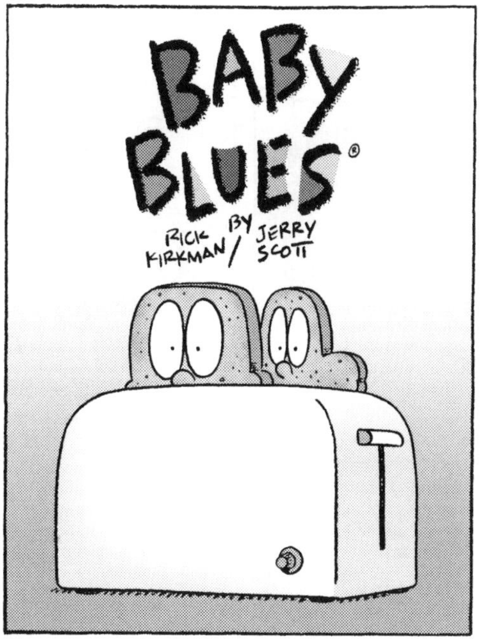
BABY BLUES®
BY RICK KIRKMAN / JERRY SCOTT

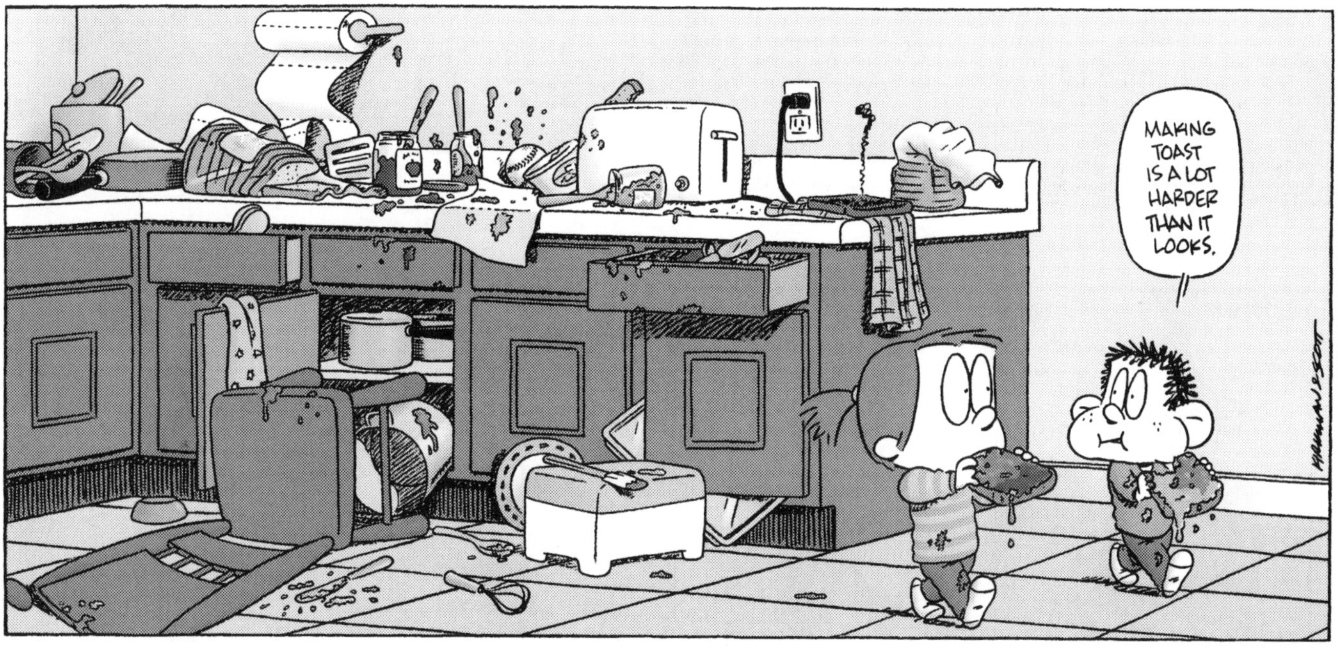
MAKING TOAST IS A LOT HARDER THAN IT LOOKS.

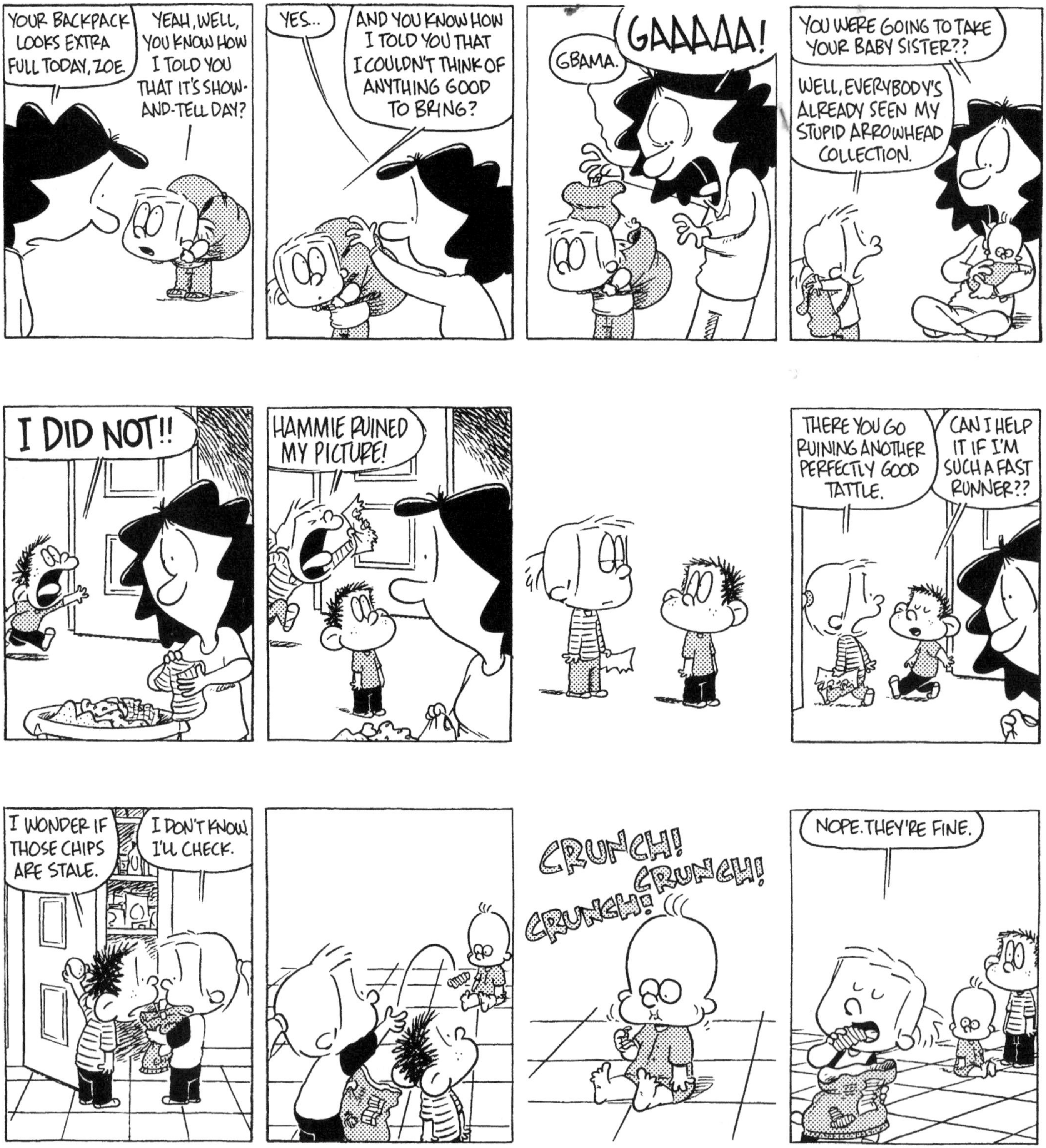
YOUR BACKPACK LOOKS EXTRA FULL TODAY, ZOE.
YEAH, WELL, YOU KNOW HOW I TOLD YOU THAT IT'S SHOW-AND-TELL DAY?
YES...
AND YOU KNOW HOW I TOLD YOU THAT I COULDN'T THINK OF ANYTHING GOOD TO BRING?
GAAAAA!
GBAMA.
YOU WERE GOING TO TAKE YOUR BABY SISTER??
WELL, EVERYBODY'S ALREADY SEEN MY STUPID ARROWHEAD COLLECTION.
I DID NOT!!
HAMMIE RUINED MY PICTURE!
THERE YOU GO RUINING ANOTHER PERFECTLY GOOD TATTLE.
CAN I HELP IT IF I'M SUCH A FAST RUNNER??
I WONDER IF THOSE CHIPS ARE STALE.
I DON'T KNOW. I'LL CHECK.
CRUNCH! CRUNCH! CRUNCH!
NOPE. THEY'RE FINE.

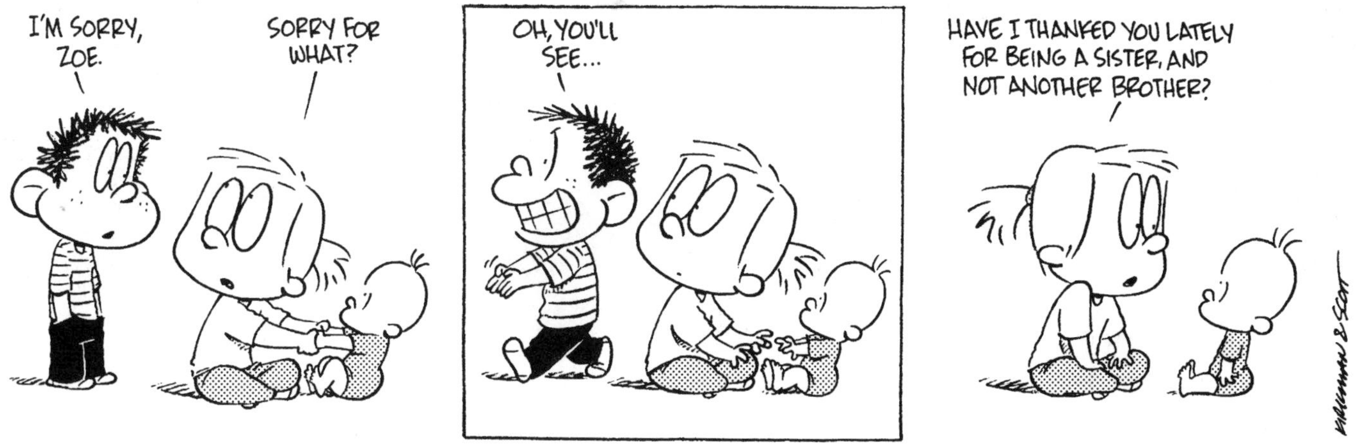
I'M SORRY, ZOE.
SORRY FOR WHAT?
OH, YOU'LL SEE...
HAVE I THANKED YOU LATELY FOR BEING A SISTER, AND NOT ANOTHER BROTHER?
KIRKMAN & SCOTT

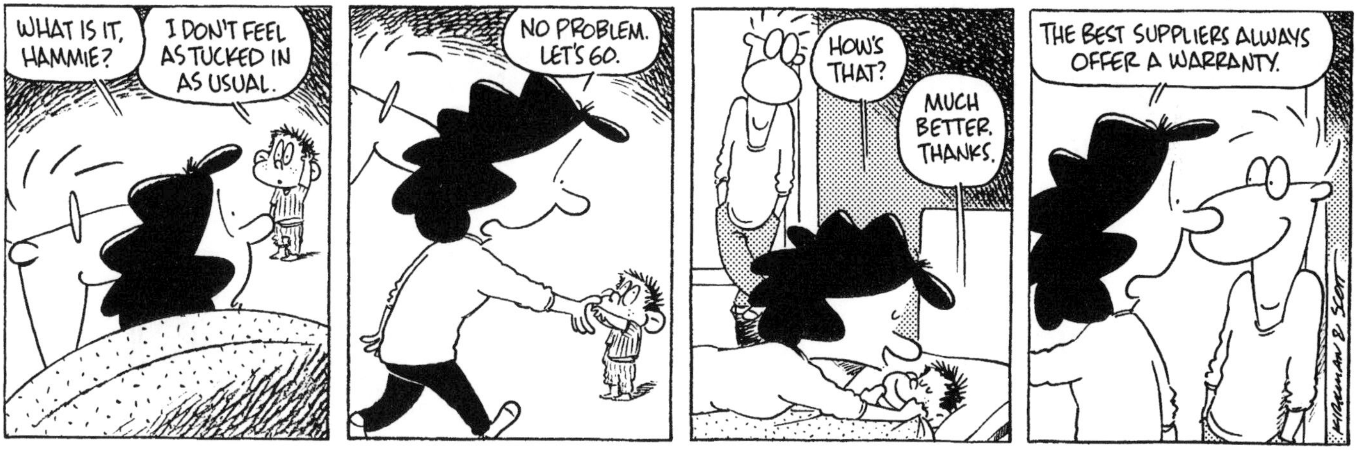
WHAT IS IT, HAMMIE?
I DON'T FEEL AS TUCKED IN AS USUAL.
NO PROBLEM. LET'S GO.
HOW'S THAT?
MUCH BETTER. THANKS.
THE BEST SUPPLIERS ALWAYS OFFER A WARRANTY.
KIRKMAN & SCOTT

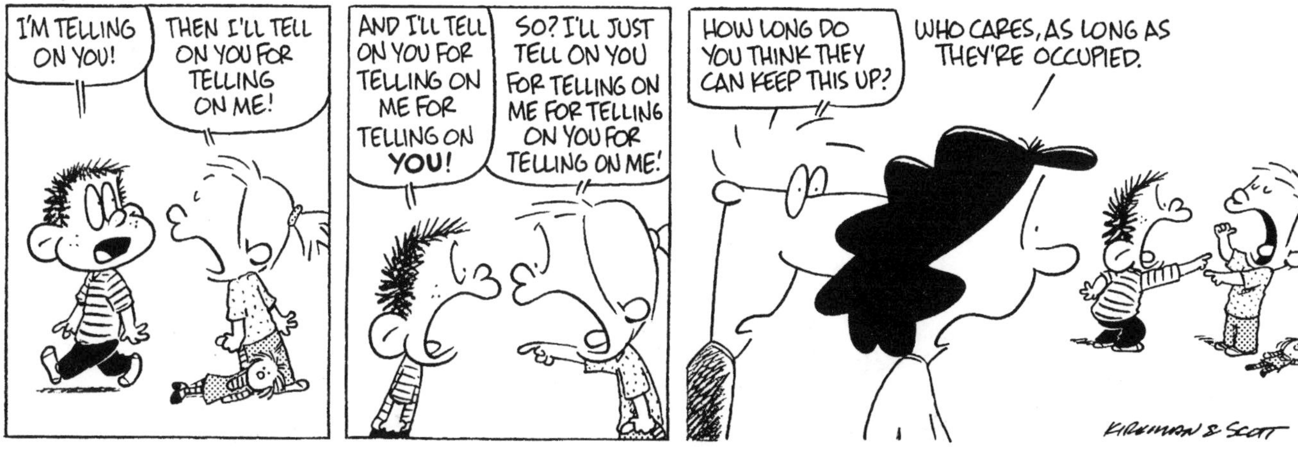
I'M TELLING ON YOU!
THEN I'LL TELL ON YOU FOR TELLING ON ME!
AND I'LL TELL ON YOU FOR TELLING ON ME FOR TELLING ON **YOU**!
SO? I'LL JUST TELL ON YOU FOR TELLING ON ME FOR TELLING ON YOU FOR TELLING ON ME!
HOW LONG DO YOU THINK THEY CAN KEEP THIS UP?
WHO CARES, AS LONG AS THEY'RE OCCUPIED.
KIRKMAN & SCOTT

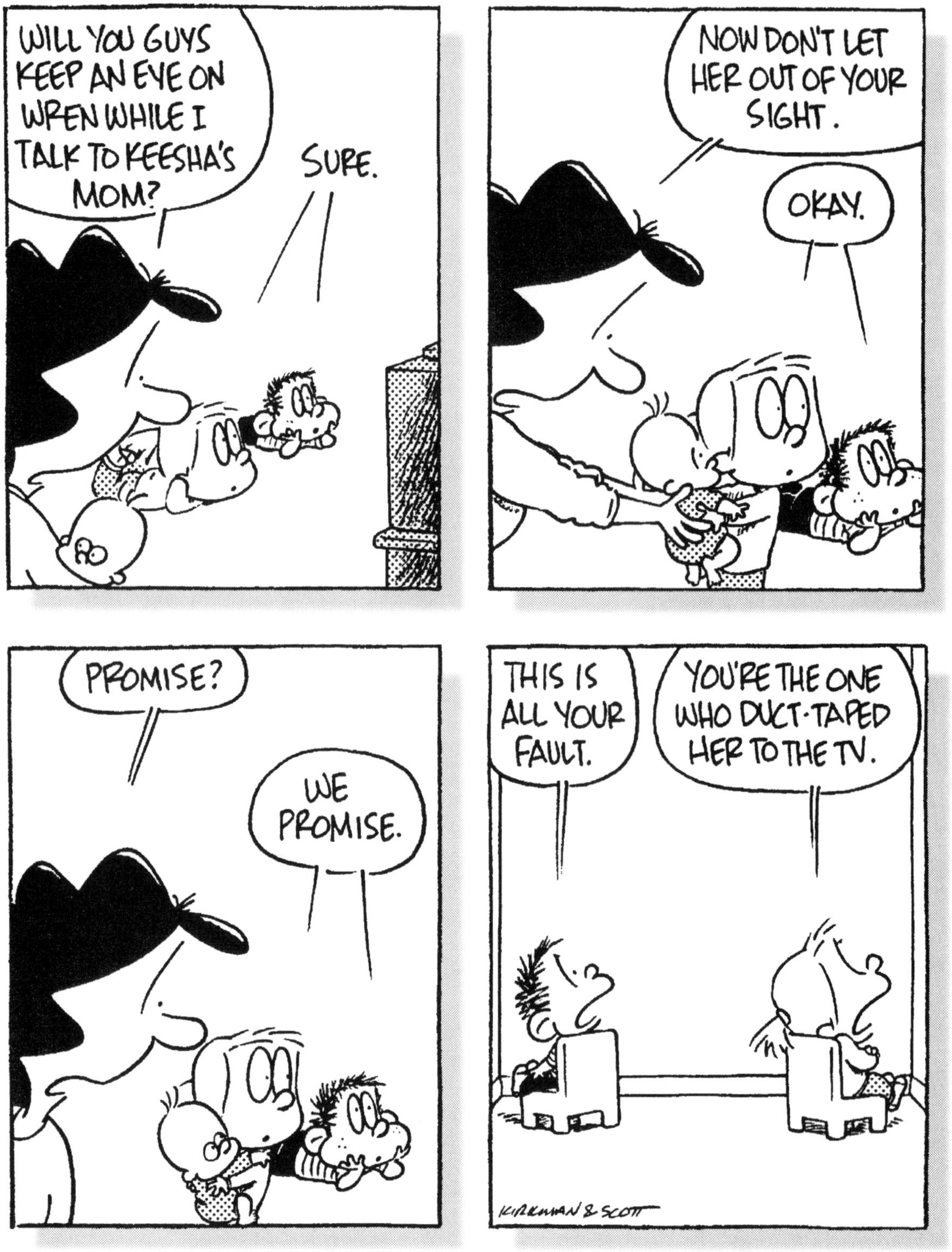
WILL YOU GUYS KEEP AN EYE ON WREN WHILE I TALK TO KEESHA'S MOM?
SURE.
NOW DON'T LET HER OUT OF YOUR SIGHT.
OKAY.
PROMISE?
WE PROMISE.
THIS IS ALL YOUR FAULT.
YOU'RE THE ONE WHO DUCT-TAPED HER TO THE TV.
KIRKMAN & SCOTT

BABY BLUES
BY
RICK KIRKMAN / JERRY SCOTT

HOW DID MY STAPLER GET IN THE FREEZER?
HAMMIE.
WHY IS THERE A PAINTBRUSH IN THE SILVERWARE DRAWER?
HAMMIE.
WHO PUT MY SLIPPERS ON THE BOOKSHELF?
HAMMIE.
THE PANCAKE SYRUP DOES NOT BELONG IN THE MAILBOX!
TELL THAT TO HAMMIE.
ZOE, IF YOU SEE YOUR BROTHER DOING ALL THIS STUFF, WHY DON'T YOU TELL HIM TO STOP?
I'M NOT AN ADVISOR... I'M A BLAMER.

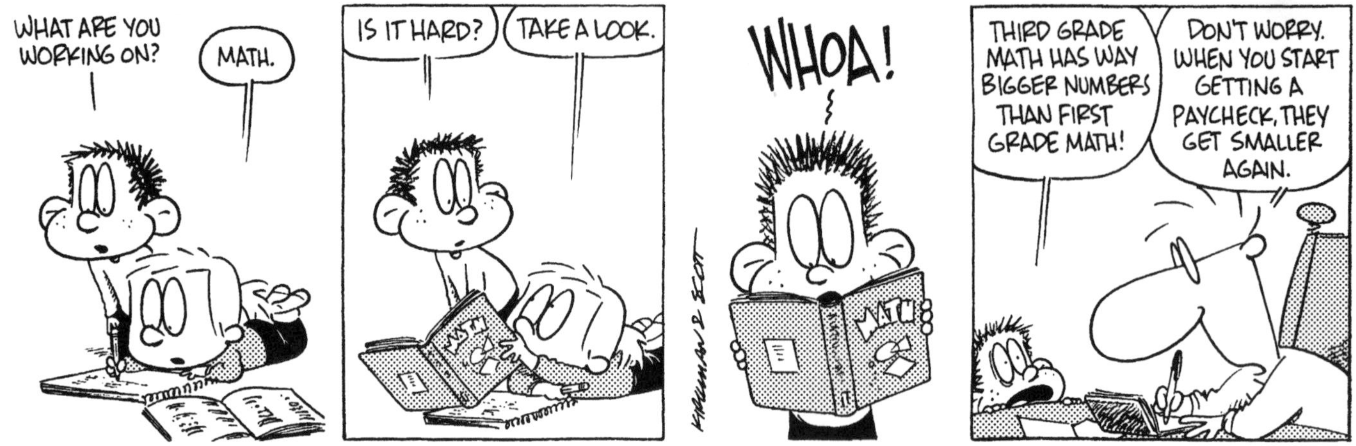
WHAT ARE YOU WORKING ON?
MATH.
IS IT HARD?
TAKE A LOOK.
WHOA!
MATH
THIRD GRADE MATH HAS WAY BIGGER NUMBERS THAN FIRST GRADE MATH!
DON'T WORRY. WHEN YOU START GETTING A PAYCHECK, THEY GET SMALLER AGAIN.
KIRKMAN & SCOTT

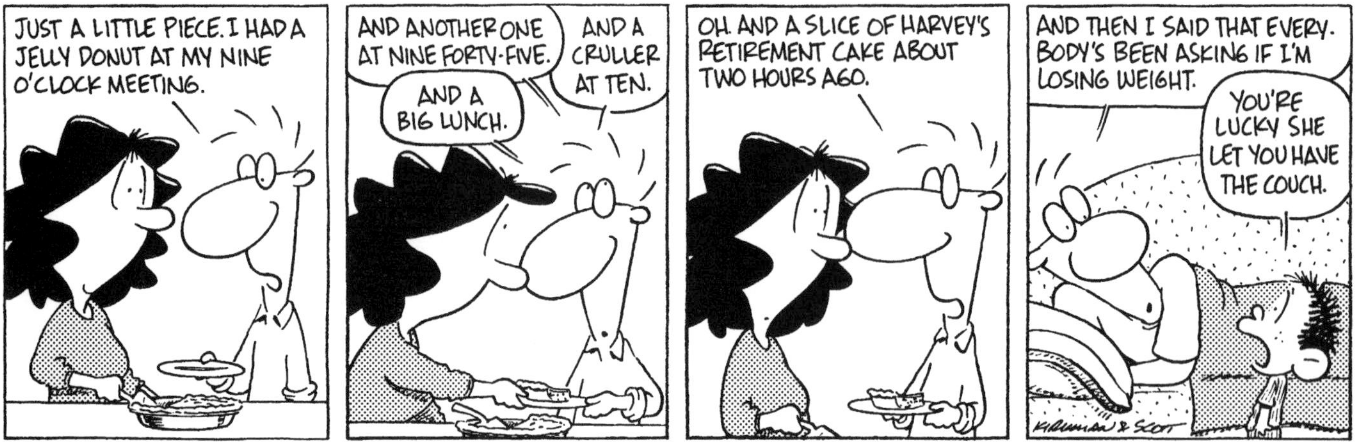
JUST A LITTLE PIECE. I HAD A JELLY DONUT AT MY NINE O'CLOCK MEETING.
AND ANOTHER ONE AT NINE FORTY-FIVE.
AND A CRULLER AT TEN.
AND A BIG LUNCH.
OH. AND A SLICE OF HARVEY'S RETIREMENT CAKE ABOUT TWO HOURS AGO.
AND THEN I SAID THAT EVERYBODY'S BEEN ASKING IF I'M LOSING WEIGHT.
YOU'RE LUCKY SHE LET YOU HAVE THE COUCH.
KIRKMAN & SCOTT

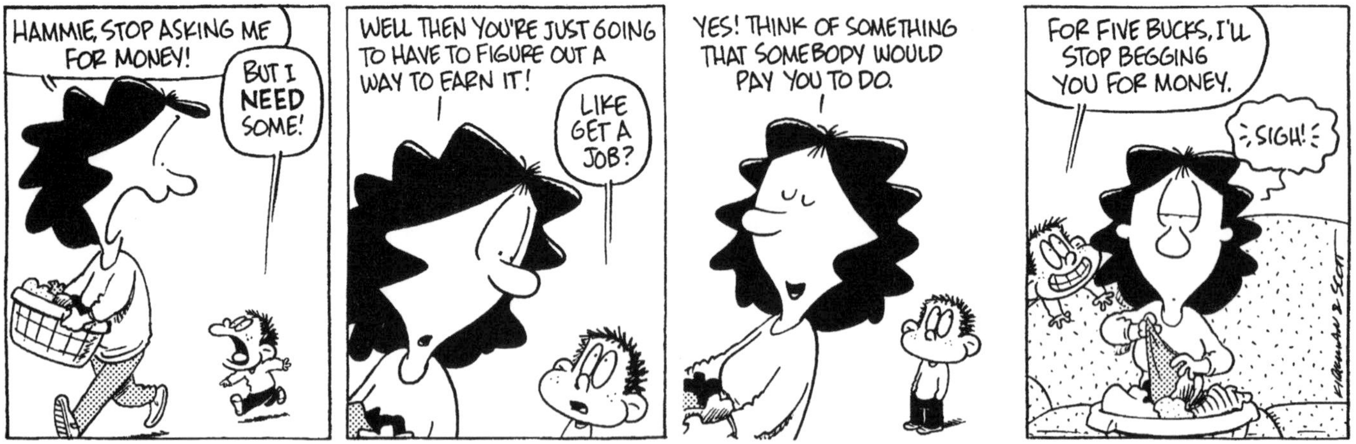
HAMMIE, STOP ASKING ME FOR MONEY!
BUT I **NEED** SOME!
WELL THEN YOU'RE JUST GOING TO HAVE TO FIGURE OUT A WAY TO EARN IT!
LIKE GET A JOB?
YES! THINK OF SOMETHING THAT SOMEBODY WOULD PAY YOU TO DO.
FOR FIVE BUCKS, I'LL STOP BEGGING YOU FOR MONEY.
SIGH!
KIRKMAN & SCOTT

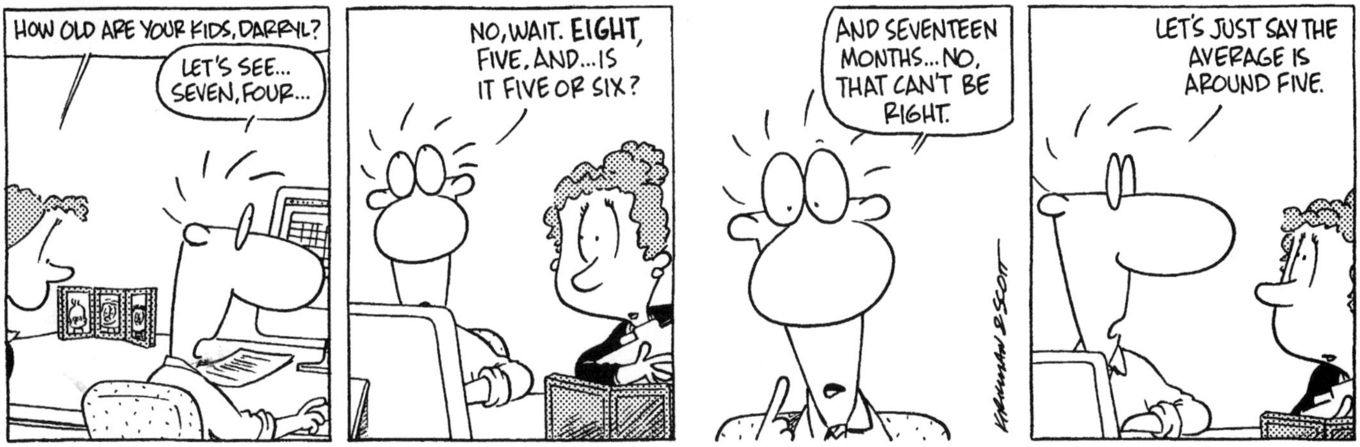
HOW OLD ARE YOUR KIDS, DARRYL?
LET'S SEE... SEVEN, FOUR...
NO, WAIT. EIGHT, FIVE, AND...IS IT FIVE OR SIX?
AND SEVENTEEN MONTHS...NO, THAT CAN'T BE RIGHT.
LET'S JUST SAY THE AVERAGE IS AROUND FIVE.

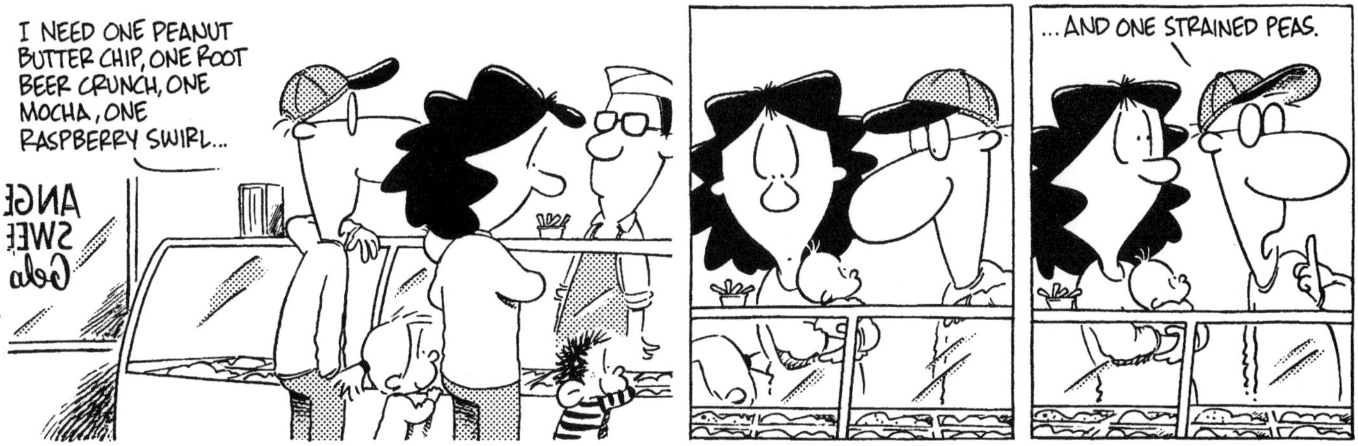
I NEED ONE PEANUT BUTTER CHIP, ONE ROOT BEER CRUNCH, ONE MOCHA, ONE RASPBERRY SWIRL...
...AND ONE STRAINED PEAS.

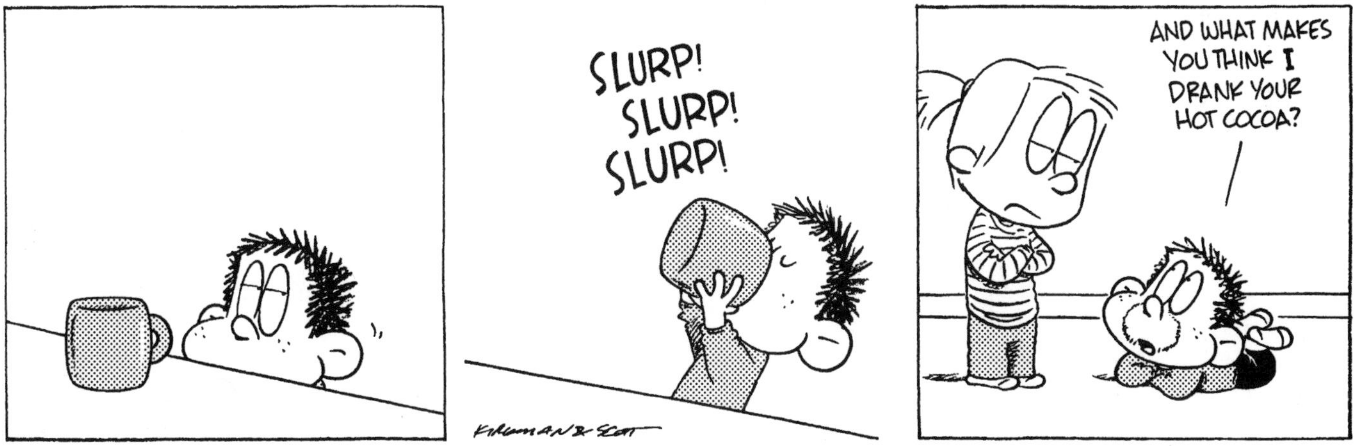
SLURP! SLURP! SLURP!
AND WHAT MAKES YOU THINK I DRANK YOUR HOT COCOA?

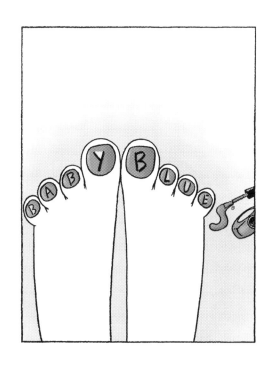

DADDY, CAN I PAINT YOUR TOENAILS?

WHAT?

I THINK YOU'D LOOK GOOD IN RED.

ZOE, I DON'T THINK—

PLEASE? PLEASE? PLEASE? PLEASE? PLEASEPLEASEPLEASE?

OKAY. OKAY.

JUST DON'T TELL ANYBODY ABOUT THIS.

DON'T WORRY, I WON'T.

ALL DONE! NOW JUST SIT THERE UNTIL THEY DRY.

YEAH, OKAY.

PHOOO... PHOOO...

DADDY?

PHOOO... WHAT? PHOOO...

SOME OF YOUR FRIENDS ARE HERE, BUT DON'T WORRY... I DIDN'T TELL THEM ABOUT THE O-NAILS-TAY.

PH—

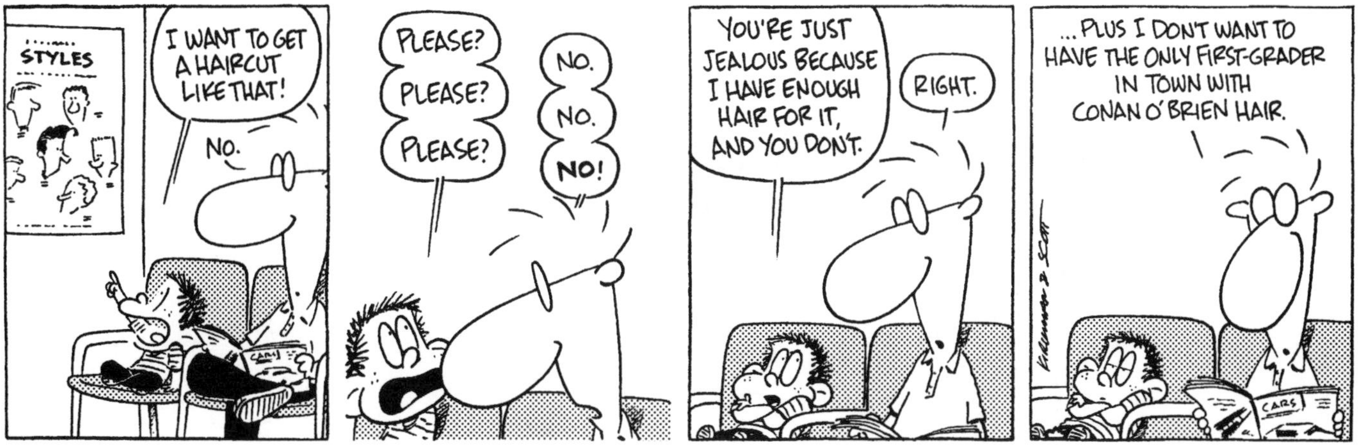
STYLES
I WANT TO GET A HAIRCUT LIKE THAT!
NO.
PLEASE? PLEASE? PLEASE?
NO. NO. NO!
YOU'RE JUST JEALOUS BECAUSE I HAVE ENOUGH HAIR FOR IT, AND YOU DON'T.
RIGHT.
...PLUS I DON'T WANT TO HAVE THE ONLY FIRST-GRADER IN TOWN WITH CONAN O'BRIEN HAIR.

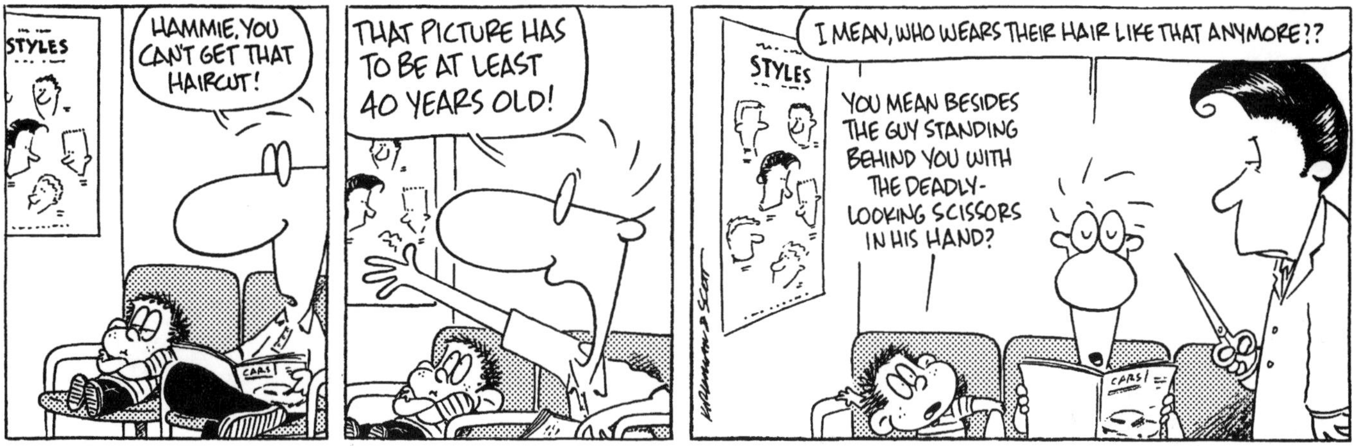
STYLES
HAMMIE, YOU CAN'T GET THAT HAIRCUT!
THAT PICTURE HAS TO BE AT LEAST 40 YEARS OLD!
I MEAN, WHO WEARS THEIR HAIR LIKE THAT ANYMORE??
YOU MEAN BESIDES THE GUY STANDING BEHIND YOU WITH THE DEADLY-LOOKING SCISSORS IN HIS HAND?

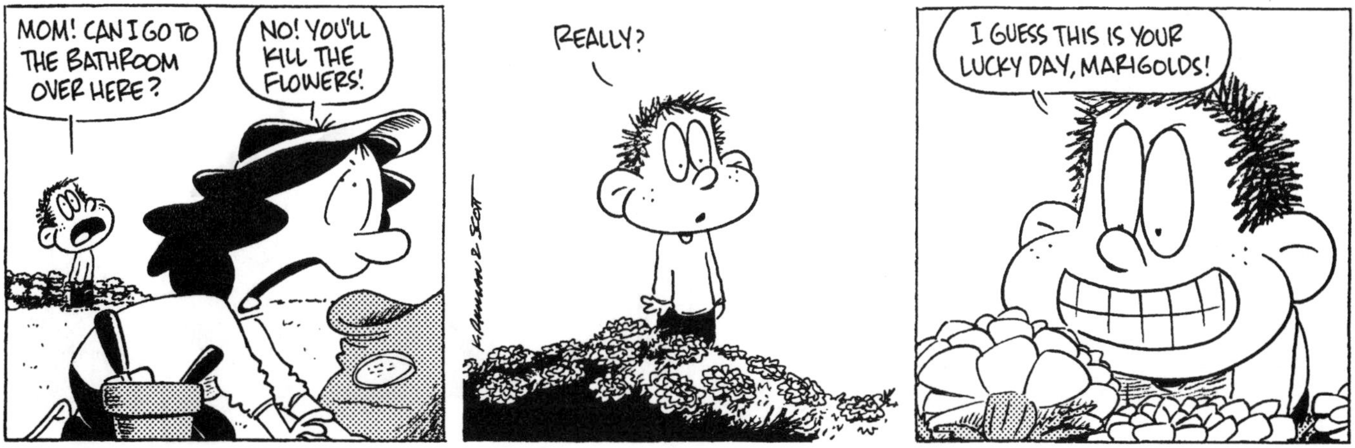
MOM! CAN I GO TO THE BATHROOM OVER HERE?
NO! YOU'LL KILL THE FLOWERS!
REALLY?
I GUESS THIS IS YOUR LUCKY DAY, MARIGOLDS!

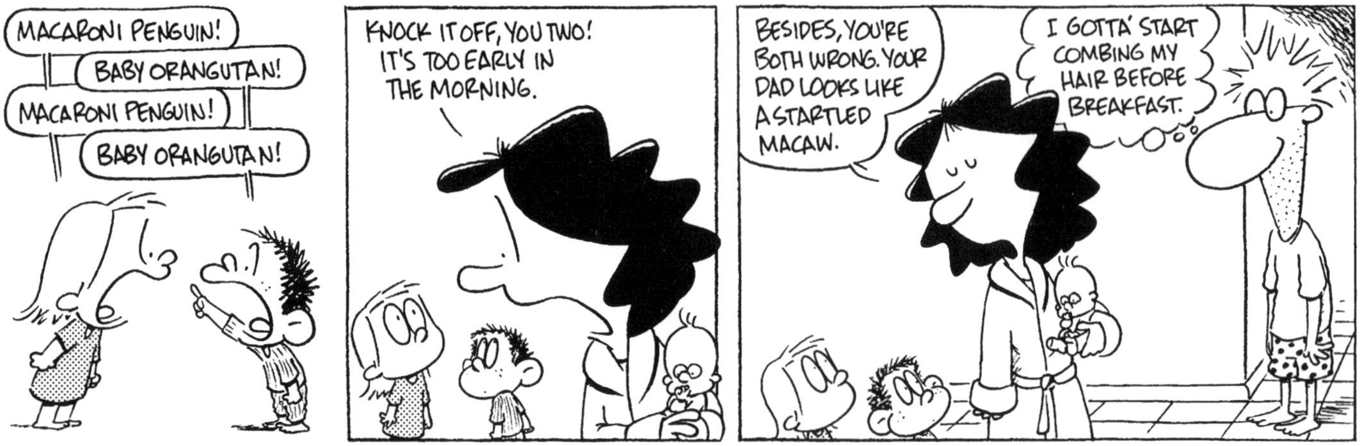
MACARONI PENGUIN!
BABY ORANGUTAN!
MACARONI PENGUIN!
BABY ORANGUTAN!
KNOCK IT OFF, YOU TWO! IT'S TOO EARLY IN THE MORNING.
BESIDES, YOU'RE BOTH WRONG. YOUR DAD LOOKS LIKE A STARTLED MACAW.
I GOTTA' START COMBING MY HAIR BEFORE BREAKFAST.

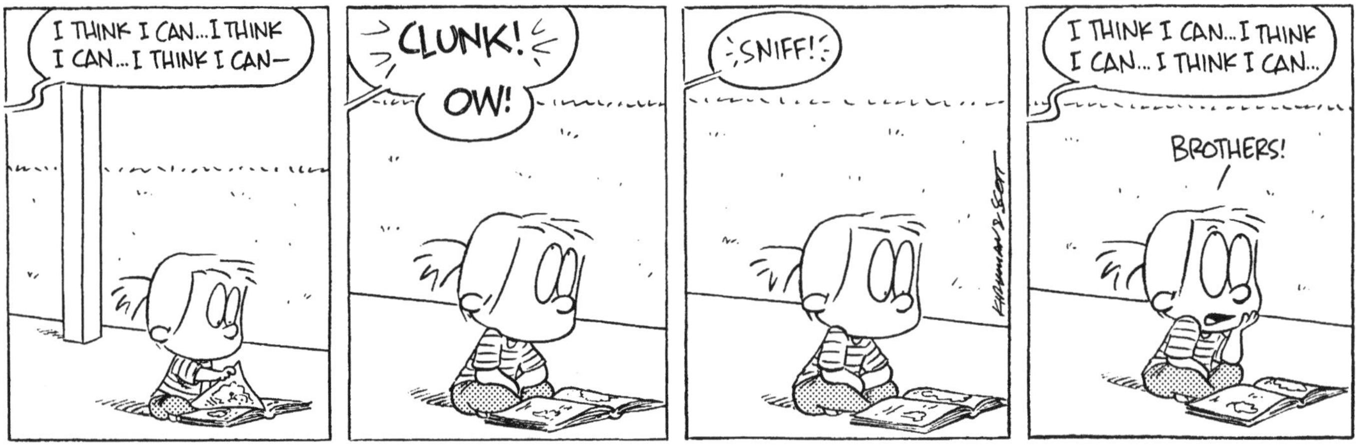
I THINK I CAN... I THINK I CAN... I THINK I CAN—
CLUNK!
OW!
SNIFF!
KIRKMAN & SCOTT
I THINK I CAN... I THINK I CAN... I THINK I CAN...
BROTHERS!

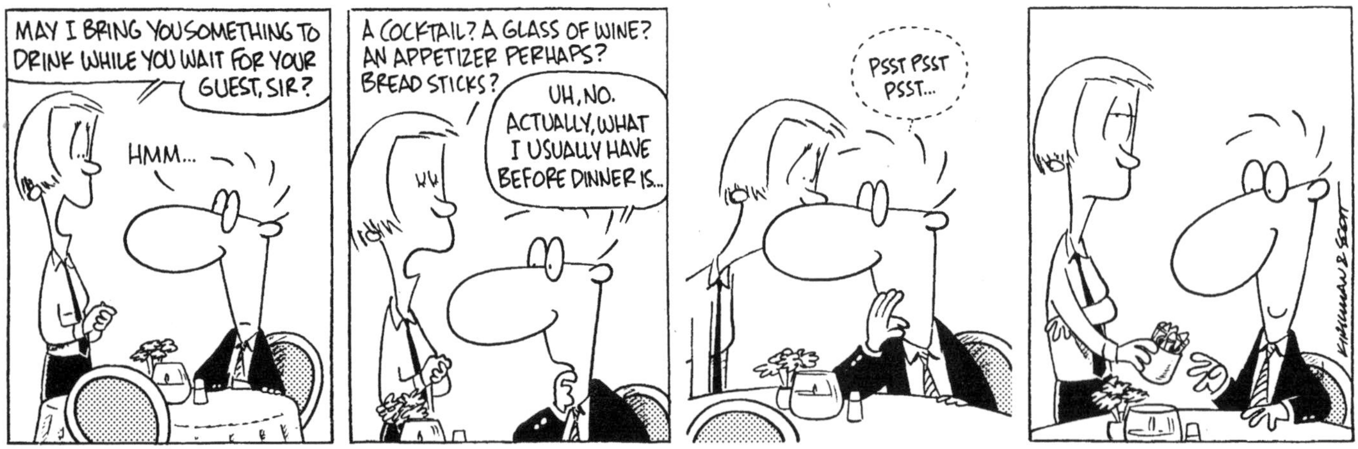
MAY I BRING YOU SOMETHING TO DRINK WHILE YOU WAIT FOR YOUR GUEST, SIR?
HMM...
A COCKTAIL? A GLASS OF WINE? AN APPETIZER PERHAPS? BREAD STICKS?
UH, NO. ACTUALLY, WHAT I USUALLY HAVE BEFORE DINNER IS...
PSST PSST PSST...
KIRKMAN & SCOTT

BABY BLUES
BY
RICK KIRKMAN / JERRY SCOTT

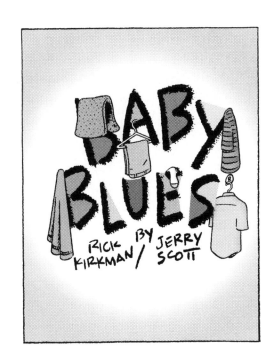

YOU KNOW I ALWAYS COMPLAINED THAT WE DIDN'T HAVE ENOUGH CLOSET SPACE? WELL, WE FINALLY GOT IT.
HOW?
AT FIRST, DARRYL WANTED TO ADD ON TO THE HOUSE, BUT THAT WAS GOING TO BE WAY TOO EXPENSIVE.
AND FOR A WHILE WE THOUGHT ABOUT TURNING THE EXTRA BEDROOM INTO A PLAYROOM/WALK-IN CLOSET, BUT I GOT PREGNANT WITH WREN.
THEN ONE DAY DARRYL JUST STUMBLED UPON THE PERFECT SOLUTION!
FEWER CLOTHES?
HE BOUGHT A TREADMILL.
KIRKMAN & SCOTT

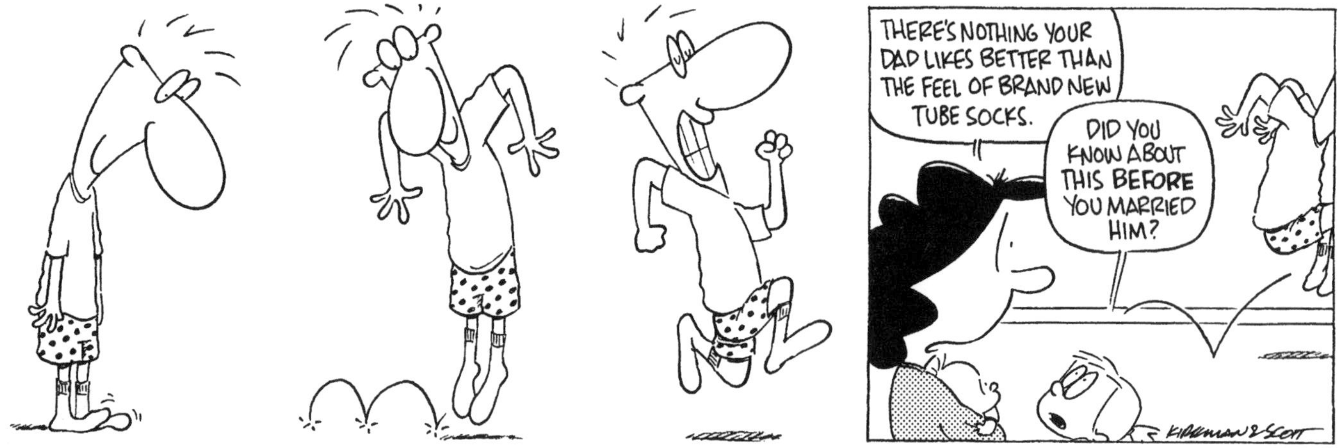
THERE'S NOTHING YOUR DAD LIKES BETTER THAN THE FEEL OF BRAND NEW TUBE SOCKS.
DID YOU KNOW ABOUT THIS **BEFORE** YOU MARRIED HIM?

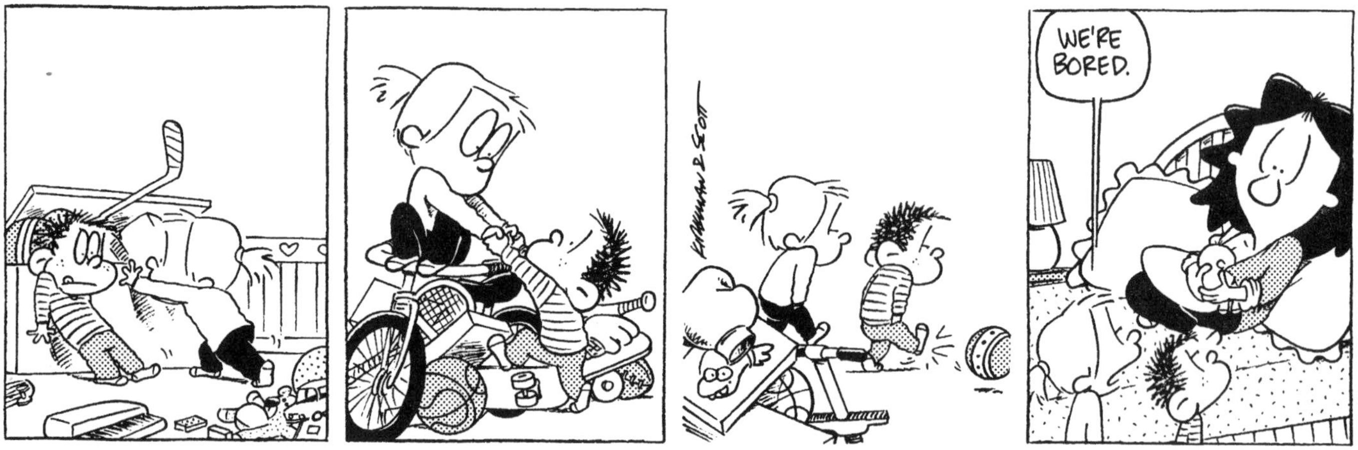
WE'RE BORED.

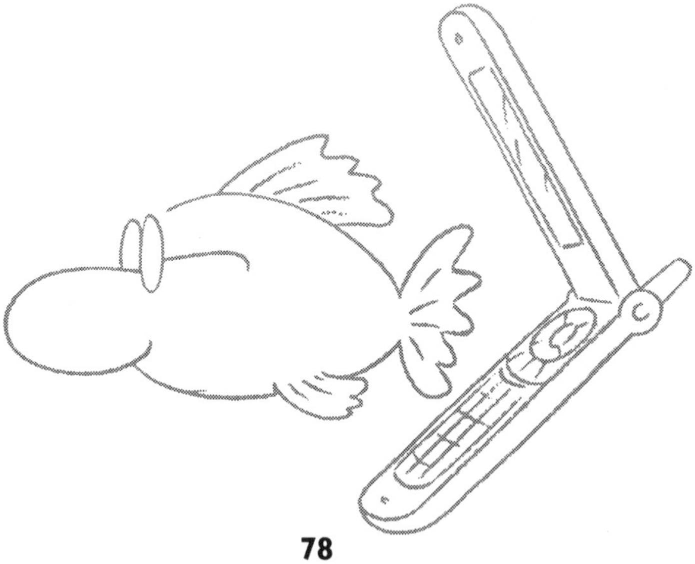

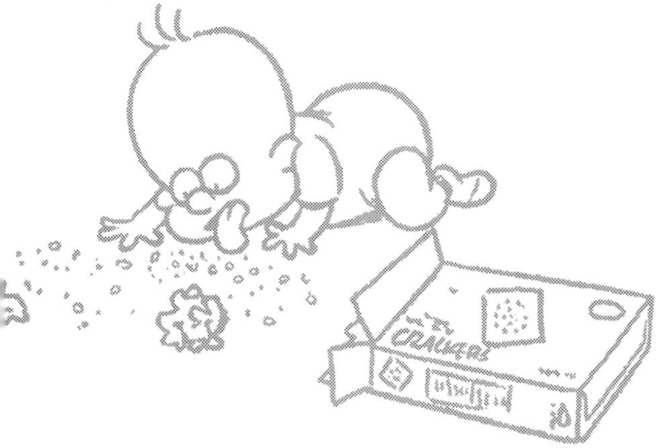

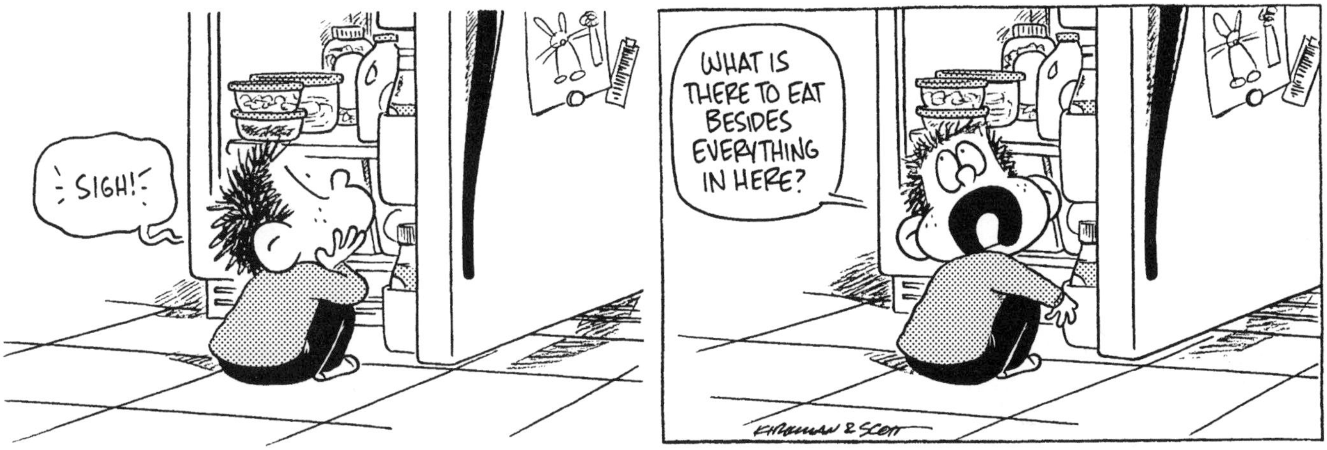
SIGH!
WHAT IS THERE TO EAT BESIDES EVERYTHING IN HERE?
KIRKMAN & SCOTT

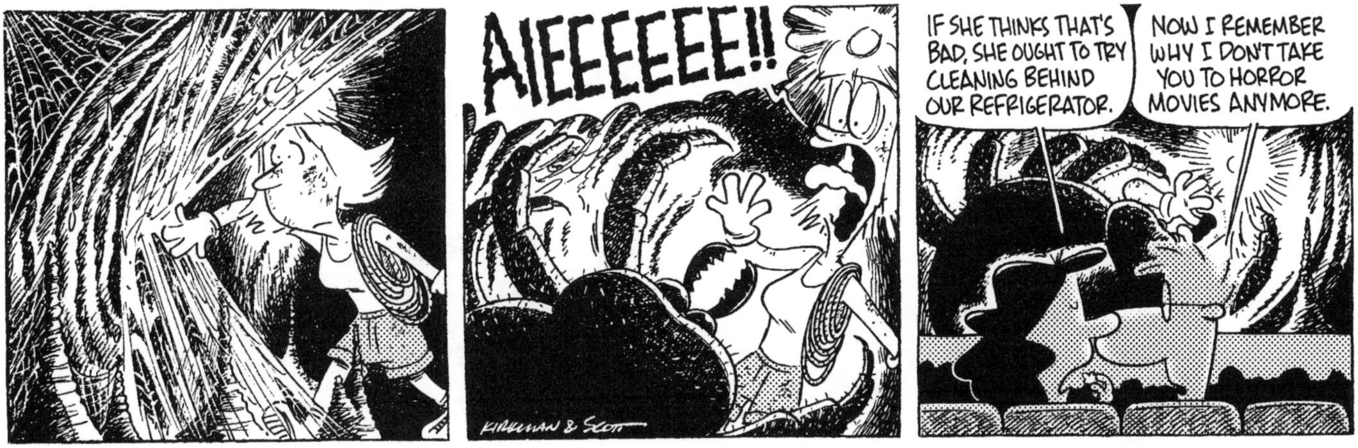
AIEEEEEE!!
KIRKMAN & SCOTT
IF SHE THINKS THAT'S BAD, SHE OUGHT TO TRY CLEANING BEHIND OUR REFRIGERATOR.
NOW I REMEMBER WHY I DON'T TAKE YOU TO HORROR MOVIES ANYMORE.

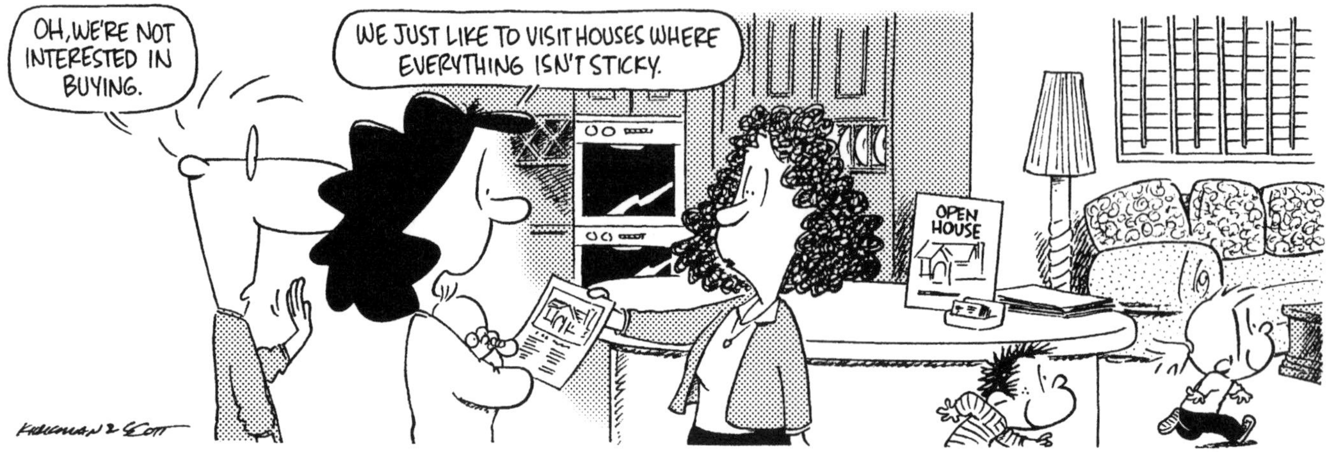
OH, WE'RE NOT INTERESTED IN BUYING.
WE JUST LIKE TO VISIT HOUSES WHERE EVERYTHING ISN'T STICKY.
OPEN HOUSE
KIRKMAN & SCOTT

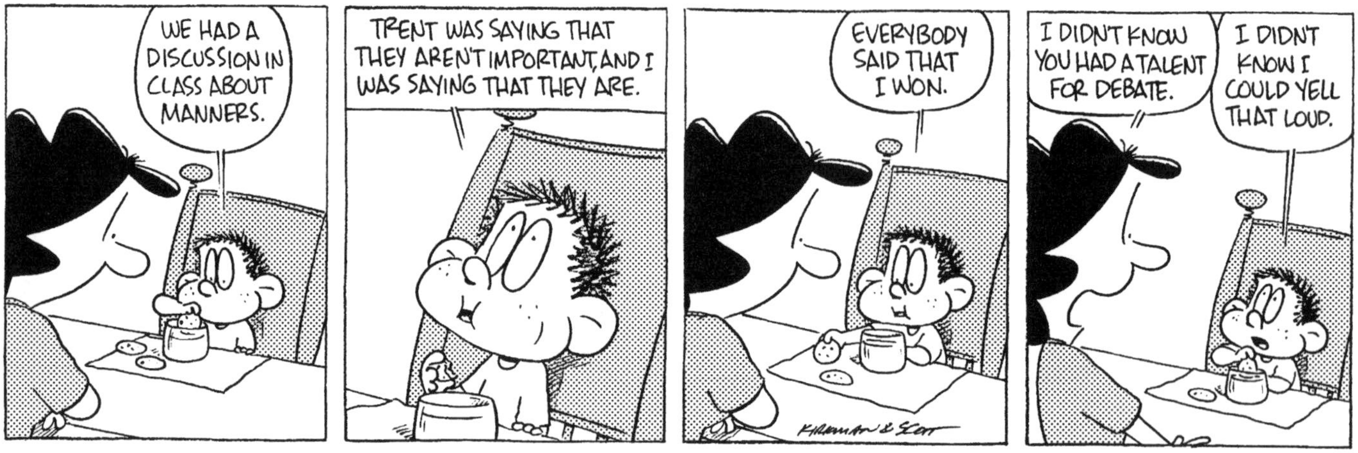
WE HAD A DISCUSSION IN CLASS ABOUT MANNERS.
TRENT WAS SAYING THAT THEY AREN'T IMPORTANT, AND I WAS SAYING THAT THEY ARE.
EVERYBODY SAID THAT I WON.
KIRKMAN & SCOTT
I DIDN'T KNOW YOU HAD A TALENT FOR DEBATE.
I DIDN'T KNOW I COULD YELL THAT LOUD.

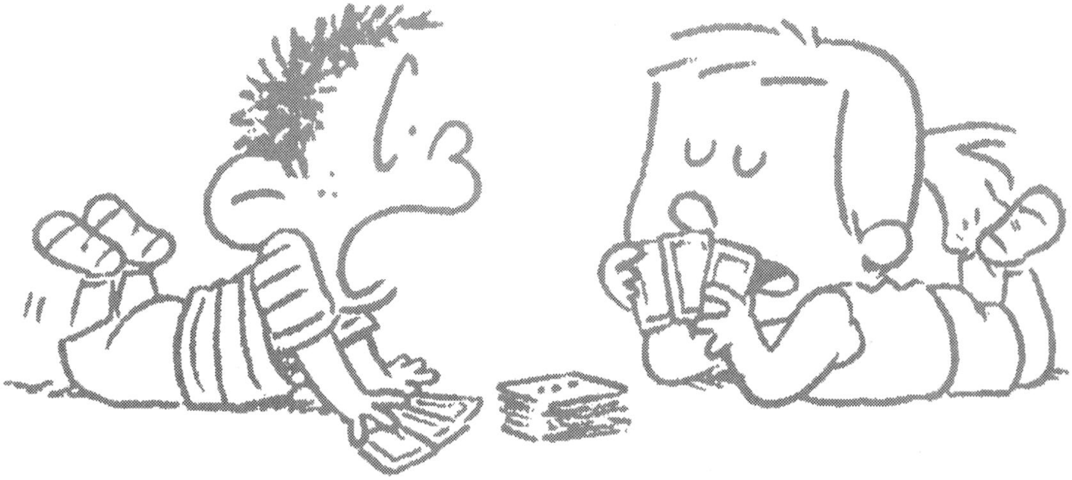

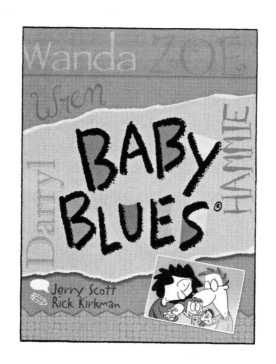

Wanda ZOE Wren Darryl HAMMIE
Baby Blues
Jerry Scott
Rick Kirkman

Panel 1: ZOE, CAN YOU HAND ME A PAIR OF SCISSORS? / WHICH ONE?

Panel 2: THE ORANGE ONE. / THIS?

Panel 3: NO, THE REGULAR ORANGE ONE. / THE BRIGHT ORANGE OR THE PALE ORANGE?

Panel 4: IT DOESN'T MATTER. THE BRIGHT ORANGE I GUESS. / THE BIG BRIGHT ORANGE OR THE LITTLE BRIGHT ORANGE?

Panel 5: JUST GIVE ME THE BIG BRIGHT ORANGE REGULAR SCISSORS, PLEASE! / OKAY! OKAY!

Panel 6: LEFT-HANDED OR RIGHT-HANDED?

Panel 7: ...AND THEN SHE JUST RAN OUT OF THE ROOM WITH A SPOOL OF RIBBON STUCK TO HER SHOE. / WHEN GOOD SCRAPBOOKERS GO BAD.

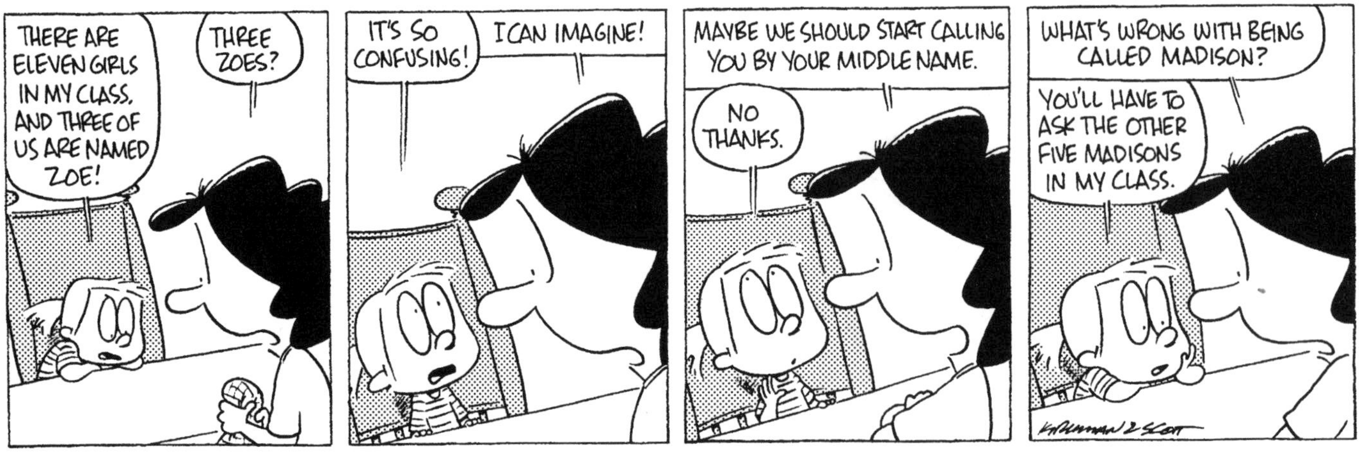
THERE ARE ELEVEN GIRLS IN MY CLASS, AND THREE OF US ARE NAMED ZOE!
THREE ZOES?
IT'S SO CONFUSING!
I CAN IMAGINE!
MAYBE WE SHOULD START CALLING YOU BY YOUR MIDDLE NAME.
NO THANKS.
WHAT'S WRONG WITH BEING CALLED MADISON?
YOU'LL HAVE TO ASK THE OTHER FIVE MADISONS IN MY CLASS.

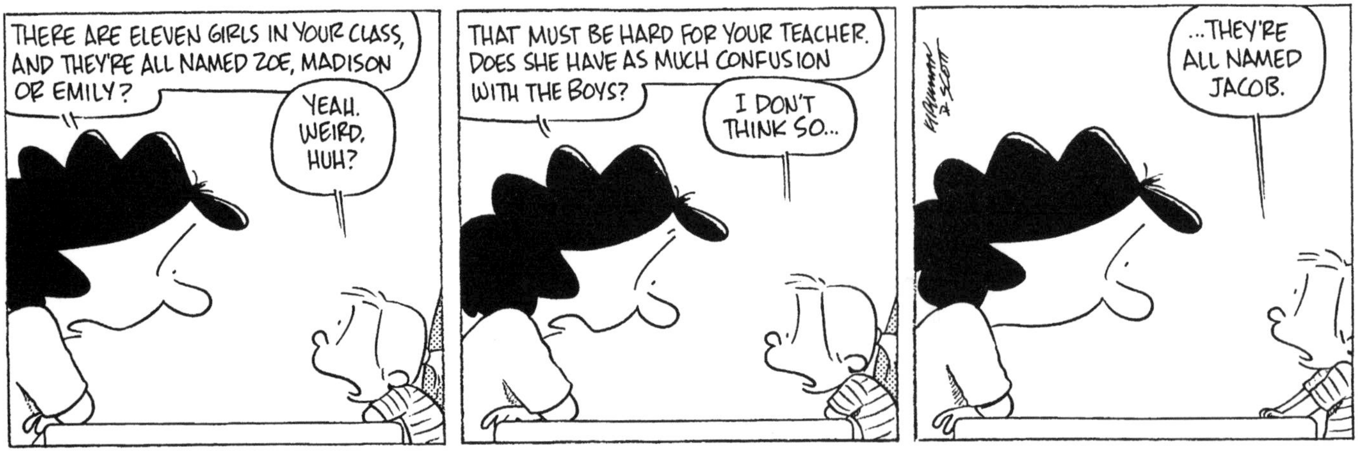
THERE ARE ELEVEN GIRLS IN YOUR CLASS, AND THEY'RE ALL NAMED ZOE, MADISON OR EMILY?
YEAH. WEIRD, HUH?
THAT MUST BE HARD FOR YOUR TEACHER. DOES SHE HAVE AS MUCH CONFUSION WITH THE BOYS?
I DON'T THINK SO...
...THEY'RE ALL NAMED JACOB.

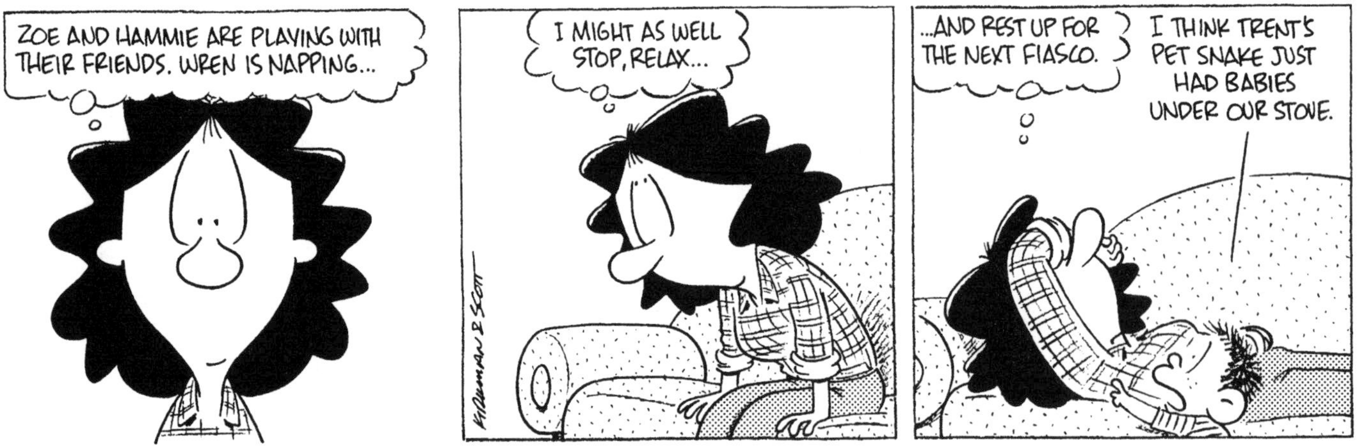
ZOE AND HAMMIE ARE PLAYING WITH THEIR FRIENDS. WREN IS NAPPING...
I MIGHT AS WELL STOP, RELAX...
...AND REST UP FOR THE NEXT FIASCO.
I THINK TRENT'S PET SNAKE JUST HAD BABIES UNDER OUR STOVE.

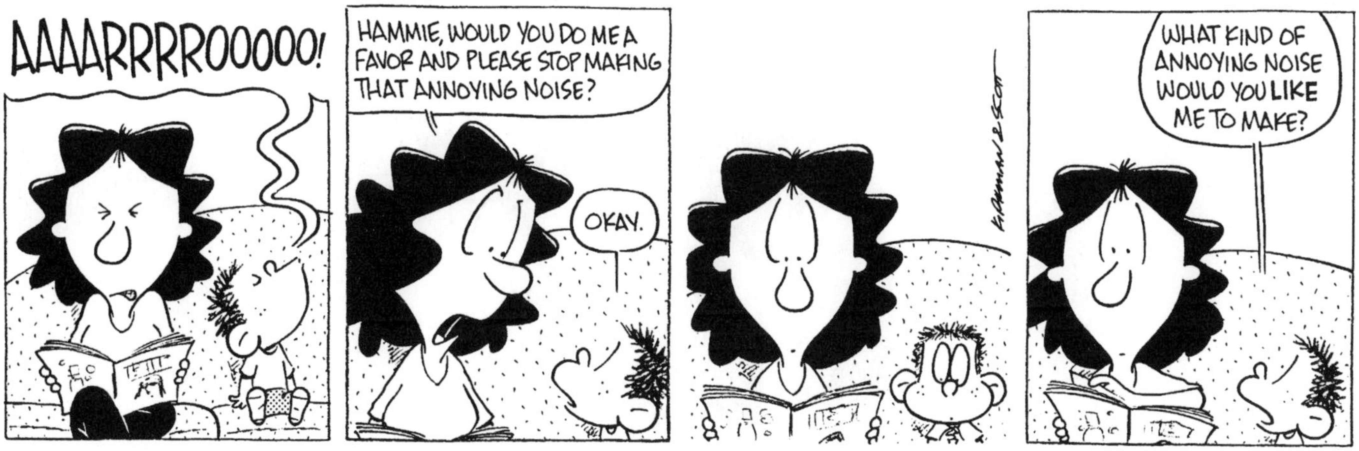
AAAARRRROOOOO!
HAMMIE, WOULD YOU DO ME A FAVOR AND PLEASE STOP MAKING THAT ANNOYING NOISE?
OKAY.
WHAT KIND OF ANNOYING NOISE WOULD YOU **LIKE** ME TO MAKE?

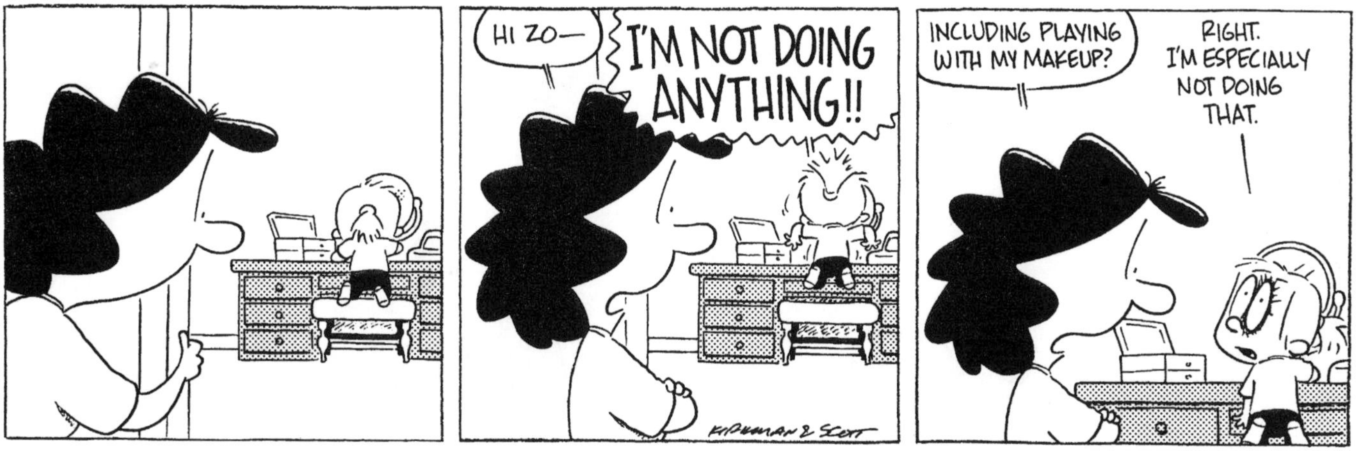
HI ZO—
I'M NOT DOING ANYTHING!!
INCLUDING PLAYING WITH MY MAKEUP?
RIGHT. I'M ESPECIALLY NOT DOING THAT.

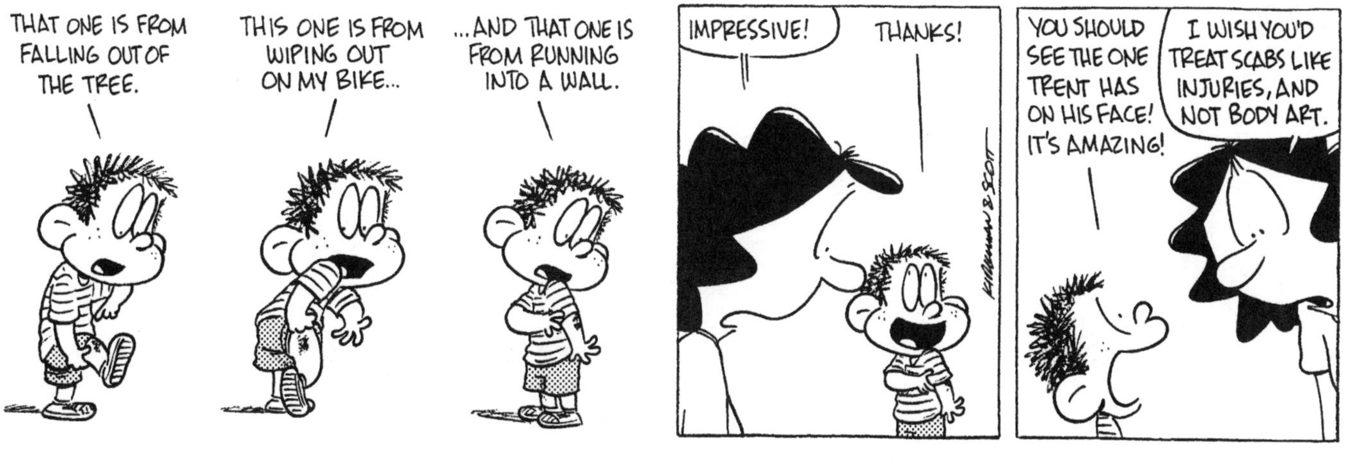
THAT ONE IS FROM FALLING OUT OF THE TREE.
THIS ONE IS FROM WIPING OUT ON MY BIKE...
...AND THAT ONE IS FROM RUNNING INTO A WALL.
IMPRESSIVE!
THANKS!
YOU SHOULD SEE THE ONE TRENT HAS ON HIS FACE! IT'S AMAZING!
I WISH YOU'D TREAT SCABS LIKE INJURIES, AND NOT BODY ART.

BABY BLUES®
BY RICK KIRKMAN / JERRY SCOTT

IT WAS REALLY NICE OF MIKE TO LEND YOU HIS PORTABLE GPS NAVIGATOR.
IN 0.2 MILES, TURN LEFT.
THIS IS SO COOL!
I CAN'T BELIEVE IT KNOWS EXACTLY WHERE WE SHOULD GO!
IN 0.1 MILES, TURN LEFT.
TURN LEFT.
NO. TURN RIGHT.
WHAT??
YOU CAN CUT THROUGH THE PARKING LOT. IT'S FASTER.
WANDA!!
BING! TURN LEFT.
WHO ARE YOU GOING TO LISTEN TO, HER OR ME?
BING! BING! BING! TURN LEFT! TURN LEFT! TURN LEFT!
SO, DID THE GPS WORK FOR YOU?
YEAH, WELL, SORTA.
WE FOUND THE MUSEUM, BUT I'LL BE SLEEPING ON THE COUCH.
KIRKMAN & SCOTT

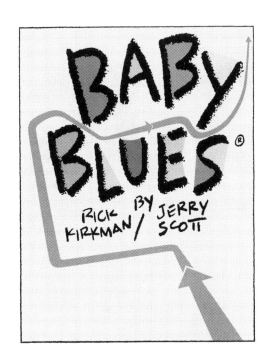

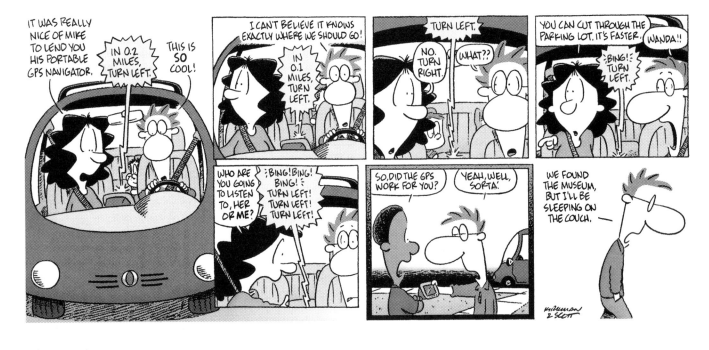

BEFORE & AFTER

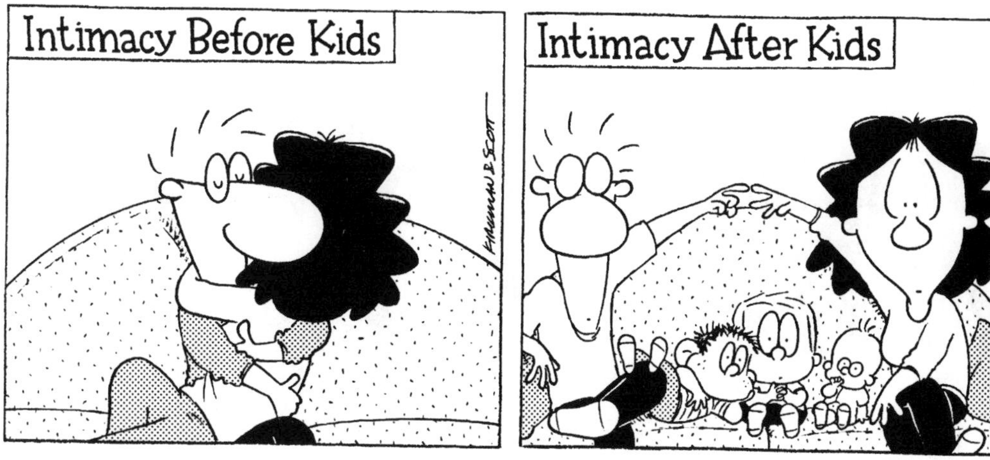
Intimacy Before Kids
Intimacy After Kids

BEFORE & AFTER

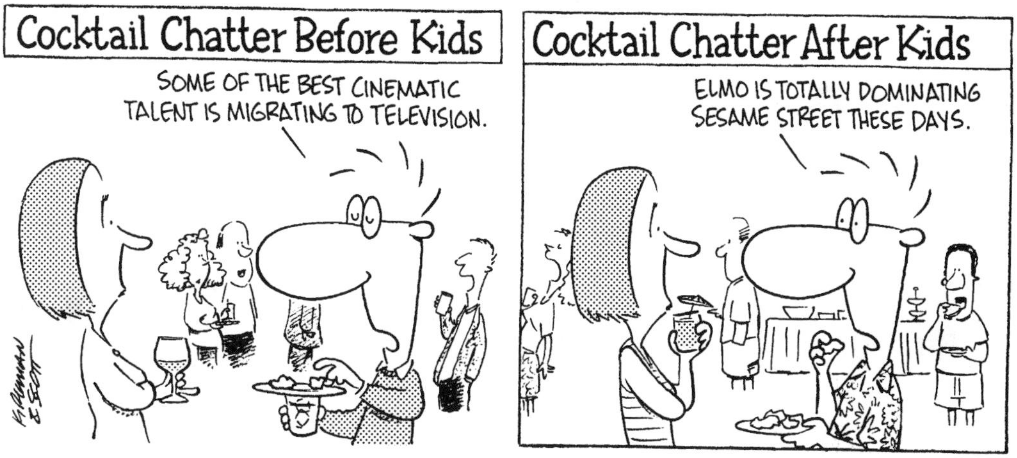
Cocktail Chatter Before Kids
SOME OF THE BEST CINEMATIC TALENT IS MIGRATING TO TELEVISION.
Cocktail Chatter After Kids
ELMO IS TOTALLY DOMINATING SESAME STREET THESE DAYS.

BEFORE & AFTER

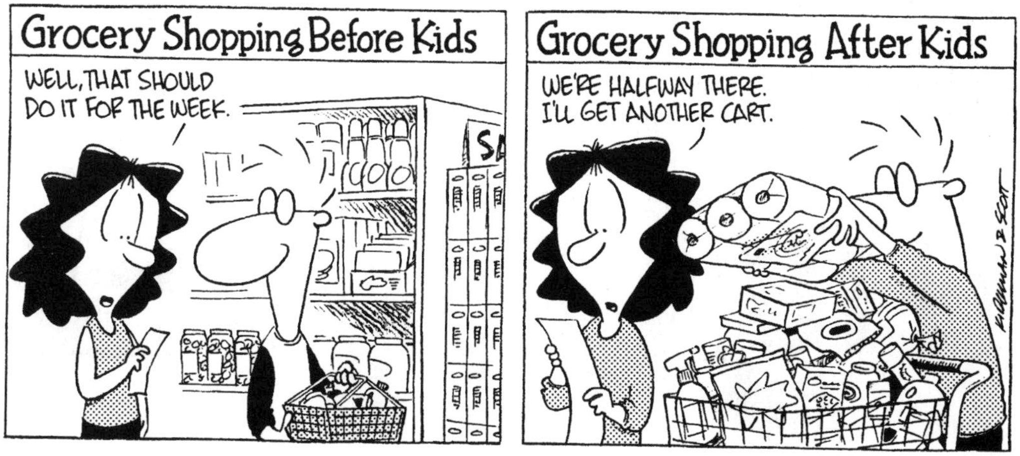
Grocery Shopping Before Kids
WELL, THAT SHOULD DO IT FOR THE WEEK.
Grocery Shopping After Kids
WE'RE HALFWAY THERE. I'LL GET ANOTHER CART.

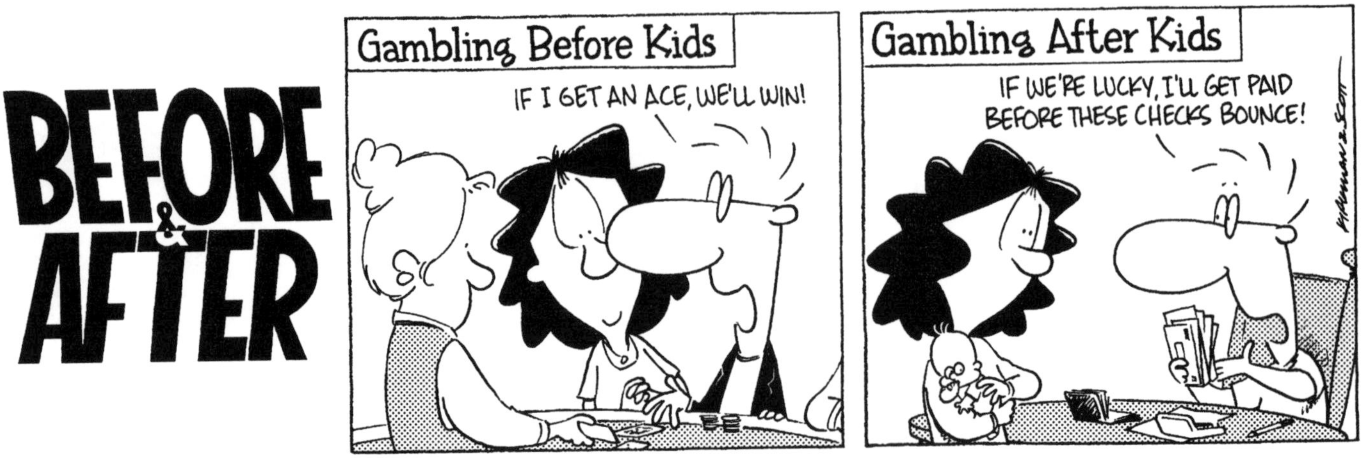
BEFORE & AFTER
Gambling Before Kids
IF I GET AN ACE, WE'LL WIN!
Gambling After Kids
IF WE'RE LUCKY, I'LL GET PAID BEFORE THESE CHECKS BOUNCE!

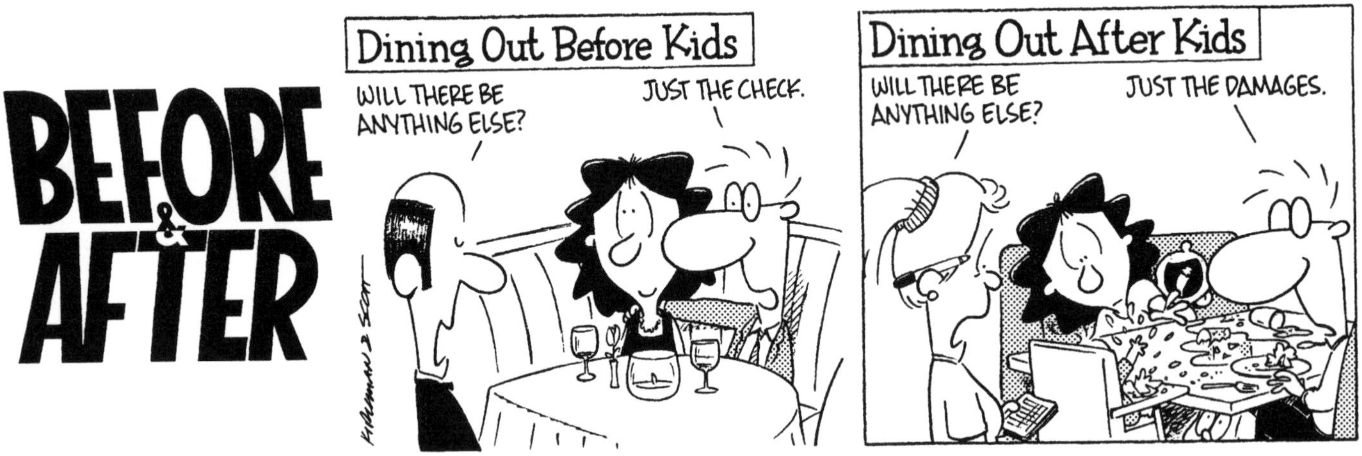
BEFORE & AFTER
Dining Out Before Kids
WILL THERE BE ANYTHING ELSE?
JUST THE CHECK.
Dining Out After Kids
WILL THERE BE ANYTHING ELSE?
JUST THE DAMAGES.

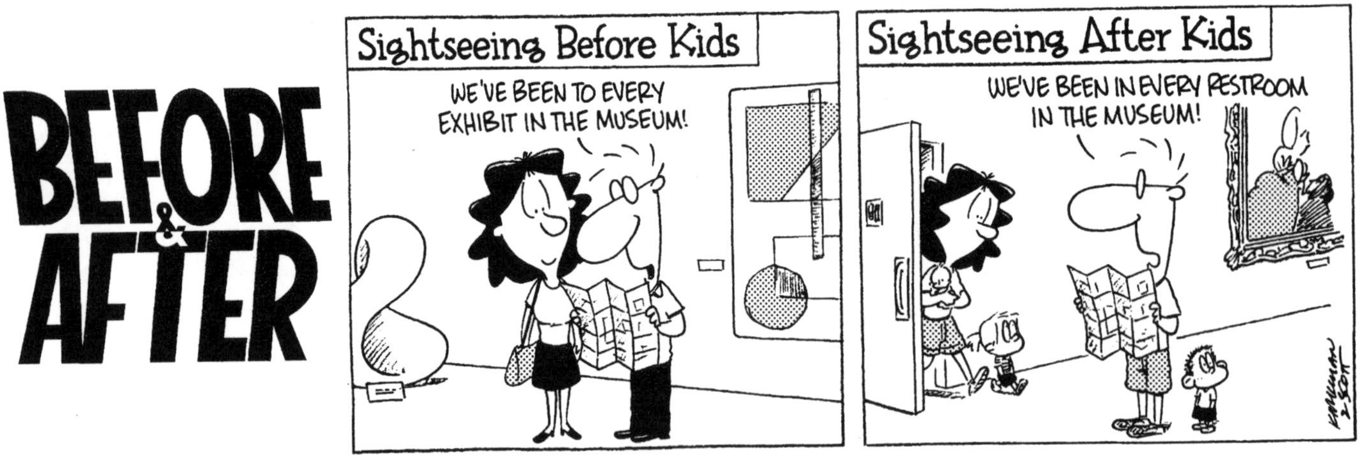
BEFORE & AFTER
Sightseeing Before Kids
WE'VE BEEN TO EVERY EXHIBIT IN THE MUSEUM!
Sightseeing After Kids
WE'VE BEEN IN EVERY RESTROOM IN THE MUSEUM!

BABY BLUES®
BY RICK KIRKMAN / JERRY SCOTT

GUYS, I JUST MOPPED THE FLOOR. TRY TO STAY OFF IT UNTIL IT DRIES.
OKAY.
ARE YOU SURE THIS IS WHAT SHE MEANT?
THAT DIDN'T SOUND LIKE A DARE TO YOU?
KIRKMAN & SCOTT

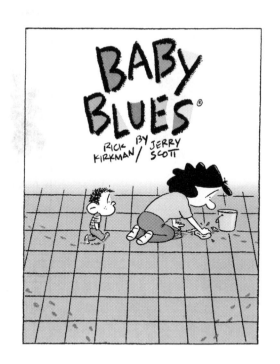

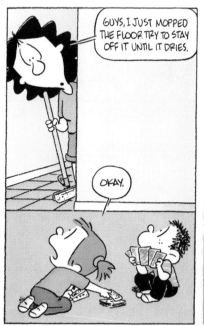

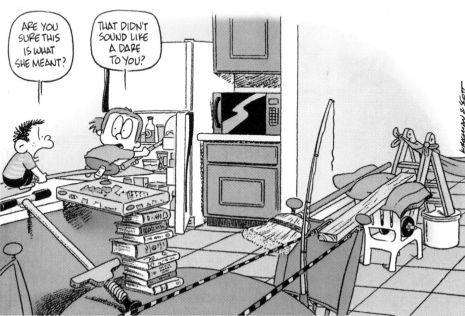

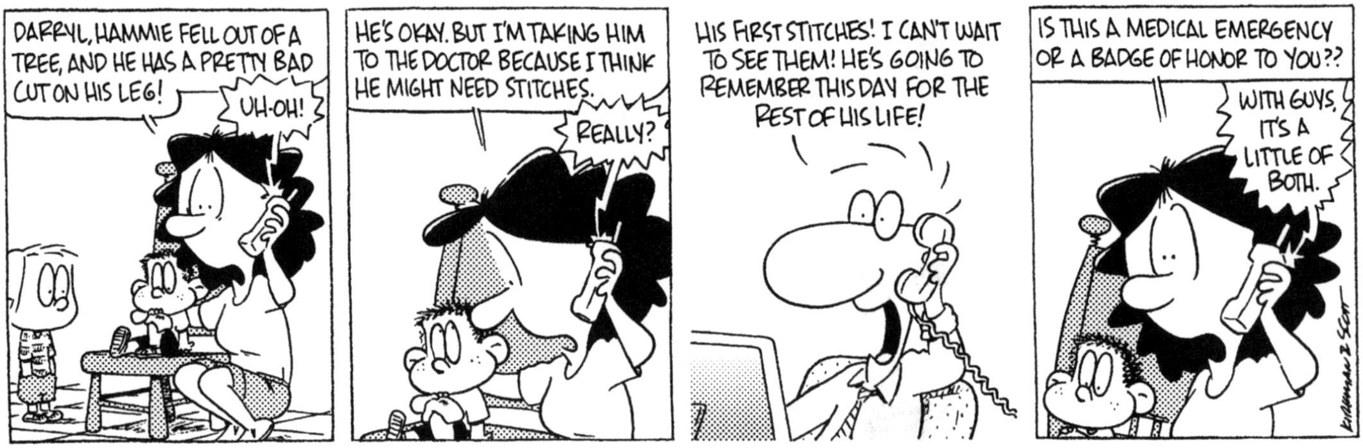
DARRYL, HAMMIE FELL OUT OF A TREE, AND HE HAS A PRETTY BAD CUT ON HIS LEG!
UH-OH!
HE'S OKAY. BUT I'M TAKING HIM TO THE DOCTOR BECAUSE I THINK HE MIGHT NEED STITCHES.
REALLY?
HIS FIRST STITCHES! I CAN'T WAIT TO SEE THEM! HE'S GOING TO REMEMBER THIS DAY FOR THE REST OF HIS LIFE!
IS THIS A MEDICAL EMERGENCY OR A BADGE OF HONOR TO YOU??
WITH GUYS, IT'S A LITTLE OF BOTH.

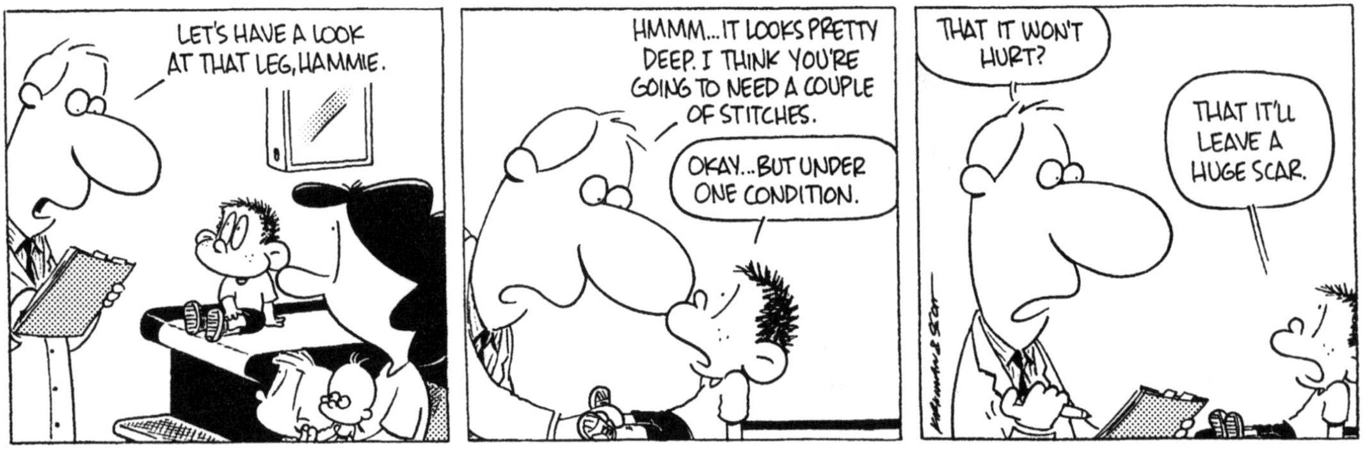
LET'S HAVE A LOOK AT THAT LEG, HAMMIE.
HMMM... IT LOOKS PRETTY DEEP. I THINK YOU'RE GOING TO NEED A COUPLE OF STITCHES.
OKAY... BUT UNDER ONE CONDITION.
THAT IT WON'T HURT?
THAT IT'LL LEAVE A HUGE SCAR.

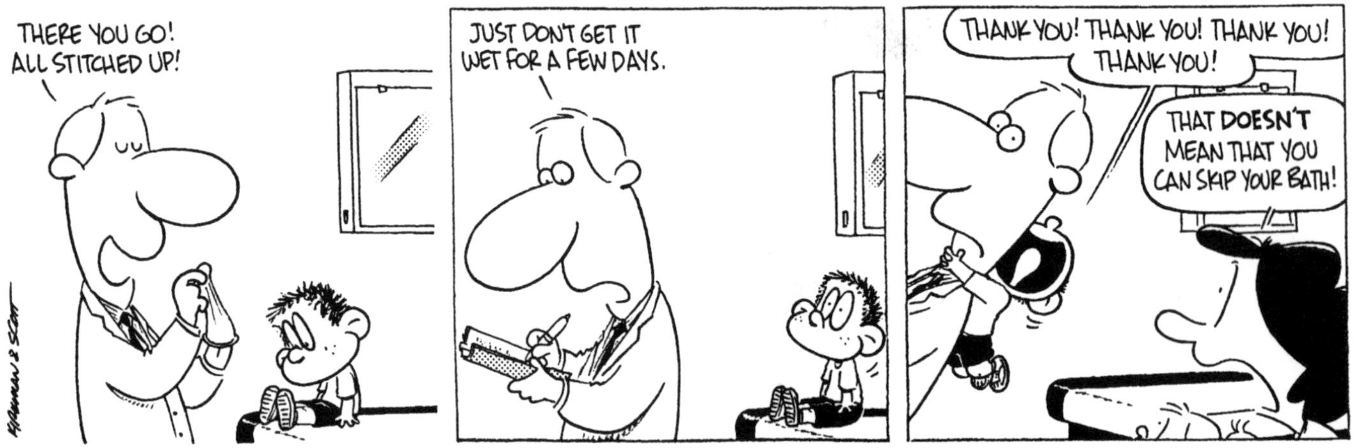
THERE YOU GO! ALL STITCHED UP!
JUST DON'T GET IT WET FOR A FEW DAYS.
THANK YOU! THANK YOU! THANK YOU! THANK YOU!
THAT **DOESN'T** MEAN THAT YOU CAN SKIP YOUR BATH!

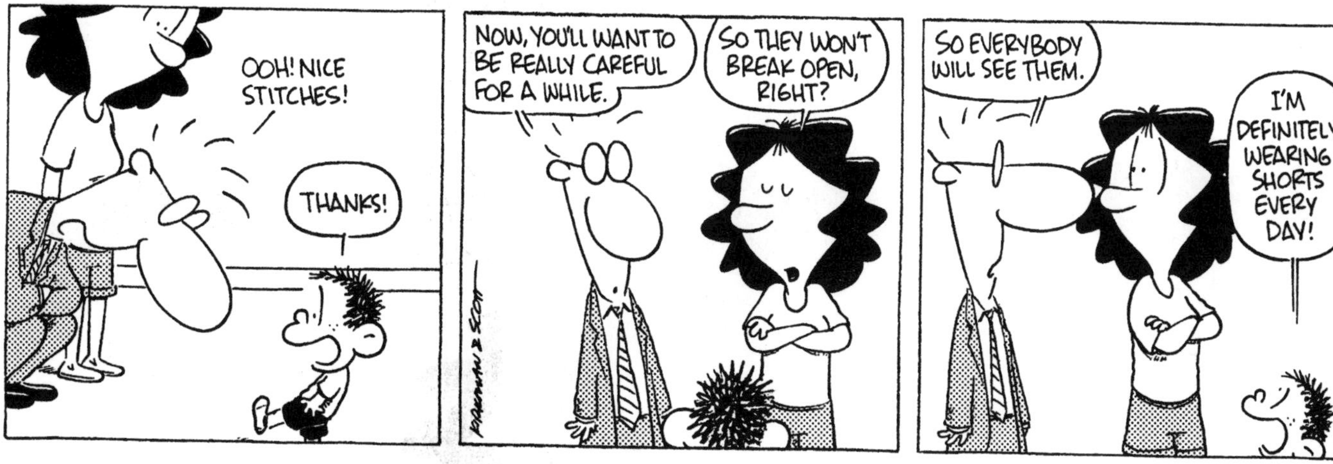
OOH! NICE STITCHES!
THANKS!
NOW, YOU'LL WANT TO BE REALLY CAREFUL FOR A WHILE.
SO THEY WON'T BREAK OPEN, RIGHT?
SO EVERYBODY WILL SEE THEM.
I'M DEFINITELY WEARING SHORTS EVERY DAY!

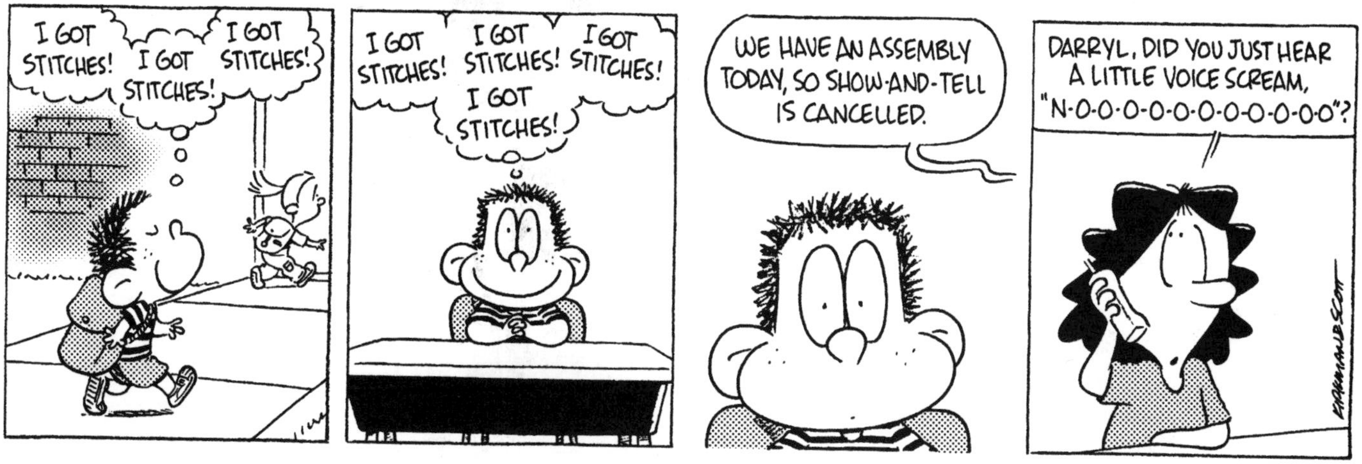
I GOT STITCHES! I GOT STITCHES! I GOT STITCHES!
I GOT STITCHES! I GOT STITCHES! I GOT STITCHES! I GOT STITCHES!
WE HAVE AN ASSEMBLY TODAY, SO SHOW-AND-TELL IS CANCELLED.
DARRYL, DID YOU JUST HEAR A LITTLE VOICE SCREAM, "N-O-O-O-O-O-O-O-O-O-O-O-O"?

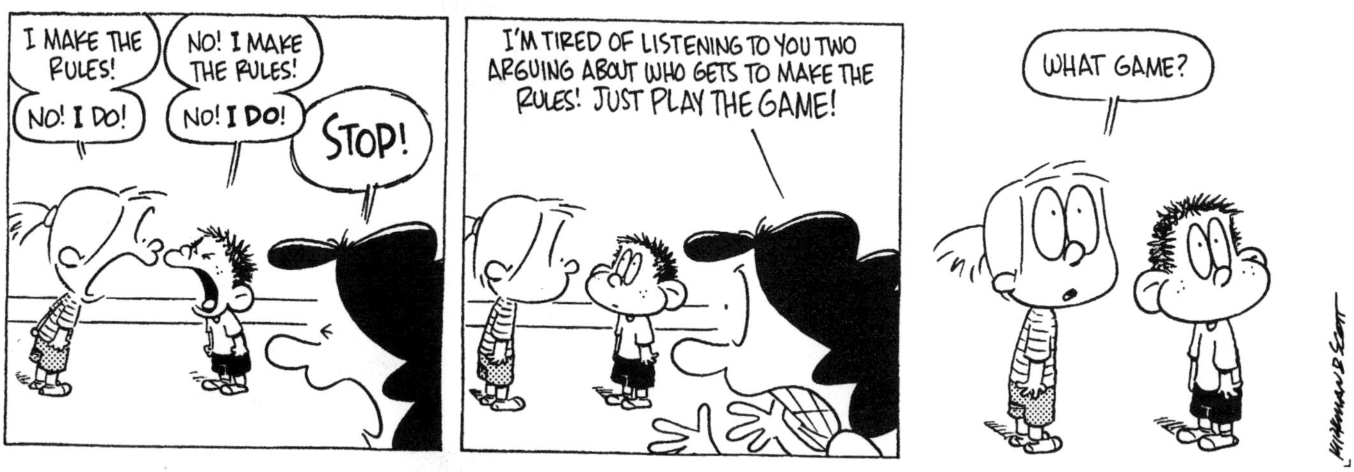
I MAKE THE RULES!
NO! I MAKE THE RULES!
NO! **I** DO!
NO! **I DO**!
STOP!
I'M TIRED OF LISTENING TO YOU TWO ARGUING ABOUT WHO GETS TO MAKE THE RULES! JUST PLAY THE GAME!
WHAT GAME?

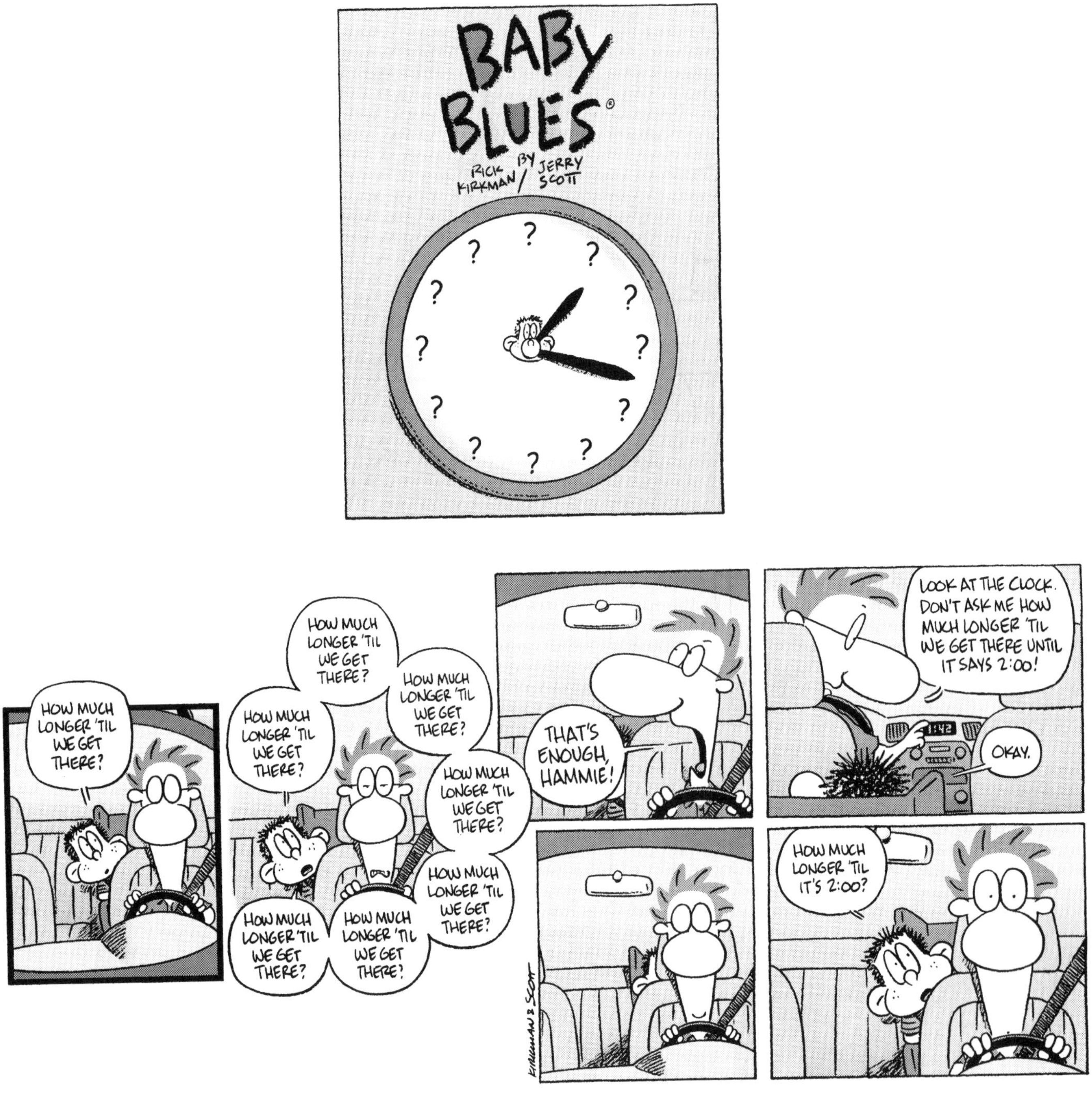

BABY BLUES®
RICK KIRKMAN / BY JERRY SCOTT
HOW MUCH LONGER 'TIL WE GET THERE?
HOW MUCH LONGER 'TIL WE GET THERE?
HOW MUCH LONGER 'TIL WE GET THERE?
HOW MUCH LONGER 'TIL WE GET THERE?
HOW MUCH LONGER 'TIL WE GET THERE?
HOW MUCH LONGER 'TIL WE GET THERE?
HOW MUCH LONGER 'TIL WE GET THERE?
HOW MUCH LONGER 'TIL WE GET THERE?
THAT'S ENOUGH, HAMMIE!
LOOK AT THE CLOCK. DON'T ASK ME HOW MUCH LONGER 'TIL WE GET THERE UNTIL IT SAYS 2:00!
1:42
OKAY.
HOW MUCH LONGER 'TIL IT'S 2:00?
KIRKMAN & SCOTT

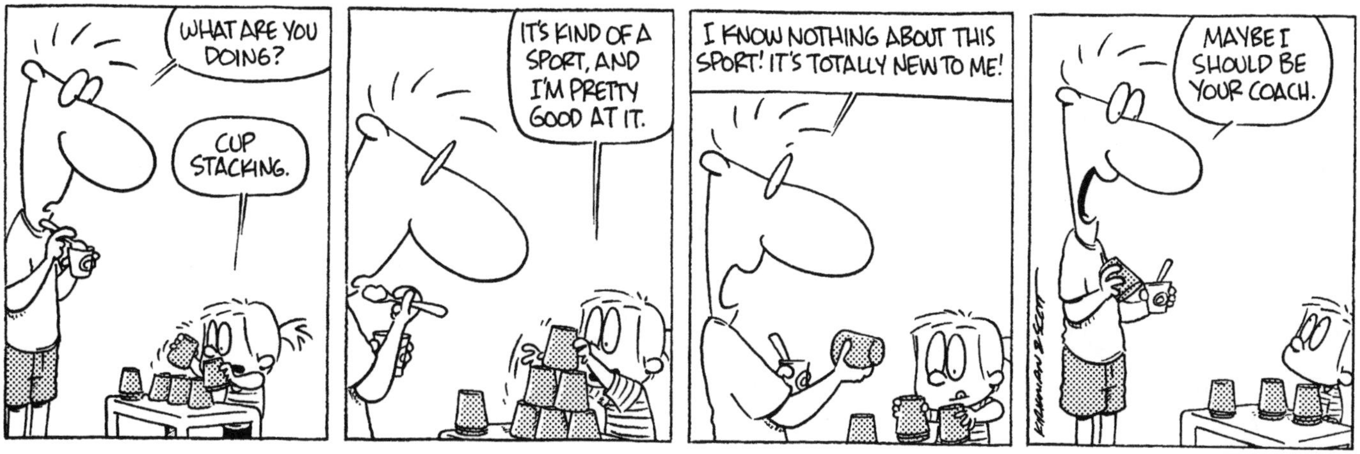

WHAT ARE YOU DOING?
CUP STACKING.
IT'S KIND OF A SPORT, AND I'M PRETTY GOOD AT IT.
I KNOW NOTHING ABOUT THIS SPORT! IT'S TOTALLY NEW TO ME!
MAYBE I SHOULD BE YOUR COACH.

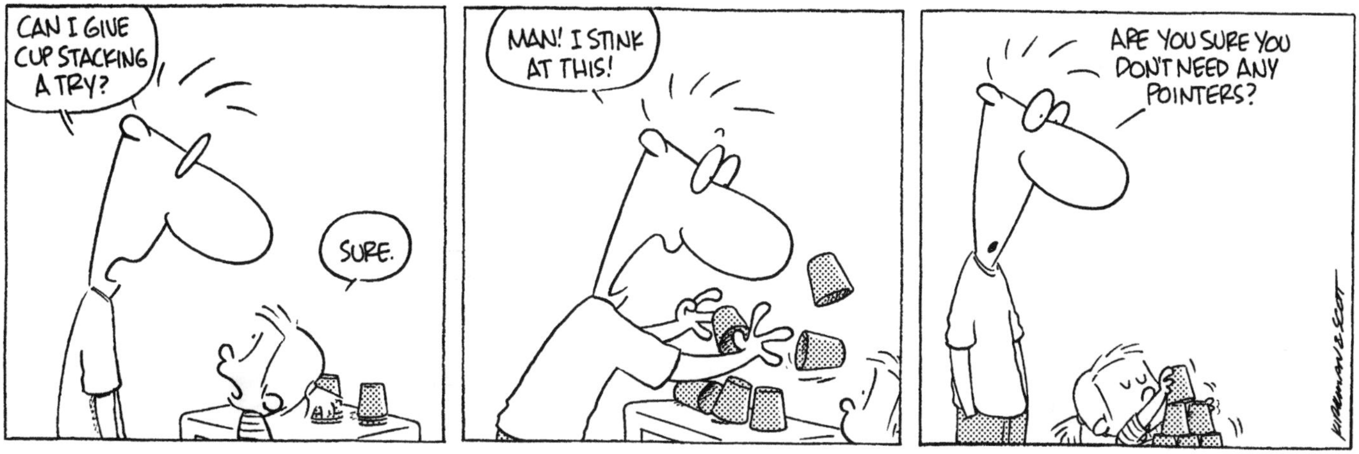

CAN I GIVE CUP STACKING A TRY?
SURE.
MAN! I STINK AT THIS!
ARE YOU SURE YOU DON'T NEED ANY POINTERS?

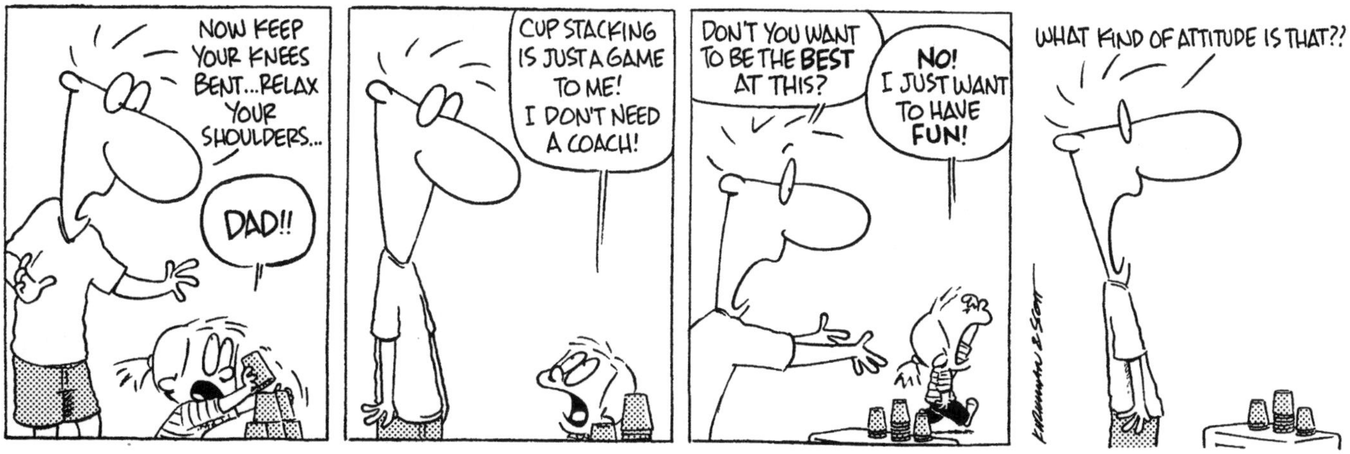

NOW KEEP YOUR KNEES BENT...RELAX YOUR SHOULDERS...
DAD!!
CUP STACKING IS JUST A GAME TO ME! I DON'T NEED A COACH!
DON'T YOU WANT TO BE THE **BEST** AT THIS?
NO! I JUST WANT TO HAVE **FUN!**
WHAT KIND OF ATTITUDE IS THAT??

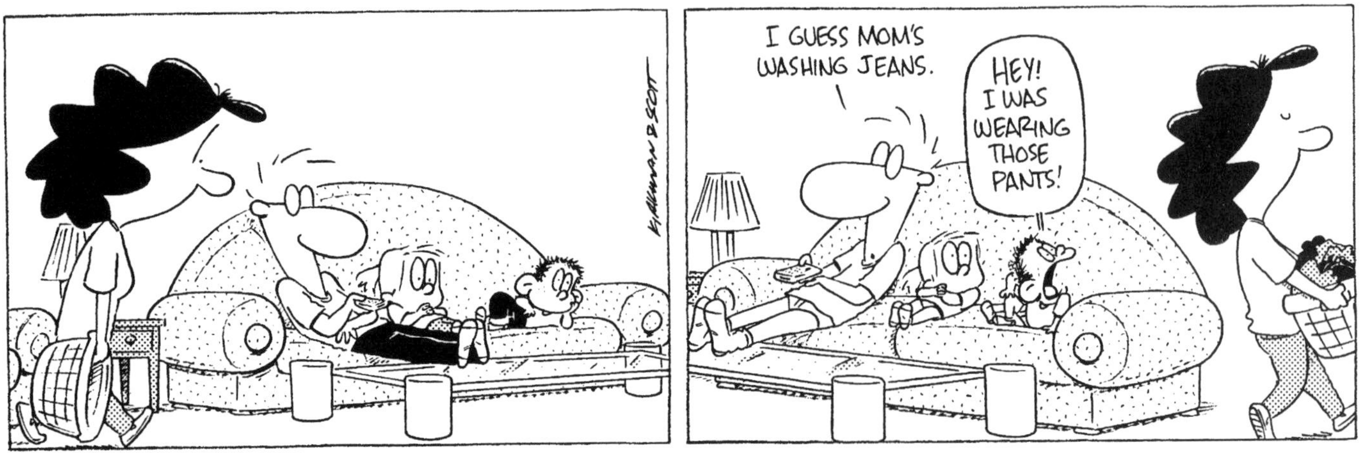
I GUESS MOM'S WASHING JEANS.
HEY! I WAS WEARING THOSE PANTS!

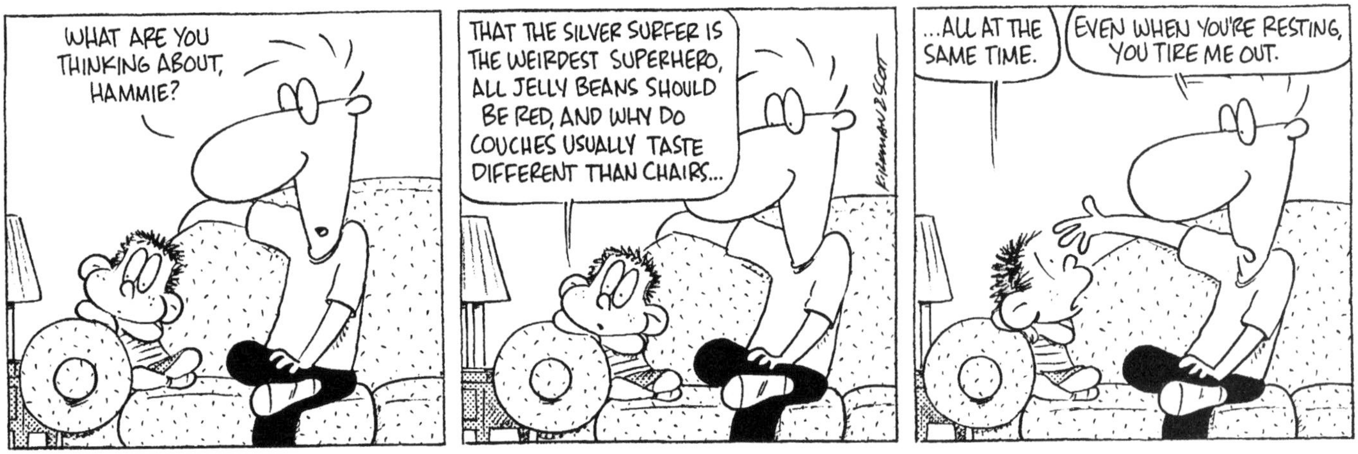
WHAT ARE YOU THINKING ABOUT, HAMMIE?
THAT THE SILVER SURFER IS THE WEIRDEST SUPERHERO, ALL JELLY BEANS SHOULD BE RED, AND WHY DO COUCHES USUALLY TASTE DIFFERENT THAN CHAIRS...
...ALL AT THE SAME TIME.
EVEN WHEN YOU'RE RESTING, YOU TIRE ME OUT.

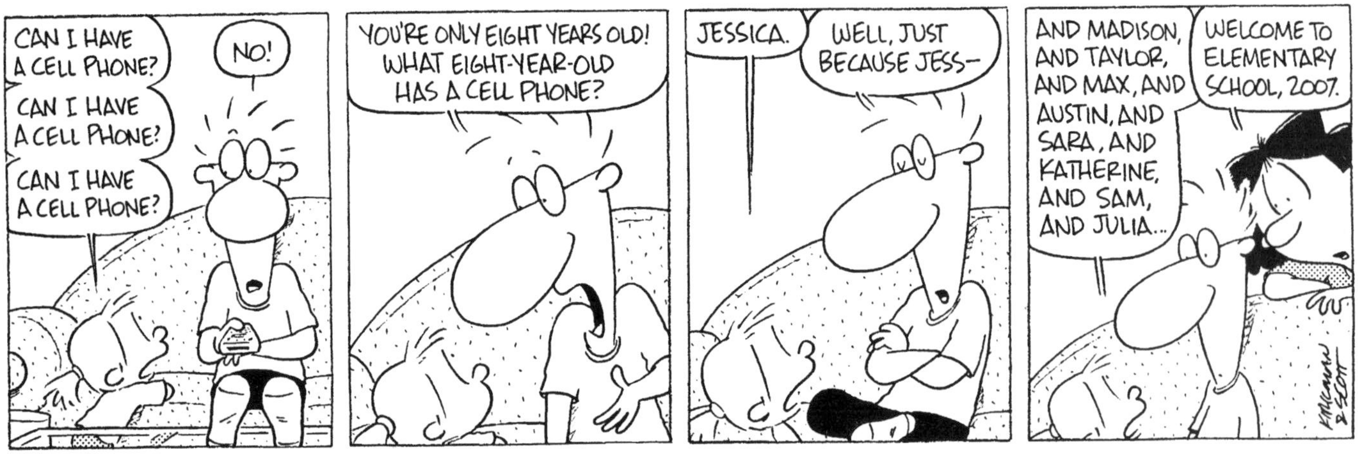
CAN I HAVE A CELL PHONE?
CAN I HAVE A CELL PHONE?
CAN I HAVE A CELL PHONE?
NO!
YOU'RE ONLY EIGHT YEARS OLD! WHAT EIGHT-YEAR-OLD HAS A CELL PHONE?
JESSICA.
WELL, JUST BECAUSE JESS—
AND MADISON, AND TAYLOR, AND MAX, AND AUSTIN, AND SARA, AND KATHERINE, AND SAM, AND JULIA...
WELCOME TO ELEMENTARY SCHOOL, 2007.

BABY BLUES®
BY RICK KIRKMAN / JERRY SCOTT
Honey
SOPAPILLA CHIPS

BZZZZZZZZZ
♫ ♪ ♫
BAM! BAM! BAM! BAM!
KIRKMAN & SCOTT
CRINKLE!
TUG! TUG!
SCRUNCH!
Honey
SOPAPILLA CHIPS
CRINKLE! SXKXX!
RUSTLE! crkkk!
R-R-R-I-I-I-P!!
Honey
THE SNACKIER THE FOOD, THE NOISIER THE PACKAGING.

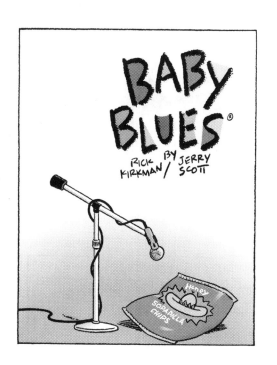

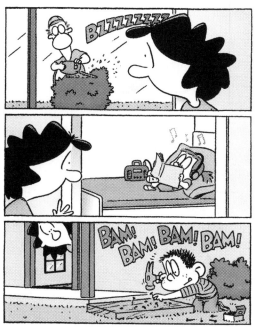

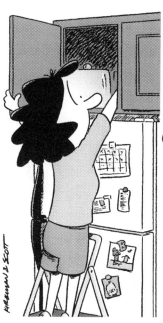

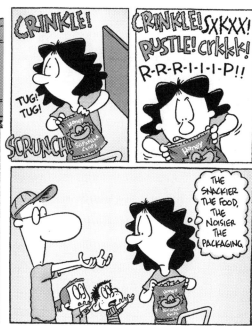

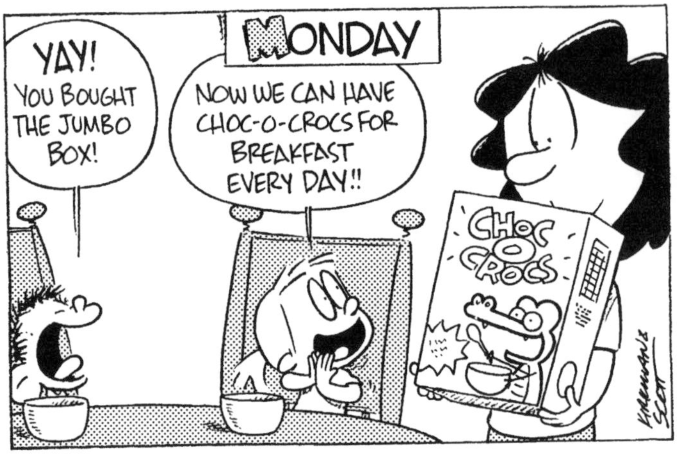
MONDAY
YAY! YOU BOUGHT THE JUMBO BOX!
NOW WE CAN HAVE CHOC-O-CROCS FOR BREAKFAST EVERY DAY!!

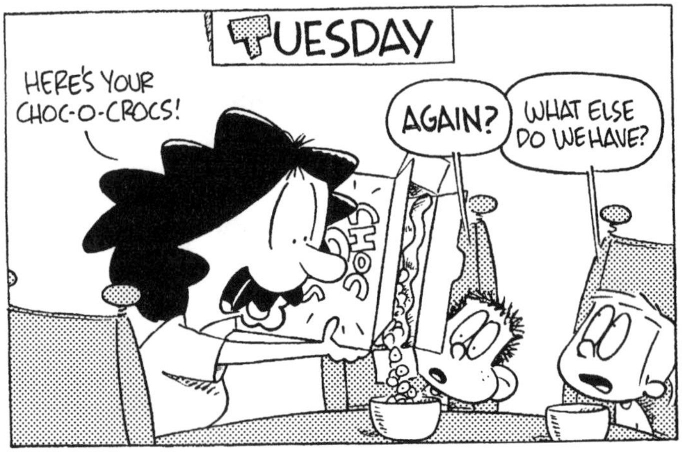
TUESDAY
HERE'S YOUR CHOC-O-CROCS!
AGAIN?
WHAT ELSE DO WE HAVE?

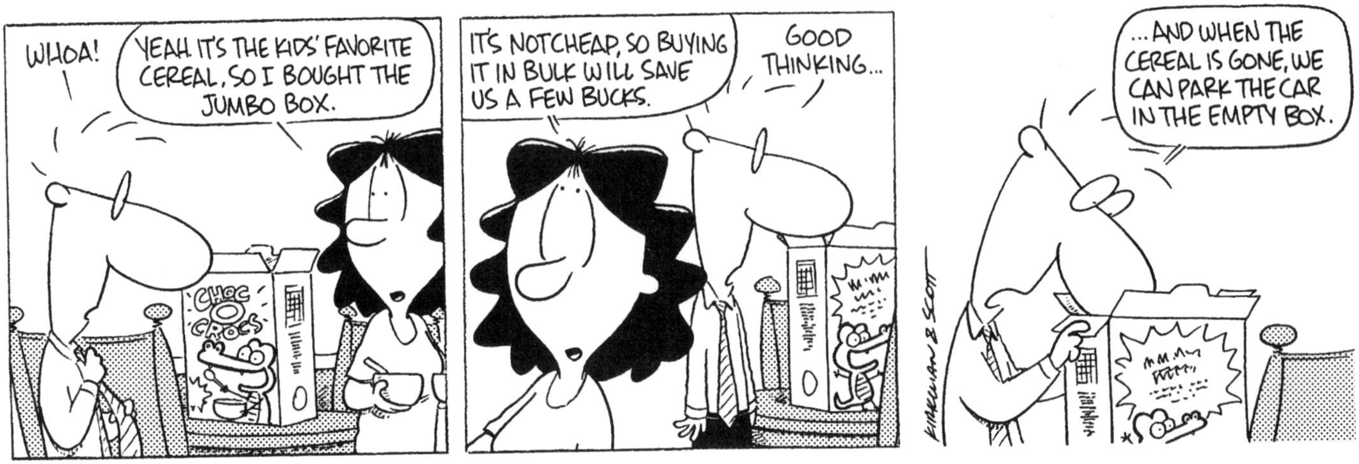
WHOA!
YEAH. IT'S THE KIDS' FAVORITE CEREAL, SO I BOUGHT THE JUMBO BOX.
IT'S NOT CHEAP, SO BUYING IT IN BULK WILL SAVE US A FEW BUCKS.
GOOD THINKING...
...AND WHEN THE CEREAL IS GONE, WE CAN PARK THE CAR IN THE EMPTY BOX.

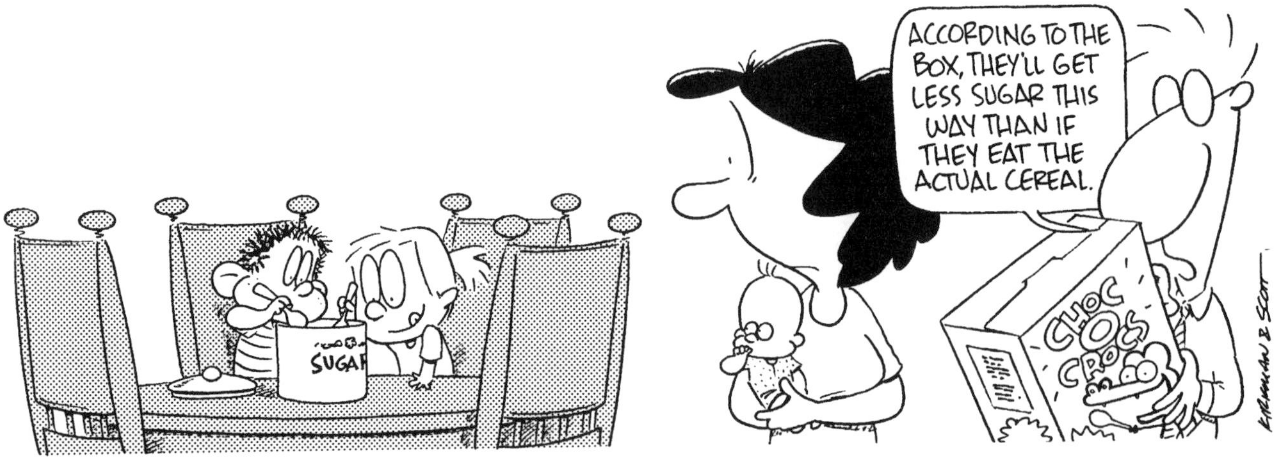
SUGAR
ACCORDING TO THE BOX, THEY'LL GET LESS SUGAR THIS WAY THAN IF THEY EAT THE ACTUAL CEREAL.

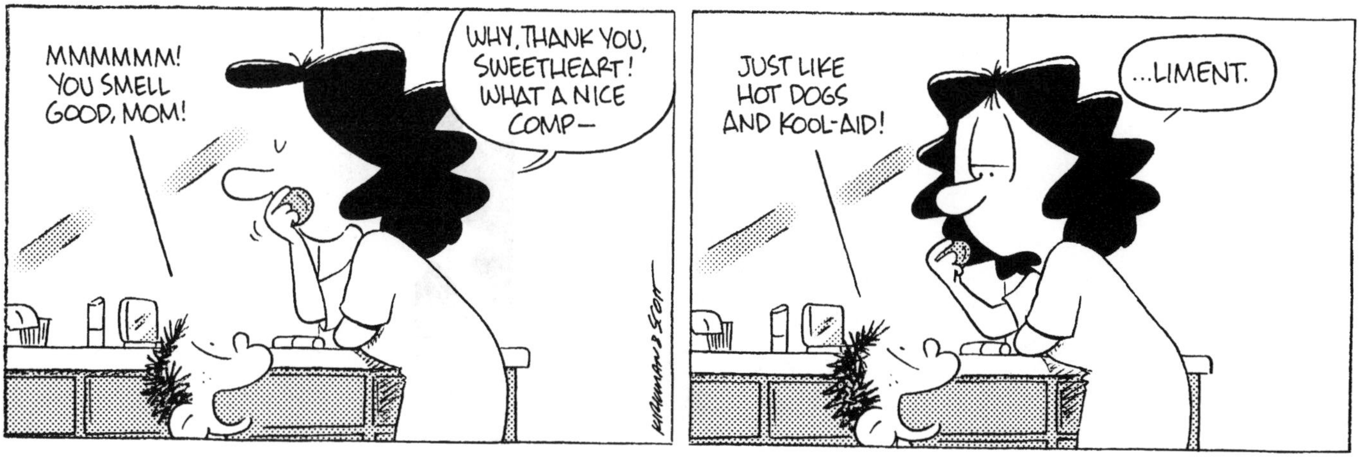
MMMMMM! YOU SMELL GOOD, MOM!
WHY, THANK YOU, SWEETHEART! WHAT A NICE COMP—
JUST LIKE HOT DOGS AND KOOL-AID!
...LIMENT.

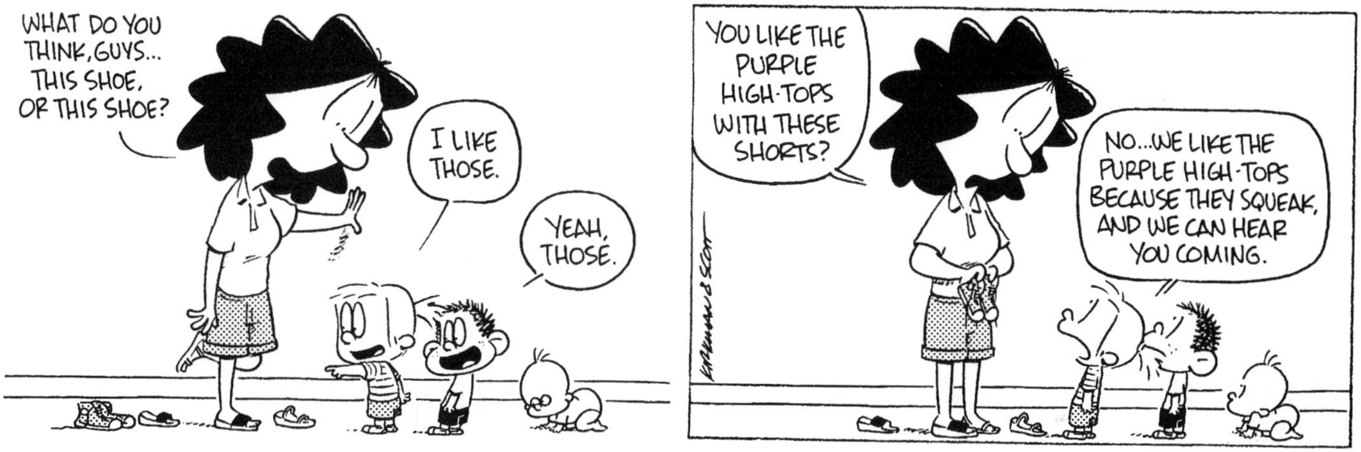
WHAT DO YOU THINK, GUYS... THIS SHOE, OR THIS SHOE?
I LIKE THOSE.
YEAH, THOSE.
YOU LIKE THE PURPLE HIGH-TOPS WITH THESE SHORTS?
NO...WE LIKE THE PURPLE HIGH-TOPS BECAUSE THEY SQUEAK, AND WE CAN HEAR YOU COMING.

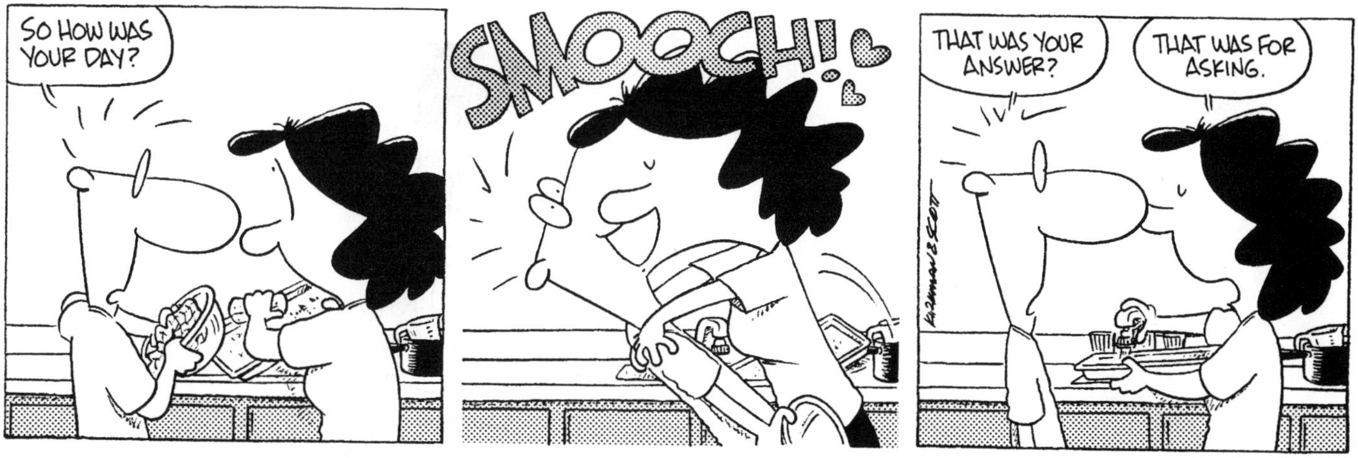
SO HOW WAS YOUR DAY?
SMOOCH!
THAT WAS YOUR ANSWER?
THAT WAS FOR ASKING.

BABY BLUES®
BY RICK KIRKMAN / JERRY SCOTT
Z
HAPPY MOTHER'S DAY!

WAAAAA!
WAAAAAA!
WEH! WEH! WEH! WEH! WEH! WEH! WEH! WEH! WEH! W—
WEH! WEH! WAAAAA!
THUP! THUP! THUP! THUP! THUP!
Z.
HAPPY MOTHER'S DAY!!
WORLD'S BEST MOM
WAAAAA
WELL ANYWAY, YOU WERE SURPRISED, RIGHT?
KIRKMAN & SCOTT

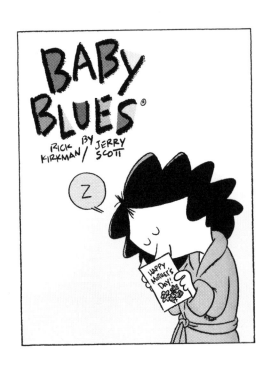

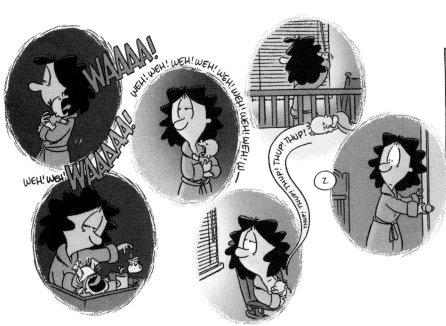

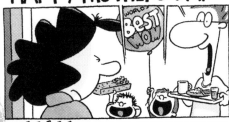

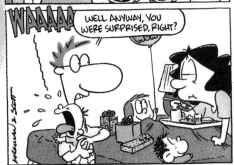

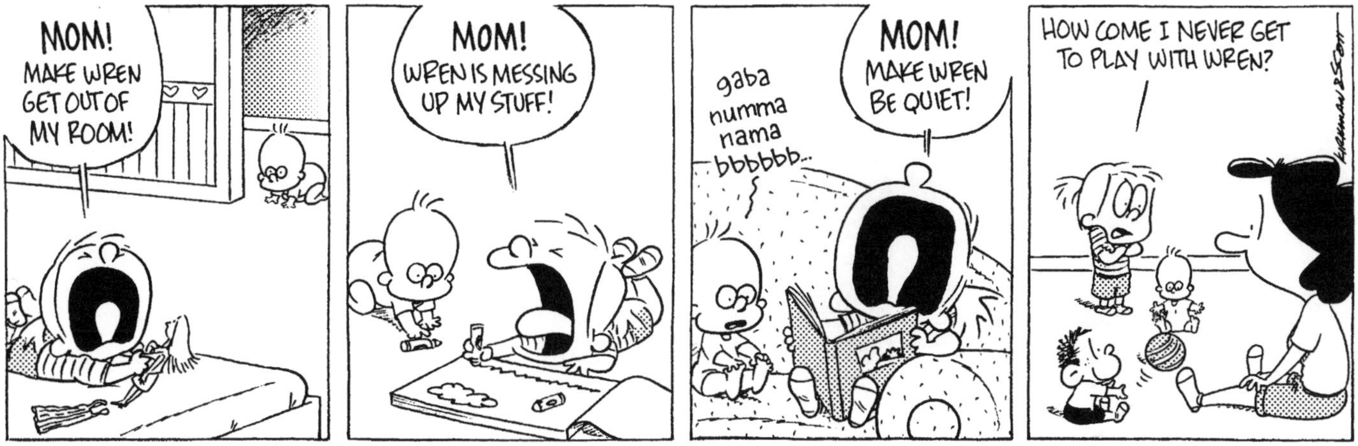
MOM!
MAKE WREN GET OUT OF MY ROOM!
MOM!
WREN IS MESSING UP MY STUFF!
gaba numma nama bbbbbb..
MOM!
MAKE WREN BE QUIET!
HOW COME I NEVER GET TO PLAY WITH WREN?
KIRKMAN & SCOTT

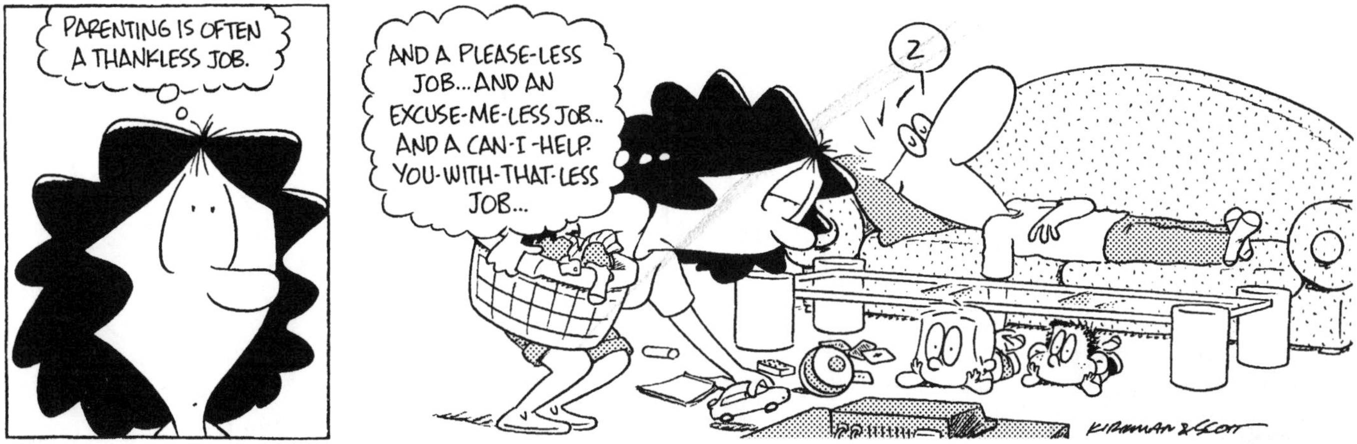
PARENTING IS OFTEN A THANKLESS JOB.
AND A PLEASE-LESS JOB...AND AN EXCUSE-ME-LESS JOB.. AND A CAN-I-HELP-YOU-WITH-THAT-LESS JOB...
Z
KIRKMAN & SCOTT

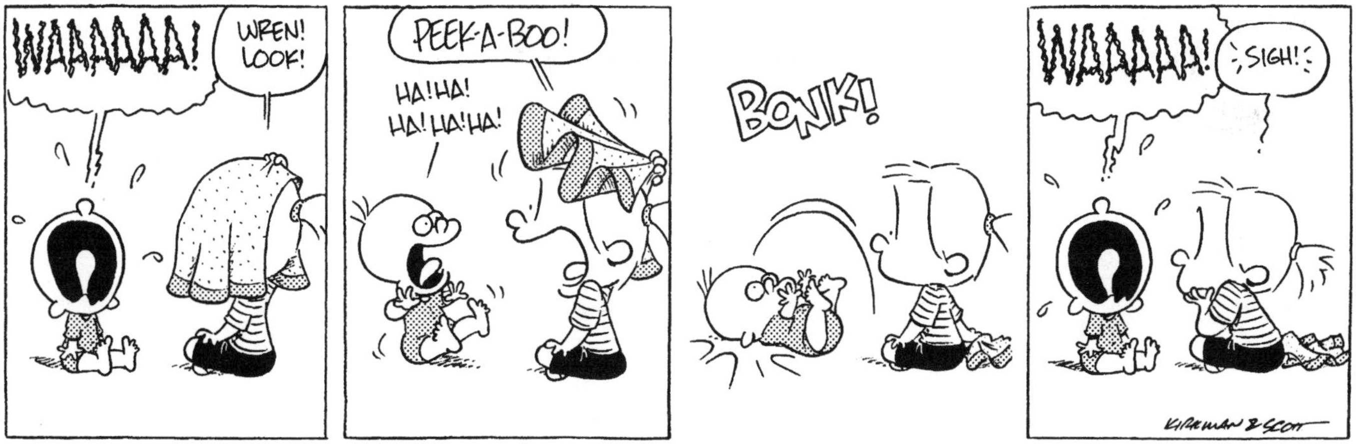
WAAAAAA!
WREN! LOOK!
PEEK-A-BOO!
HA! HA! HA! HA! HA!
BONK!
WAAAAA!
SIGH!
KIRKMAN & SCOTT

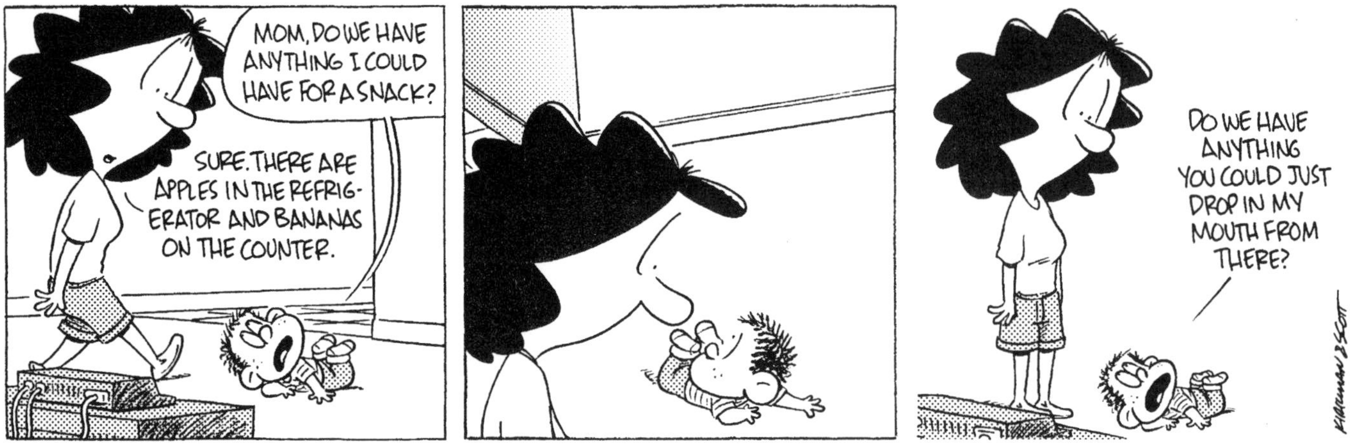
MOM, DO WE HAVE ANYTHING I COULD HAVE FOR A SNACK?
SURE. THERE ARE APPLES IN THE REFRIGERATOR AND BANANAS ON THE COUNTER.
DO WE HAVE ANYTHING YOU COULD JUST DROP IN MY MOUTH FROM THERE?

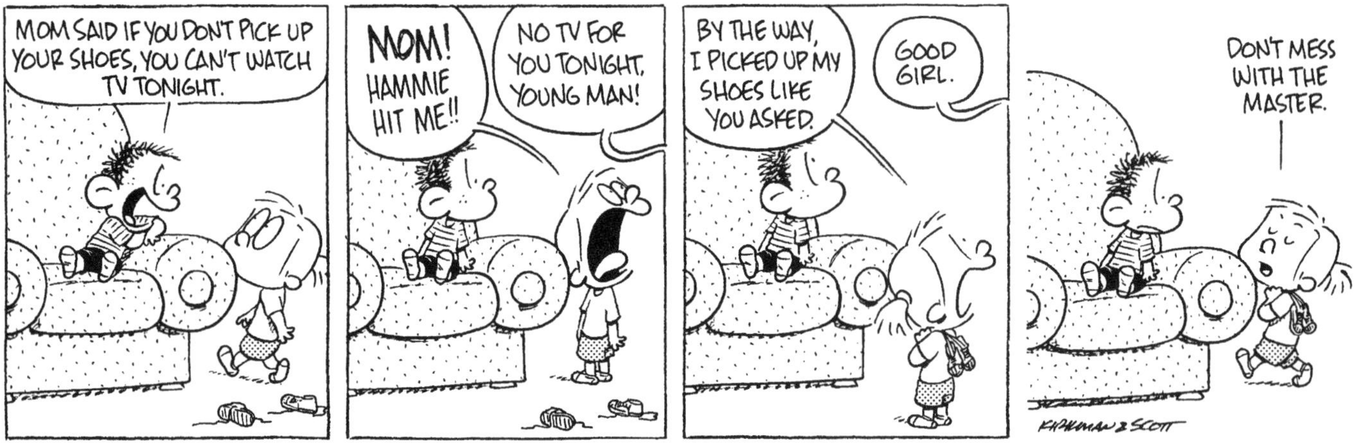
MOM SAID IF YOU DON'T PICK UP YOUR SHOES, YOU CAN'T WATCH TV TONIGHT.
MOM! HAMMIE HIT ME!!
NO TV FOR YOU TONIGHT, YOUNG MAN!
BY THE WAY, I PICKED UP MY SHOES LIKE YOU ASKED.
GOOD GIRL.
DON'T MESS WITH THE MASTER.

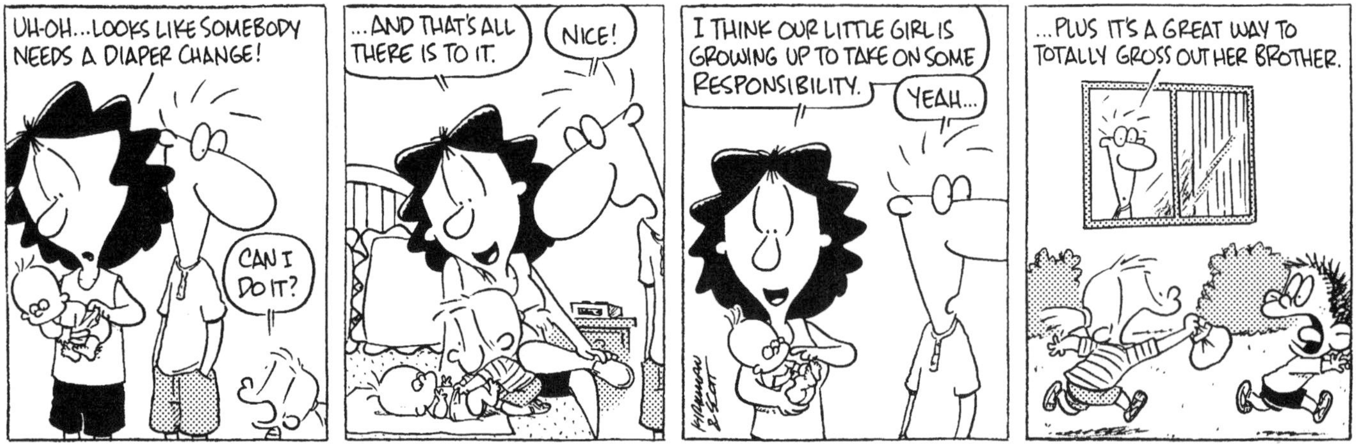
UH-OH... LOOKS LIKE SOMEBODY NEEDS A DIAPER CHANGE!
CAN I DO IT?
...AND THAT'S ALL THERE IS TO IT.
NICE!
I THINK OUR LITTLE GIRL IS GROWING UP TO TAKE ON SOME RESPONSIBILITY.
YEAH...
...PLUS IT'S A GREAT WAY TO TOTALLY GROSS OUT HER BROTHER.

BABY BLUES®
BY RICK KIRKMAN / JERRY SCOTT

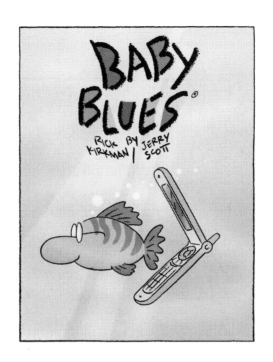

I CAN'T FIGURE OUT HOW TO ADJUST THE VOLUME, SET THE WALLPAPER, DOWNLOAD RINGTONES OR LOCK THE KEYPAD ON THIS NEW CELL PHONE!
LET ME SEE IT.
BIP! BIP! BUP! BEEP!
I GOT THE VOLUME ADJUSTED, BUT I DON'T KNOW HOW TO SET THE WALLPAPER.
LET ME TRY.
BUP! BIP! BIP!
I SET THE WALLPAPER, BUT I CAN'T DOWNLOAD RINGTONES.
LET ME SEE IT.
BEEP! BIP! BOOP!
HMM... I GOT THE RINGTONES DOWNLOADED, BUT THE KEYPAD WON'T LOCK...
NYNGH! NYNGH! NYNGH!
NOW IT'S LOCKED. YOU'RE ALL SET, DAD.
HAPPY?
ABOUT WHAT? THAT MY PHONE IS SET UP, OR THAT I'M AT THE BOTTOM OF THE TECHNOLOGY FOOD CHAIN.
KIRKMAN & SCOTT

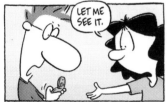

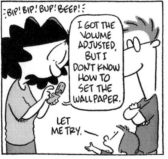

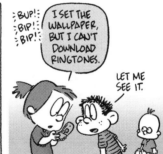

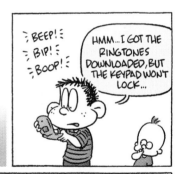

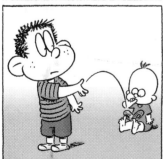

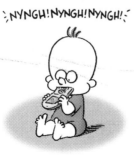

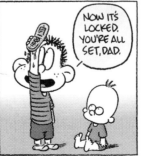

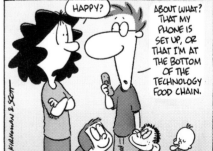

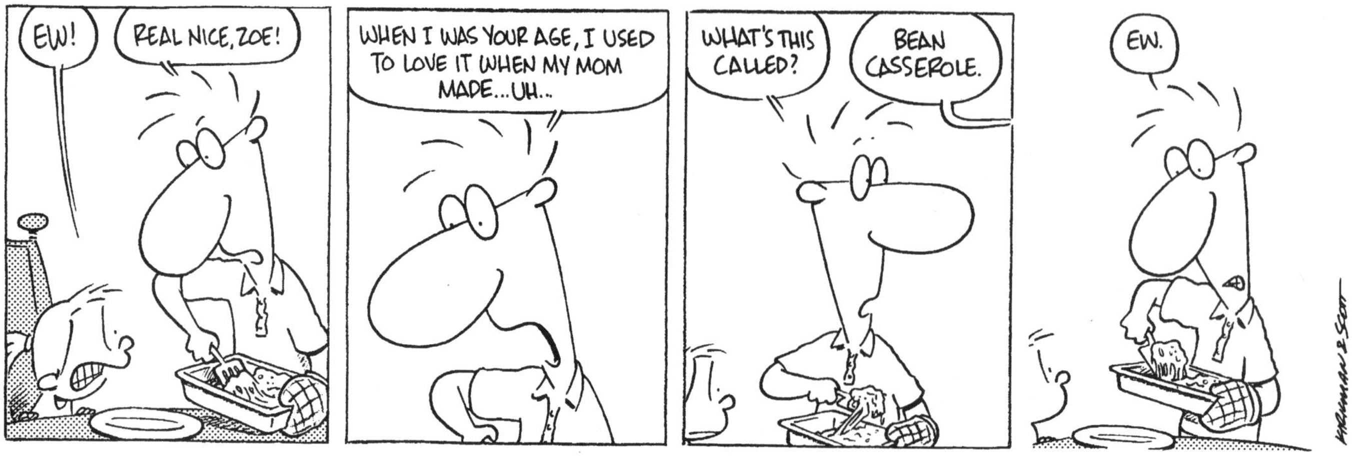
EW!
REAL NICE, ZOE!
WHEN I WAS YOUR AGE, I USED TO LOVE IT WHEN MY MOM MADE... UH...
WHAT'S THIS CALLED?
BEAN CASSEROLE.
EW.

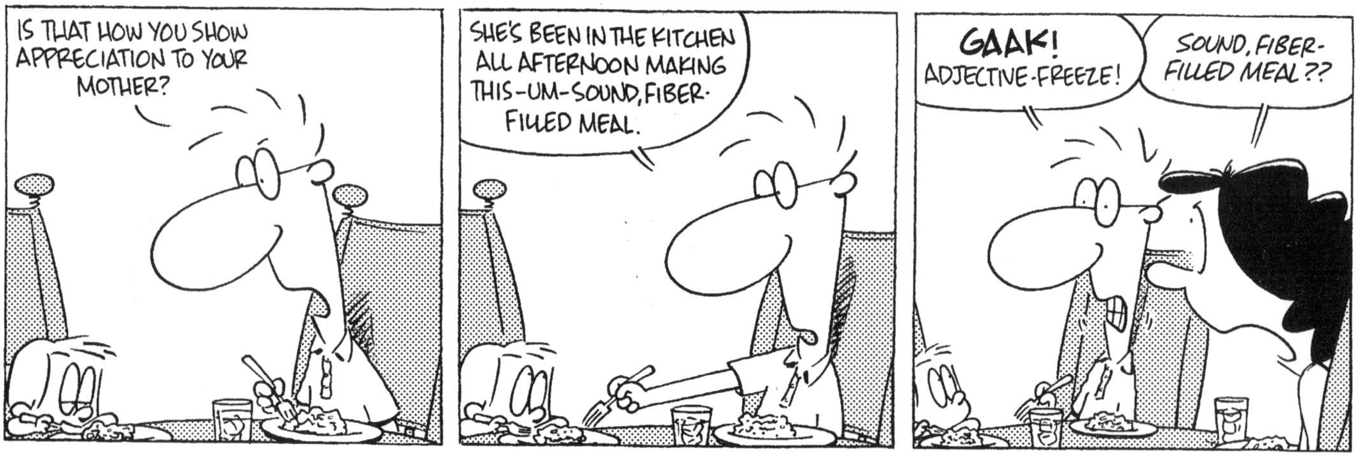
IS THAT HOW YOU SHOW APPRECIATION TO YOUR MOTHER?
SHE'S BEEN IN THE KITCHEN ALL AFTERNOON MAKING THIS-UM-SOUND, FIBER-FILLED MEAL.
GAAK!
ADJECTIVE-FREEZE!
SOUND, FIBER-FILLED MEAL??

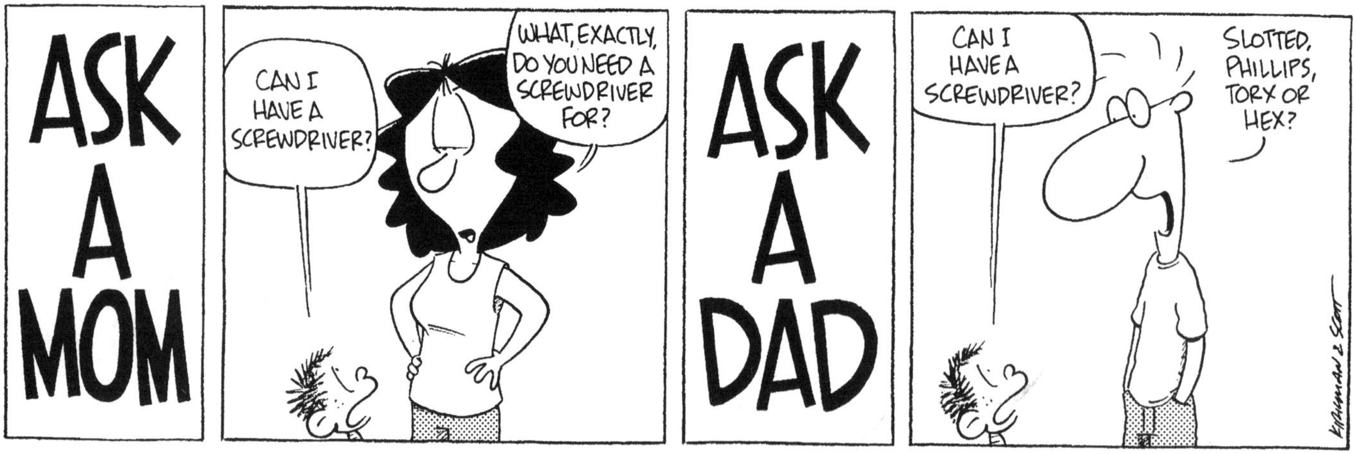
ASK A MOM
CAN I HAVE A SCREWDRIVER?
WHAT, EXACTLY, DO YOU NEED A SCREWDRIVER FOR?
ASK A DAD
CAN I HAVE A SCREWDRIVER?
SLOTTED, PHILLIPS, TORX OR HEX?

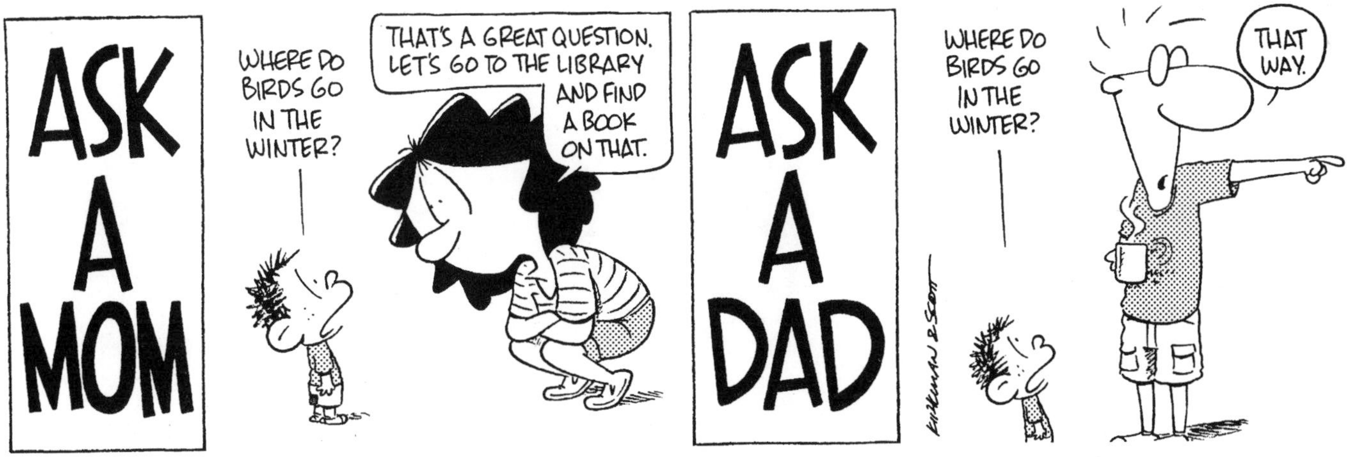
ASK A MOM
WHERE DO BIRDS GO IN THE WINTER?
THAT'S A GREAT QUESTION. LET'S GO TO THE LIBRARY AND FIND A BOOK ON THAT.
ASK A DAD
WHERE DO BIRDS GO IN THE WINTER?
THAT WAY.
KIRKMAN & SCOTT

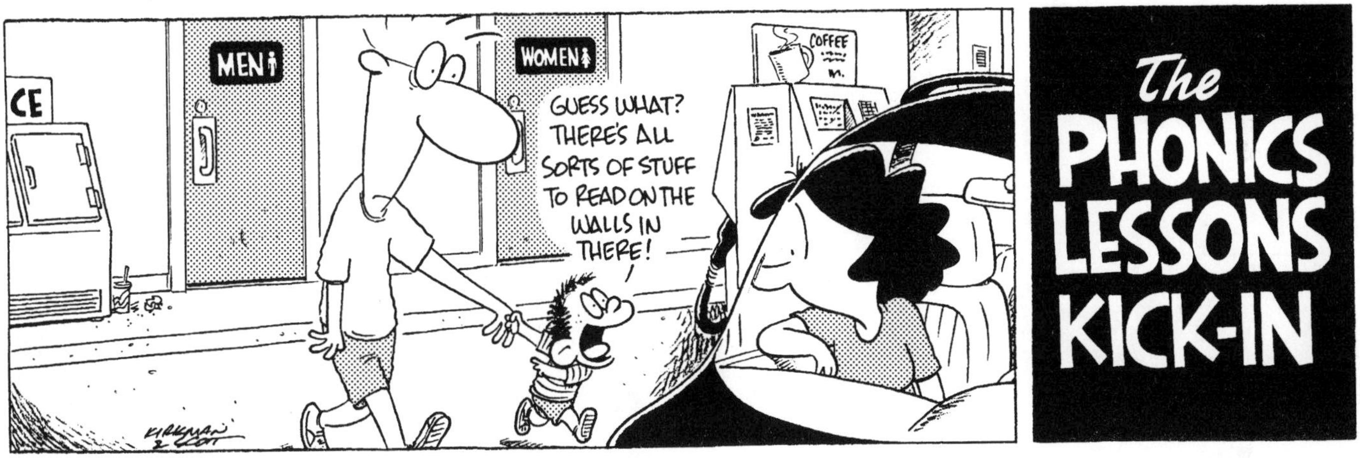
CE
MEN
WOMEN
COFFEE
GUESS WHAT? THERE'S ALL SORTS OF STUFF TO READ ON THE WALLS IN THERE!
KIRKMAN & SCOTT
The PHONICS LESSONS KICK-IN

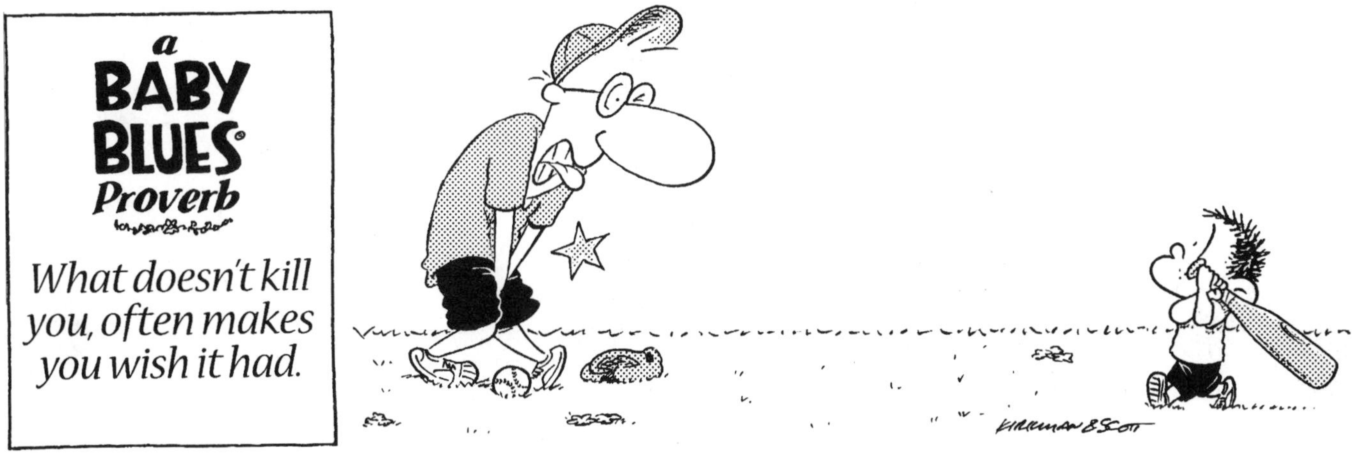
a BABY BLUES® Proverb
What doesn't kill you, often makes you wish it had.
KIRKMAN & SCOTT

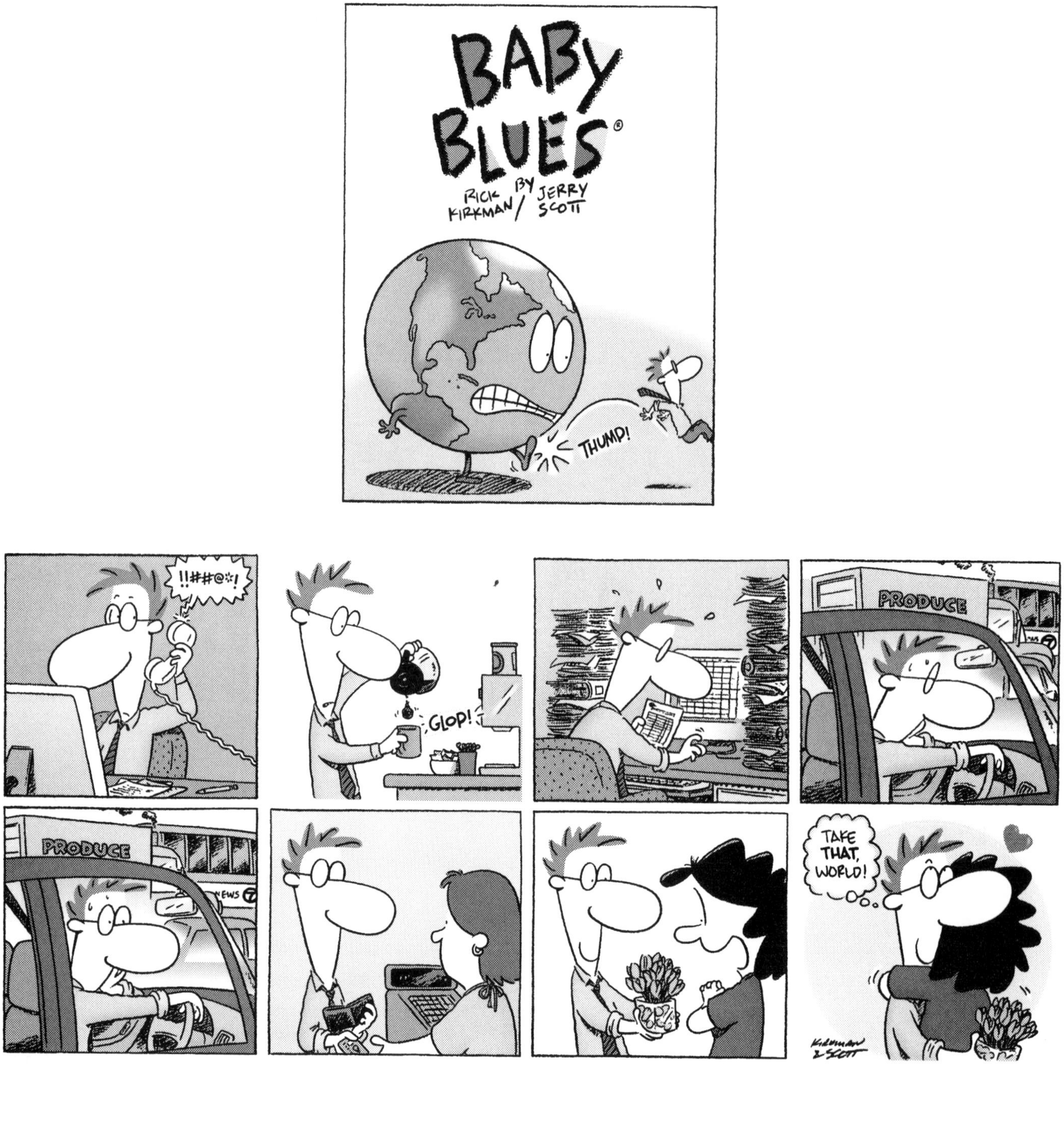
BABY BLUES®
BY RICK KIRKMAN / JERRY SCOTT
THUMP!
!!#@*!
GLOP!
PRODUCE
PRODUCE
TAKE THAT, WORLD!
KIRKMAN & SCOTT

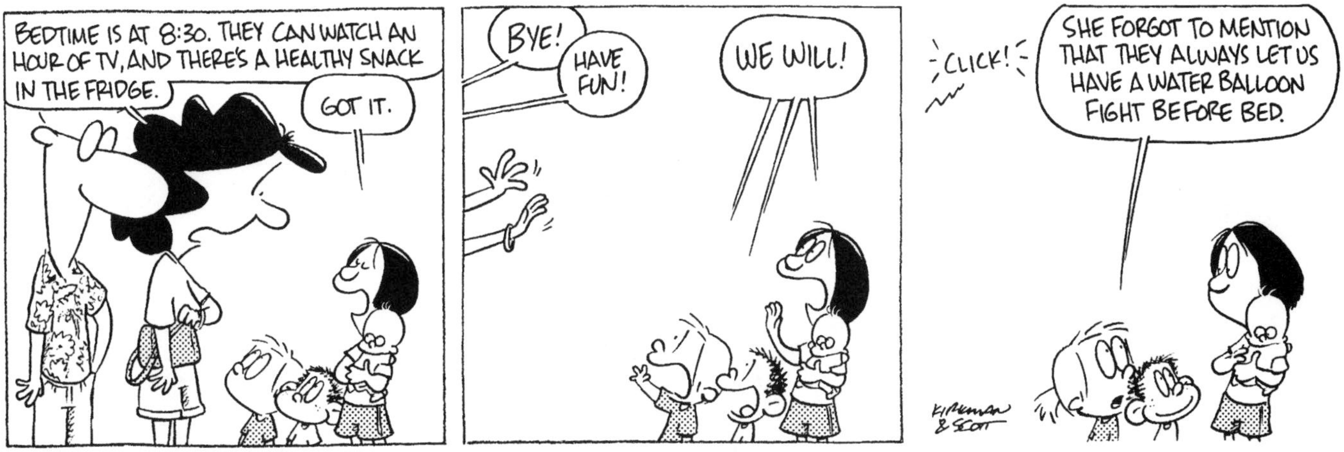
BEDTIME IS AT 8:30. THEY CAN WATCH AN HOUR OF TV, AND THERE'S A HEALTHY SNACK IN THE FRIDGE.
GOT IT.
BYE!
HAVE FUN!
WE WILL!
CLICK!
SHE FORGOT TO MENTION THAT THEY ALWAYS LET US HAVE A WATER BALLOON FIGHT BEFORE BED.
KIRKMAN & SCOTT

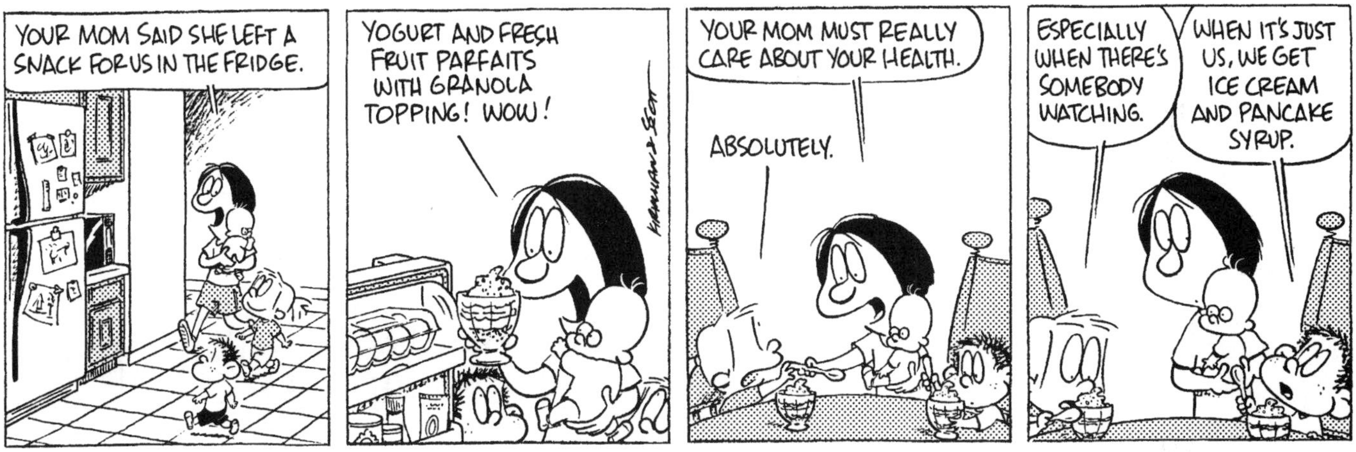
YOUR MOM SAID SHE LEFT A SNACK FOR US IN THE FRIDGE.
YOGURT AND FRESH FRUIT PARFAITS WITH GRANOLA TOPPING! WOW!
KIRKMAN & SCOTT
YOUR MOM MUST REALLY CARE ABOUT YOUR HEALTH.
ABSOLUTELY.
ESPECIALLY WHEN THERE'S SOMEBODY WATCHING.
WHEN IT'S JUST US, WE GET ICE CREAM AND PANCAKE SYRUP.

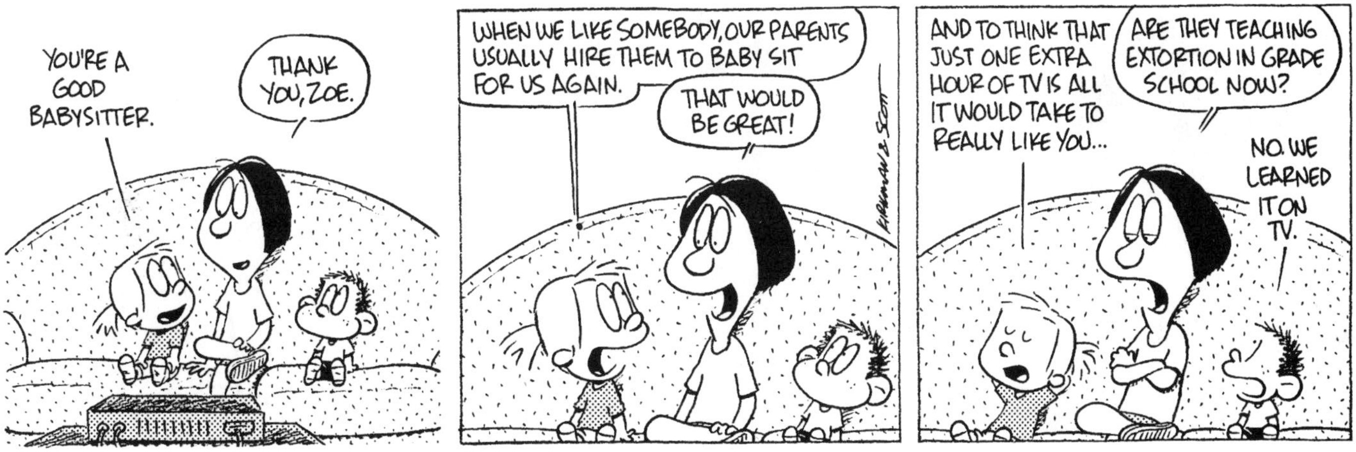
YOU'RE A GOOD BABYSITTER.
THANK YOU, ZOE.
WHEN WE LIKE SOMEBODY, OUR PARENTS USUALLY HIRE THEM TO BABY SIT FOR US AGAIN.
THAT WOULD BE GREAT!
KIRKMAN & SCOTT
AND TO THINK THAT JUST ONE EXTRA HOUR OF TV IS ALL IT WOULD TAKE TO REALLY LIKE YOU...
ARE THEY TEACHING EXTORTION IN GRADE SCHOOL NOW?
NO. WE LEARNED IT ON TV.

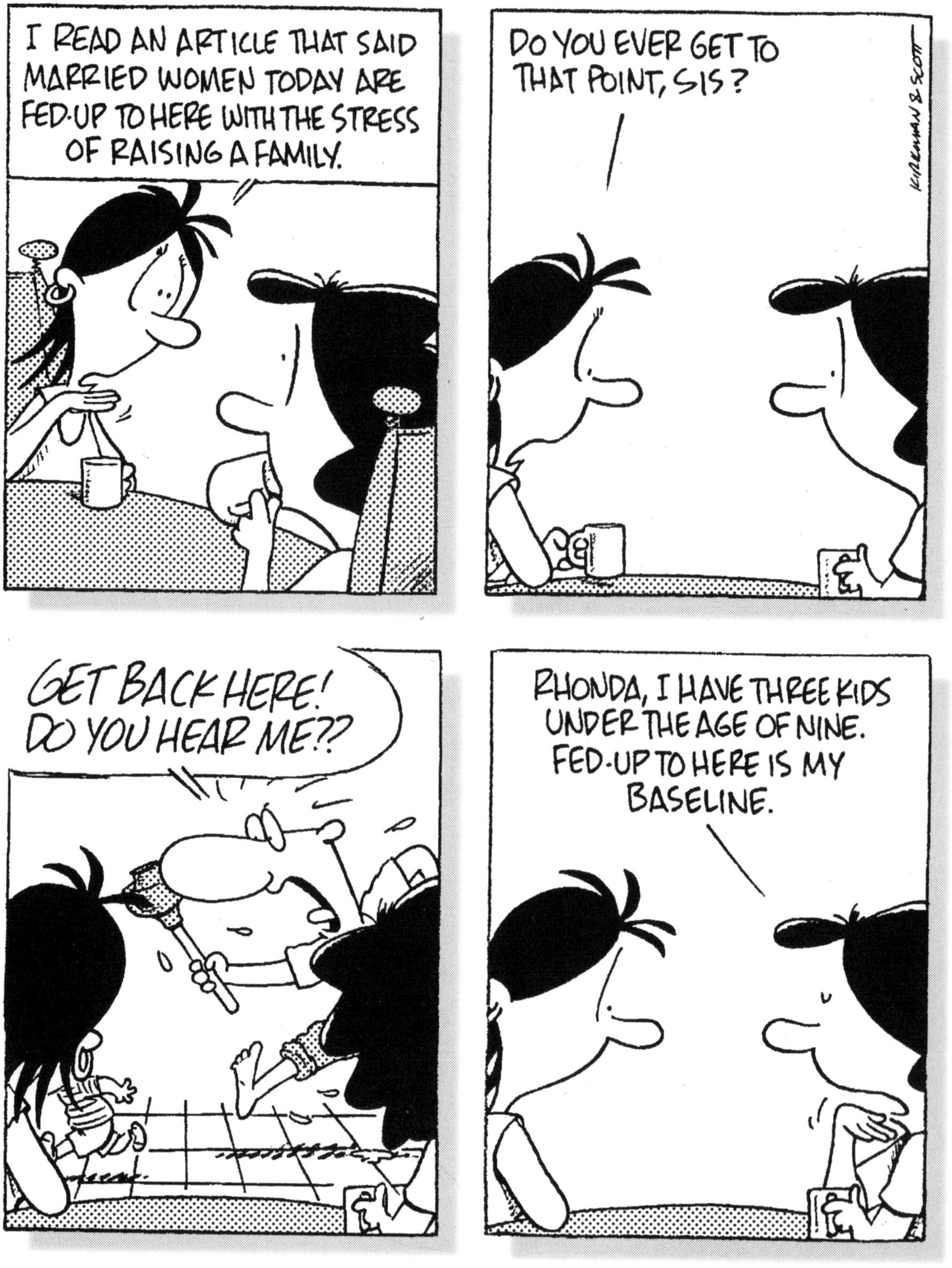
I READ AN ARTICLE THAT SAID MARRIED WOMEN TODAY ARE FED-UP TO HERE WITH THE STRESS OF RAISING A FAMILY.
DO YOU EVER GET TO THAT POINT, SIS?
KIRKMAN & SCOTT
GET BACK HERE! DO YOU HEAR ME??
RHONDA, I HAVE THREE KIDS UNDER THE AGE OF NINE. FED-UP TO HERE IS MY BASELINE.

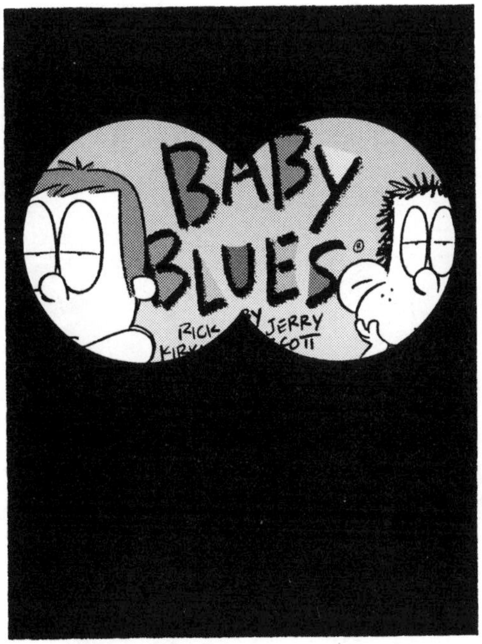
BABY BLUES®
RICK
JERRY

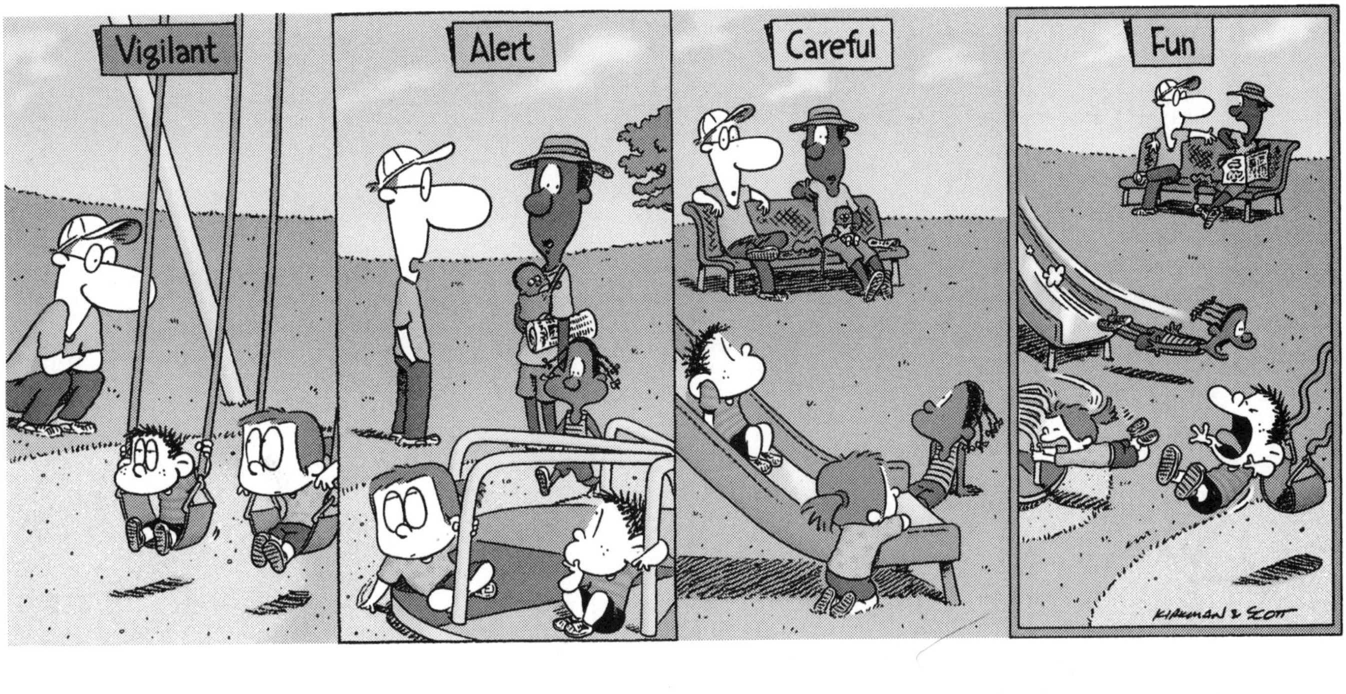
Vigilant
Alert
Careful
Fun
KIRKMAN & SCOTT

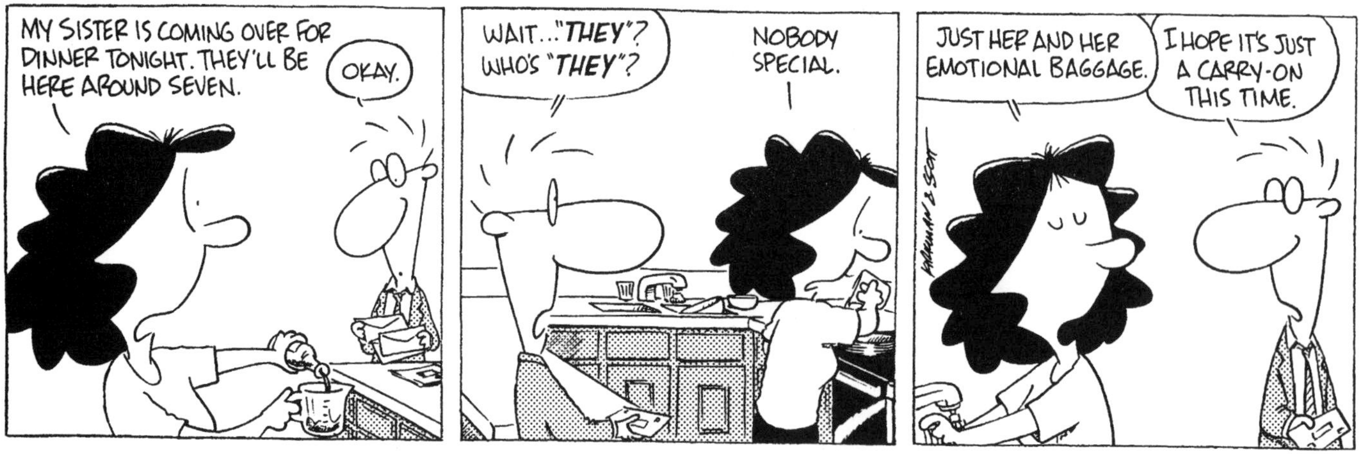
MY SISTER IS COMING OVER FOR DINNER TONIGHT. THEY'LL BE HERE AROUND SEVEN.
OKAY.
WAIT..."THEY"? WHO'S "THEY"?
NOBODY SPECIAL.
JUST HER AND HER EMOTIONAL BAGGAGE.
I HOPE IT'S JUST A CARRY-ON THIS TIME.

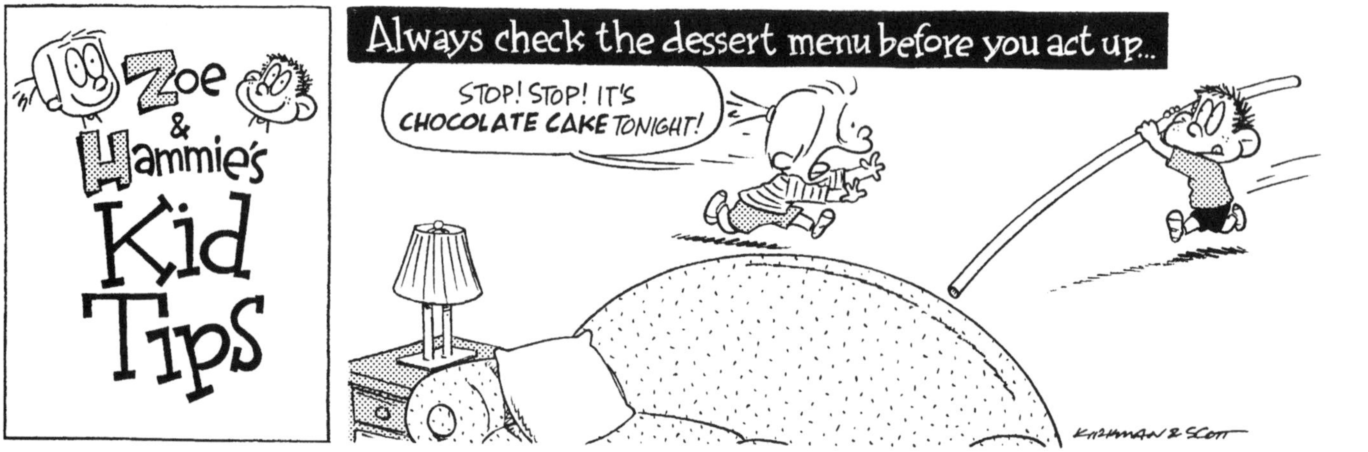
Zoe & Hammie's Kid Tips
Always check the dessert menu before you act up...
STOP! STOP! IT'S CHOCOLATE CAKE TONIGHT!
KIRKMAN & SCOTT

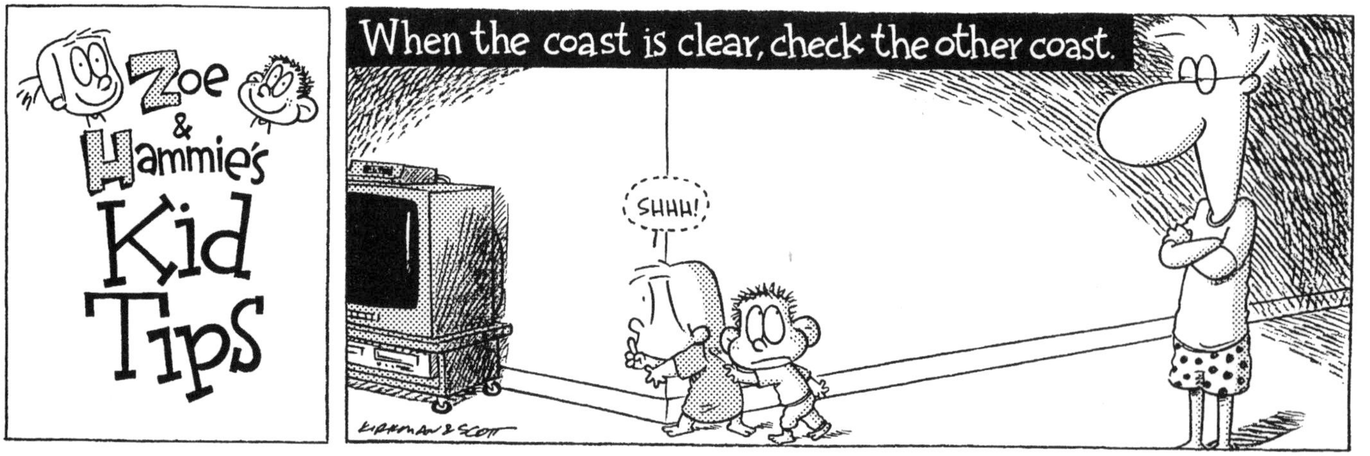
Zoe & Hammie's Kid Tips
When the coast is clear, check the other coast.
SHHH!
KIRKMAN & SCOTT

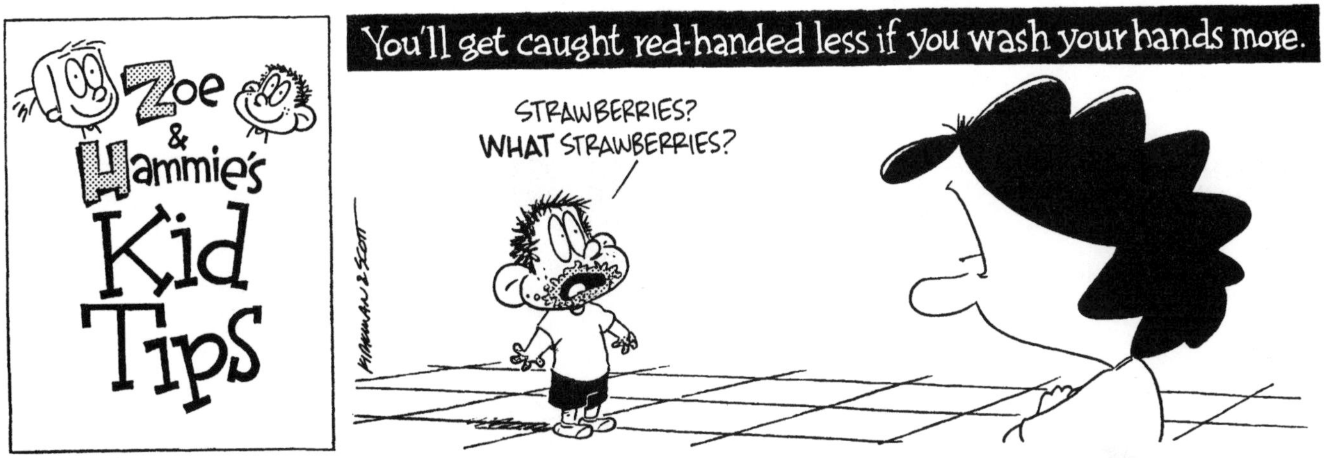
Zoe & Hammie's Kid Tips
You'll get caught red-handed less if you wash your hands more.
STRAWBERRIES? WHAT STRAWBERRIES?

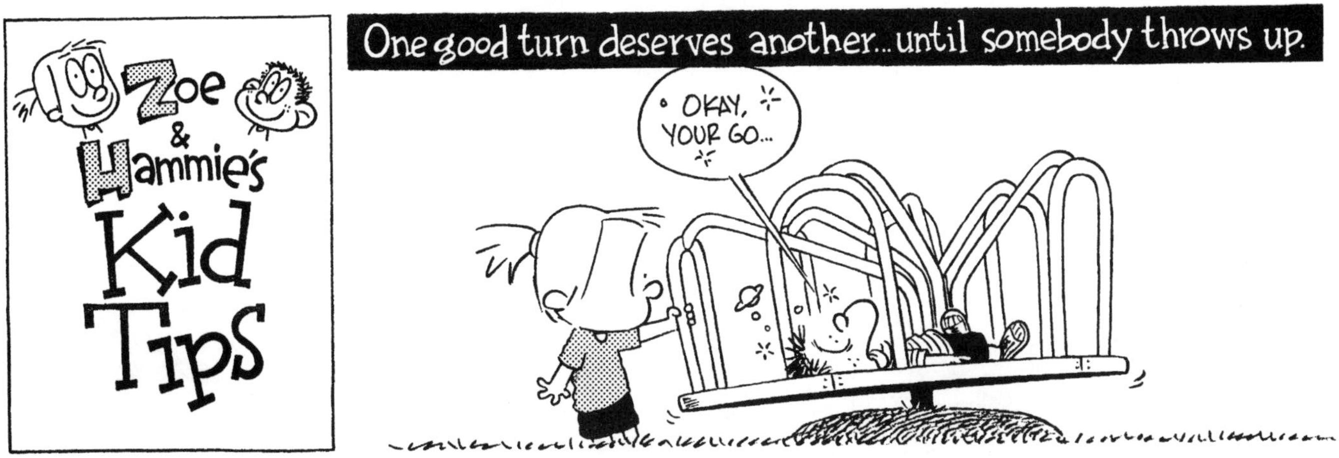
Zoe & Hammie's Kid Tips
One good turn deserves another...until somebody throws up.
OKAY, YOUR GO...

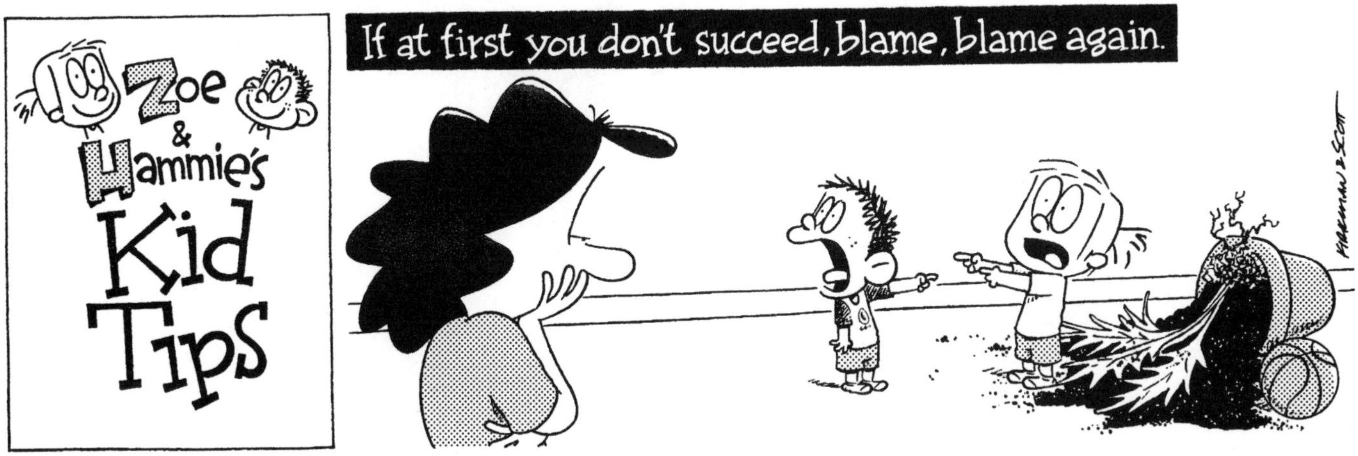
Zoe & Hammie's Kid Tips
If at first you don't succeed, blame, blame again.

BABY BLUES®

NOW THAT'S A NICE-LOOKING MEATLOAF!
WE'RE HAVING MEATLOAF??
OH, MAN!
WHAT'S WRONG WITH MEATLOAF?
WE HATE MEATLOAF!
WHY CAN'T YOU MAKE SOMETHING ELSE?
LIKE WHAT?
HAMBURGERS.
MEATLOAF IS HAMBURGER, AND HAMBURGER IS MEATLOAF! WHAT'S THE DIFFERENCE??
I GUESS IT WOULD HAVE TO BE THE BUN.
YEAH. THE BUN.
KIRKMAN & SCOTT
UM...
NOW DON'T YOU START!

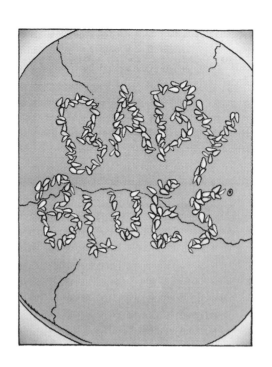

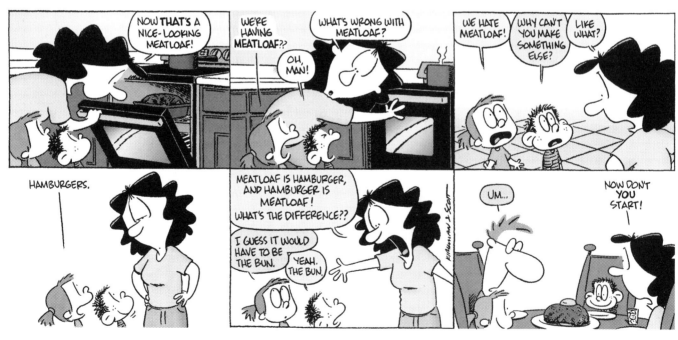

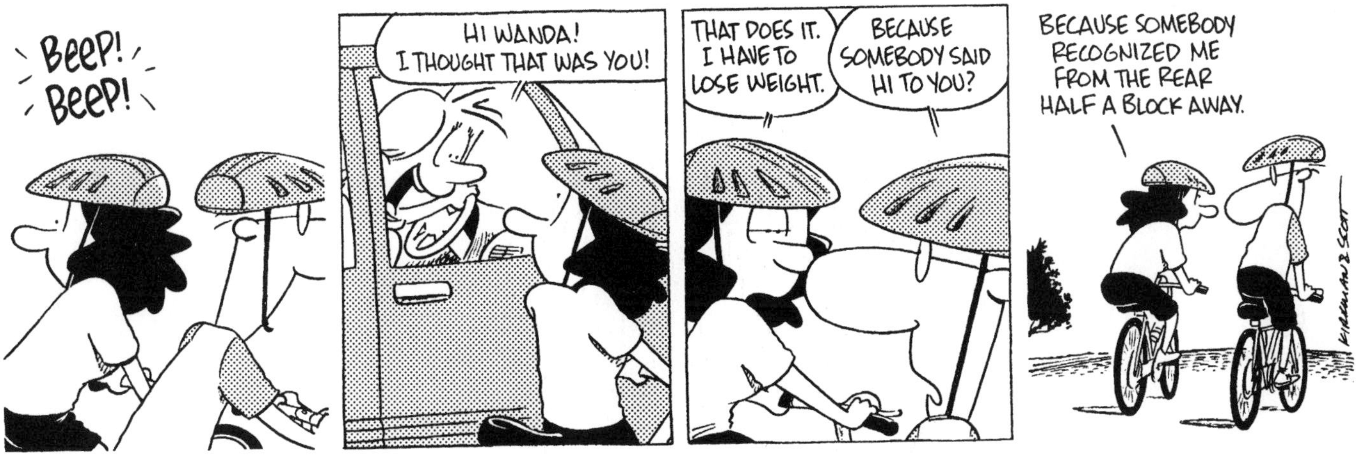
Beep! Beep!
HI WANDA! I THOUGHT THAT WAS YOU!
THAT DOES IT. I HAVE TO LOSE WEIGHT.
BECAUSE SOMEBODY SAID HI TO YOU?
BECAUSE SOMEBODY RECOGNIZED ME FROM THE REAR HALF A BLOCK AWAY.
KIRKMAN & SCOTT

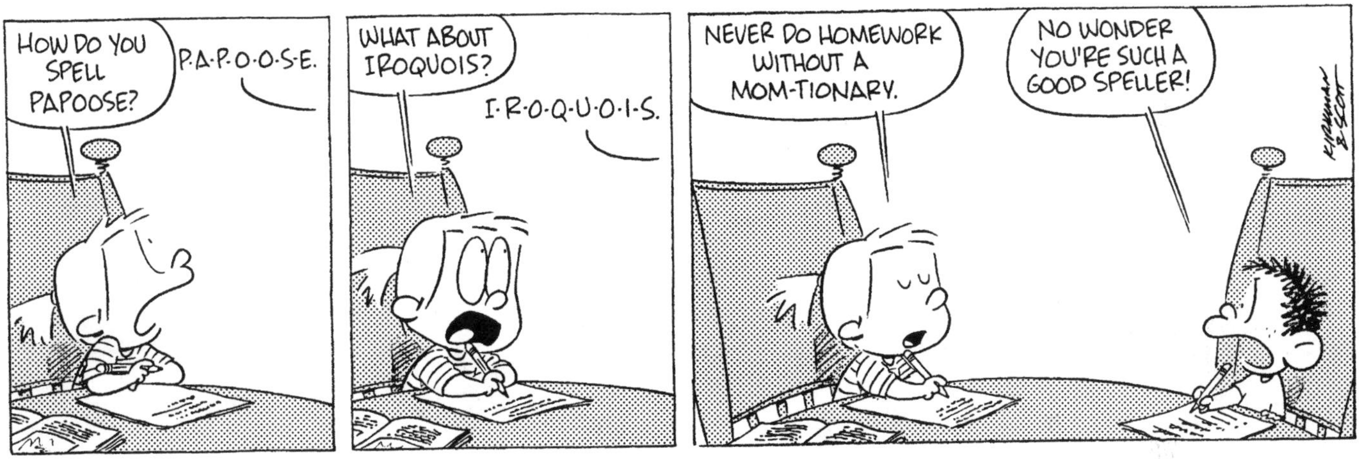
HOW DO YOU SPELL PAPOOSE?
P-A-P-O-O-S-E.
WHAT ABOUT IROQUOIS?
I-R-O-Q-U-O-I-S.
NEVER DO HOMEWORK WITHOUT A MOM-TIONARY.
NO WONDER YOU'RE SUCH A GOOD SPELLER!
KIRKMAN & SCOTT

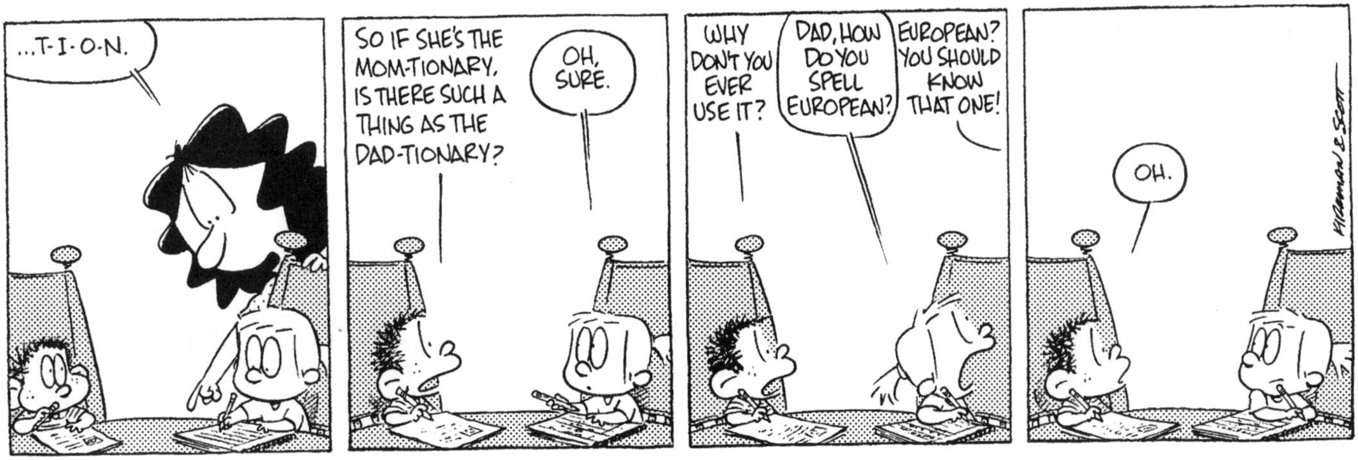
...T-I-O-N.
SO IF SHE'S THE MOM-TIONARY, IS THERE SUCH A THING AS THE DAD-TIONARY?
OH, SURE.
WHY DON'T YOU EVER USE IT?
DAD, HOW DO YOU SPELL EUROPEAN?
EUROPEAN? YOU SHOULD KNOW THAT ONE!
OH.
KIRKMAN & SCOTT

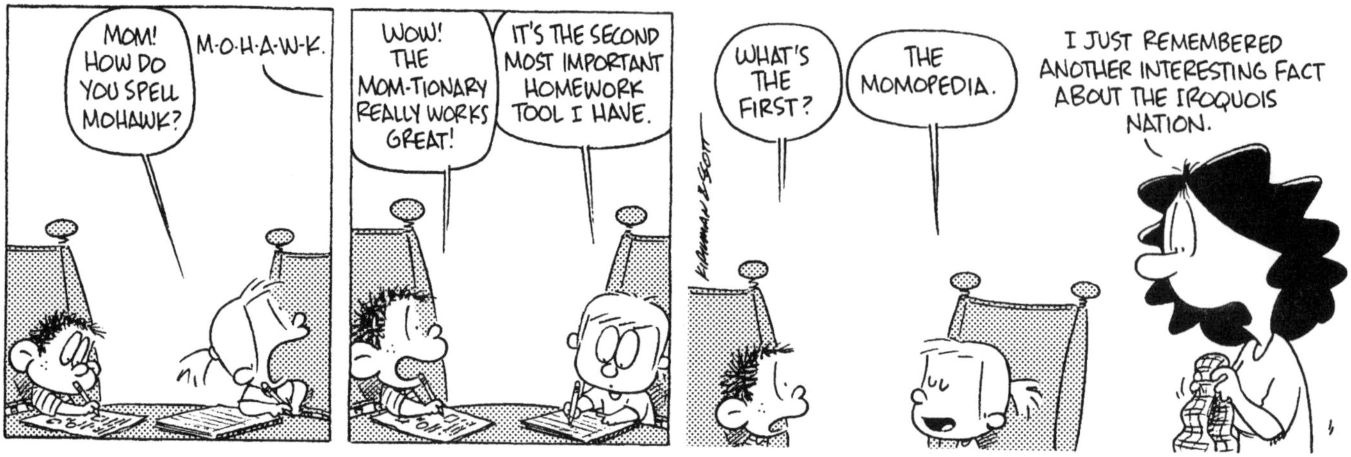
MOM! HOW DO YOU SPELL MOHAWK?
M-O-H-A-W-K.
WOW! THE MOM-TIONARY REALLY WORKS GREAT!
IT'S THE SECOND MOST IMPORTANT HOMEWORK TOOL I HAVE.
WHAT'S THE FIRST?
THE MOMOPEDIA.
I JUST REMEMBERED ANOTHER INTERESTING FACT ABOUT THE IROQUOIS NATION.

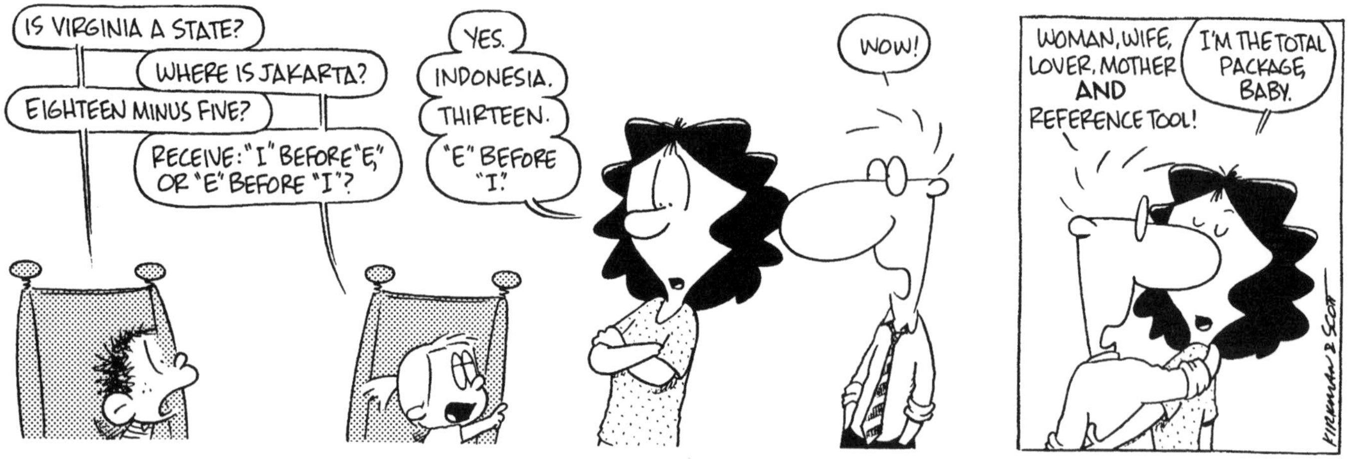
IS VIRGINIA A STATE?
WHERE IS JAKARTA?
EIGHTEEN MINUS FIVE?
RECEIVE: "I" BEFORE "E," OR "E" BEFORE "I"?
YES.
INDONESIA.
THIRTEEN.
"E" BEFORE "I."
WOW!
WOMAN, WIFE, LOVER, MOTHER **AND** REFERENCE TOOL!
I'M THE TOTAL PACKAGE, BABY.

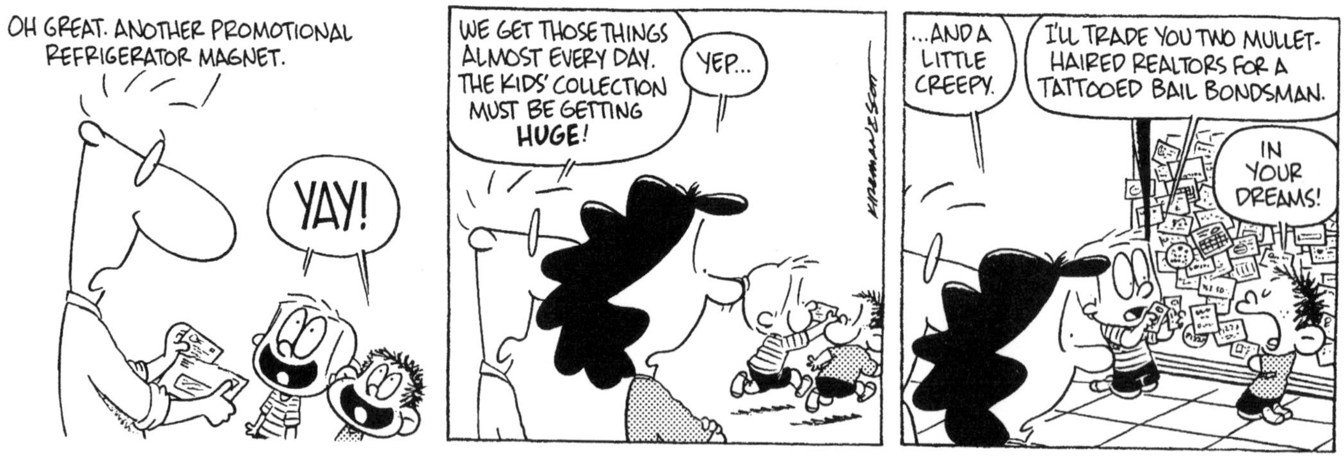
OH GREAT. ANOTHER PROMOTIONAL REFRIGERATOR MAGNET.
YAY!
WE GET THOSE THINGS ALMOST EVERY DAY. THE KIDS' COLLECTION MUST BE GETTING **HUGE**!
YEP...
...AND A LITTLE CREEPY.
I'LL TRADE YOU TWO MULLET-HAIRED REALTORS FOR A TATTOOED BAIL BONDSMAN.
IN YOUR DREAMS!

BABY BLUES®
BY RICK KIRKMAN / JERRY SCOTT
LITTLE PINK SHIRT LITTLE PINK SHIRT
APOLOGIES TO PATRICK McDONNELL

MOM! I CAN'T FIND A PINK SHIRT!
HERE'S ONE.
THAT HAS SPARKLES. I WANT ONE WITH NO SPARKLES.
HOW ABOUT THIS?
THAT ONE HAS A HEART ON IT.
AND THAT ONE HAS SLEEVES. I WANT ONE WITH NO SPARKLES, HEARTS OR SLEEVES.
THEN—
NO. I DON'T WANT SPAGHETTI STRAPS, RUFFLES OR POCKETS, EITHER.
WELL, I DON'T KNOW WHAT ELSE TO TELL YOU...
THAT'S OKAY. I HAVE A SOLUTION.
WE NEED TO GO SHOPPING.
CAN I GO, TOO? I NEED MORE TRUCKS.
KIRKMAN & SCOTT

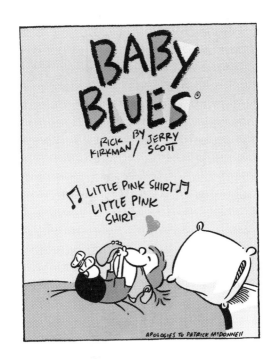

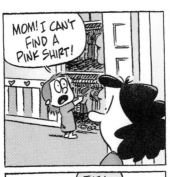

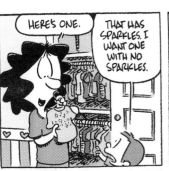

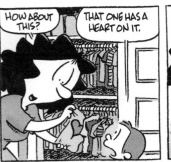

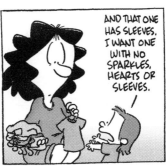

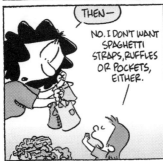

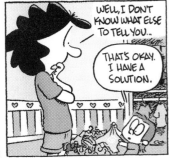

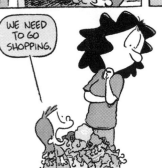

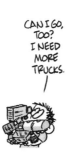

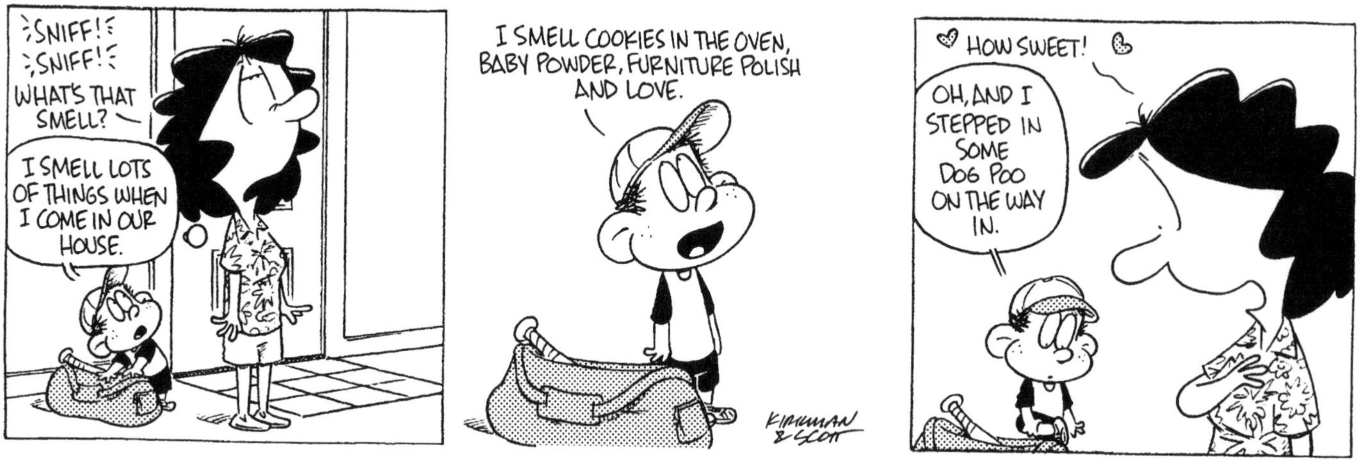
SNIFF!
SNIFF!
WHAT'S THAT SMELL?
I SMELL LOTS OF THINGS WHEN I COME IN OUR HOUSE.
I SMELL COOKIES IN THE OVEN, BABY POWDER, FURNITURE POLISH AND LOVE.
KIRKMAN & SCOTT
HOW SWEET!
OH, AND I STEPPED IN SOME DOG POO ON THE WAY IN.

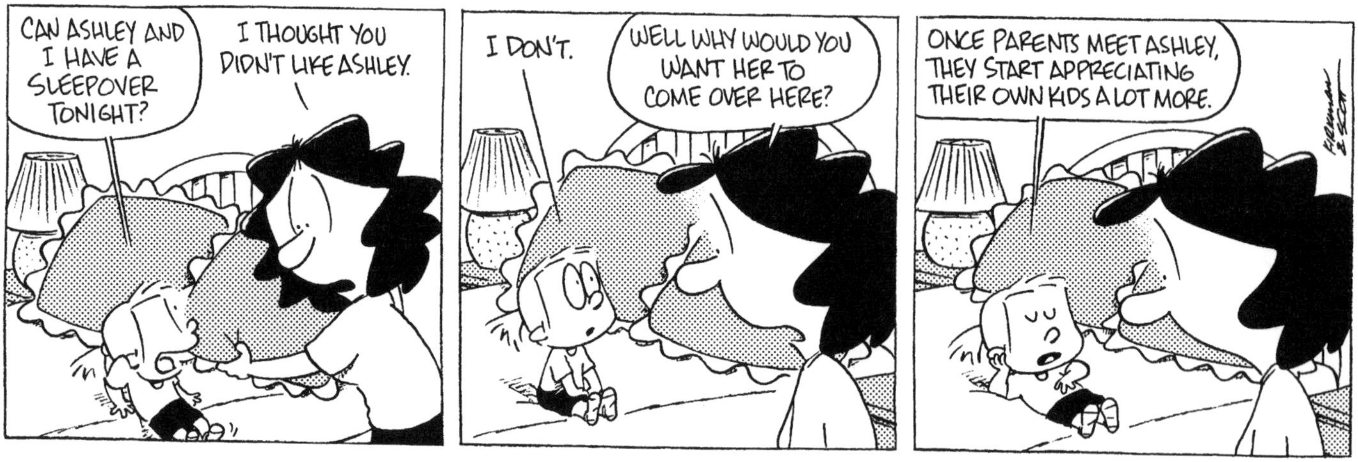
CAN ASHLEY AND I HAVE A SLEEPOVER TONIGHT?
I THOUGHT YOU DIDN'T LIKE ASHLEY.
I DON'T.
WELL WHY WOULD YOU WANT HER TO COME OVER HERE?
ONCE PARENTS MEET ASHLEY, THEY START APPRECIATING THEIR OWN KIDS A LOT MORE.
KIRKMAN & SCOTT

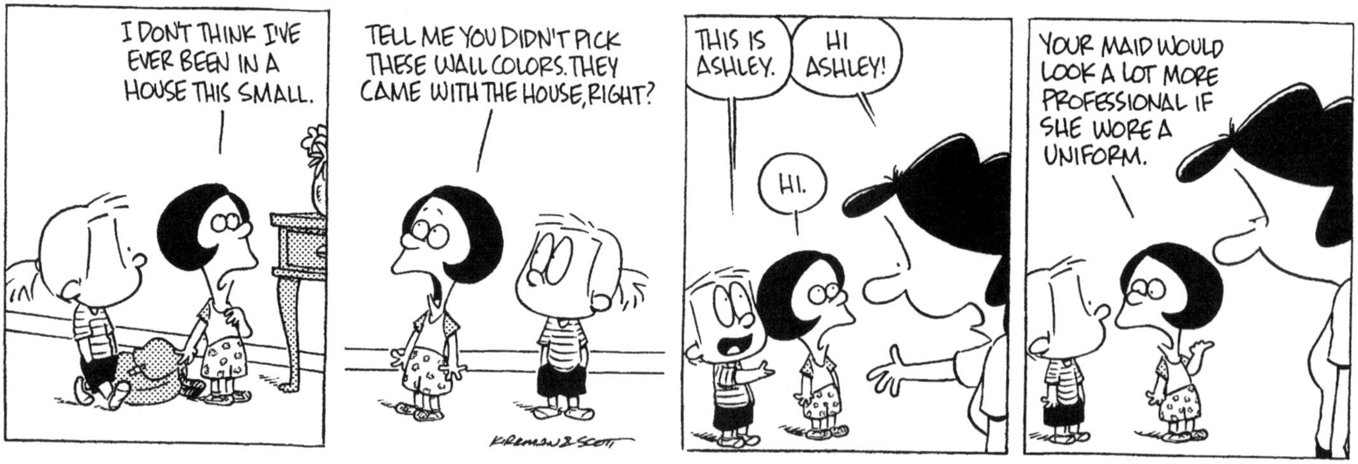
I DON'T THINK I'VE EVER BEEN IN A HOUSE THIS SMALL.
TELL ME YOU DIDN'T PICK THESE WALL COLORS. THEY CAME WITH THE HOUSE, RIGHT?
KIRKMAN & SCOTT
THIS IS ASHLEY.
HI ASHLEY!
HI.
YOUR MAID WOULD LOOK A LOT MORE PROFESSIONAL IF SHE WORE A UNIFORM.

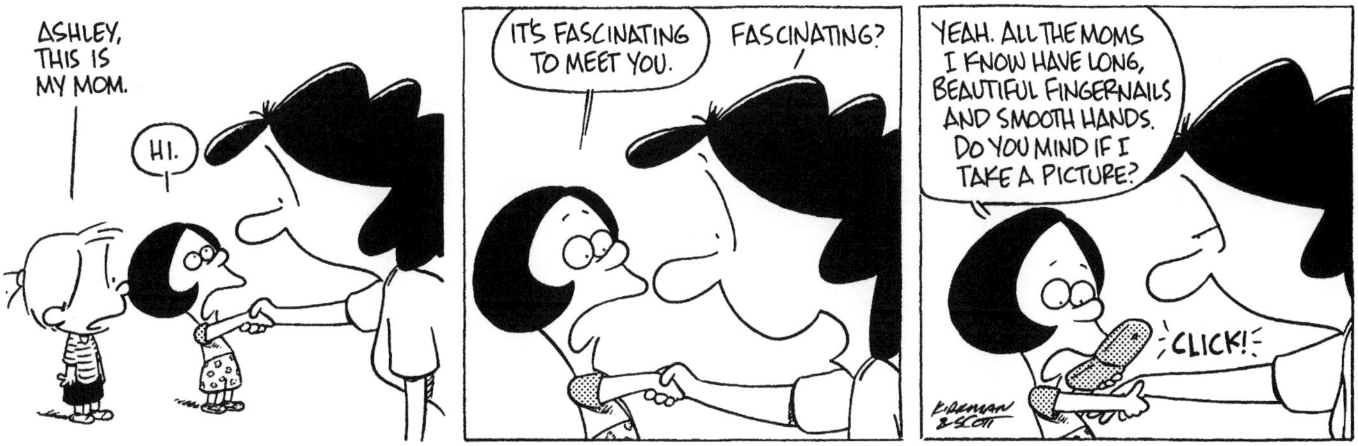
ASHLEY, THIS IS MY MOM.
HI.
IT'S FASCINATING TO MEET YOU.
FASCINATING?
YEAH. ALL THE MOMS I KNOW HAVE LONG, BEAUTIFUL FINGERNAILS AND SMOOTH HANDS. DO YOU MIND IF I TAKE A PICTURE?
CLICK!
KIRKMAN & SCOTT

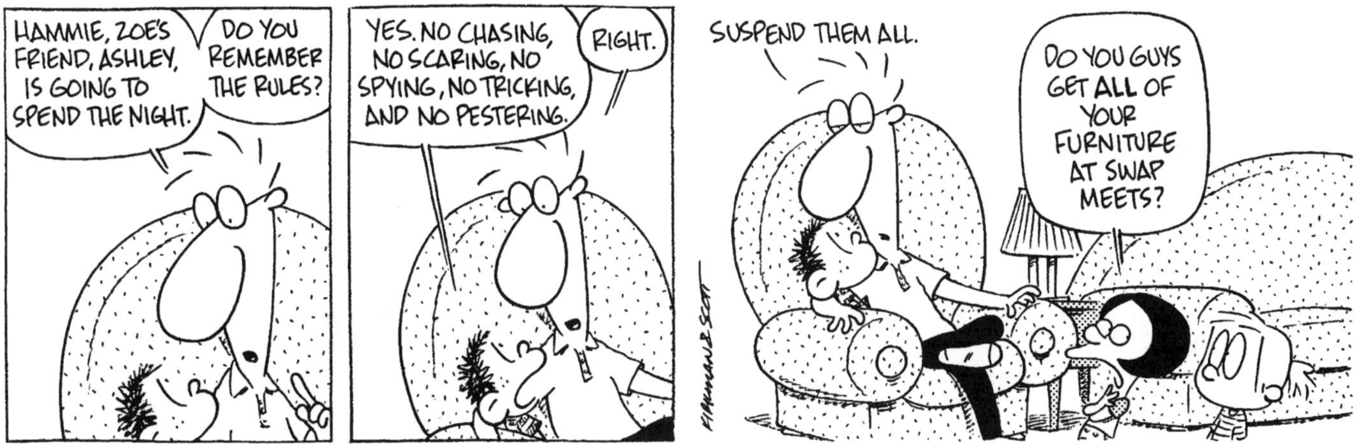
HAMMIE, ZOE'S FRIEND, ASHLEY, IS GOING TO SPEND THE NIGHT.
DO YOU REMEMBER THE RULES?
YES. NO CHASING, NO SCARING, NO SPYING, NO TRICKING, AND NO PESTERING.
RIGHT.
KIRKMAN & SCOTT
SUSPEND THEM ALL.
DO YOU GUYS GET **ALL** OF YOUR FURNITURE AT SWAP MEETS?

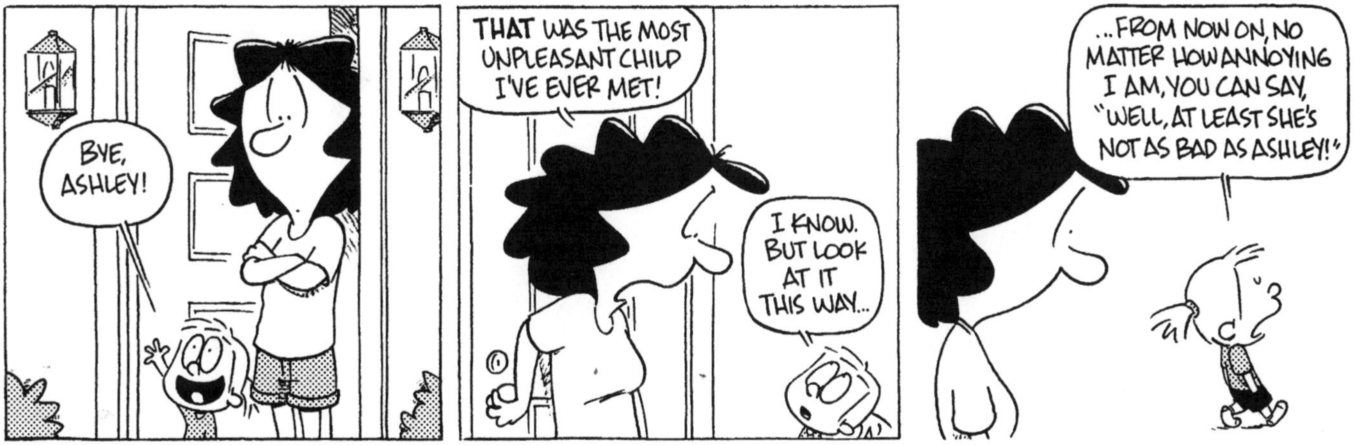
BYE, ASHLEY!
THAT WAS THE MOST UNPLEASANT CHILD I'VE EVER MET!
I KNOW. BUT LOOK AT IT THIS WAY...
...FROM NOW ON, NO MATTER HOW ANNOYING I AM, YOU CAN SAY, "WELL, AT LEAST SHE'S NOT AS BAD AS ASHLEY!"

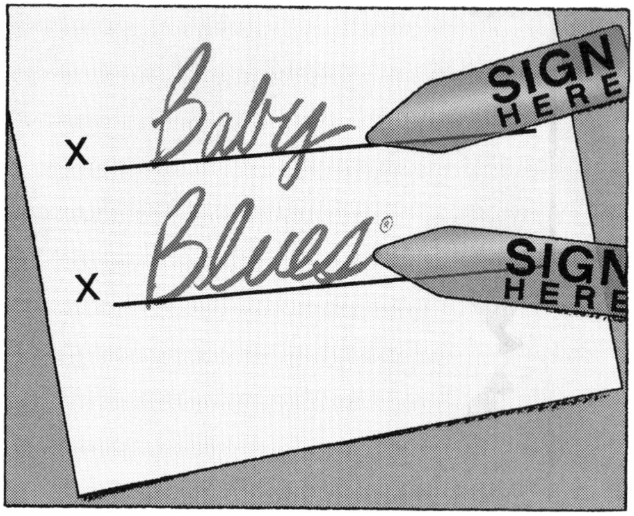
Baby Blues®
SIGN HERE
SIGN HERE
x
x

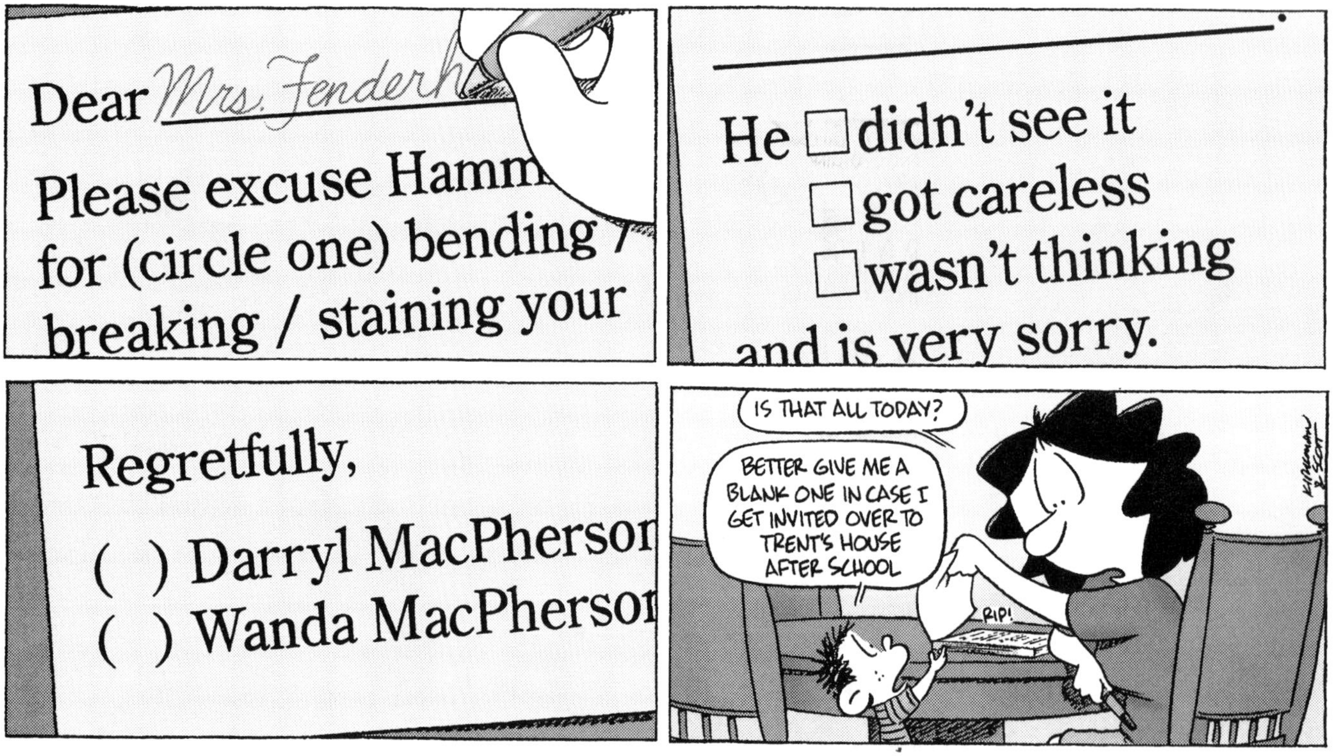
Dear Mrs. Fenderh
Please excuse Hamm
for (circle one) bending /
breaking / staining your
He ☐ didn't see it
☐ got careless
☐ wasn't thinking
and is very sorry.
Regretfully,
( ) Darryl MacPherson
( ) Wanda MacPherson
IS THAT ALL TODAY?
BETTER GIVE ME A BLANK ONE IN CASE I GET INVITED OVER TO TRENT'S HOUSE AFTER SCHOOL
RIP!

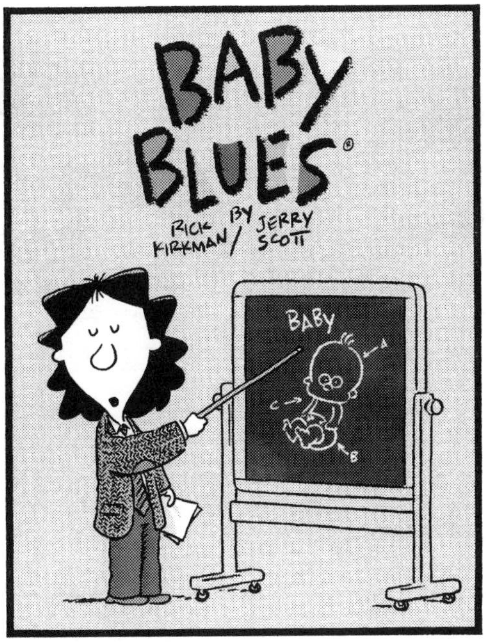
BABY BLUES®
BY RICK KIRKMAN / JERRY SCOTT
BABY
A
B
C

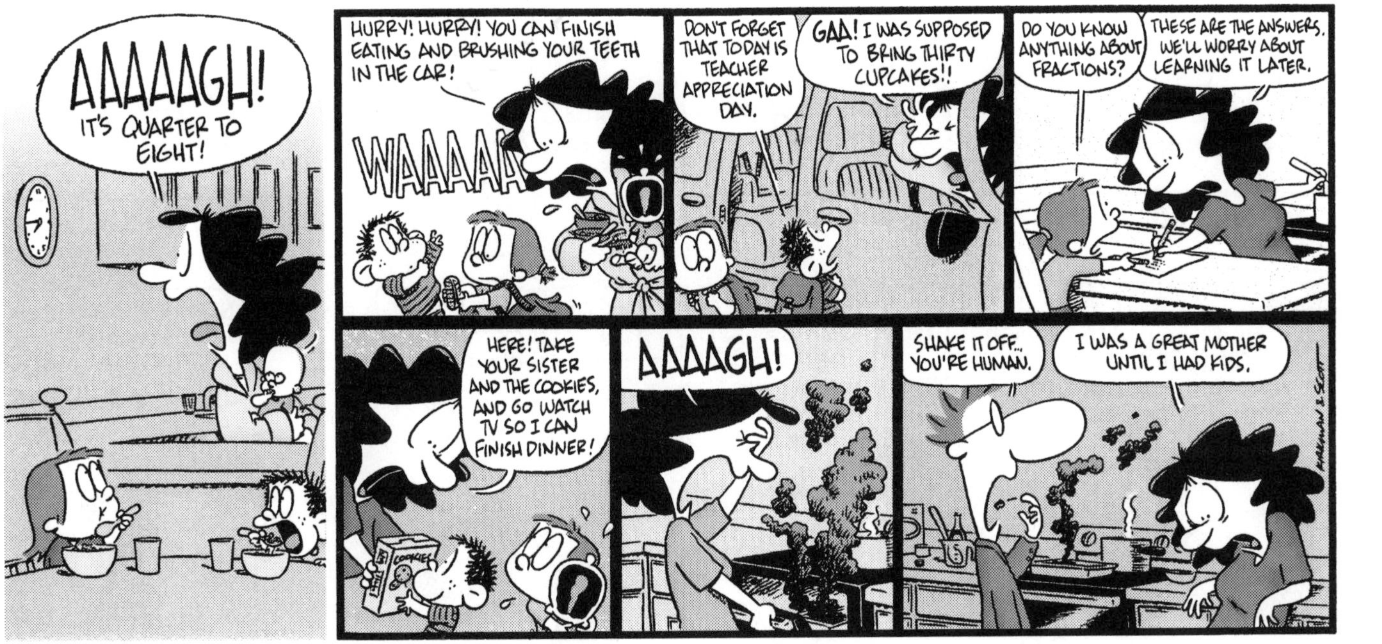
AAAAAGH! IT'S QUARTER TO EIGHT!
HURRY! HURRY! YOU CAN FINISH EATING AND BRUSHING YOUR TEETH IN THE CAR!
WAAAAA
DON'T FORGET THAT TODAY IS TEACHER APPRECIATION DAY.
GAA! I WAS SUPPOSED TO BRING THIRTY CUPCAKES!!
DO YOU KNOW ANYTHING ABOUT FRACTIONS?
THESE ARE THE ANSWERS. WE'LL WORRY ABOUT LEARNING IT LATER.
HERE! TAKE YOUR SISTER AND THE COOKIES, AND GO WATCH TV SO I CAN FINISH DINNER!
COOKIES
AAAAGH!
SHAKE IT OFF... YOU'RE HUMAN.
I WAS A GREAT MOTHER UNTIL I HAD KIDS.

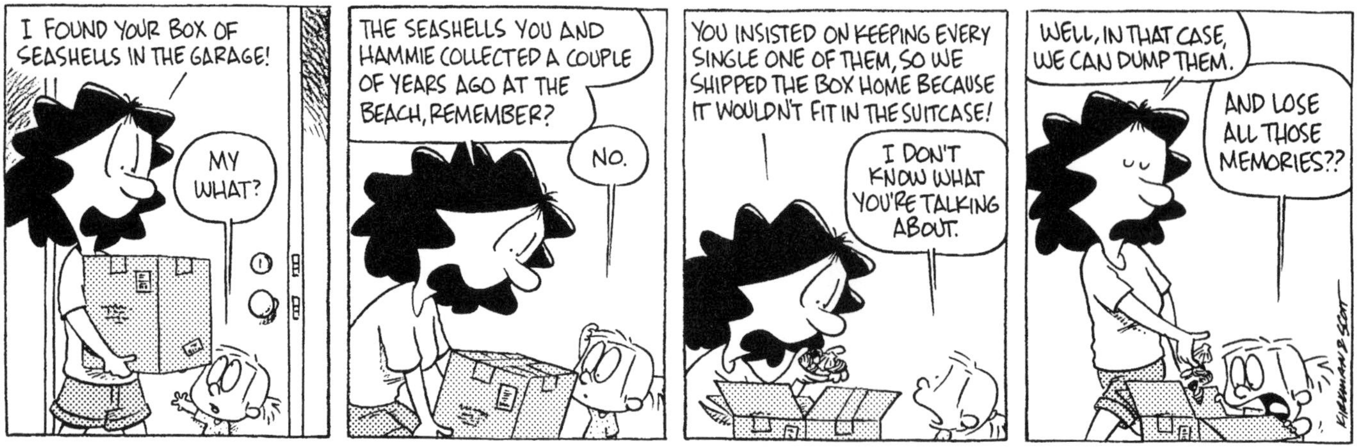
I FOUND YOUR BOX OF SEASHELLS IN THE GARAGE!
MY WHAT?
THE SEASHELLS YOU AND HAMMIE COLLECTED A COUPLE OF YEARS AGO AT THE BEACH, REMEMBER?
NO.
YOU INSISTED ON KEEPING EVERY SINGLE ONE OF THEM, SO WE SHIPPED THE BOX HOME BECAUSE IT WOULDN'T FIT IN THE SUITCASE!
I DON'T KNOW WHAT YOU'RE TALKING ABOUT.
WELL, IN THAT CASE, WE CAN DUMP THEM.
AND LOSE ALL THOSE MEMORIES??

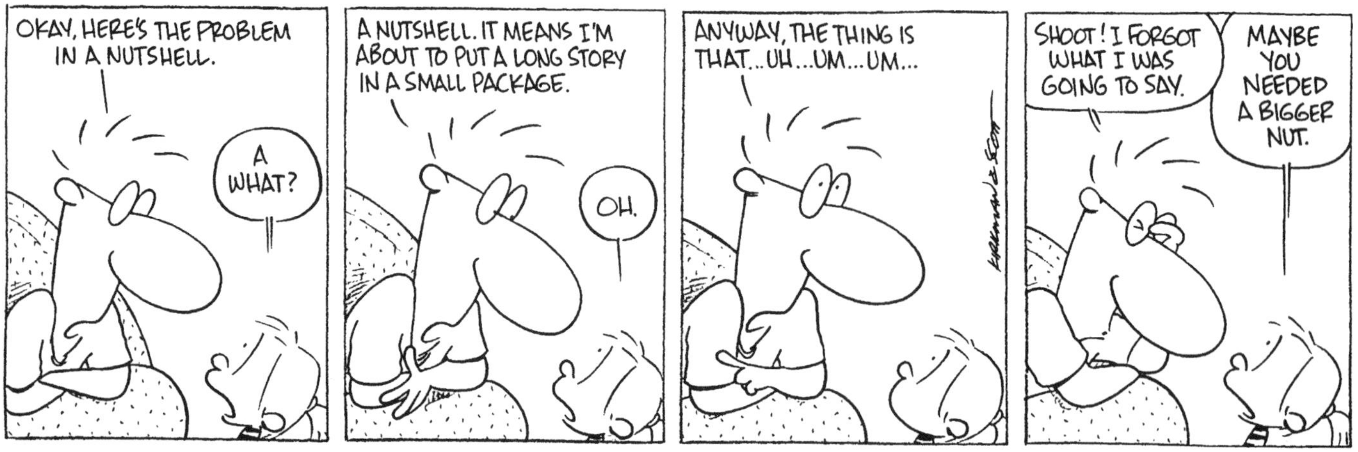
OKAY, HERE'S THE PROBLEM IN A NUTSHELL.
A WHAT?
A NUTSHELL. IT MEANS I'M ABOUT TO PUT A LONG STORY IN A SMALL PACKAGE.
OH.
ANYWAY, THE THING IS THAT...UH...UM...UM...
SHOOT! I FORGOT WHAT I WAS GOING TO SAY.
MAYBE YOU NEEDED A BIGGER NUT.

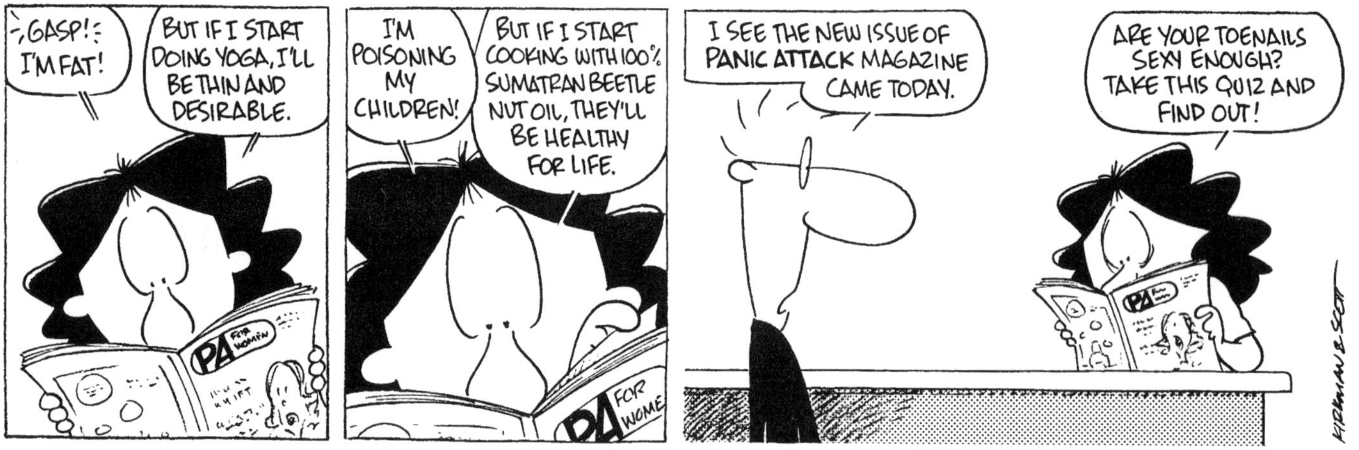
GASP! I'M FAT!
BUT IF I START DOING YOGA, I'LL BE THIN AND DESIRABLE.
I'M POISONING MY CHILDREN!
BUT IF I START COOKING WITH 100% SUMATRAN BEETLE NUT OIL, THEY'LL BE HEALTHY FOR LIFE.
I SEE THE NEW ISSUE OF PANIC ATTACK MAGAZINE CAME TODAY.
ARE YOUR TOENAILS SEXY ENOUGH? TAKE THIS QUIZ AND FIND OUT!

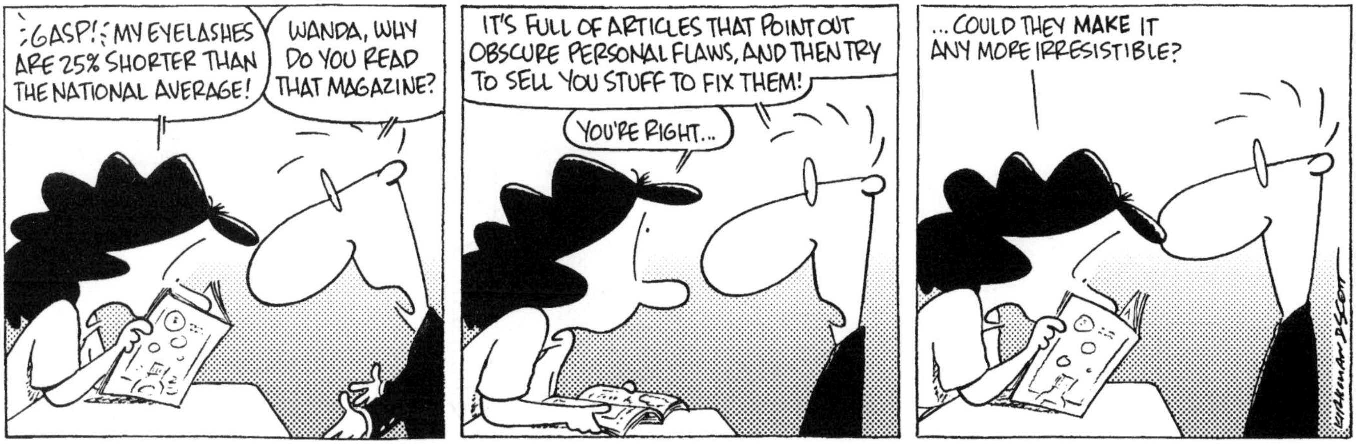
GASP! MY EYELASHES ARE 25% SHORTER THAN THE NATIONAL AVERAGE!
WANDA, WHY DO YOU READ THAT MAGAZINE?
IT'S FULL OF ARTICLES THAT POINT OUT OBSCURE PERSONAL FLAWS, AND THEN TRY TO SELL YOU STUFF TO FIX THEM!
YOU'RE RIGHT...
...COULD THEY MAKE IT ANY MORE IRRESISTIBLE?

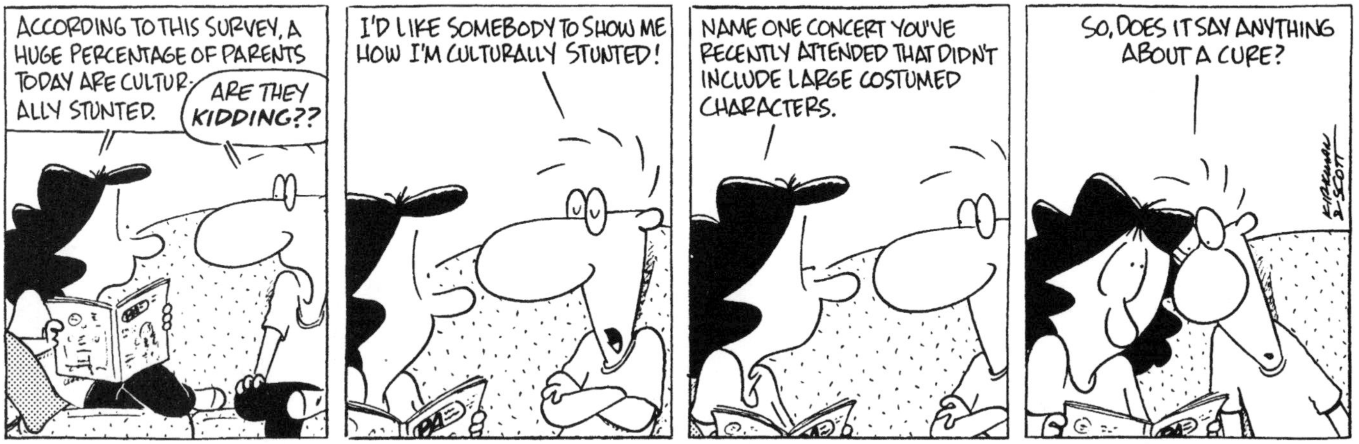
ACCORDING TO THIS SURVEY, A HUGE PERCENTAGE OF PARENTS TODAY ARE CULTURALLY STUNTED.
ARE THEY KIDDING??
I'D LIKE SOMEBODY TO SHOW ME HOW I'M CULTURALLY STUNTED!
NAME ONE CONCERT YOU'VE RECENTLY ATTENDED THAT DIDN'T INCLUDE LARGE COSTUMED CHARACTERS.
SO, DOES IT SAY ANYTHING ABOUT A CURE?

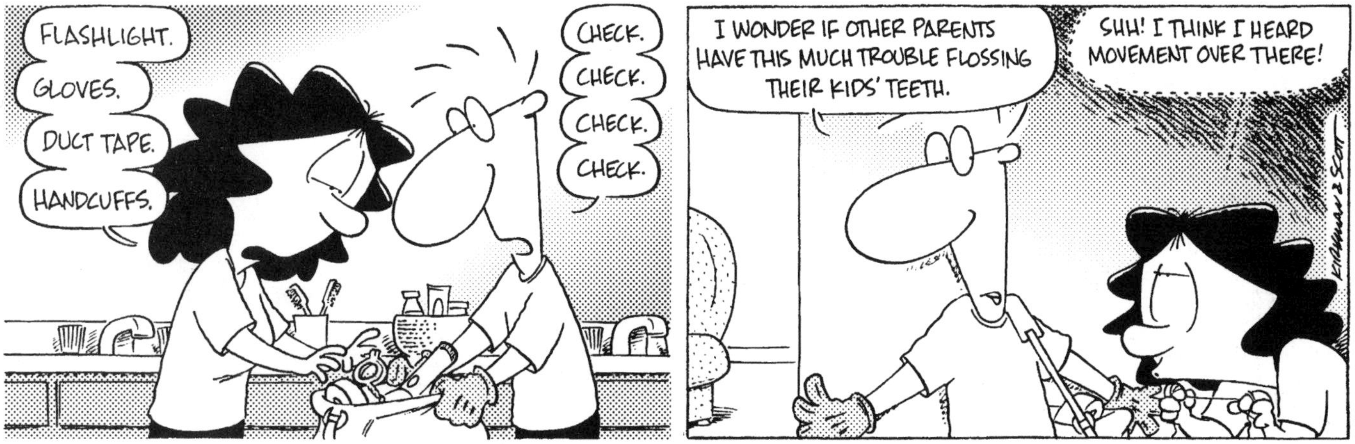
FLASHLIGHT.
CHECK.
GLOVES.
CHECK.
DUCT TAPE.
CHECK.
HANDCUFFS.
CHECK.
I WONDER IF OTHER PARENTS HAVE THIS MUCH TROUBLE FLOSSING THEIR KIDS' TEETH.
SHH! I THINK I HEARD MOVEMENT OVER THERE!

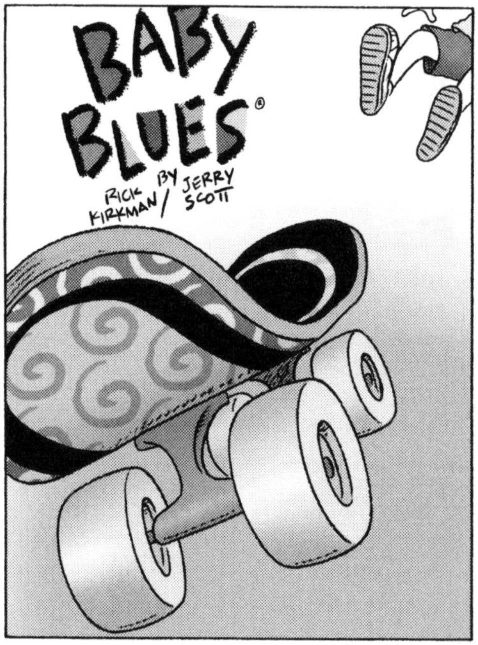
BABY BLUES®
BY RICK KIRKMAN / JERRY SCOTT

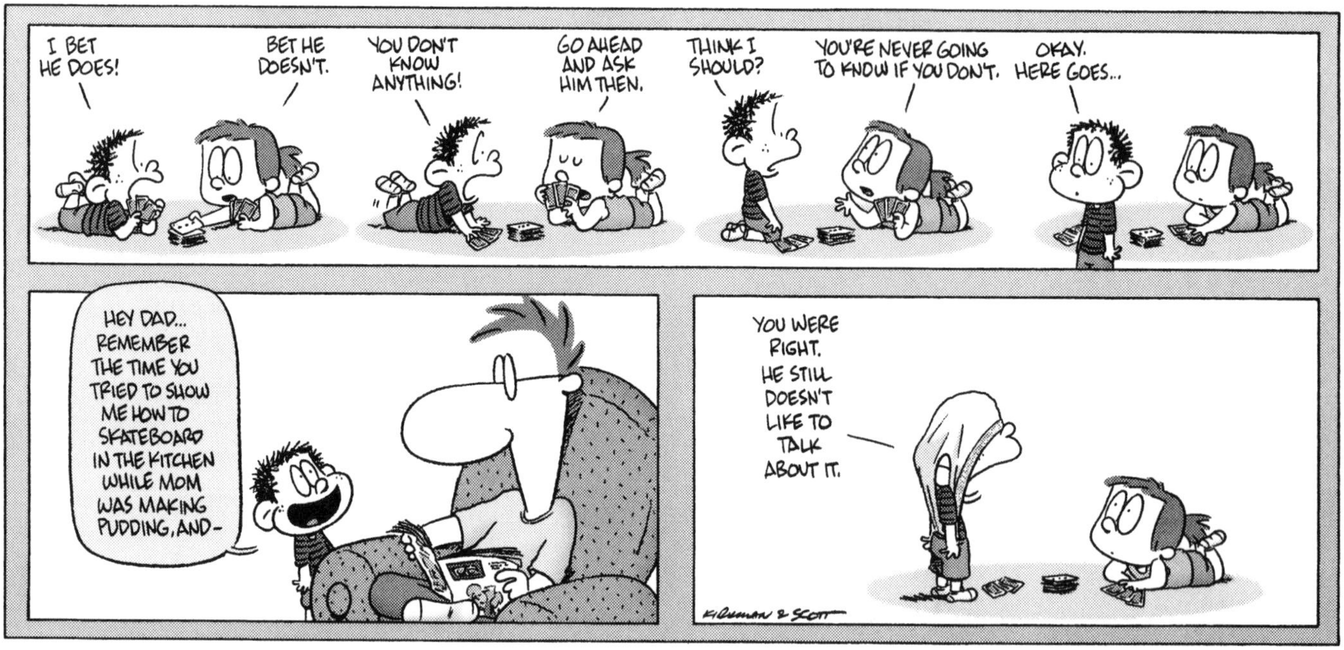
I BET HE DOES!
BET HE DOESN'T.
YOU DON'T KNOW ANYTHING!
GO AHEAD AND ASK HIM THEN.
THINK I SHOULD?
YOU'RE NEVER GOING TO KNOW IF YOU DON'T.
OKAY. HERE GOES...
HEY DAD... REMEMBER THE TIME YOU TRIED TO SHOW ME HOW TO SKATEBOARD IN THE KITCHEN WHILE MOM WAS MAKING PUDDING, AND–
YOU WERE RIGHT. HE STILL DOESN'T LIKE TO TALK ABOUT IT.
KIRKMAN & SCOTT

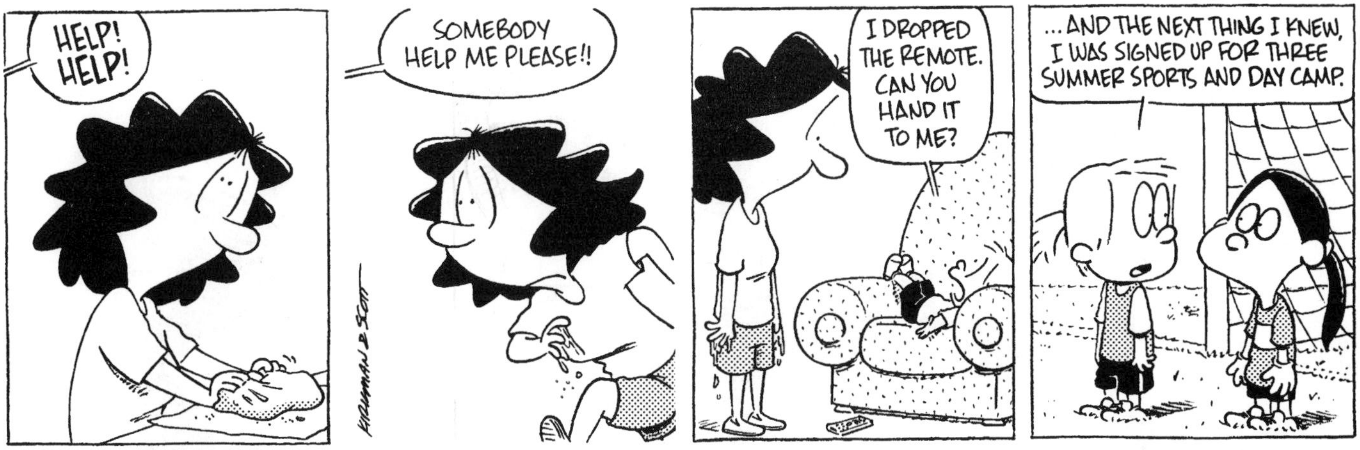
HELP! HELP!
SOMEBODY HELP ME PLEASE!!
I DROPPED THE REMOTE. CAN YOU HAND IT TO ME?
... AND THE NEXT THING I KNEW, I WAS SIGNED UP FOR THREE SUMMER SPORTS AND DAY CAMP.

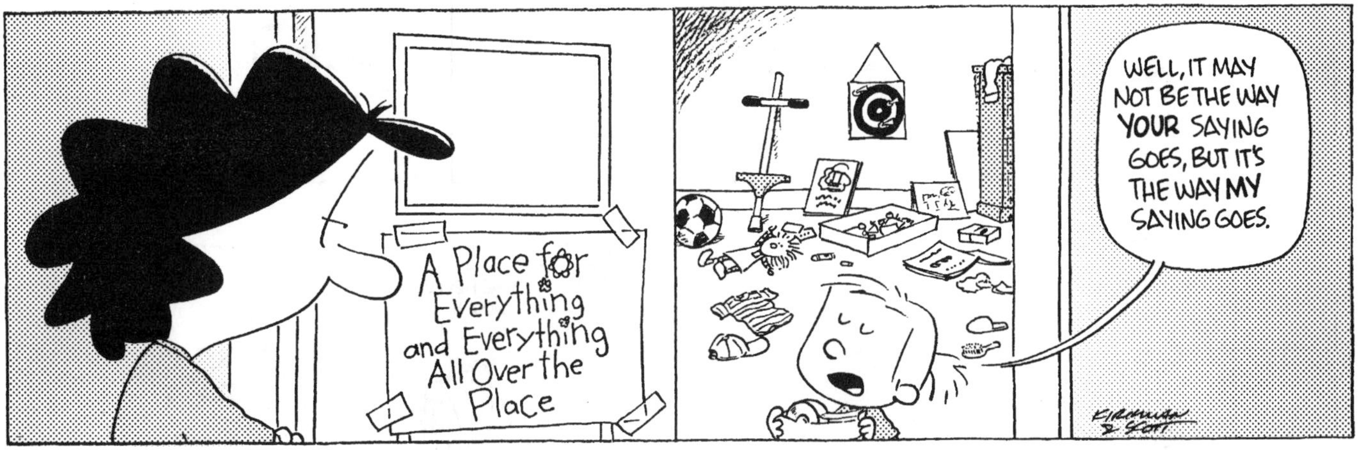
A Place for Everything and Everything All Over the Place
WELL, IT MAY NOT BE THE WAY YOUR SAYING GOES, BUT IT'S THE WAY MY SAYING GOES.

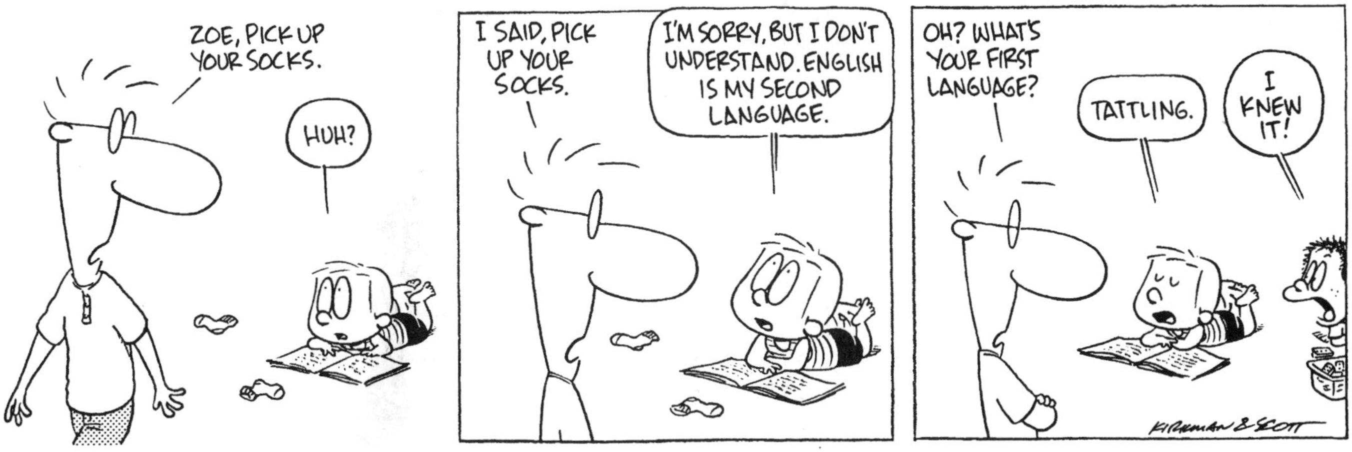
ZOE, PICK UP YOUR SOCKS.
HUH?
I SAID, PICK UP YOUR SOCKS.
I'M SORRY, BUT I DON'T UNDERSTAND. ENGLISH IS MY SECOND LANGUAGE.
OH? WHAT'S YOUR FIRST LANGUAGE?
TATTLING.
I KNEW IT!
KIRKMAN & SCOTT

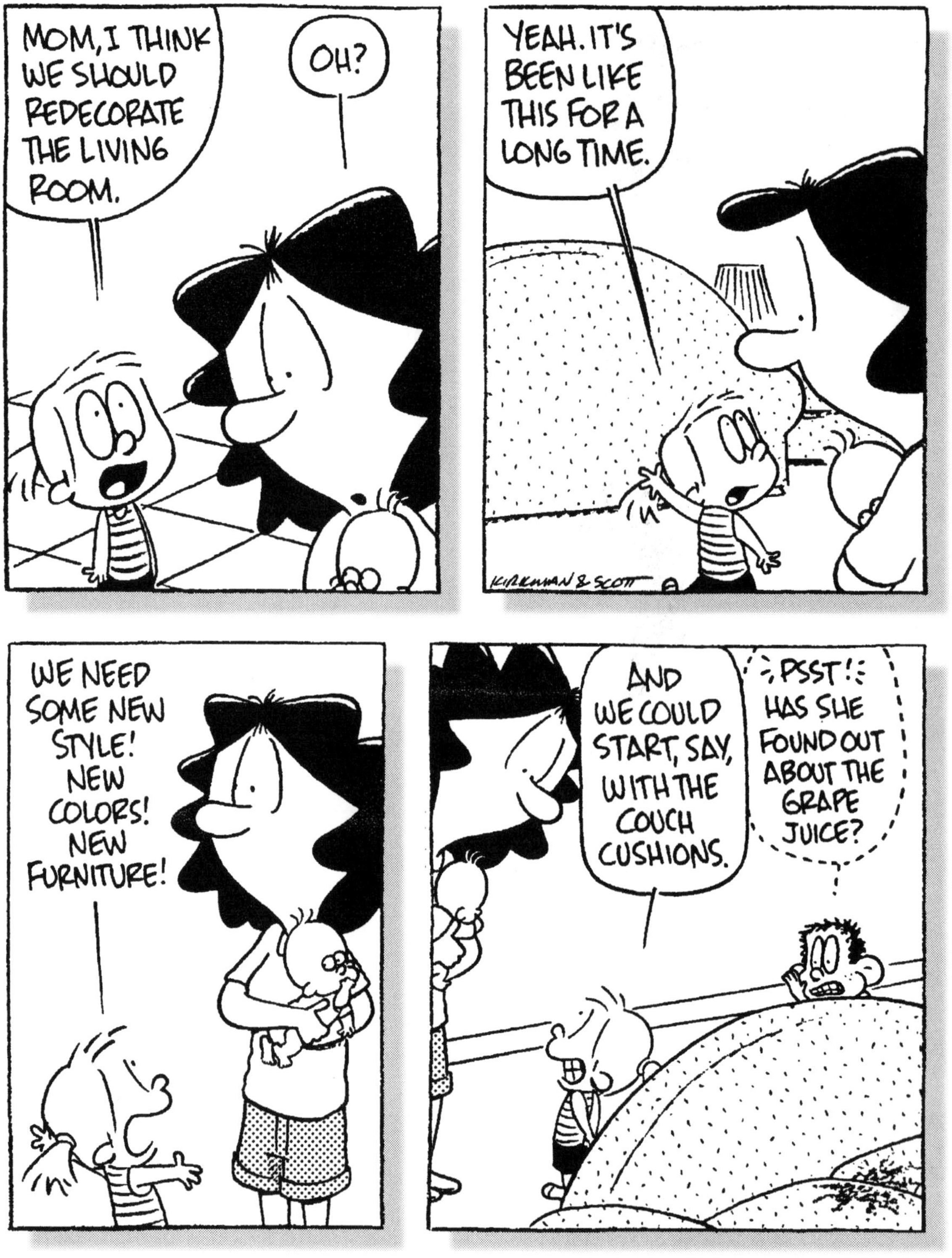
MOM, I THINK WE SHOULD REDECORATE THE LIVING ROOM.
OH?
YEAH. IT'S BEEN LIKE THIS FOR A LONG TIME.
KIRKMAN & SCOTT
WE NEED SOME NEW STYLE! NEW COLORS! NEW FURNITURE!
AND WE COULD START, SAY, WITH THE COUCH CUSHIONS.
PSST! HAS SHE FOUND OUT ABOUT THE GRAPE JUICE?

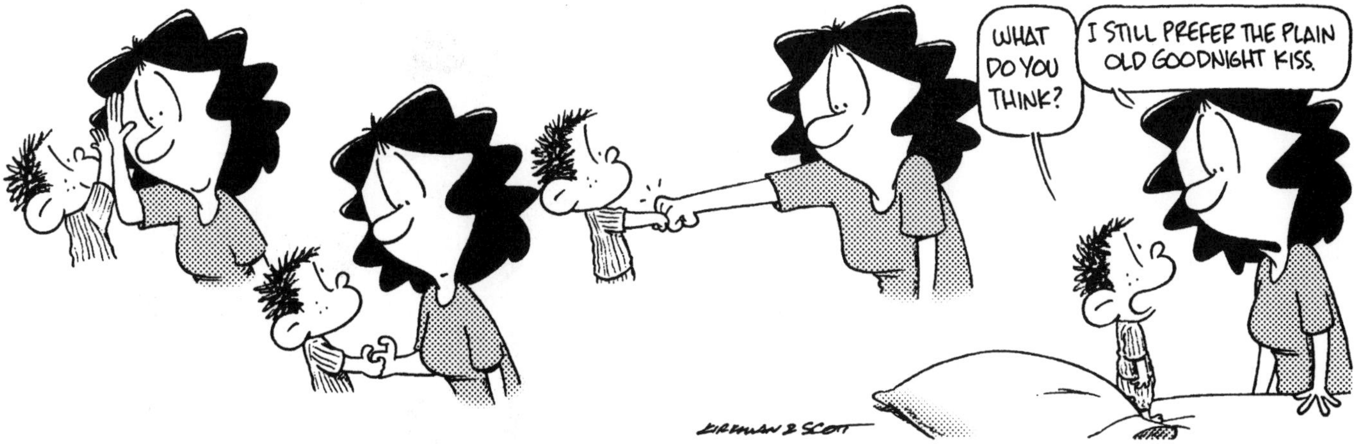
WHAT DO YOU THINK?
I STILL PREFER THE PLAIN OLD GOODNIGHT KISS.
KIRKMAN & SCOTT

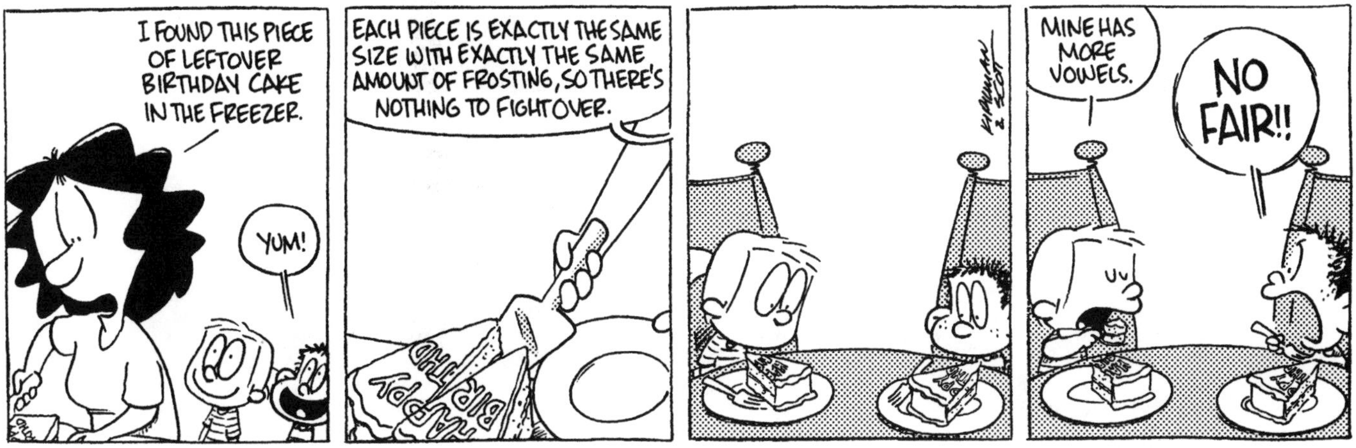
I FOUND THIS PIECE OF LEFTOVER BIRTHDAY CAKE IN THE FREEZER.
YUM!
EACH PIECE IS EXACTLY THE SAME SIZE WITH EXACTLY THE SAME AMOUNT OF FROSTING, SO THERE'S NOTHING TO FIGHT OVER.
HAPPY BIRTHD
MINE HAS MORE VOWELS.
NO FAIR!!

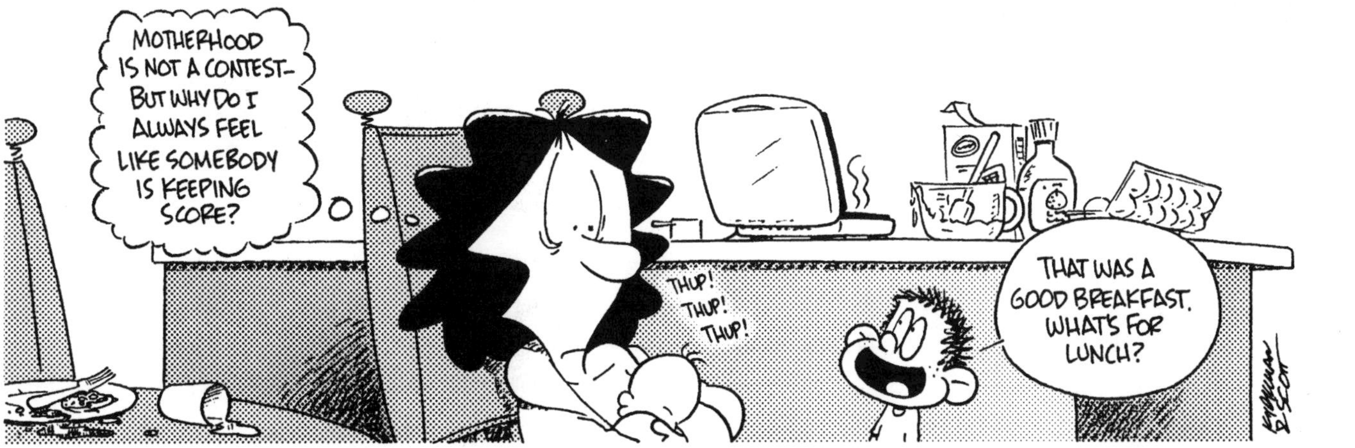
MOTHERHOOD IS NOT A CONTEST- BUT WHY DO I ALWAYS FEEL LIKE SOMEBODY IS KEEPING SCORE?
THUP! THUP! THUP!
THAT WAS A GOOD BREAKFAST. WHAT'S FOR LUNCH?

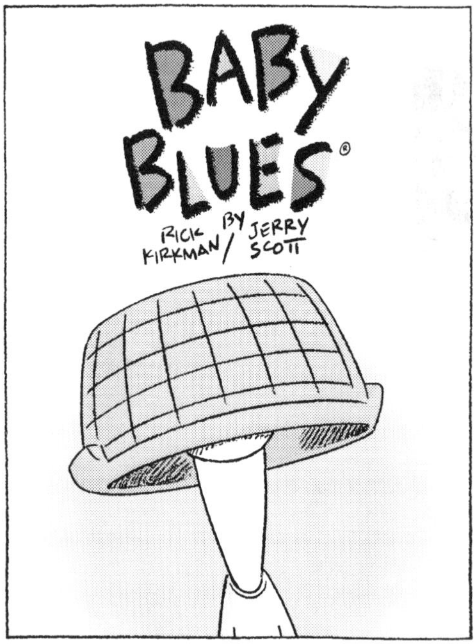
BABY BLUES®
BY RICK KIRKMAN / JERRY SCOTT

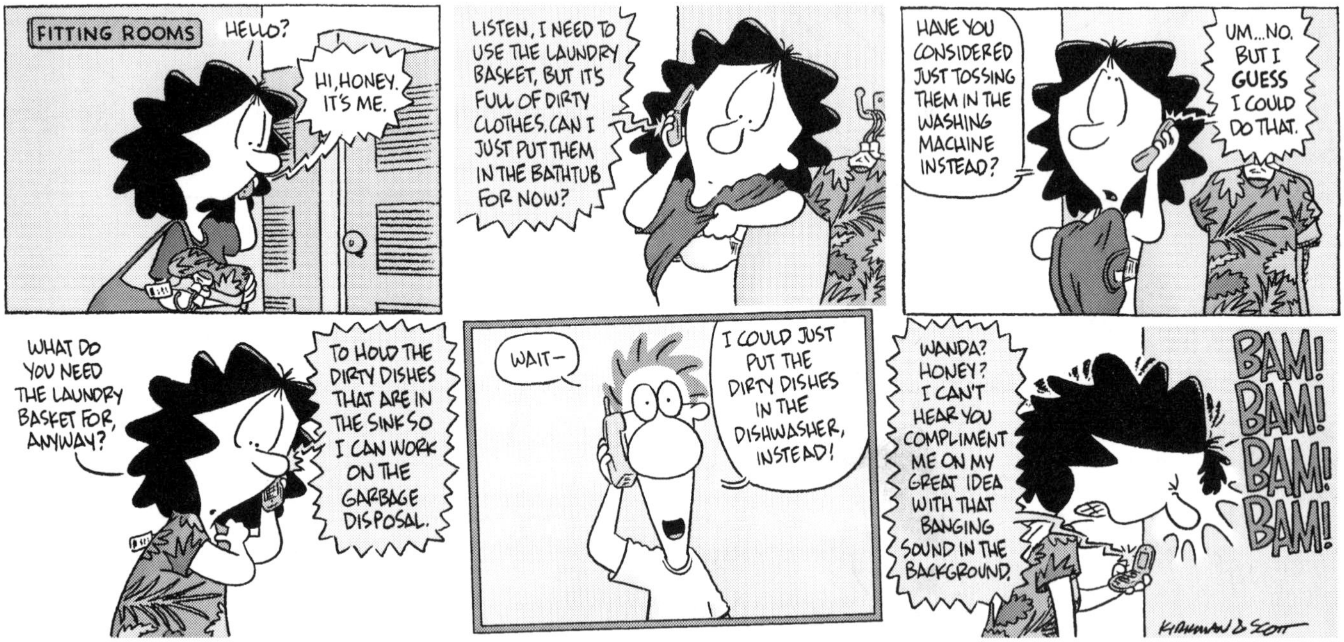
FITTING ROOMS
HELLO?
HI, HONEY. IT'S ME.
LISTEN, I NEED TO USE THE LAUNDRY BASKET, BUT IT'S FULL OF DIRTY CLOTHES. CAN I JUST PUT THEM IN THE BATHTUB FOR NOW?
HAVE YOU CONSIDERED JUST TOSSING THEM IN THE WASHING MACHINE INSTEAD?
UM...NO. BUT I GUESS I COULD DO THAT.
WHAT DO YOU NEED THE LAUNDRY BASKET FOR, ANYWAY?
TO HOLD THE DIRTY DISHES THAT ARE IN THE SINK SO I CAN WORK ON THE GARBAGE DISPOSAL.
WAIT—
I COULD JUST PUT THE DIRTY DISHES IN THE DISHWASHER, INSTEAD!
WANDA? HONEY? I CAN'T HEAR YOU COMPLIMENT ME ON MY GREAT IDEA WITH THAT BANGING SOUND IN THE BACKGROUND.
BAM! BAM! BAM! BAM!
KIRKMAN & SCOTT

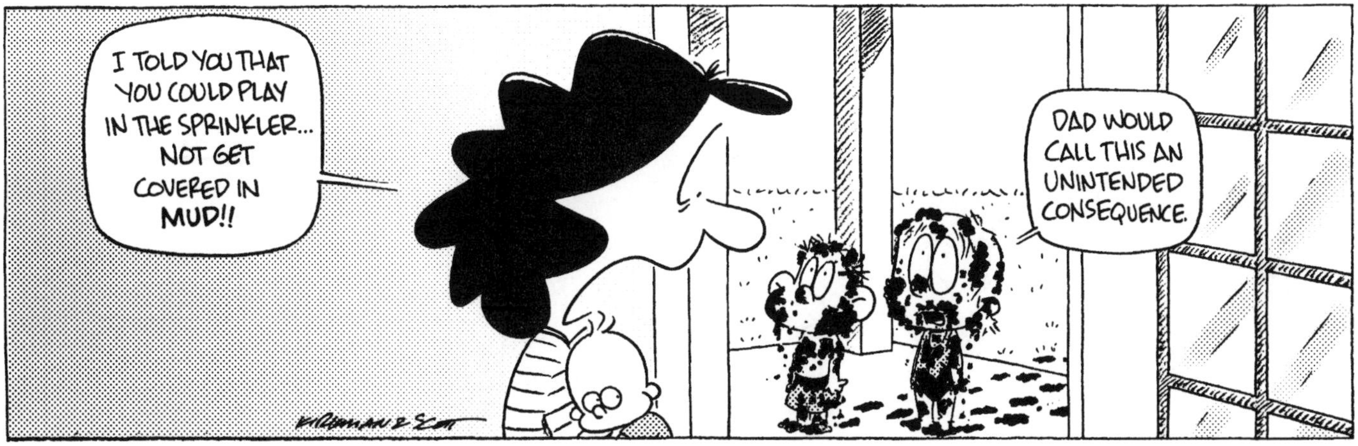
I TOLD YOU THAT YOU COULD PLAY IN THE SPRINKLER... NOT GET COVERED IN MUD!!
DAD WOULD CALL THIS AN UNINTENDED CONSEQUENCE.

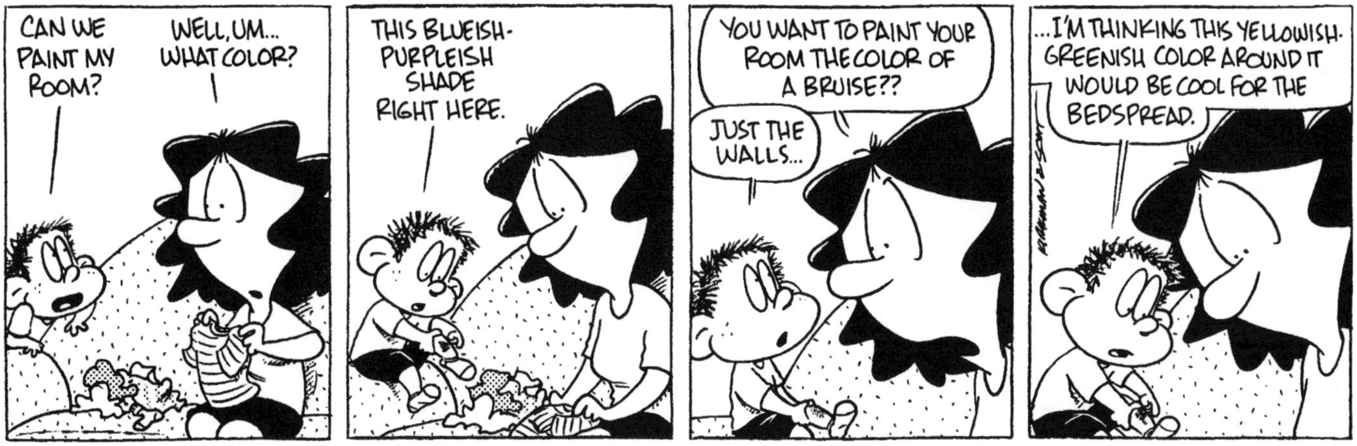
CAN WE PAINT MY ROOM?
WELL, UM... WHAT COLOR?
THIS BLUEISH-PURPLEISH SHADE RIGHT HERE.
YOU WANT TO PAINT YOUR ROOM THE COLOR OF A BRUISE??
JUST THE WALLS...
...I'M THINKING THIS YELLOWISH-GREENISH COLOR AROUND IT WOULD BE COOL FOR THE BEDSPREAD.

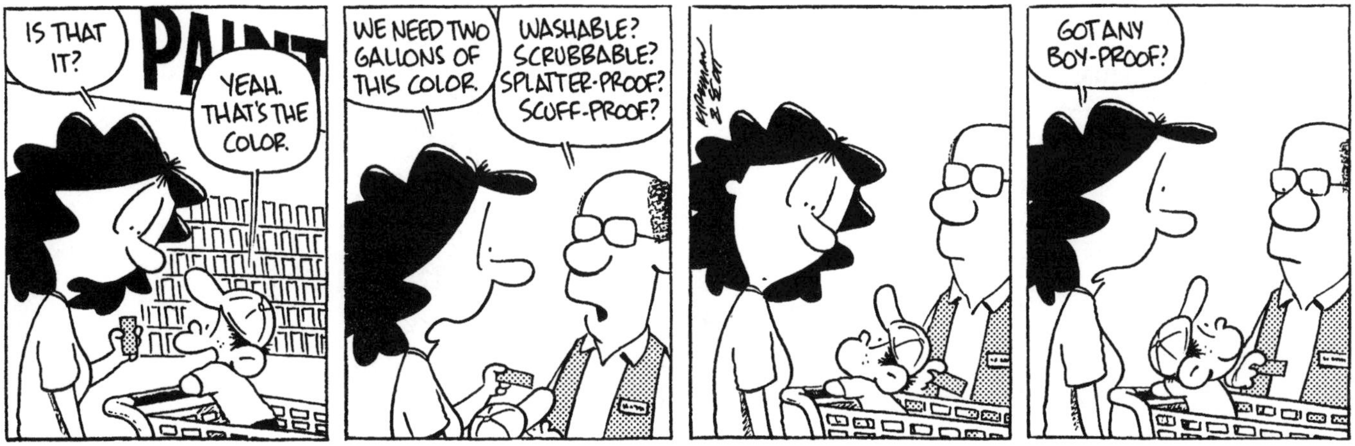
PAINT
IS THAT IT?
YEAH. THAT'S THE COLOR.
WE NEED TWO GALLONS OF THIS COLOR.
WASHABLE? SCRUBBABLE? SPLATTER-PROOF? SCUFF-PROOF?
GOT ANY BOY-PROOF?

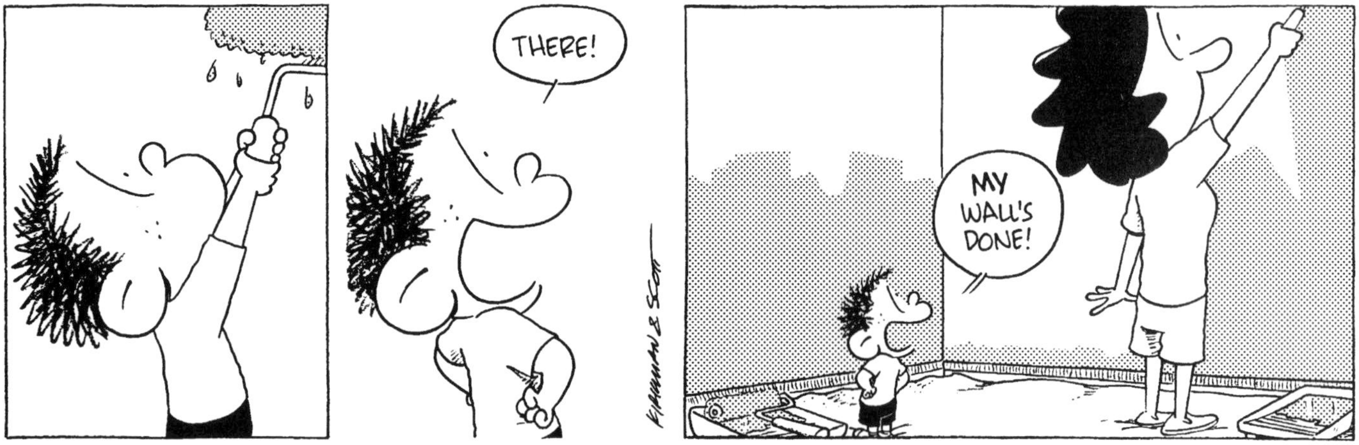
THERE!
MY WALL'S DONE!

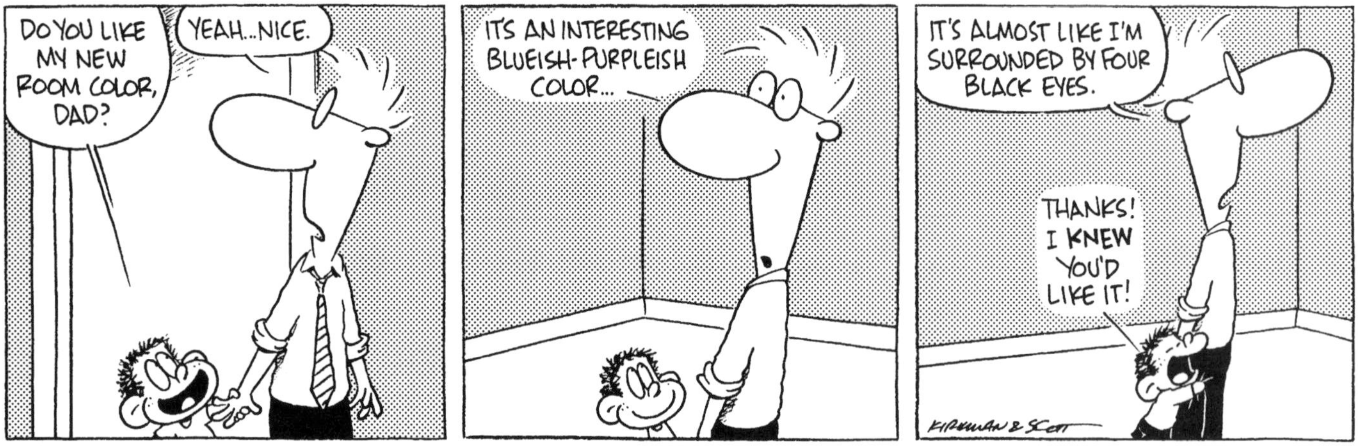
DO YOU LIKE MY NEW ROOM COLOR, DAD?
YEAH...NICE.
IT'S AN INTERESTING BLUEISH-PURPLEISH COLOR...
IT'S ALMOST LIKE I'M SURROUNDED BY FOUR BLACK EYES.
THANKS! I **KNEW** YOU'D LIKE IT!
KIRKMAN & SCOTT

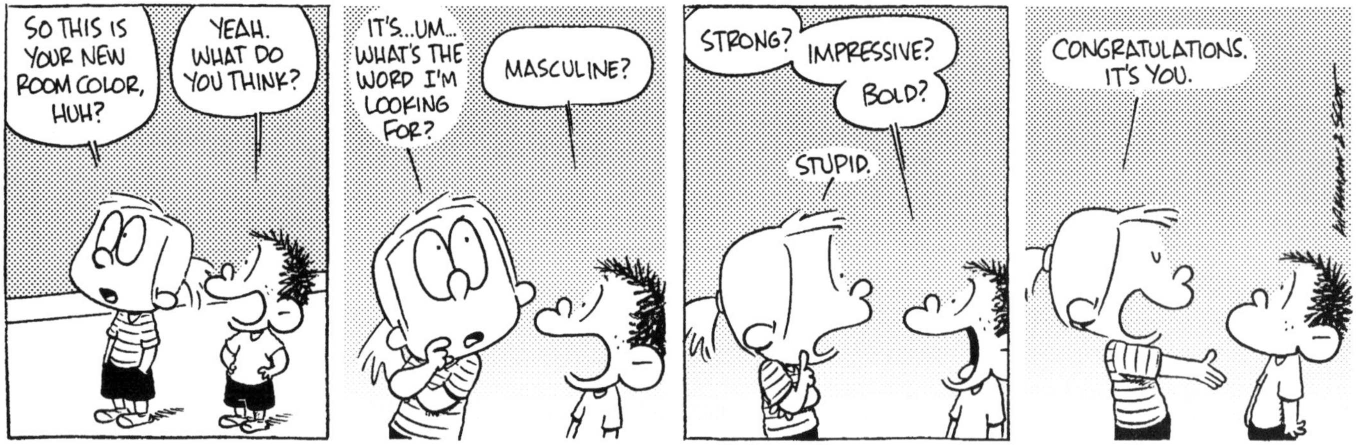
SO THIS IS YOUR NEW ROOM COLOR, HUH?
YEAH. WHAT DO YOU THINK?
IT'S...UM... WHAT'S THE WORD I'M LOOKING FOR?
MASCULINE?
STRONG?
IMPRESSIVE?
BOLD?
STUPID.
CONGRATULATIONS. IT'S YOU.

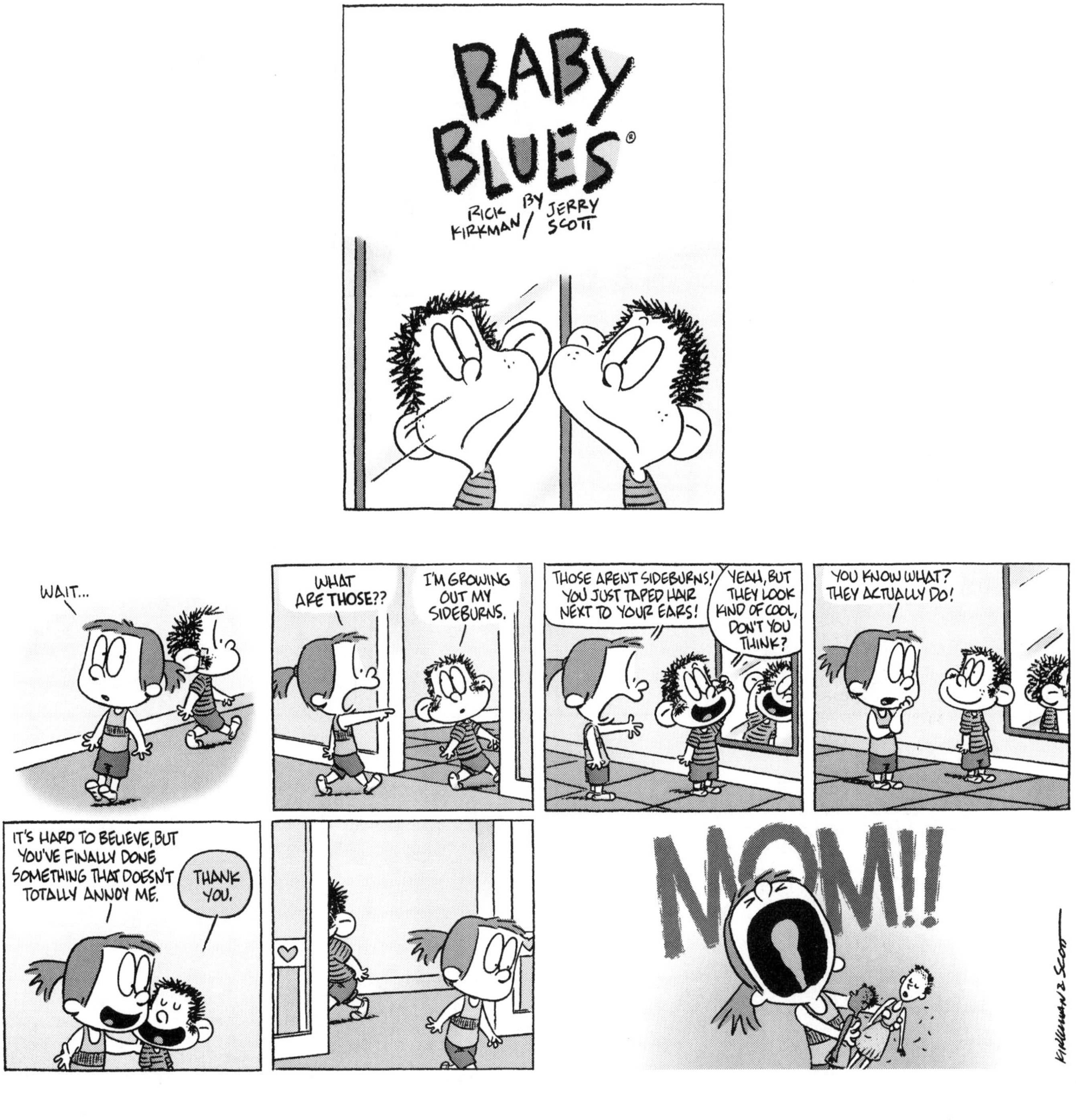
BABY BLUES®
BY RICK KIRKMAN / JERRY SCOTT
WAIT...
WHAT ARE THOSE??
I'M GROWING OUT MY SIDEBURNS.
THOSE AREN'T SIDEBURNS! YOU JUST TAPED HAIR NEXT TO YOUR EARS!
YEAH, BUT THEY LOOK KIND OF COOL, DON'T YOU THINK?
YOU KNOW WHAT? THEY ACTUALLY DO!
IT'S HARD TO BELIEVE, BUT YOU'VE FINALLY DONE SOMETHING THAT DOESN'T TOTALLY ANNOY ME.
THANK YOU.
MOM!!
KIRKMAN & SCOTT

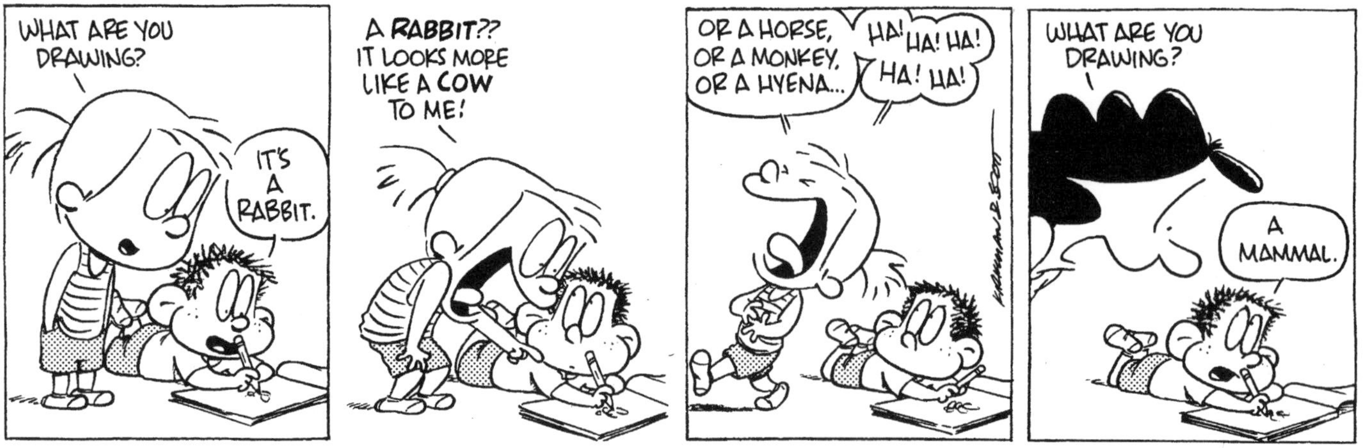
WHAT ARE YOU DRAWING?
IT'S A RABBIT.
A **RABBIT**?? IT LOOKS MORE LIKE A **COW** TO ME!
OR A HORSE, OR A MONKEY, OR A HYENA...
HA! HA! HA! HA! HA!
WHAT ARE YOU DRAWING?
A MAMMAL.
KIRKMAN & SCOTT

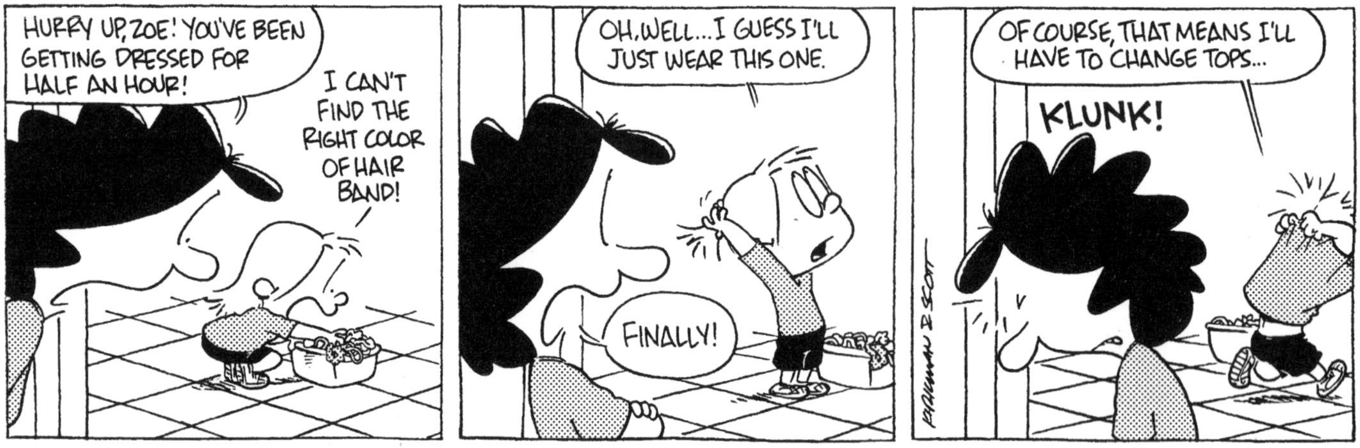
HURRY UP, ZOE! YOU'VE BEEN GETTING DRESSED FOR HALF AN HOUR!
I CAN'T FIND THE RIGHT COLOR OF HAIR BAND!
OH, WELL... I GUESS I'LL JUST WEAR THIS ONE.
FINALLY!
OF COURSE, THAT MEANS I'LL HAVE TO CHANGE TOPS...
KLUNK!
KIRKMAN & SCOTT

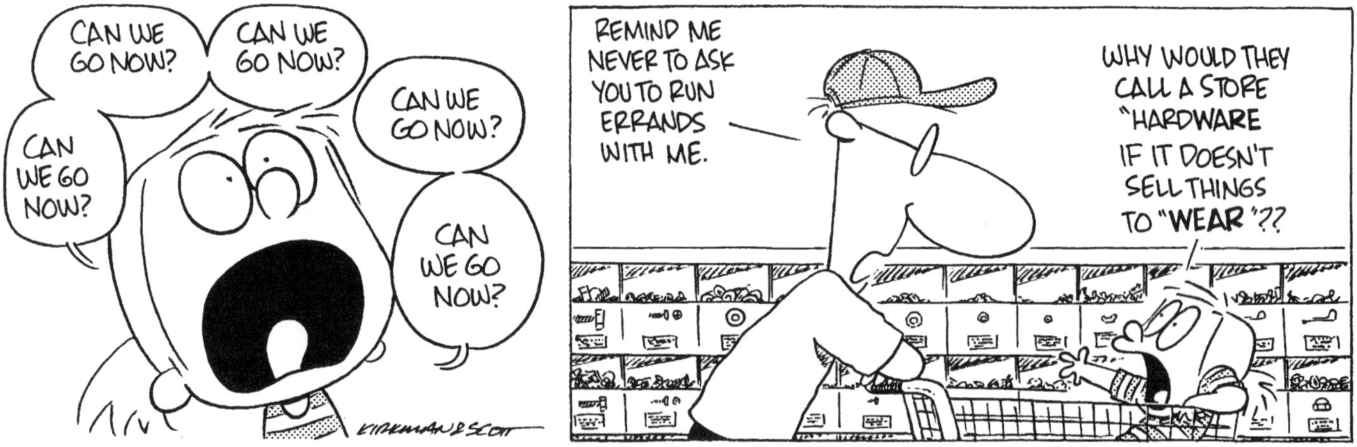
CAN WE GO NOW?
CAN WE GO NOW?
CAN WE GO NOW?
CAN WE GO NOW?
CAN WE GO NOW?
KIRKMAN & SCOTT
REMIND ME NEVER TO ASK YOU TO RUN ERRANDS WITH ME.
WHY WOULD THEY CALL A STORE "HARD**WARE** IF IT DOESN'T SELL THINGS TO "**WEAR**"??

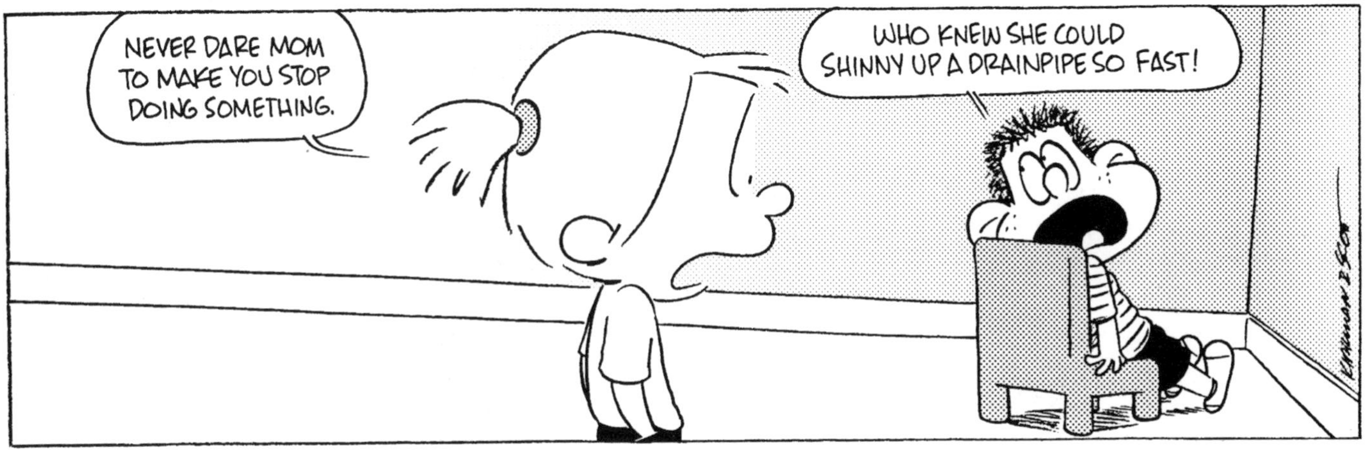
NEVER DARE MOM TO MAKE YOU STOP DOING SOMETHING.
WHO KNEW SHE COULD SHINNY UP A DRAINPIPE SO FAST!

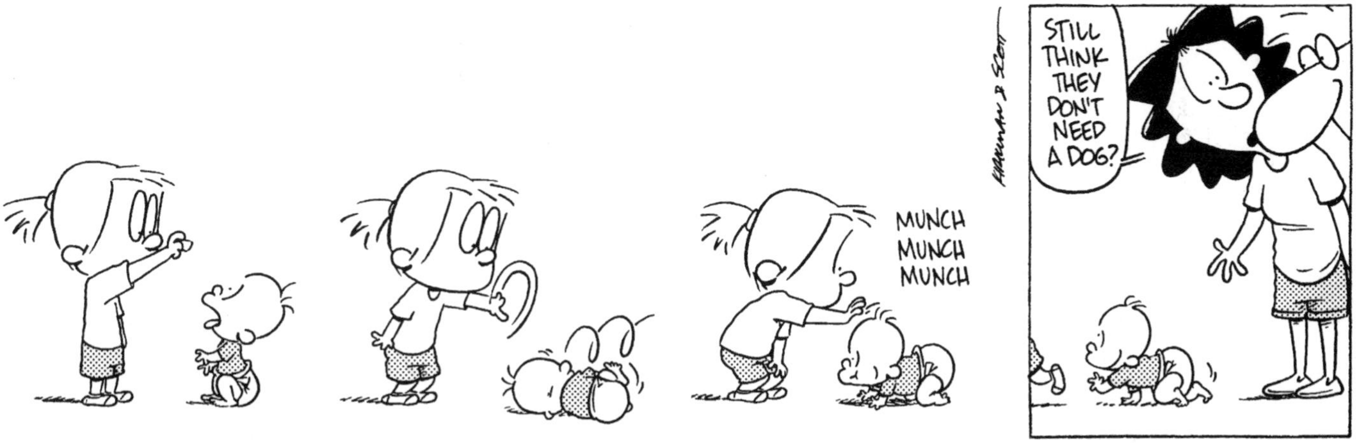
MUNCH MUNCH MUNCH
STILL THINK THEY DON'T NEED A DOG?

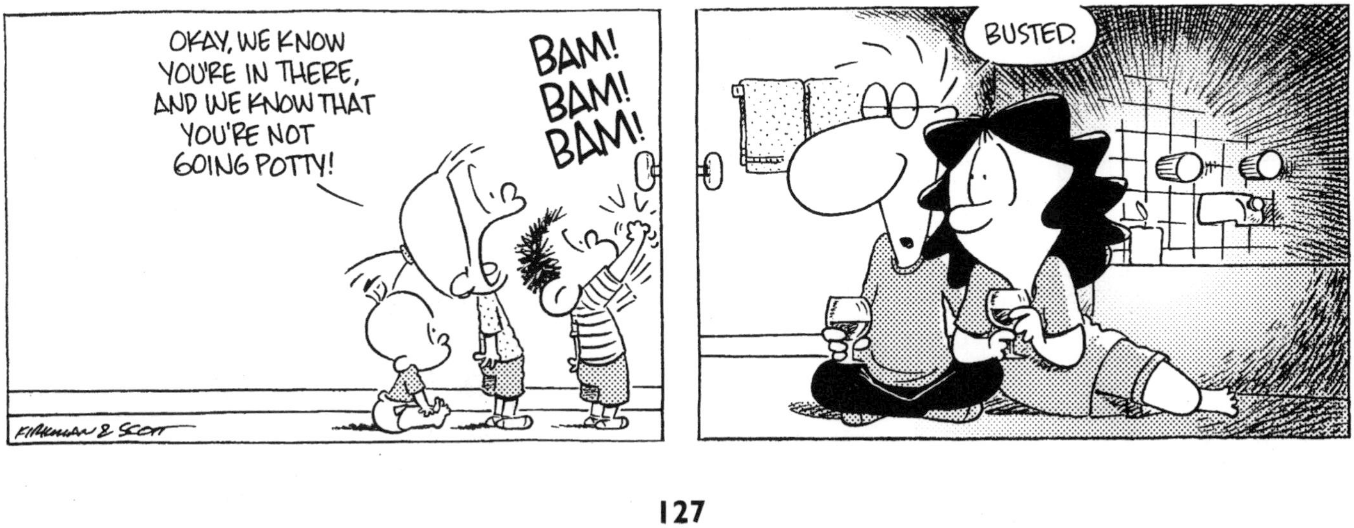
OKAY, WE KNOW YOU'RE IN THERE, AND WE KNOW THAT YOU'RE NOT GOING POTTY!
BAM! BAM! BAM!
BUSTED.

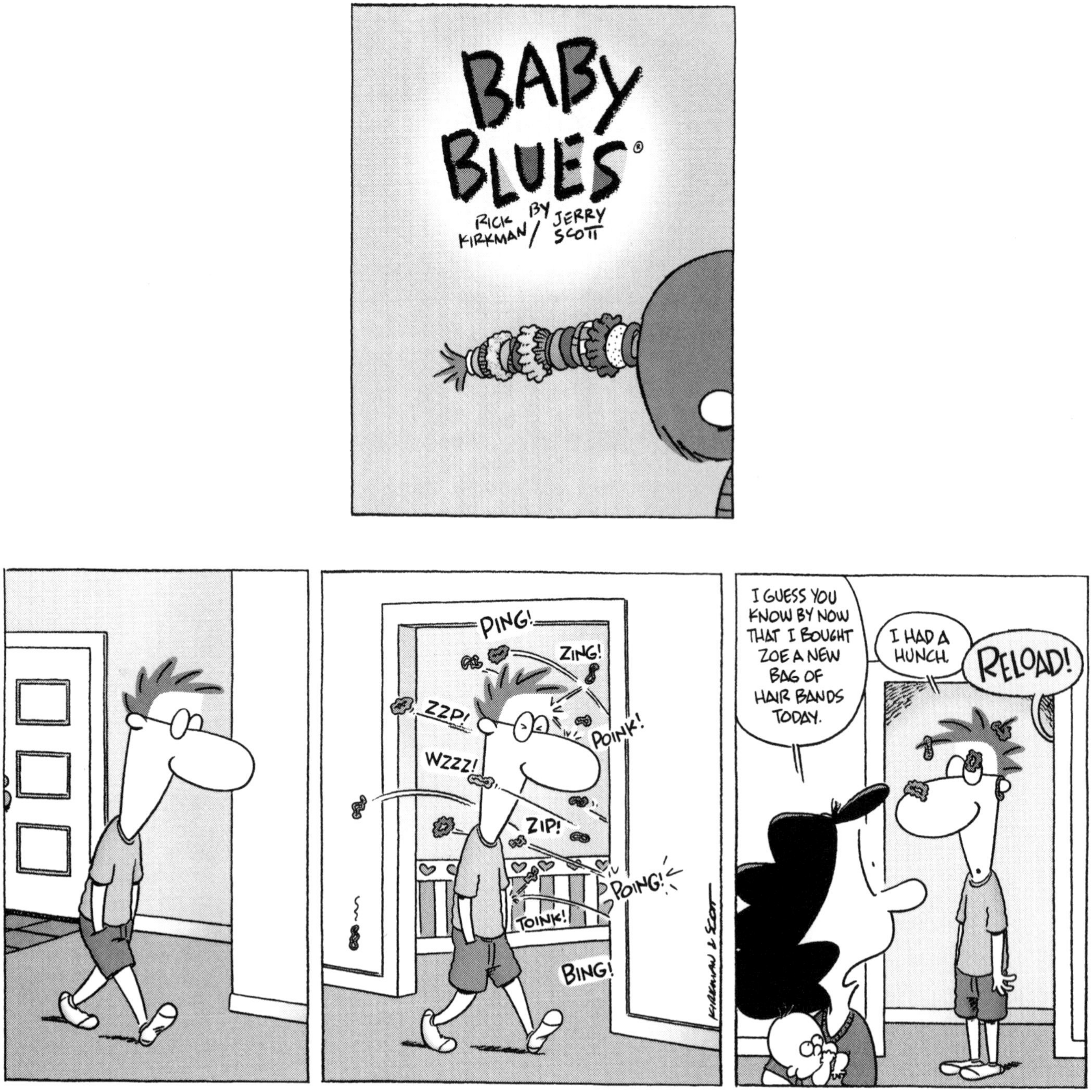
BABY BLUES®
RICK KIRKMAN / BY JERRY SCOTT
PING!
ZING!
ZZP!
POINK!
WZZZ!
ZIP!
POING!
TOINK!
BING!
KIRKMAN & SCOTT
I GUESS YOU KNOW BY NOW THAT I BOUGHT ZOE A NEW BAG OF HAIR BANDS TODAY.
I HAD A HUNCH.
RELOAD!

6 140